is democracy a lost cause?

paradoxes of an imperfect invention

Alfio Mastropaolo

Translated by Clare Tame

ecpr PRESS

First published by the ECPR Press in 2012

The translation of this work has been funded by:

S E P S

SEGRETARIATO EUROPEO PER LE PUBBLICAZIONI SCIENTIFICHE

Segretariato Europeo per le Pubblicazioni Scientifiche
Via Val d'Aposa 7 – 40123 Bologna – Italy
seps@seps.it – www.seps.it
and
The University of Turin, Department of Cultures, Politics and Society,
Via Giolitti, 33 – 10123 Torino – Italy

The ECPR Press is the publishing imprint of the European Consortium for Political Research (ECPR), a scholarly association, which supports and encourages the training, research and cross-national cooperation of political scientists in institutions throughout Europe and beyond.

ECPR Press
University of Essex
Wivenhoe Park
Colchester
CO4 3SQ, UK

Typeset by ECPR Press

Printed and bound by Lightning Source

British Library Cataloguing in Publication Data A catalogue record for this book is available from the British Library

Paperback ISBN: 978-1-907301-38-4

www.ecprnet.eu/ecprpress

Series Editors:
Dario Castiglione (University of Exeter)
Peter Kennealy (European University Institute)
Alexandra Segerberg (Stockholm University)
Peter Triantafillou (Roskilde University)

Publications from the ECPR Press

ECPR Essays:
Just Democracy (ISBN: 9781907301148) Philippe Van Parijs
Hans Kelsen and the Case for Democracy (ISBN: 9781907301247) Sandrine Baume

ECPR Classics:
Beyond the Nation State: (ISBN: 9780955248870) Ernst Haas
Citizens, Elections, Parties: Approaches to the Comparative Study of the Processes of Development (ISBN: 9780955248887) Stein Rokkan
Democracy: Political Finance and State Funding for Parties (ISBN: 9780955248801) Jack Lively
Electoral Change: Responses to Evolving Social and Attitudinal Structures in Western Countries (ISBN: 9780955820311) Mark Franklin,Thomas Mackie, and Henry Valen
Elite and Specialized Interviewing (ISBN: 9780954796679) Lewis Anthony Dexter
Identity, Competition and Electoral Availability: The Stabilisation of European Electorates 1885-1985 (ISBN: 9780955248832) Peter Mair and Stefano Bartolini
Individualism (ISBN: 9780954796662) Steven Lukes
Modern Social Policies in Britain and Sweden: From Relief to Income Maintenance (ISBN: 9781907301001) Hugh Heclo
Parties and Party Systems: A Framework for Analysis (ISBN: 9780954796617) Giovanni Sartori
Party Identification and Beyond: Representations of Voting and Party Competition (ISBN: 9780955820342) Ian Budge, Ivor Crewe, and Dennis Farlie
People, States and Fear: An Agenda for International Security Studies in the Post-Cold War Era (ISBN: 9780955248818) Barry Buzan
Political Elites: (ISBN: 9780954796600) Geraint Parry
Political Theory and Political Science (ISBN: 9781907301025) Martin Landau
State Formation, Parties and Democracy (ISBN: 9781907301179) Hans Daalder
System and Process in International Politics (ISBN: 9780954796624) Morton Kaplan
Territory and Power in the UK: Territory and Power in the UK (ISBN: 9780955248863) James Bulpitt
The State Tradition in Western Europe: A Study of an Idea and Institution (ISBN: 9780955820359) Kenneth Dyson

Please visit www.ecprnet.eu/ecprpress for up-to-date information about new publications

contents

To T.

acknowledgements

In my experience, a book is first of all the product of meetings, reflections and discussions with others. This time has been no exception and there are many colleagues and friends to whom I am indebted. I will limit myself here to thanking those who have read and commented on the manuscript of the Italian edition, which I have thoroughly revised for its publication in English: Irene Bono, Anna Caffarena, Mario Cardano, Loris Caruso, Dario Castiglione, Giuseppe Di Palma, Jean-Pierre Gaudin, Oscar Mazzoleni, Duncan McDonnell, Vittorio Mete, Nino Palumbo, Davide Pellegrino, Filippo Sabetti and Rocco Sciarrone. Obviously, any remaining errors in the book are my own responsibility.

Translating the thoughts and words of someone else is never easy. I therefore wish to thank Clare Tame for undertaking this task and, in particular, for the immense patience she has shown while doing it. Finally, I would like to express my gratitude to Ildi Clarke for her careful editing of the translation and for compiling the index.

Alfio Mastropaolo
Turin, July 2012

introduction

*'It seems you don't understand that words are the labels we stick on
things, not the things themselves, you'll never know what the things
are really like, nor even what their real names are, because the
names you gave them are just that, the names you gave them ...'*

José Saramago, *Death With Interruptions*, 2005

It is an oft-forgotten fact, but democracy is a human invention and therefore a historical fact. It claims to be the supreme good, but it is not. Neither is it the fate of the human race, or even a necessity. It originated somewhere, from where it is spread widely, changing and adapting, and it is destined to have an end.[1] As with all historical facts, its birth, success and misfortunes are characterised by a broad margin of uncertainty.

In spite of this, nowadays democracy stands out for its inexhaustible ambition. It has become a sacred icon, resistant to any reservations and that sanctifies everything it touches.[2] The message that its name contains – that of transforming the governed into governors and thus abrogating power – has only been taken seriously by a few. It would be a mistake to deny the successes and virtues of which democracy can genuinely be proud. But neither should we forget that its practice, whatever the preferences of each, has often been rather disappointing. Indeed, it is sometimes so modest that one might even stop considering democracy as the best form of government, even morally superior to all others. Yet, some still take it as a point of arrival in human history and the aim of history. In the 1990s, when the devastating collapse, of what had for over half a century been considered democracy's most feared contender, 'real socialism', someone solemnly announced nothing less than the 'end of history' and that the magic place where its labours would cease had finally been reached.[3]

---

1   James Bryce recalled this in *Modern Democracies* (New York, Macmillan, 1921, vol. II, p. 597). To the question of whether democracy is 'the final form' of government, he responded that 'for whatever else history teaches, it gives no ground for expecting finality in any human institution'.

2   It is difficult to question something that is considered positive *per se*, free from any critical reflection. See Quentin Skinner, 'The Empirical Theorists of Democracy and their Critics: A Plague on Both their Houses', *Political Theory* 1(3), 1973, 287–306. See also John Dunn, *Setting the People Free. The Story of Democracy* (London, Atlantic Books, 2005).

3   Francis Fukuyama, *The End of History and the Last Man* (New York, The Free Press, 1992).

Now that democracy is 'the only game in town',[4] even for its old adversaries, it has been consecrated as a universal norm. Even the big international institutions, once rather inattentive to democracy, now propagandise it zealously. And time-honoured democratic regimes feel authorised to give to non-democratic regimes, lessons in democracy, with or without their leave. Statistics, after all, certify that over sixty per cent of the population on the planet is governed democratically. Democracy has even conquered regions always considered off-limits: from Eastern Europe to Latin America, from the Far East to parts of Africa.[5] Nevertheless, if we look at the diffusion of democratic regimes on a planetary scale with the least bit of attention, what we find is an enormous mound of approximations and uncertainties, frequent second thoughts and denials. At this point the frontier between the happy territories of democracy and the desolate regions of non-democracy becomes extremely confused.

For a while reassuring news circulated according to which on the southern shores of the Mediterranean, peoples formerly considered doggedly incompatible with democracy, have finally reawakened and are demanding institutions and democratic rights. But is it really democracy that Tunisians and Egyptians want, or just better life conditions and a ruling class that is less greedy and corrupt?

The spread of democracy is therefore problematic. Western observers have gradually become aware of this and have coined precautionary labels: 'hybrid regimes', 'low-intensity democracies', purely 'electoral democracies'.[6] We have witnessed changes, the brutal dictatorships of the past are disappearing, but this is not enough to hide the absence of some basic conditions, that as a rule are expected from a democratic regime. Would we ever have imagined that it would be so difficult to become democratic?

Unfortunately, there is not much to rejoice about even in the West. At first glance, the lethal economic and financial crises that are currently shaking the most developed countries do not seem to be challenging democracy. When they can, the *indignados* occupy streets and piazzas and protest parties gain votes, but no-one questions democracy. For the time being there are no upheavals comparable to those that took place in Europe between the two World Wars. In spite of this, things which are not in the least bit edifying take place in even the most renowned democracies.

---

4   Giuseppe Di Palma, *To Craft Democracies: An Essay on Democratic Transitions* (Los Angeles: University of California Press, 1990, p. 113).

5   For an accurate comparative analysis see Davide Grassi, *Le nuove democrazie. I processi di democratizzazione dopo la caduta del Muro di Berlino* (Bologna, Il Mulino, 2008).

6   Larry Diamond, 'Thinking about Hybrid Regimes', *Journal of Democracy* 13(2), 2002, 21–35 and *Developing Democracy: Toward Consolidation* (Baltimore MD, Johns Hopkins University Press, 1999). The confusion is increased by the cases where the polls have given birth to democratically exemplary outcomes, which are not welcomed by the more long-standing democracies. This was the case of the Palestinian elections in early 2006 which saw the landslide victory of Hamas. Yet the Hamas victory was rejected.

The latest reports from Freedom House describe how in a country like Italy elections are not manipulated, but the parliamentary majority simply rewrites electoral legislation to suit themselves, while the control of the media is concentrated in too few hands. The treatment of migrants who flock to Europe to escape poverty and violence, by many democratic European regimes, is, to say the least, inhuman. The *patria* of the *Declaration of the Rights of Man and the Citizen* has been accused of deporting eight thousand Roma, and Britain has been criticised for the severity of its anti-terrorism laws. In America, the crisis in the press with the closure of many local newspapers, is seen as a threat against freedom of information. Finally, there are the countless cases where police forces have brutally repressed even peaceful protests. Not to speak of countries that practice torture and the death sentence.

Yet, if some are scandalised by these issues, others only consider them minor shortcomings, and yet others do not even consider them that. Provided that the electoral rites are celebrated, and the rights that the West likes to define as human and universal are consecrated, there is no wrong that cannot be pardoned. The problem is that we all use the same term and adopt the same institutions, but not everyone means the same thing by democracy, or uses its institutions in the same way or with the same results.

Forgive the imprecision regarding dates, but social change has a hard time making appointments and hardly ever fixes them everywhere at the same time. Yet, recently something new has occurred. In the past, the application of democratic rules and principles has progressively extended. More recently, even in the oldest and most well-established democratic regimes, inroads have been made by the idea that it is better to limit democracy for its own good. It appears that everything is democratically in order. But the electoral principle seems no longer fashionable in democratic regimes and policy-making is increasingly removed from electorally legitimated authorities and entrusted to technical or neutral authorities, or to negotiations between public and private actors typical of so-called governance.

The world changes, the scale of government changes and it is inevitable that places and ways of decision-making are modified. However, there are plenty of reasons to argue that democracy now has a worrying propensity to take its leave of citizens. It does so claiming to do it in their best interests. In the meantime the return of oligarchies is being reported everywhere. Oligarchies have always existed and it is difficult to imagine a world without them. But for some time new social groups had found an audience in the places of power, renewing, at least in part, the sociological composition of the ruling class. Inverting the trend, the recruitment pool for political leadership now tends to be closed from the top down and towards the lower classes, allowing the wealthier strata to recoup a large part of lost ground.

In parallel to the democratisation of political personnel recruitment, democratic regimes had adopted incisive policies to redistribute wealth – and of political power – for the benefit of the popular classes, and maybe even more, for the middle class. For quite a long time the course has been reversed and the redistribution has started to work the other way around. Inequalities are again on the rise, with a consequent tangible deterioration of the living conditions of a sizeable quota of the population.[7] The fact that all this is taking place in respect to democratic rules is in no way reassuring. Indeed, we are tempted to ask whether the rules have not been adapted in such a way that the losers cannot oppose them, if they have not simply been trained to assent.

The problem of oligarchies is even posed on a global scale. The choices of a state have always conditioned the fate of other states and countries but now this occurs ever more frequently, and it also seems that the consequences – in terms of economy, energy, environment and so forth – are much more exacting than in the past. In spite of this, democratic regimes do not seem to pay it too much attention. Besides, not even the global and regional collaboration to which the states are increasingly subject, confer them considerable decision-making responsibility, or are particularly concerned about the will, interests or needs of the governed. In the first place, the institutions that guide them carefully avoid placing rulers, chosen and invested by the ruled, at their top echelons. When they have – this is the case of the European Parliament – its tasks have been strictly defined and complicated and it has been distanced as far as possible from the electors. And what can we say about the transnational oligarchies which sport the guise of the financial markets and are currently taking some democratic regimes hostage, dictating, together with big international financial institutions, conditions so drastic as to condemn entire populations to poverty?

No trend is irreversible, but at the same time the costs are high. In consolation, some appreciable progress is reported in the field of human rights and in the internationalisation of their protection. This is proclaimed solemnly, together with a promise to protect them in all directions. There are countries which are internationally authorised to violate any right with impunity and which may, even in the name of rights, let slip a war too many. In spite of this, the little has that been realised for human rights is not completely irrelevant, but it is certainly not enough to glimpse the germs of a future planetary democracy in the attention paid to human rights.

Let us be realistic. The life of the thing we call democracy, and the regimes that we consider democratic, have always been complicated. It has always been a tangle of gains and successes, great and small, but also of humiliation, defeat, compromise, as well as dramatic denials, and, in the words of Norberto Bobbio, 'broken promises' and unexpected obstacles.[8] What is currently happening to democracy in the new millennium should come as no surprise. Precisely for this reason it would be more honest, and perhaps more profitable, to take democracy down from the altars and to treat it with a bit of realism, or at least to recognise it as an intrinsically unfinished accomplishment.

---

7   It is enough to flick through the pages and the data in the OECD report *Growing Unequal? Income Distribution and Poverty in OECD Countries* (Paris, OECD, 2008).

8   Norberto Bobbio, *The Future of Democracy: A Defence of the Rules of the Game* (Cambridge, Polity Press, 1987).

The criterion of incompleteness is that used by Robert H. Dahl, one of the most authoritative theorists of twentieth-century democracy. He singled out a mechanism in democracy which sub-divides and dissipates power. Awareness of the incompleteness, pushed him to revoke even the name of democracy as being too pretentious, and suggesting the more modest term of 'polyarchy'.[9] The proposal was immediately archived. A humbler term might satisfy some critically inclined intellectual, but would do a disservice to the democratic rhetoric and would be scandalous for the ordinary citizen. This was also the opinion of a jurist of adamantine democratic faith, Hans Kelsen. When democracy was undergoing the dramatic test of its existence in Austria and Germany, Kelsen upheld the need to cultivate the idea, however false or imprecise, that the people governs itself, albeit indirectly.[10] It is unlikely that the people, although flattered, are fooled, but the idea is worth endorsing.

In other words the democratic rhetoric has too much seductive capacity to be discarded. But even if it might be reasonable to leave democracy its name, the obligation not to pontificate remains. Democracy makes admirable promises, but maintains very few of them, and the confines with non-democracy are uncertain and badly defended. Neither should we forget that autocracy is not the only imaginable alternative to democracy. It would therefore be wise for the so-called democratic regimes to stop giving lessons. This book is, first of all, an invitation to caution.[11]

What this book proposes, in a special way, is to approach and reorganise some of the many elements that theory and research have recently accumulated on democratic regimes and their condition. Each reorganisation, however, implies a broad margin of arbitrariness. It may be convincing, and in fact it would be better if it was, but it will not be convincing for everyone. Other more convincing readjust-

---

9   Robert A. Dahl, *A Preface to Democratic Theory* (Chicago Ill., University of Chicago Press, 1956, pp. 75–81).

10 Hans Kelsen, 'On the Essence and Value of Democracy', in Arthur Jacobson, Bernhard Schlink. (eds.), *Weimar. A Jurisprudence of Crisis* (Berkeley, University of California Press [1929] 2000, p. 97).

11 For at least a decade there has been a steadily increasing flow of critical reflection, from different points of view, on the state of democracy. Admitting some syntony with the authors, despite their differences see: Marcel Gauchet, *La démocratie contre elle-même* (Paris, Gallimard, 2002); Colin Crouch, *Post-Democracy* (Cambridge, Polity Press, 2004); Pierre Rosanvallon, *Counter-Democracy. Politics in an Age of Distrust* (Cambridge, Cambridge University Press, 2008); Guy Hermet, *L'hiver de la démocratie ou le nouveau régime* (Paris, Colin, 2007); Sheldon S. Wolin, *Democracy Incorporated: Managed Democracy and the Specter of Inverted Totalitarianism* (Princeton NJ, Princeton University Press, 2008); Massimo Salvadori, *Democrazia senza democrazia* (Rome/Bari, Laterza, 2009); John Keane, *The Life and Death of Democracy* (New York, Simon & Schuster, 2009); Giuseppe Di Palma, *Viaggio nelle modernità. Rischio sociale e solidarietà dall'assolutismo al neoliberalismo e oltre* (Soveria Mannelli, Rubbettino, 2011).

ments are always feasible. We know that the best readjustments take place when taken calmly and rationally, or when all is said and done, and everything is known. This is certainly not our case, we can seldom reason on similar themes calmly, or pretend to do so.

What is certain is that democracy is a historical fact and that in a precise historical moment, and in particular circumstances, something bearing its name came into being. New circumstances have gradually transformed it, leaving the name intact, but making something different of it. This book deals with the applications of Western democracy, especially within Europe, and obviously feels the impact of the tormented dealings of the particular democratic regime that hosts its author.

In the light of their extremely problematic nature, the first two chapters deal with the disputes that intertwine around the definitions of democracy, the first and basic problem being the word itself. Its meaning has been defined a thousand times, and very authoritatively. But its success has made it extremely controversial. Politics, or the innumerable political actors – and not only professional politicians – pull it in every direction and self-assuredly bend it to their own needs.

Chapter 1 discusses how the word 'democracy' is used and how its meaning has broadened or contracted, depending on changing political conditions. Chapter 2 examines the government of the people. Letting the people govern is a magnificent promise, but one which is difficult to realise, among other things, because every different political actor will want to enlist the people for its own cause.

In the rest of the volume the reasoning on the recent transformations of democratic regimes is divided into four different chapters. Chapter 3 deals with the changes to the social fabric on which democracy rests. Chapter 4 considers the evolutions of democratic theory. Mid-twentieth century it understood democracy in one way, but a quarter of a century later it has completely different expectations. Chapter 5 and Chapter 6 examine the transformations undergone by the two basic mechanisms used by democracy mid-century – the state and political parties – and their important impact on institutional democratic structures.

How have the governed reacted to these changes? Chapter 7 questions the resentment that, according to the prevailing interpretation, citizens seem to have regarding democratic politics. Chapter 8 focuses on the appearance of political entrepreneurs who expressly cultivate this resentment: entrepreneurs who oppose not only other, already established, entrepreneurs, but who paradoxically even come from the ranks of the established. Chapter 9 is dedicated to the image and composition of the elective leaderships. The old concept of political class has been retrieved from the archives of theory, while some exacting adjustment has been made to the theory and practice of representation. Finally, Chapter 10 examines the multiple and complex manoeuvres used to face the alleged discontent of the governed, but perhaps directed solely at perfecting the changes which have taken place in the last thirty years.

At first sight this book offers a linear review on how theories, society, the state, parties and so forth, change. The problem is that these accounts intersect and that each of them has a multiplicity of versions and interpretations, that often differ and even rival each other. There are narratives formulated by actors and there are those drafted by observers, who are in fact also actors. The narratives are in turn politically-oriented filters through which we identify and observe phenomena. It is a well-known fact that we do many rather challenging things with words. That is to say, that the disputes – theoretical, but contextually political – and negotiations that take place around words, meanings, classifications and also ideas, theories and reviews that make words, are a vital element not just in the observation of the phenomena, but of the phenomena themselves.

Moreover, the part recited by professional observers of social and political phenomena should not be underrated. As specialists of narratives, interpretations and theories, they act in a field of their own, with its own operational rules and its own rites of admission, promotion and exclusion. Their relation with politics is an extremely complicated game, which needs to be reconstructed case by case. Sometimes they are ahead of events, sometimes they remain behind and are preceded by politics. Sometimes they back it, sometimes they contradict it. Intellectuals are never unanimous, and draw their political preferences and values from their biographies and from the contingent situation in which they live and work. They can be an organic part of a political formation or not, and can be associated with different schools of thought. These divisions also intersect. But in the moment when they describe, denominate, classify or explain, contributing to give an intelligible form and sense to what is observed – what we generically refer to as theory – sides with, and competes to set horizons of possibility, or to trace the limits of what is true, preferable, advisable, dutiful or prohibited.

They are not the only ones, but the intellectuals, especially those who are well-known, have always enjoyed particular professional acclaim. We do not know if this condition is likely to last. In the intellectual *milieux*, the school and university in first place, values and rules of behaviour differ from those commonly found elsewhere. Some segments of these ambits have adapted to the latter. Others are conditioned by their media visibility. But this has not happened to all. This may be why for some time now, politics has shown less appreciation for intellectual and academic activities and polemicises heavily with their rules of functioning, trying to bend them. It often does this through assessment procedures, promoting values – first of all competitiveness – imported from other ambits and at that moment more esteemed. At this moment, the theory is still an influential social practice and its involvement in the political game – not necessarily to the benefit of a particular part – is in any case an aspect to consider. We should also remember that the claim of being scientific, that social theory solemnly puts forward, is also a political move.

The book ends with a question for which it has no answer: once the word has been confirmed, what sort of democracy does the future have in store? The signs are uncertain. Furthermore, the capacity to predict the future is limited, also for the social sciences, while, as always, many unexpected things, not necessarily negative, are concealed in the fabric of the present. So, it is better to say it immediately, the final game – but surely similar matches never end – still has to be played.

chapter one | controversial definitions and uncertain boundaries

A human invention

Democracy, it seems, is the ultimate good, there being no better way to govern human beings. Yet, despite its success, we do not even a have a universally shared definition of what it actually means. There are a great many definitions, but as a rule they are vague. When they are not, they are problematic. What is the essence of democracy? The word is polysemic, changes meaning over time and can have more than one meaning at the same time. Even the definitions used to reduce the risks of controversy and to obtain maximum consensus, and referred to as minimal, are problematic.

Nevertheless, the choice of minimal definitions appears the least controversial, at least among scholars. Among these definitions, the one formulated by Norberto Bobbio stands out. Coming from a generation which had a direct and devastating experience of autocracy, Bobbio conceived of democracy as a threshold of inalienable conditions. By the time the disasters produced by democracy's main contender, socialism, had become apparent, Bobbio reunited and refined another two – minimal and renowned – definitions, that of Hans Kelsen,[1] and Joseph A. Schumpeter.[2] Yet, Bobbio preferred the realistic – but not resigned – minimalism of the former to the sceptical reductivism of the latter. Nowadays one cannot go far wrong defining democracy in this way, but how long this will last remains to be seen.

Bobbio's minimal definition is based more on the experience of twentieth-century democratic regimes than on theoretical premises. He stipulates the importance of 'who' decides in democracy and 'how', excluding any regulation of 'what' is to be decided, and he dictates three basic pre-conditions, or 'rules of the game'. The first rule stipulates that all citizens, or a very large number of them, must be entitled to vote. The second rule stipulates that all decisions must be taken by a majority. A third and final rule stipulates that the choice of voters must be exercised freely and made from among genuine alternatives.[3]

---

1   Hans Kelsen, 'On the Essence and Value of Democracy', in Arthur Jacobson, Bernhard Schlink (eds.), *Weimar. A Jurisprudence of Crisis* (Berkeley, University of California Press, [1929] 2000) and *General Theory of Law and State* (Cambridge MA, Harvard University Press, [1929] 1945).

2   Joseph A. Schumpeter, *Capitalism, Socialism and Democracy* (New York/London, Harper & Brothers, 1942).

3   Norberto Bobbio, *The Future of Democracy* (Cambridge, Polity Press, 1987, pp. 29–54).

These preconditions appear minimal and simple. Yet, in the present historical context, characterised by the failure of the socialist alternative and the rapid increase in the number of democratic regimes - even if it is a generally held belief that such regimes must necessarily conform to these preconditions, and that without them there can be no democracy – a great many problems remain unsolved. The boundaries appear clear, and in the real world of democratic regimes where the theories that justify, legitimate or criticise such regimes are devised, agreement on the minimal rules that Bobbio formulated is unanimous, or almost. This unanimity does not, however, extend to the interpretation and application of such rules.

Let us take the question of the majority principle. To begin with, what decisions is it applied to? What is an electoral majority? Is it the majority of those who actually vote, or the majority of those eligible to vote? Is it acceptable for voters' decisions to condition the lives of those who did not vote? Is it really fair that silence implies consent and that a non-vote has no value? Furthermore, since someone has to govern, is it acceptable that democratic regimes adopt electoral rules that often transform a relative majority of voters, that is, a substantial minority – but still minority – into a majority of parliamentary seats? Even if this occurs in the noblest democratic regimes, and we are accustomed to it, we are dealing with a subterfuge, justifiable in many ways, but a subterfuge nonetheless.

Moreover, let us consider the principle of choosing between different alternatives. What is meant by this? What is the appropriate degree of competition in order to define the choice of voters as democratic? A choice between two candidates, between ten candidates, between a thousand candidates? What rules must be used to carry out the electoral competition and who must the contestants be – individuals or parties? This is quite apart from the difficulties faced by voters. How much are they supposed to be informed about individual and collective contestants so as to choose, consciously, between them? What criteria should electors use when making their choice? Finally, and alluding to the current problem of the media, what is the threshold beyond which mass media interference becomes interference with the vote

The right to vote is in itself problematic. We can only talk of democracy in the full sense in conditions of universal suffrage. In Europe this occurred between the end of the nineteenth century and the mid-twentieth century. But even the criterion of the universality of the vote remains uncertain. First of all, the rules of access to the right to vote – and the way in which it is exercised – vary more than a little from one democratic regime to another. Some, for example, require that each individual applies to be registered on the electoral roll, and this is clearly an obstacle for some social strata. There is, moreover, a lack of agreement as to who is entitled to vote. As a rule, we do not make too much of the delay in the introduction of female suffrage, so as not to shorten the history of democratic regimes too much. But today the age of majority is still being discussed, and even the question of giving children the vote via their parents, has been raised.[4] Above all, today there is the question of whether a person born beyond the national boundaries, but who works, pays taxes, uses public services within those same boundaries, is entitled to vote or not.

Things become even more difficult when we try to explore this in more depth. The definition proposed by Bobbio, albeit minimal, is not intended to be void of values. Its rules are simple and essential, but not dictated by chance. They are derived from an onerous historical experience and are legitimated in the light of a particular conception of the world, and on the values that the modern Western world has raised to the level of its constituent values. Bobbio's definition has a normative thread running through it that makes it much more exacting than it seems. His definition recognises the equal dignity of human beings, and their ability to decide freely. It is furthermore based on the notion that human beings are able to take decisions, also together, regarding their destiny. This includes freedom of thought, speech, association and so forth. At the same time the democratic rules presuppose that conflict can be resolved in a civil way, through discussion and voting. If not why would we elect governments through free elections, or advocate the majority decision?

Once democratic procedures have been adopted, the next obvious step is to promote these values, but this is not always – and not sufficiently – the case. This is also because agreement on the meaning of such values is even more problematic than in the case of rules. What does freedom of thought mean? What is the meaning of tolerance? Who must democratic regimes extend this tolerance to? To all human beings? To their citizens? Or to whoever it is provisionally convenient? Agreement is lacking, and even in the West ideas of what these basic rights mean is somewhat divergent.

In other words, neither the rules formulated by Bobbio, nor the principles underpinning these rules, are decisive. All use the same word, all have given it with a miraculous meaning, but they do not all mean the same thing. Not in the least, is Robert A. Dahl satisfied with the fact that what he refers to, more submissively, as polyarchies, resemble, or try to meet his preconditions, stipulated in terms not very different from those by Bobbio.[5] But the ploy has had little success and the doubt

4   Philippe C. Schmitter, *How to Democratize the European Union…and Why Bother?* (Lanham, Rowman & Littlefield, 2000, pp. 40–41).

5   Bobbio's minimal definition of democracy is not the only one. See, for example, Robert A. Dahl, who established eight rules for polyarchy: each member of the organisation should be able to express his vote preference freely; the vote of each member should have the same weight; the alternative with the greatest number of votes will be the winner; before the vote all members have the right to add their own preference to the list of those standing for election; all citizens should be equally well informed about the options available; after the elections the alternative (leaders or policies) with the greatest number of votes takes precedence over those with less votes; citizens must accept the choice of who has been elected; between one election and another the choices adopted with the vote take precedence over all else, that is, they must correspond to the precedent conditions. See Dahl, *A Preface to Democratic Theory* (Chicago IL, University of Chicago Press,

remains as to what is democratic and what is not.

In return, democracy is based on the presumption that it is always preferable to non-democracy. Indeed, it is not at all certain that democratic regimes will always win when measured against non-democratic regimes, especially if we have the honesty to admit that the borderlines are porous. Democratic regimes are proud of the fact that the governors consult the governed regularly and that those in government alternate, following the choice of the governed. At the same time, the pluralistic nature of opinions, interests and also dissent are recognised, and coercion and violence are minimised in the political struggle. But perhaps we should not exaggerate. Non-democratic regimes, old or new, do not always correspond to autocracy, nor are they always brutal. Also in non-western and non-democratic regimes, government can be exercised with the consensus of the governed, and with respect to religious, linguistic, ethnic and cultural pluralism.[6]

Stripped of its *hauteur*, democracy is nothing more than one of the many 'technologies of power', of the legitimisation of power, and the resolution of conflicts. Separating democracy from the values that inspire and legitimate it is clearly a serious error. Historically democracy is the child of these values, no less than it is the child of pluralism and conflict. It is however a solution devised in historical conditions, where no actor was able to predominate over others, and where all considered it convenient to recognise pluralism, to accept the official and peaceful competition for political authority, and to involve the governed in the action of government. Historically this option may even have been imposed by whoever was temporarily the stronger grouping, in order to facilitate cohabitation between individual and collective actors on the one hand, and government on the other.

Once pluralism and competition for authority had been officially acknowledged, they then needed to be regulated. Following in the steps of the representative system, which is their legitimate forefather,[7] democratic regimes officially grant all the politically relevant actors a generous dose of autonomy. Nevertheless, these regimes dictate also rather strict rules of behaviour and subject actors to rules that are no less severe when it comes to competing for power. In contrast to the coercion and explicit constraints of autocracy, democratic regimes prefer internalised, invisible and less stringent constraints, that allow them to raise the

---

1956, p. 84). The minimal definitions also include that of Bernard Manin, according to which representative and democratic government should hold elections of representatives at regular intervals, and should be, at least partially, independent, opinions should be freely held, and decisions should be taken on the basis of discussion; see Manin, *The Principles of Representative Government* (Cambridge, Cambridge University Press, 1995, pp. 161–192).

6   Amartya Sen reminds us of this in 'Democracy as a Universal Value', *Journal of Democracy* 10(3) 1999, 3–17. For an interesting review somewhere between anthropology and historiography, of procedural assembly and government through discussion that involves members of the social body, also beyond the West, see Marcel Detienne (eds.), *Qui veut prendre la parole?* (Paris, Seuil, 2003).

7   Manin, *Principles of Representative Government.*

flags of freedom and equality.[8] The constraints, however, exist regardless.

Once democratic governors had reconciled to cyclical turnover, they also had to tolerate the enlargement of their pool of recruitment, and the range of interests and values deemed politically relevant. However, democratic regimes, like any other regime, do not react well to anything unexpected and therefore do manage to protect themselves carefully against unexpected prospects of change and unexpected forms of pluralism.

The opponents of universal suffrage feared its consequences and it was only introduced because realism prevailed. Universal suffrage was, however, subject to various filtering devices such as electoral rules, parliamentary regulations, and all sorts of ideological and cultural constraints. These regulated it and mitigated the much-feared risks. Above all, the realists knew from the outset that they could profit from the composite nature of the electorate and from the persistence of some traditional forms of deference, such as voters in rural areas, catholics and women. It was this that probably allowed the realisation of something we agree on calling democracy. However, from the outset democracy has always hosted an oligarchic claim. This is relaxed whenever the political struggle registers vigorous thrusts from below, and resumes, perhaps dressed up in new words and forms, when routine is re-established.

Authoritarian regimes have taken a totally different direction: that of the official negation of pluralism. Instead of containing it, they simply negate it. This is done primarily with coercion, but also with non-violent methods. There are many ways to obtain conformity and acquiescence from the governed, and authoritarian regimes turn out to be much less coherent and compact than their rhetoric would have us believe. There is no authoritarian regime that has not been torn by fierce power struggles and authoritarian regimes tend to repress pluralism, but to varying degrees. One thing is the Soviet regime, another is nazism, and yet others are fascism or franchism, that, for example, conceded ample space to the Roman Catholic church. It is important to recognise these differences as well as the variations within each of these regimes through time, space and policy areas.[9]

In conclusion, however much democracy is polemically mirrored in autocracy, and raises the flags of freedom and equality. In the real world authoritarianism and democracy are not necessarily mutually exclusive, but learn one from one another and are reciprocally influencing each other. We can imagine them as the two ends of a continuum whose unifying feature or legitimating principle is 'the people'. In the middle are a great many diverse forms of hybridisation.[10]

---

8   This is what Pierre Bourdieu rather crudely refers to as 'symbolic violence' in *Pascalian Meditations* (Stanford, Stanford University Press, 2000, pp. 49–84). On how modernity has enlarged the spaces of these limitations unwittingly, see Norbert Elias's classic, *The Civilizing Process, The History of Manners* (Oxford, Blackwell, 2006).

9   For an example full of the possible expressions of power and consensus see Béatrice Hibou, *Anatomie politique de la domination* (Paris, La Découverte, 2011).

10   The question of the hybridisation has been raised by Michel Camau and Gilles Massardier (eds.),

Democratic regimes govern in the name of the people, but so do authoritarian regimes. The idea that these two regime types have of the people is clearly very different. The people of democratic regimes is made up of individual bearers of basic and inalienable rights. The people of non-democratic regimes is the people *in toto*, understood organically – and at times ethnically – and that prevails over individuals. Nevertheless it is significant that modern non-democratic regimes in Europe – the dictatorships of Cromwell, Napoleon I and Napoleon III, Mussolini and Hitler – all openly evoked the notion of the people, albeit in different ways.

The shift from one notion of the people to the other is not particularly difficult. It is enough to invoke some higher need of the collective body, or the people, in order to suppress pluralism and to weaken the defence of individuals. The good of what is defined the people predominates over the good of its parts, and the latter can be sacrificed – revoked, suspended, distorted or restricted. Experience teaches us that democratic rulers can resort to similar expedients not only in the presence of a real threat to democracy, but also when it is convenient to invent such a threat. This occurs, for example, when a dangerous adversary appears, or with the arrival of unknown and ill-defined forms of pluralism which are difficult to assimilate.

The opponents of universal suffrage considered the imperfection and the incompleteness of democracy to be congenital. Indeed, for them democracy was a mystification, a deception, and an illusionary and unrealisable promise, which it would be better to be free of. In the long run similar arguments have been silenced and the opponents of universal suffrage, or their heirs, have generally adapted to democracy. The fact remains that democratic systems are extremely imperfect, or are bursting with 'broken promises'. They evoke ideals that legitimate them and that have historically inspired many attempts to perfect them, but these go largely unheeded, not only because they are controversial, but because democracy itself makes them controversial. If nothing else, this is good to know, and we can take comfort from the great virtue of the rules of the democratic game. Irrespective of how one limits the application of the rules, it is impossible to silence every critical voice. These can be blocked, but not suppressed. It is also difficult to prevent actors from working to perfect democracy, to renew its content and to bring its practice nearer to its principles[11].

Démocraties et autoritarismes. Fragmentation et hybridation des régimes (Paris, Karthala, 2009). See, in particular, the introduction by the editors: 'Revisiter les régimes politiques'. See also Gilles Massardier, Olivier Dabène, Vincent Geisser, *Autoritarismes démocratiques et démocraties autoritaires au XXIe siècle: Convérgences Nord-Sud* (Paris, La Découverte, 2009).

11 Bobbio, *The Future of Democracy*, pp. 34–37.

Procedure and substance

The rules laid down by Bobbio are few and simple, but become fragile and controversial when it comes to their interpretation and application. One can imagine how controversial attempts to broaden democracy are, which establish that in order to speak of democracy we need to satisfy other conditions.

Let us start from the historical experience. Once instituted, democratic regimes have been progressively enriched by a body of measures designed to reduce inequalities and to guarantee all citizens work, education, housing, healthcare and pensions. The differences between one country and another are striking, but in the second postwar period all democratic regimes set up more or less reliable safety nets of guarantees to protect citizens against life's uncertainties.

Once Bobbio had identified a first type of democracy, under the labels of 'rules of the game', 'formal democracy' or 'procedural democracy', he then identified a second type, thanks to the egalitarian policies introduced especially in the second half of the twentieth century, and which he refers to as 'substantive democracy'. The democracy of who decides and how decisions are made, is flanked by a democracy of what must be decided. But does democracy really dictate constraints on the level of political choices in the direction of equality and social justice that sets it apart from all other forms of government?

Bobbio was a convinced proponent of liberal socialism. Nevertheless he sustained that the marriage between formal and substantive democracy, albeit desirable, was not indispensable. Democracy, in his opinion, consisted solely of the 'rules of the game'.[12] Taking this reasoning to the level of values, according to Bobbio, democracy must pursue both equality and justice, but without ever sacrificing liberty. First of all, democracy must safeguard the rules of the game and the opportunity to play according to these rules. In any case the latter allow us to adopt policies that help promote greater justice and equality. Bobbio instructs us to stick to who and how and to leave to all decisions on what to the electoral contest and the majority principle, i.e. to politics.

It is paradoxical, but among those tending towards an enrichment of the meaning of democracy – holding egalitarian policies to be one of its constituent elements – we find some of democracy's enemies, particularly those who had worked most

---

12 For the dilemma between procedural and substantive democracy, see Bobbio, *The Future of Democracy.* It is worth recalling how Bobbio proposed his minimal definition of democracy. In 1975 he was concentrating on the procedural aspects with his interlocutor, the Italian Communist Party (PCI), then driven to the threshold of government by electoral results, but still accused by some of a preference for democratic substantivism not accompanied by a sufficient focus on procedures. The text was published in *Which Socialism?: Marxism, Socialism and Democracy* (Cambridge, Polity Press, [1975] 1987). For an accurate presentation of Bobbio's ideas and of the context in which he expressed them see Corina Yturbe, 'On Norberto Bobbio's Theory of Democracy', *Political Theory* 25(3), 1997, 377–400.

to prevent its realisation. The case of a conservative thinker like Gaetano Mosca is exemplary[13] – universal suffrage and a democratic regime would not only have given a voice to the less-educated, but would have also meant political measures leading to an upheaval in the distribution of property and wealth, and thus an upheaval of the social order itself.

As we know, this upheaval never took place. What occurred was more peaceful and unpretentious, like the redistributive policies of welfare. The conservatives became resigned to it when they discovered that democracy was not disturbing property and social order, and therefore it earned a virtuous reputation and a significant surplus of legitimacy. What remains to be seen, however, is whether this legitimacy is transferred automatically into the redistributive policies promoted by socialist-led or popular parties, and even maintained by conservative parties for a long time, making them a truly inalienable component of democracy itself. Some democratic theorists assert this, while others resolutely deny it, demonstrating very clearly that the difference between procedure and substance is not an elegant theoretical controversy, but the stake of a much more exacting contention that affects relations between democracy and the market in a special way. Politics is also a way to gain and to distribute resources. Why else would it mean defining substantive democracy as democratic if not to establish that a public intervention of readjustment, specifically designed to balance out market-generated inequalities, is democratically legitimate and even a political due?

When the recommendations of the Beveridge Report were being implemented by Clement Attlee's Labour government, with its theory of citizens' rights, Thomas H. Marshall considered this sort of intervention, and the egalitarian action of the state, to be completely legitimate.[14] Rights have a complicated history. They were initially acclaimed as limits to the powers of the state. They circumscribed an untouchable sphere of citizens' autonomy which limited the action of the state in guaranteeing the physical wellbeing of its citizens and the protection of their material goods. Over time the action of the state *vis-à-vis* its citizens has been extended for a range of reasons. This is not necessarily to the benefit of the citizens themselves (as in the case of education or healthcare), so much as to the benefit of the state, or in the interests of a well-ordered collective existence and social stability. Yet, in the long-term the idea that key services provided by the state could benefit citizens and should, in particular, help remove the inequalities that divide

---

13 Gaetano Mosca, 'Cause e rimedi della crisi del regime parlamentare', in *Partiti e sindacati nella crisi del regime parlamentare* (Bari, Laterza, 1949, p. 98).

14 Thomas H. Marshall, *Citizenship and Social Class, and Other Essays* (Cambridge, Cambridge University Press, 1950). Marshall anchored rights in citizens rather than the individual. In reality, the problem of citizenship and its limits has only recently become a pressing issue, due to the migratory processes which have hit Europe. In Marshall's reasoning, the word 'citizenship' does not have a restrictive meaning. On the contrary, it means the full inclusion of the popular classes following the introduction of universal suffrage.

them, became a strategic theme of political struggle. In the end these services come to be considered mandatory and were consecrated by extending the concept of rights. As a tribute to the Whig historiographic tradition, what Marshall called, social, rights thus became the fulfilment of a precise evolutionary course – and of egalitarian convergence – which had been undertaken with the introduction of civil and political rights, and of which 'social rights' were the obvious next step. But what was obvious for Marshall – and not only for him – is not taken for granted by all.

For example, a quarter of a century earlier Hans Kelsen who, despite his social-democratic inclinations, and having differentiated 'political' democracy from 'social' democracy, carefully distanced himself from the latter. In line with his notion of the state, and in dispute with Marxism-Leninism then experimenting with the revolution of the soviets, Kelsen considered democracy a 'method of creation' of the social order, open to egalitarian outcomes, but not limited to realising them.[15]

This adhesion to proceduralism, where equality and social justice are cut short, can be seen as a first defeat for democracy. But one can also, realistically, suppose that, without the priority of the formal dimension, what we today call democracy would never have overcome the opposition of its adversaries. Apart from his hostility to Marxism, this was Kelsen's idea. At the time and place in which he was writing, binding democracy to egalitarian content would have provoked reactions, even violent reactions, that would simply have swept it away. The theoretical toll paid by Kelsen was, as we know, insufficient, because Weimar democracy did not manage to avoid such reactions. But the dilemma still stands.

On the other hand, supporting the priority of procedures does not automatically entail sufficient guarantees for democratic vitality. For a strict proceduralist such as Bobbio, redistributive policies were democratically healthy and even indispensable.[16] With the same decision, Dahl has also raised the question of the inequalities that afflict democratic regimes which he invites us to resolve through what he calls 'economic' democracy.[17] Lastly, Luigi Ferrajoli is quite peremptory in his monumental piece of research devoted to democracy and democratic rights. 'Yes', he argues, 'political' democracy is the minimal threshold for 'constitutional' democratic regimes, but this threshold, even if necessary, is 'completely insufficient'. What is needed is 'multi-dimensional' democracy that includes other key dimensions, such as social rights.[18]

---

15 Kelsen, 'On the Essence and Value of Democracy' , p. 98.

16 See, for example, Norberto Bobbio, 'Eguaglianza', *Enciclopedia del Novecento* (Rome, Istituto dell'Enciclopedia Italiana, 1977, vol. II).

17 Robert A. Dahl, *A Preface to Economic Democracy* (Berkeley, University of California Press, 1985).

18 Luigi Ferrajoli, *Principia juris. Teoria del diritto e della democrazia 1* (Bari, Laterza, 2009, vol. II, 20–23). Ferrajoli traces the boundaries between substantive democracy and procedural democracy

Not all proceduralists, however, are so open to discussion and conciliatory. There are some for whom substantive democracy, or the policies identified with it, constitute a redundant and inappropriate addition to democracy, since they would place democratically unacceptable restrictions on basic freedoms. For others, the democracy of 'what' could impose burdensome constraints on democratic decisions, limiting the present and future opportunities of the choices made by the democratically elected and their electors.[19]

The second argument is not uncommon and merits careful examination. Apart from regarding substantive democracy as inalienable, to what point is it opportune for the advocates of justice and equality that one or more political actors, temporarily majoritarian (also to a great degree, as is normally the case for constitutional decisions), are allowed to claim preferences that have matured in a given historical moment, and are thus the fruit of a historically contingent equilibrium of power as a democratic due, in the form of rights and constitutional provisions. And if at the first suitable occasion, other political actors claimed to deconsecrate these principles democratically and to consecrate as rights other preferences: free competition in the place of social rights and who knows what else? The concept of justice is democratically controversial, as are rights. The European Union has already promoted market competition as an inalienable democratic requirement and sooner or later someone may propose making it a right. Some democrats of very dubious credentials, have also tried to transform the cultural rights of repressed minorities, such as native Americans or native Australians, into a more generalised 'right to identity' which can also be used against ethnic and religious minorities in order to ban the Islamic headscarf or the building of mosques. Perhaps we should not exaggerate when it comes to rights.

What some proceduralists still mind beyond the restrictions that the attribution of some substance to democracy would impose on freedom – of the more fortunate classes or strata – is the overall inadequacy of the scheme. Procedural democracy, they argue, is realistic because the individual civil and political rights on which it is based have no cost, while the same cannot be said of social rights and policies. The argument is both debatable and debated. The substantivists reply, and not without good reason, that their egalitarian democracy is not only desirable, but also realistic, because, at least in part, it has already existed somewhere and generated benefits for collective life. The great postwar economic development was, to a great extent, powered by the policies of the welfare state. Furthermore, it is not true that civil and political rights are cost-free. The protection of all

---

in terms which differ from those used by Bobbio. For Ferrajoli fundamental rights introduce constraints and obligations regarding what democracy can do, and consequently already belong to the sphere of substantive democracy (Ferrajoli, pp. 13–18).

19   Anna Pintore reproposed this perspective with great polemical *verve*, but using rather stringent arguments. See 'Insatiable Rights', *International Journal for the Semiotics of Law* 14(3), 2001, 277–297.

rights, including civil and political rights, entails considerable costs.[20] How can we exercise the right to own property without public services and infrastructure, which are also an inevitable burden on the social body? And how can we ignore the fact that since Western democratic regimes have adopted policies that reshape welfare policies and reduce taxation, the investments in law-and-order policies appear to have increased considerably? Is this really coincidental? Reducing social policies can often prove socially, but also financially, costly.

Where equality and justice are officially recognised as necessary elements of democracy, and are inseparable from its procedures, the question of costs would not arise, and nor would the question of the limitations to freedom. Some degree of reduction of the freedoms of socially or economically advantaged minorities, or the reduction of a democratically debatable right (also in the light of the principles which support the procedures listed by Bobbio) such as that of property, might be tolerable disadvantages if the freedom and dignity of the greater number benefit. Can a regime legitimately define itself as democratic when the freedom and dignity of its members are a function of their income level? Can citizens in need, or those suffering from ignorance or illness, really exercise democratic freedom?

Similar arguments may be persuasive, but do not to convince everyone. It is precisely this sort of question that authors like Thomas H. Marshall have been posing and trying to answer for a quarter of a century from 1945 until around 1970, together with the fathers of the postwar constitutions and charters, for whom democracy was a body of procedural regulations, but also a body of content, that democratic regimes were held to respect.

It is true that there was a period when some advocates of substantive democracy made absolutely liquidating declarations against procedural democracy. What is the value, they said, of procedure without substance? But that season, when it was held that democracy could also exist with procedures other than those indicated by Bobbio, is now long past. It came to an end after the experience of pure substantivism proved catastrophic in regimes that were defined (or auto-defined), as 'popular democracies' thus confirming the disputed and flexible nature of the term.[21] Since then the substantivists have resisted, but they have now reached a compromise with proceduralism, albeit without getting much in return.

---

20 Stephen Holmes and Cass R. Sunstein argue that rights always entail costs: see *The Costs of Rights. Why Liberty Depends on Taxes* (New York, W. W. Norton, 1999). See also Liam Murphy and Thomas Nagel, *The Myth of Ownership. Taxes and Justice* (Oxford, Oxford University Press, 2000).

21 A very well-known work by an authoritative French specialist of public law and political science, George Burdeau, includes 'Marxist' and, according to the way they defined themselves, 'popular', democracies in his classification of democratic regimes (Georges Burdeau, *La démocratie. Essai synthètique*, Bruxelles, Office de la publicité, 1956, pp. 73–86). In 1968, another authoritative French specialist dedicated course lessons to Marxist democracies: see Georges Vedel, *Les démocraties soviétiques et populaires* (Paris, Cours de droit de l'Université de Paris, 1968).

Despite the fact that it is not short-lived, not even the historical experience of welfare policies has helped halt the controversy. The successes of welfare have helped convert the substantivists to the benefits of proceduralism, while maintaining substantive democracy as the condition of the full functionality of procedural democracy. But the pure proceduralists refuse to reciprocate. The convergence on procedures has gratified them, but not converted them and is seriously detrimental to the substantivists. Once the latter recognised the procedures as a priority, albeit minimal and insufficient, they surrendered. While proceduralists have become more rigid, having won, thanks to the neo-liberal turn and policies inspired by it, why do they need to be conciliatory with the vanquished?

Notwithstanding all attempts at conciliation in both the political and theoretical ambits, the controversy between formal democracy and substantive democracy remains unresolved. Or rather the substantivists resist, but the proceduralists have had the better of them: practically no-one now doubts the need for procedures to identify democratic regimes.[22] A conflict of values and a power struggle, as mentioned, clearly underlie the semantic contention. The democratic regimes which emerged after World War II chose to combine the two meanings of the word democracy in their constitutional provisions, but this agreement turned out to be temporary and the two meanings collided.

Certainly, a regime that does not protect equality and justice sufficiently may not please some, or even many, who will define it as non-democratic, but nowadays the most they can do is to try to persuade voters. Declaring the egalitarian policies of welfare democratic, and defining them in terms of basic and universal rights, is a political fact that has a very high value for some. It gives a universalistic character to social rights, to anchor social policies in the dignity of the individual, without reducing them to charitable assistance for those in conditions of hardship, and tracing debatable lines of division between the 'haves' and the 'have-nots'. But at the moment, democratically speaking, egalitarian policies remain an intent and an ambition. Current events are witnessing how social rights are anything but an irreversible conquest.

While attempts to deconsecrate social rights, and to consecrate expectations and claims of quite another tenor as rights, seem destined to succeed – if they have not already done so – proceduralists should however ask themselves whether, by chance, the basic freedoms do not also run a risk of being deconsecrated. At first sight it is easier to protect the rights of freedom than it is to guarantee social rights: the complexity of modern society supports them. But what will happen if the living standards of a large part of the population are not sufficiently protected by democracy? Will citizens remain loyal to the democratic rules and concerned about what happens to them? At the practical level the fate of basic rights is not, by any chance, favoured by that of social rights?

22　A substantivist perspective was recently reproposed by Philippe Van Parijs in *Just Democracy. The Rawls-Machiavelli Programme* (Colchester, ECPR Press, 2011).

The paradox is that once democracy has been reduced to procedures, we cannot be sure that some substance will not be excluded from its policies. If we strip democracy of all obstacles to popular sovereignty and majority declarations,[23] even then, once it has been reduced to just a few rules and some minimal assumptions, it would still have a robust content. If procedural democracy is a way to regulate political competition, not setting limits to 'what' implies that democracy is open-ended: it can adopt egalitarian welfare policies, but it can also adopt their opposite. Substance is thus prescribed for democratic policies even when there is a ban on substance. Defining the non-intervention of governments in the face of poverty, illness and ignorance, as democratically legitimate, and trusting all restorative interventions to impulsive electoral verdicts, means recognising the democratic legitimacy of inequalities, especially after the decades of welfarist protection.

Once again the controversy is not just theoretical. Today we know that, irrespective of whether we consider it a right or not, an acceptable implementation of social policies requires much more time than the interval between one general election and another, and that therefore, entrusting such policies to the majority of the day means jeopardising these policies for a good while. A strict proceduralist will remain indifferent and maintain his position. We can, however, be certain that the beneficiaries of social policies will suffer some non-secondary problems, not without significant advantages for the well-off.

Not all procedures are equal

Today, the idea of a minimum threshold of democracy, irrespective of how debatable, is certainly one of the most generally shared ideas. However, not only does the minimum threshold host some binding content, but it can vary a great deal, although very little is said about this. There are procedures and procedures, and they are anything but interchangeable. Democratic regimes have an infinite variety of rules of the game, each with their own interpretation and application. These allow us to decline the democracy of 'who' and 'how' in an infinite number of ways, with striking consequences for the 'what': that is, for politics. It is a well-known fact that rules condition the game and its results, and that they are also, and not incidentally, the object of fierce theoretical debates and even more heated political disputes.

There are procedures that provide for the collegial action of the executive and others that prefer monocratic leadership. There are procedures that subject the executive to parliament, others that place the two organs on the same level, and yet others that subject parliament to the executive. Within elected assemblies, there are decisions that can be taken by majority declaration, whereas others, on particular questions, require a qualified majority. Some procedures encourage conciliation

---

23 Jeremy Waldron, *The Dignity of Legislation* (Cambridge, Cambridge University Press, 1999).

between different points of view, whilst others discourage it. The current debate on so-called 'deliberative democracy'[24] would re-legitimate and promote public debate at all levels. It views procedural revisions to reinforce – also in parliaments – opportunities for conciliation, which have been on the decline for some time due to the primacy attributed to the executive and its supporting majority. There are also single-chamber regimes and bicameral regimes, symmetrical bicameralism and asymmetrical bicameralism, centralised regimes and federal regimes.

Turning to the norms regulating elections, these too, are very different. Looking at electoral law, who has the right to vote? How does a citizen enrol to vote? Who is entitled to be a candidate? Who presides over electoral operations? How are they carried out, and how are the results checked?[25] Then there are the electoral systems *stricto sensu*, that transform votes into parliamentary seats. Some photograph the distribution of political preferences of the electorate, albeit in a rather approximate fashion. Other electoral systems simplify elector preferences in various ways, and yet others reduce them to two options or thereabouts. Proportional systems favour a multiplication of the political supply and more accurate mirroring of the political orientations of voters in the representative institutions, whereas majoritarian systems transform a minority of votes into a majority of seats.[26]

According to the advocates of this second solution, it is not very important to represent all political opinions. After all, it is better to suppress a part, forcing the voters to adopt positions that are useless or pretentious from among the prevalent orientations. Opinions can be expressed in other ways and in other spaces. The values that need to be protected, it is claimed, are government stability, which is a guarantee of efficiency, or the popular will. It is also preferable that the political colour of the executive, and the way it operates, depend on voters' choices rather than the alchemy of parties and parliament. Whenever voters are dissatisfied they can retaliate by voting for the other side at the next elections.

Different types of electoral regime also imply different strategies by those competing in elections, and different behaviour on the part of voters.[27] In proportional systems parties need to have national and local strategies at the same time. In single or double-turn uninominal systems political forces need to concentrate on marginal constituencies, by adopting propagandistic strategies targeted at the local level. The overall constitutional architecture is not irrelevant. In France semi-presidentialism encourages national electoral strategies, where

---

24 For a first definition see John Elster (ed.), *Deliberative Democracy* (Cambridge, Cambridge University Press, 1998).

25 For a comparative review see Louis Massicotte, Andre Blais, Antoine Yoshinaka, *Establishing the Rules of the Game: Election Laws in Democracies* (Toronto, University of Toronto Press, 2004).

26 Arend Lijphart and Bernard Grofman (eds.), *Electoral Laws and Their Political Consequences* (New York, Agathon Press, 1986).

27 See the very broad comparison carried out by Pippa Norris, *Electoral Engineering: Voting Rules and Political Behaviour* (Cambridge, Cambridge University Press, 2004).

the vote for the President nearly always acts as a driving force for parliamentary elections. To reinforce this effect, the two electoral deadlines have now coincided, or almost. In the American system the election of the President is decided at the level of swing states, while in Italy the national party leaderships count to such an extent, that the system introduced in 2006 only allows voters to vote on blocked lists.

In proportional regimes the elector is usually free to vote for who he prefers, whereas in uninominal regimes he is invited to vote for the party and the candidate whose ideas are least far from his own, and who is most likely to win. In recent times the structure of political competition has been modified, placing a majoritarian bias on nearly all electoral regimes.

Furthermore, there are procedures which neither encourage nor discourage participation, others that make the vote more difficult (e.g. by making citizens responsible for registering on the electoral roll), and yet others that stimulate participation beyond electoral deadlines, through parties or associations.[28]

It is clear that when one procedure is adopted rather than another, what is at stake is not so much – as officially claimed – the freedom and equality of voters, the stability and efficiency of government action, or the greater or lesser capacity of the governed to influence the work of government *ex ante* and to monitor it *ex post*. It is not even – an old argument recently reproposed – the morality of politics, that no procedure is able to guarantee.[29] The rules are not established by an independent authority, but the players themselves provide them. It is no accident that the contention surrounding them is so intense: what is at stake are the power relations between the political forces and, as a consequence, the policies that they can carry out, precisely because one or other procedure will produce very different political equilibria: tending to favour certain actors and certain policies over others. We should ask ourselves whether the downsizing suffered by welfare does not have something to do with the majoritarian turn taken by democratic regimes.[30]

---

28 Primaries, for example, encourage occasional participation. For a broad reconnaissance of the variables that influence participation see Laura Morales, *Joining Political Organisations: Institutions, Mobilisation and Participation in Western Democracies* (Colchester, ECPR Press, 2009).

29 It is no coincidence that the reasons adopted in the public debate to cancel the proportional electoral regime in Italy in the early 1990s were much the same as those used to introduce it in 1919.

30 In addition to the already cited articles by Arend Lijphart, see *Patterns of Democracy: Government Forms and Performance in Thirty-Six Countries* (New Haven CT, Yale University Press, 1999). For an examination of the book's hypotheses, and one that does not refute its conclusions, see Klaus Armingeon, 'The Effects of Negotiation Democracy: A Comparative Analysis', *European Journal of Political Research* 41(1), 2002, 81–105. In the same number of the *EJPR* see Arend Lijphart, 'Negotiation Democracy versus Consensus Democracy: Parallel Conclusions and Recommendations', *European Journal of Political Research* 41(1), 2001, 107–113.

This is why the dispute over procedures deserves no less attention than the dispute between procedure and substance. As to procedures, during the twentieth century democratic regimes registered a triple movement which was not without consequences. The first movement was universal suffrage: new social classes infiltrated the citadel of power and made their presence felt, even if not in the way feared by the opponents of such suffrage. The second movement was the extension and intensification of democracy. Political equality has been corroborated with a discrete dose of social and economic equality and also with procedures suited to the political parties which favour it. Institutional incentives have also been introduced to encourage participation and collective mobilisation. These help balance the advantages enjoyed by the well-off and educated, and many regimes preferred procedures that promoted broad-based, multi-party coalitions.

In spite of those who considered it irreversible, the transition from procedure to substance, and the transition from a slight and hasty procedure to an intense procedure encouraging participation, has nevertheless come to a end. During the closing years of the twentieth century politics imposed a third movement – or counter-movement – on democratic regimes. Procedures were adopted that reduced the mobilisation potential of the 'big numbers' and broke down their opposition to the downsizing of welfare policies. This counter-movement included the tendency to limit the spaces where democratic procedures can be applied.[31]

Even democratic regimes with the best credentials have instituted and enlarged the spaces reserved for apparently non-political institutions, but whose decisions are always political. Democratic regimes have restricted the spaces for electoral competition, for the dialectic between parties, and for social conflict, and have multiplied the number of independent regulatory agencies, the forms of non-elected representation and the negotiations of governance, to which only the so-called 'stakeholders' are admitted. Let us not forget also the various participatory and deliberative procedures, which are strictly non-partisan. Furthermore, we should add the introduction of privatistic-managerial criteria in public administration and the restitution of the supply of some basic public services to the market. We should also recall the strengthening of executive power, at the cost of that of parliaments and parties, the evolution of the latter as agencies of electoral marketing, and the adoption of electoral rules that have a reductive impact on party pluralism. The list is likely to get longer.

The counter-movement finally accelerated, through the more frequent adoption of emergency procedures by governments. Similar procedures have always existed, but the combined pressure of a terrorist threat and migratory fluxes have given them a powerful impetus. We have however been witnessing a multiplication of

---

31 Michael Saward, 'Reconstructing Democracy: Current Thinking and New Directions', *Government and Opposition* 36(4), 2001, 559–581. In his now classic work, Danilo Zolo was among the first to point out this evolution clearly in *Democracy and Complexity. A Realist Approach* (Cambridge, Polity Press, 1992).

national instances of when the ordinary rules are suspended. Natural catastrophes, economic crises, or the realisation of particularly complex public works, all are excellent opportunities to do so. It is arguable that the rhetoric which stigmatises the 'exception-as-the-rule', the emancipation of politics from law, and thus the authoritarian turn taken by democratic regimes – both treacherous and striking – is probably overrated.[32] But only up to a certain point. There is reason to believe that the application of rules, principles and democratic rights is undergoing a severe downward revision.

---

32 For an alarmist perspective see Giorgio Agamben, *State of Exception* (Chicago IL, University of Chicago Press, 2005). For a critique see Jef Huysmans, 'The Jargon of Exception. On Schmitt, Agamben and the Absence of Political Society', *International Political Sociology* 2(2), 2008, 165–183.

chapter two | the government of the people

Invented by chance

With no disrespect for those who coined the term around two thousand years ago, democracy is in fact an invention of Western modernity. The first grounds for its originality is the binding promise which its name contains and displays: if power cannot be abolished, then at least it should be entrusted to its beneficiaries. Indeed, this ambitious promise, with which democracy adorns itself, is certainly part of it as a technology of power, albeit not without some drawbacks. If, on the one hand, this promise has great legitimising capacity, on the other hand, democratic rulers remain imprisoned by it. In other words, the term 'democracy' is grounds for both its strengths and weaknesses.

The origins of the word 'democracy' date back a long way,[1] but, after Rousseau's *Social Contract*, it was the American Revolution[2] and the French Revolution – which often used it warily and preferring the term of republic – that brought the term back into the world's eye.[3] The historical course taken by modern democratic regimes dates instead, back to the mid-seventeenth century, when the English Revolution initiated, not democratic government, but representative government. A regime where power was exercised by the King, and the oligarchy that flanked him, was replaced by a regime that officially enthroned the people,[4] albeit through Parliament. Claiming legitimacy based on the participation of the governed, or rather, of an authorised and restricted portion of the governed, that new regime pledged to pursue their interests.[5]

---

1   On the term 'democracy' see, for example, Moises I. Finley, *Democracy Ancient and Modern* (New Brunswick, Rutgers University Press, 1975). But Greek democracy was very different from modern democracy: see Paul Veyne, 'Did the Greeks Know Democracy?', *Economy and Society* 34(2), 2005, 322–245. The tormented route taken by the term and the concept has been summed up at last by John Dunne in, *Setting the People Free: The Story of Democracy* (London, Atlantic Books, 2005). For an impressive reconstruction of the long and arduous path taken by democracy from its origins to the present day, see John Keane, *The Life and Death of Democracy* (London, Simon & Schuster, 2009). According to Keane, democracy's origins are even more ancient than the Greek ones.

2   Robert R. Palmer, 'Notes on the Use of the Word "Democracy", 1789–1799', *Political Science Quarterly* 95(2), 1953, 203–226.

3   Raymonde Monnier, 'Démocratie et révolution française', *Mots. Les langages du politique* 59(9), 1999, 47–68.

4   Margaret Canovan, *The People* (Cambridge, Polity Press, 2005, pp. 16–19).

5   For an accurate and fascinating account of this affair see Edmund S. Morgan, *Inventing the People*:

No-one wanted the upheaval of the social hierarchy: what the Parliament had in mind was the Venetian oligarchy, and this was the bugbear of Charles I.[6] But King and Parliament both pronounced the name of the people. Parliament called the people to its aid against the absolutist claims of Charles I. Keen to follow the example of the French and Spanish sovereigns, and to cancel the age-old feudal and estatist dualism that had until then juxtaposed Parliament to the King, Charles I invoked the good of the people and his royal obligations towards them. No-one anticipated radical outcomes, or expected that the name of the people, hurled back and forth between Parliament and King, would change its meaning in the course of events, or that the abstract entity they evoked would actually materialise.[7]

The procedure then in use was rough and ready, but the Parliament that rose up against the King had been chosen following a bitter electoral struggle with the party that supported the monarchy.[8] The King, no less than Parliament, tried to stir up a broad popular mobilisation around their disputes, which happened to continue the religious mobilisation already taking place. While the people of London protested on the streets and designated Parliament as their spokesperson, the Puritans called for the universal priesthood of believers and the equal dignity of human beings. Finally, in the thick of the Civil War, the *Agreement of the People* appeared[9] and its authors proclaimed themselves the true and unmediated voice of the people. Not be mitigated by pre-existing representative mechanisms, this voice sketched the profile of a people made up of individuals equal among themselves, who would regularly elect their own representatives, subject to just and unarbitrary laws, equal before those laws, and free to profess their own faith. This heralded the arrival of a new protagonist on the scene, and set in motion the archiving of a very old technology of power and the adoption of a rather different one.

Rulers had always taken those they ruled into account. Involving the people, whether openly or not, was a very old, and oft-used and abused, resource in the political struggle. In spite of this, the role that the English Revolution officially attributed to the people, and the new rhetoric of power that it introduced, radically renewed the way in which the governed were treated and the form of their subjection. Once the governed were represented, and represented *qua* people, they became the beneficiaries of nothing less than sovereignty and the way in which power would be exercised and debated could not remain the same.

The Rise of Popular Sovereignty in England and America (New York/London, Norton & Co., 1988). On the concept and the fate of the people see also Margaret Canovan, *The People*.

6   John Adamson, *The Noble Revolt. The Overthrow of Charles I* (London, Phoenix, 2007, pp. 212, 226).

7   Morgan, *Inventing the People*.

8   R. N. Kershaw, 'The Elections for the Long Parliament, 1640', *The English Historical Review* 152(38), 1923, 496–508.

9   London, 1647–1649.

Clearly, the vicissitudes and the dramatic political debate that preceded it and accompanied it along its course, are not the only reasons we can give for revolution. It is easy to establish a link between the demand for self-government in the religious sphere and the attribution of a legal title, to holding power on behalf of the people.[10] Furthermore, there are economic and demographic reasons. The emerging market economy and the revolution in education and communication, promoted both by royal centralisation and religious unrest, pushed new actors and new social groups to the top of collective life.[11] The processes of social mobility had to be strong enough to induce those with political ambitions, on the edge of the aristocracy and at the margins of emerging social groups, to present a demand for co-participation in power for the latter. This claim will constitute a model and similar demands will be put forward in the future by new and aspiring spokespersons for new social groups, until the final outcome of universal suffrage.

Oddly enough, the epicentre of English events was an old institution, inclined to caution by way of its structure and composition – the Parliament. It was more than just the protagonist of the rebellion against the King and became the central pillar of an unexpected institutional *bricolage* heralding great developments. At the end of the conflict Parliament constituted a hugely successful precedent, and was to become the symbolic meeting place of the rulers with the ruled. Had the English Revolution turned out differently, or had it never taken place, the problem of reinforcing communication between rulers and ruled would have taken another direction and the technology of power would have followed other developments.

In this situation political theory made an important contribution, elaborating a repertoire of words and arguments, not limited to adorning the effigies of the new regime, but forming a constituent part of it. The idea of the people, for example, dates back to the Roman *res publica* and was already back in fashion in the Middle Ages. Political theory opened up a new scenario, one that models the individual as a basic constituent of collective life, with inputs from different sources. Regarding self-government and representation, the contribution of the *Agreement of the People* was amateurish, albeit fed by intense theological reflection. By contrast, Hobbes' contribution was more professional. What he designed in his writings was a complex and well-argued model which recognised the individual's right to life, and legitimised this to underwrite the social contract and to constitute the authority of the state.

Moreover, the English innovation, perfected by what will be called the Glorious Revolution, proved contagious. The ruling class – or aspiring ruling class – of other countries thought it expedient to replicate it. This sort of new technology

---

10 Alessandro Pizzorno, 'Mutamenti nelle istituzioni rappresentative and sviluppo dei partiti', in Paul Bairoch, Eric J. Hobsbawn (eds.), *Storia dell'Europa contemporanea* (Turin, Einaudi, 1996, pp. 960–1031).

11 Revolution in education is Jean-Philippe Genet's theme in *La genèse de l'État moderne. Culture et société politique en Angleterre* (Paris, Puf, 2003).

hardly ever takes root entirely without problems. The circumstances and the context in which it is imported always impose significant adaptations. Nevertheless, this did not stop the new technology from being disseminated, even though initially nothing had given any idea of its eventual success.

To tell the truth, not many expected that the wide use of the name of the people would lead to self-government, either in the present, or in some distant future. During the Revolution the people, and in particular the population of London, had rallied and played an important role. But like the divine right of Kings before it, it soon became clear that self-government by the people was a fiction and, in the best hypothesis, a remote regulatory ideal.[12] When a century and a half later the people were again evoked and celebrated on the other side of the Channel, the part assigned them would not be very different.

The challenges of the people

Evoking the people is not enough to make them a political actor, and yet this is what involuntarily occurred. But once sovereignty had been attributed to the people, this immediately postulated an intricate tangle of problems. These were destined to weigh on representative regimes first, and on democratic ones later. Indeed, not only is self-government by the people one of the many fictions dreamt up by political imagery, and by political and constitutional theory, but the people itself was, and remains, a fiction. Where politics, and political theory, place the people, there is in fact something else, and this is the population. If we consider it as an object and, even more so, as a subject of government, it poses at least four problems, none of which is easy to resolve.

The first problem is one of numbers. If we go beyond even a very small number of citizens, self-government becomes impracticable. When the decisions to be taken become the least bit complex, no collective body is able to decide collectively, and no collective body has the time to do so.

The second, and major, problem is the irrevocably composite and pluralistic nature of the population. On the factual level, the population was already plural before the great upheavals of modernity with its incessant emphasis on pluralism, and this is still the case with post-modernity. In these conditions, if we recognise a political technology specifically designed to cope with pluralism in democracy, how do we keep the many parts that constitute the people united, and how do we obtain a will that can be accredited as collective and legitimate to govern?

The third problem is incompetence. Is each man really the best judge of his own interests? If we look at the facts, not only are there insurmountable difficulties in recomposing the different expressions of the will of the electors in a collective choice, but political competences are asymmetrically distributed across the popu-

---

12 Morgan, *Inventing the People*.

lation. There are citizens who are well-educated and informed, but there are many more who are not. Not even the numeric relation between them is important, given that in democracy the will of one or other citizen has the same value. Even if the incompetent were just a minority, every collective choice would be irremediably compromised.

The fourth and final problem is manipulation. The incompetent can be manipulated, but also the competent, who are not competent on everything. The questions which politics deals with are extremely complex and it is very difficult to anticipate the future and how current problems will evolve. Finally, we should not forget neither the intrinsic incompleteness of information, nor its manipulability.

Democratic regimes, and liberal regimes before them, have adopted a whole range of devices to cope with similar problems. Some of these are official and legitimate, others unofficial and, at times, illegitimate. Unofficial and illegitimate devices sometimes become official and *vice versa*. The most obvious, and oldest, move is to circumscribe the population demographically. Who is part of the people and who is not? Where must you be born, or live, to be part of the people? This question has been raised again in response to the migratory flows that have recently disturbed Western societies. It is a particularly delicate question, tightly linked to the functioning of the oldest device used to give voice to, to govern, and to settle the problems of the people. In other words, representation. Who is entitled to vote and to be represented?

We know that representation is older than modern representative and democratic regimes. When dealing with the challenges of numbers, pluralism, incompetence and manipulation, it first of all reduces the population to a symbol that represents it: that is, the people. The population is plural and to represent it as the people already means representing its unity.

But even if a word or symbol may count a great deal, it is still not sufficient, especially when the people have been promised self-government. The solution used has been 'political' representation but even this has not been sufficient. Even if modern political representation is designed to resolve all challenges at the same time, starting with pluralism, they are mitigated, but not resolved, as modern political representation is, by nature, pluralistic and contrived in such a way as to foster pluralism.

The premodern *ständliche* representation served the same aim, but represented a society based on preconstituted and independent bodies. It was also a simpler world, where the relations of power were more direct and where it was feasible to have a contractual management of the relations between estates and princes. It is only starting from the fifteenth century that the princes expressed their intolerance of the constraints that the estates had erected against them and against their claims establishing monarchical absolutism. Modern political representation is the child of a more complex world in which pluralism developed to the point of making absolutism inapplicable, as well as the previous representative contractual formula.

Society is made up of parts – local communities, religious faiths, associations, parties and interests of all sorts. These parts exist, at most, in the latent state until

some political entrepreneur arrives to constitute them,[13] to circumscribe their interests, and to give them a name. In other words, what is needed is someone who
will act as spokesperson for the latent parts, and represent them, making them
present to themselves and to others, and mobilising them in the direction of common objectives.[14]

In the first place pluralism is thus the fruit of the performative action of what can
be termed spontaneous representation. The modern version of political representation, trying to restrain pluralism in ways that differ from representation by estates,
contrasts with it. With respect to the representation by estates, modern political
representation works to reconstitute the unity of the collective body, and to periodically verify the condition of pluralism.[15] It is this dynamic dimension, based on
the regularity of elections, that allows modern parliaments to accredit themselves
officially as representative, not of separate parts, but of the people as a whole.

At first sight, political representation appears to be an effect of the pluralistic
configuration of the population. But there are excellent reasons to suspect that the
relationship has to be inverted. It is not representation that has been invented to
make the people govern, but the people which has been invented to allow the
representatives to govern.[16] The people serve to legitimise the ambitions of new
political entrepreneurs and hence the spontaneous representation of new social
groups and interests.

---

13 The definition of political enterprise and political entrepreneur is proposed by Max Weber. See,
    for example, 'The Profession and Vocation of Politics', in Peter Lassman and Ronald Speirs
    (eds.), *Max Weber: Political Writings* (Cambridge, Cambridge University Press, [1918] 1994).
    A similar metaphor is used by Joseph A. Schumpeter, who explains that group-wise volitions 'do
    not as a rule assert themselves directly. Even if strong and definite they remain latent, often for
    decades, until they are called to life by some political leader who turns them into political factors'
    (*Capitalism, Socialism and Democracy*, p. 270).

14 In the words of Hanna F. Pitkin, author of one of the most interesting and well-formulated
    contributions on the theme: representation means 'making present *in some sense* something
    that however is *not* present, literally or in fact'. See *The Concept of Representation* (Berkeley,
    University of California Press, 1967, pp. 8–9). For a sociological reading of representation see
    Pierre Bourdieu, 'Political Representation. For Elements of a Theory of the Political Field', now
    in Bourdieu, *Language and Symbolic Power* (Cambridge MA, Harvard University Press, [1981]
    1991). See also Daniel Gaxie, *La démocratie représentative* (Paris, Montchréstien, 2004).

15 For a general review of the developments and contradictions of the theory of representation, see
    Didier Mineur, *Archéologie de la représentation politique. Structure et fondement d'une crise*
    (Paris, Presses de SciencesPo, 2010).

16 Edmund S. Morgan, 'Government by Fiction: The Idea of Representation', *Yale Review* 72, 1983,
    32–39. Paul Veyne puts the question in these terms: 'the indirect democracy of the modern West is
    a way of legitimising the power exercised by professional politicians over a passive population':
    see Paul Veyne (2005), 'Did the Greeks Know Democracy?', *Economy and Society* 34(2), 322–
    345, 334.

Nevertheless, discipline and the regulation of pluralism was, and remains, a vain labour of Sisyphus in spite of the efforts made by theory and political practice. Immediately modern political theory – Edmund Burke, for instance[17] – intervened to urge the represented to concede autonomy of judgement and action to their representatives. This was in order to avoid the contractual degeneration of their reciprocal relations that would have complicated the government of pluralism. Some institutional constraints have been thought out to this end, such as the independence of representatives and the ban on the imperative mandate. Another well-known expedient – primarily theoretical, but also practical – consists of breaking down the people into its most basic units, that is individuals. This was done in the hope of unifying the people and transcending it more easily. This was Sieyès' idea. The revolutionary Le Chapelier law, which in 1791 banned workers associations, was a product of this climate.

Sieyès was a master of elegant but implausible abstract geometry. He imagined political representation as a radical synthesis, according to a perspective not very different from that of Hobbes, who had reduced the relation between individuals and the sovereign to a single social contract. In the Hobbesian pact the people only exist in so far as the sovereign represents it. To dispel any doubt, Sieyès instead made representation the representation of a representation: the nation represents the people and the parliament represents the nation. Once reduced to individuals, abstracted from their context, electors indeed are allowed to vote. But the official principle of representation, and the depository of sovereignty, is not the people, but the nation. Here the nation is understood as a collective entity where individuals are dissolved and whose exclusive spokesperson is the representative assembly in its unity, through which the nation itself is constituted. According to Sieyès the election of the representative assembly should come about through a procedure of radical abstraction. In order to purge the representative body of any reference to a previous will, such as a social group or territorial collectivity, which could question the indivisible unity of the nation, Sieyès went so far as to plan an electoral regime that divided France up into a perfect chessboard of equally-sized electoral constituencies.[18]

Using different formulas, a hypothesis of synthesis comparable to that of the nation reappears many times in the theory of representation. The German doctrine, not devoid of organicistic influences, makes representation a function of the authority of the state, which selects the elected, but does not give them a mandate.

---

17 See, for instance, Edmund Burke, 'Mr. Edmund Burke's Speeches at His Arrival at Bristol and at the Conclusion of the Poll', in Burke, *The Writings & Speeches of Edmund Burke* (New York, Cosimo, vol. 2, [1774] 2008).

18 Emmanuel-Joseph Sieyès, 'Observations sur le rapport du comité de constitution, concernant la nouvelle organisation de la France', in Sieyès, *Écrits politiques* , edited by Roberto Zapperi (Paris, Edition des archives contemporaines, [1789] 1985).

The outcomes in French and Italian political theory are not dissimilar.[19] According to this perspective, law-making was not the product of representation, and of a contingent political majority given by the electors, but the manifestation of the law embodied in the state and of which inalienable individual rights are part.

Yet, even if the theory appears well-founded, the empirical politics that followed teems always with a host of unofficial representatives, impervious to attempts to unify or abstract them. To complicate things, it is modernity itself that legitimates individuals in asserting their diversity of values and interests, while the society on which the modern political representation stands, is legitimately recognised as pluralistic and heterogeneous.

Once again the theory of representation recognised the existence of the problem. The revolutionary Sieyès imagined representation as representation of the totality, and thus as an abstraction with respect to the real people. Instead, a liberal like Benjamin Constant, believed that representation should describe the people truthfully as they are:[20] once revolutionary abstractions were set aside, the task of representatives was to act as spokespersons for their electors, after accurately filtering them according to property, income and education requirements. It was the job of the parliamentary debate to transcend particularistic interests. A not very dissimilar perspective was held by the *maitre à penser* of the orleanist monarchy, François Guizot. According to Guizot, parliaments are places to debate and to compare arguments, where representatives can speak publicly, before the citizens, in order to 'search for the truth together'.[21]

But is this really what happened? It is the great theme of an unfinished debate. The realists deny it and the critics of representative government, in particular, consider it a device that multiplies and stimulates particularistic interests. According to Gaetano Mosca the political class does not consist of virtuous and disinterested men, in pursuit of the general interest, but of political actors working to maintain their parliamentary seats, inevitably induced to back the electors and even to provoke particularistic interests.[22] In the mid-twentieth century Schumpeter specified that it is the same electoral competition that encourages pluralism. As already

---

19 See respectively Paul Laband, *Deutsches Reichsstaatsrecht* (Tübingen, Mohr, 1907); Raymond Carré de Malberg, *Contribution à la théorie générale de l'État* (Paris, Sirey, 1920) and Vittorio Emanuele Orlando, 'Sulla rappresentanza politica', in Orlando, *Diritto pubblico generale: scritti varii, 1881–1940, coordinati in sistema* (Milan, Giuffrè, [1895] 1954).

20 Benjamin Constant, *Principles of Politics*, now in *Political Writings* (Cambridge, Cambridge University Press, [1815] 1988, pp. 201–207).

21 François Guizot, *Histoire des origines du gouvernement représentatif en Europe* (Paris, Didier, 1851, vol. II, p. 14). Carl Schmitt cited him, obviously, to support his – idyllic – image of liberal parliamentarism. See *The Crisis of Parliamentary Democracy* (Cambridge MA, MIT Press, [1923] 1985, 35).

22 Gaetano Mosca, *Sulla teorica dei governi e sul l governo parlamentare. Studii storici and sociali* (Palermo, Loescher, 1884, p. 306).

mentioned, how do contenders compete in the competition if not by hunting down interests that only exist in the latent state, in order to give them shape and to use them to their advantage?[23] For Mosca the conclusion was that parliamentary government was necessarily spoilt and that it would be better to be rid of it,[24] while Schumpeter believed in the need for other precautions to govern pluralism, such as the culture of the ruling class and competent bureaucracies.

Not by chance, representative democratic regimes devised so many sophisticated precautions to contain pluralism.[25] At the same time, as with all representation, political representation works with selective intentionality. The principles and rules, beginning with electoral rules, are established precisely to this end. The electors are counted and classified, and must be authorised to exercise their right. Progressively we observe the introduction of the secret vote, the single national ballot paper, voting cubicles, strict procedures for the count, while the choice of the elector became just a sign or a name on a ballot paper. The divergence between the constituent parts of pluralism are also subject to a process of abstraction in the vote count, expressed concretely in well-ordered and aseptic statistical summaries. Requirements and well-codified forms of conduct are also required of candidates.[26] Some potential competitors are excluded from the start as being too outlandish, whilst electoral regimes work to reduce the choices offered to those who decide to vote.

Where this is not enough, representation officialises interests and conflicts. In so doing it forces them to converge within a common space where they are obliged to express themselves according to the strict code of official politics. We will return to this later on. In the same way that maps, anything but casually, reduce the asperity of the world they represent to marks,[27] so political representation, even when it promises faithfully to reproduce pluralism – as in the case of proportional electoral regimes – returns a version which is stylised, well-ordered, measurable, artificial and that inevitably risks being defined, depending on the case, as defective, or redundant, by those who are likely to benefit, or to be disadvantaged, politically.

---

23 Schumpeter, *Capitalism, Socialism and Democracy,* p. 270.

24 Nevertheless, when fascism satisfies his wish, Mosca will regret liberal parliamentarism. See Gaetano Mosca, *Partiti and sindacati nella crisi del regime parlamentare* (Bari, Laterza, 1949)

25 A scientific formulation is also needed. See Oliver Ihl, Martine Kaluszynski, Gilles Pollet, *Les sciences de gouvernement* (Paris, Economica, 2003).

26 On the standardisation of the vote in France, see Alain Garrigou, *Le vote et la vertu. Comment les français sont devenus électeurs* (Paris, Presses de la Fondation nationale des sciences politiques, 1992). More in general on the complexity of a phenomenon which is only simple in appearance, see Oliver Ihl, *Le vote* (Paris, Montchrestien, 2000) and Yves Déloye, Oliver Ihl (eds.), *L'acte de vote* (Paris, Presses de SciencesPo, 2008).

27 On the correspondence between representation and the maps see Franco Farinelli, *Critica della ragione geografica* (Turin, Einaudi, 2009, pp. 188–191).

To conclude, representation, like the people, is a well-studied fiction.[28] But if it fails to resolve definitively the challenge of pluralism, it is also an imperfect device when it comes to circumventing the incompetence of the people and the electors. James Madison fooled himself that the remedy for such incompetence was to entrust the task of 'refin[ing] and enlarge[ing] the public views by passing them through the medium of a chosen body of citizens, whose wisdom may best discern the true interest of their country'.[29] But if there is any prospect that the representatives are more informed and more competent than those they represent, that likelihood is not a certainty. Thus, in order to protect against the risk – and not only – that uninformed and incompetent electors make disastrous choices, liberal regimes have, for a long time, tightened the defining limits of the people. For a long while a sizeable part of the population was obliged to risk its life in the service of the nation, but the nation refused it the right to vote. This right was instead reserved for a minority considered representative – what a surprise! – of the population, since the precondition of property and education select its *melior pars*, the sole part considered fit to represent the people and to be represented in parliament.[30]

The government of the people will also resort to other, more in-depth, measures. The best known, which is also aimed at reducing the heterogeneity of the people, is a symbolic policy which transforms the people into a nation. In so doing the people is not only rebaptised, as Sieyès did, but is deliberately promoted as having a shared identity, designed not to regulate pluralism, but to contrast it.[31] To this end liberal regimes, just like Absolutism had done before, adopt unifying symbols and rules which establish clear differences when compared with other countries and peoples, and adopt educational policies to make the population linguistically homogeneous, and to give it common cultural horizons. The first social policies, from assistance for the poor to public healthcare and labour protection, have the same aim. These policies, did not have egalitarian ends, but were primarily created on the grounds of public order and to prevent conflict.[32]

---

28 Not by chance, for Hans Kelsen representation is a 'crass fiction'. See, 'On the Essence and Value of Democracy' in Arthur Jacobson, Bernhard Schlink (eds.), *Weimar. A Jurisprudence of Crisis* (Berkeley, University of California Press, [1929] 2000, p. 98). This is like saying that the crisis is congenital to representation: stressed recently by Didier Mineur, *Archéologie de la représentation politique*.

29 James Madison, 'Federalist 10', in Alexander Hamilton, James Madison, John Jay, *The Federalist Papers*, edited by Lawrence Goldman (Oxford, Oxford University Press, [1788] 2008, p. 53).

30 See, for instance, Benjamin Constant, *Principles of Politics*, pp. 214–215.

31 Ernest Gellner, *Nations and Nationalism* (Ithaca, Cornell University Press, 1983). See also Benedict R. O. Anderson, *Imagined Communities: Reflections on the Origins and Spreads of Nationalism* (London, Verso, 1991).

32 For a reconstruction of the development of the welfare state see Peter Flora and Arnold J. Heidenheimer (eds.), *The Development of Welfare States in Europe and America* (New Brunswick

Furthermore, in contrast to the dispersion provoked by networks of notables, the first 'parties of notables' as Max Weber calls them,[33] worked empirically to aggregate the elected around shared values and interests. The people, or the minority entitled to vote, remained heterogeneous, but these primitive parties served, at least, to reduce the heterogeneity of the elected.

Of course the efficiency of the latter as an instrument is limited in time. Within only a few decades the practice needed to be revised, following the expansion of suffrage, demanded in the name of the people not only by socialist parties, but by whoever could mobilise reserves of traditional deference to their advantage, particularly in rural areas where the socialist parties were unable to make inroads. Irrespective of the compliance of a good part of the newly enfranchised electors, thus contradicting those who attributed subversive effects to universal suffrage, the latter nevertheless aggravated the problems of numbers, heterogeneity, incompetence and manipulability of the people, and triggered the invention of more new instruments. A very successful device was found immediately, substituting the parties of notables with the so-called mass parties, which in any case raised other problems. On the one hand, mass parties functioned extremely well in reorganising the increased heterogeneity of the people. On the other hand, they intersected with political representation, and disturbed its practical mechanisms, together with its theory.

The parties of notables were fluid structures, whereas mass parties were large, solid, political and professionally-run enterprises,[34] whose aim was to conquer power, but that, in order do this, gave form to – mobilising and representing – large segments of the electorate, around collective plans regarding the state of the world. Mass parties did not obtain a single will shared by all the people from the diversity of interests and particular wills, but, if nothing else, they obtained a more limited and less abstract plurality of wills.

Here again, it remains to be seen whether the rationed plurality represented by mass parties facilitated political synthesis or not. For a long period of time, on both the empirical and theoretical level, this ability has been officially recognised for parties, considering them as new 'intermediate bodies' which 'rationalise' pluralism and representation,[35] and give citizens, and hence the people, an otherwise unobtainable voice.

In principle, anyone could set up a party. Very democratically, it was the number of voters that each party and its programme managed to attract that decreed its success and measured its political weight. Moreover, parties frequently formed

---

NJ, Transactions, 1998).

33 Weber, 'The Profession and Vocation of Politics', p. 335.

34 Starting frome Weber's definition of the political entrepreneur, see Michel Offerlé, *Les parties politiques* (Paris, Puf, 2002) and Gaxie, *La démocratie représentative*.

35 Pierre Rosanvallon, *Le peuple introuvable. Histoire de la représentation démocratique en France* (Paris, Gallimard, 1998, p. 183).

alliances or alternated in power. Therefore, the theory also recognised that if the principle of majority established which interests and values would have been satisfied by government action, from the outset minorities would have the opportunity to be satisfied in the future, while the interaction between parties, parliamentary discussion and the public in general, appeared quite reliable as devices to stipulate compromises and transcend the particularism of interests.[36]

Yet, this mechanism was neither perfect nor stable, also because its political consequences were not universally welcomed. The success of parties would soon encounter regret for the esteemed virtues of liberal parliamentarism. This regret was instrumental. The critics of parties, however, accused them of betraying the principles of representation, insofar as parties rigidified the contrasts between interests and superimposed the specific advantage of whoever led them professionally, to the will of the people.[37]

The argument was exacerbated, above all, by those who did not appreciate the fact that it was parties that produce some advantages for the popular strata by organising the 'big numbers'. Among other things, mass parties radically renewed the mechanisms of selection for their political personnel and of generating consensus, thus achieving egalitarian effects. Parties not only recruited and trained political personnel from the working class, but they also steered policies to their advantage in order to win their consensus: and this was obviously not to the advantage of all.

Nevertheless, once universal suffrage had been achieved, democratic regimes not content with parties, adopted other measures to reduce the heterogeneity and incompetence of the population. Not only was the national principle maintained – albeit subject to competition from the ideological options of socialist parties, that were united in favour of the nation during World War I – but educational policies were confirmed and strengthened and, above all, after World War II, welfare state policies, which included strengthened educational policies, were adopted. The influence of the popular parties made itself felt. The official objective of such policies was to reduce inequality, and to complete, to use the terminology of Thomas H. Marshall, the trajectory of citizenship through the introduction of social rights.[38] But once again their main mission was to prevent social conflict and to govern pluralism.

---

36 Kelsen, 'Essence and Value of Democracy', and *General Theory of Law and State* (Cambridge MA, Harvard University Press, 1945, 288).

37 See Carl Schmitt's well-known critique of the parties and his hypocritical defence of liberal parliamentarism in *The Crisis of Parliamentary Democracy*. For a direct reply to Carl Schmitt see Kelsen, 'Das Problem des Parlamentarismus', in *Soziologie und Sozialphilosophie. Schriften der Soziologischen Gesellschaft in Wien* (Wein/Leipzig, W. Braumüller, 1925, vol. III).

38 Thomas H. Marshall, *Citizenship and Social Class, and other Essays* (Cambridge, Cambridge University Press, 1950).

The story does not end here. Even the solution offered by mass parties will turn out to be provisional. In the first place, because parties change over time for a variety of reasons. Secondly, because the opponents of parties found a way to make themselves heard. As always in these cases, by evoking the health of democracy, even the democracy of parties will become redundant.[39] The next step for representation – and the instruments used to defend representative and democratic regimes against the overhasty attribution of sovereignty to the people – consists in outflanking parties through organised interests and lobbies, and in attributing a representative function straight to the head of the executive, often elected directly by the citizens.

This last evolution occurred in many ways at the end of the twentieth century, openly recognising the right and ability of the people to express its will fully. If electoral choice is reduced to a binary option, it seems that the challenges of numbers, complexity and incompetence suddenly disappear. The will of the people is *tout court* the will of the electoral majority. The minority is temporarily silent, in exchange for the chance to become a majority at the next elections. This is what is called 'majoritarian democracy'.[40] In its most recent version, based on the electoral designation of the head of the executive, and that has been with some imprecision assimilated to American presidentialism,[41] it matters relatively little that the majority has been artificially produced by the electoral rules. What is important is that the people find a voice, not necessarily unique, but certainly pre-eminent in who leads the executive on the direct choice of the electors.

In this way the simplification of pluralism is really drastic: perhaps too drastic. We should even ask whether such simplification does not resemble Carl Schmitt's radical remedy – also stimulated by universal suffrage – that challenges the people and can be defined as 'plebiscitary democracy', rather than the tradition of political representation. Plebiscitary democracy is the model formulated by Schmitt when he defined the fundamental trait of democracy, not as heterogeneity, but as the unity and homogeneity of the people – as well as identity between the rulers and the ruled – currently jeopardised by parties and organised interests. In this democratic model the challenges of numbers, competence and complexity are cancelled, entrusting the task of embodying the popular will to a plebiscitary leader acclaimed by the people.[42] Is there, by any chance, a risk that this model may be coming back in fashion?

---

39 Bernard Manin, *The Principles of Representative Government* (Cambridge, Cambridge University Press, 1995).

40 Arend Lijphart, *Democracies: Patterns of Majoritarian and Consensus Government in Twenty-one Countries* (New Haven CT, Yale University Press, 1984).

41 Thomas Poguntke and Paul Webb (eds.), *The Presidentialization of Politics. A Comparative Study of Modern Democracies* (Oxford, Oxford University Press, 2005).

42 Of the many works by Carl Schmitt which deal with this perspective see *Constitutional Theory* (Durham NC, Duke University Press, [1928] 2008) and *Legality and Legitimacy* (Durham NC, Duke University Press, [1932] 2004).

The majority principle and the rule of law

Schmitt's solution is both extreme and democratically incompatible, despite claiming to be called democracy. But it is to avoid a similar drift that representative and democratic regimes are not satisfied with regulating the people. Conscious of the danger inherent in any form of power – popular or otherwise – these regimes have always faced the question from the other end. Attempts to regulate power are indeed very old: not as old as power itself, but still very old. They are so old that neither representative nor democratic regimes have any exclusive ascendancy in the matter. On the contrary, they largely make use of antecedent efforts.[43] When the representative regime first saw the light of day during the English Revolution, few ideas were as clear as the need to circumscribe the exercise of power. The first thing to do was to subject power, symbolically, and not solely, to the people and to the general interest. But at the same time, other limits were set. The effectiveness of these limits is still debated.

In a regime based on the election of rulers, the first instrument used to limit power is the decision-making procedure. For representative and democratic regimes the procedure *par excellence* are the elections and the majority principle used to make all collective choices.[44] This substitutes monarchic, aristocratic and oligarchic principles. Collective choices must be shared, if not by all, then at least by the majority of the governed, or those who represent them. Nevertheless, this is only a partial solution. How can majorities be prevented from abusing the power conferred on them to the detriment of minorities?

A complement to the antidote, that is in fact part of it, is thus the cyclical holding of elections. Governors can be replaced, every majority is by definition reversible and all choices made by a majority are by definition provisional, only we cannot be certain that reversibility of choice is an absolute guarantee. A choice that is damaging for the minority cannot always be remedied by simply revoking it. Its not even certain that absolute reversibility is always wise. Revoking choices can also have a destabilising impact. This is the case, for example, for procedures. It is not worthwhile having procedures that can be too easily revoked, while what is needed, very often, are procedures that are strengthened by the additional legitimation that their duration in time gives them.

Another crucial antidote, that has been available long before the introduction of elections and the majority principle, is designating spaces where power is not

---

43 See Charles H. McIlwain's classic work *Constitutionalism Ancient and Modern* (Cornell, Cornell University Press, 1940).

44 On the history of the majority principle and the theoretical dilemmas that it raises, see Edoardo Ruffini (*Il principio maggioritario. Profilo storico* (Milan, Adelphi, [1927] 1976). On the problematic nature of the principle see Norberto Bobbio 'La regola di maggioranza: limiti and aporie', in Bobbio, Claus Offe, Siro Lombardini, *Democrazia, maggioranza and minoranze* (Bologna, Il Mulino, 1981).

authorised to decide. This was precisely the intention of the English Parliament when it rose up against Charles I, in full agreement moreover, with the *Agreement of the People*. Both demanded clear limits to power – that is, freedom and rights – that the governors would have to respect. Once the principle of limited power had been recorded in the genetic code of representative regimes, democratic regimes were keen to maintain it.

The 'rule of law' subjects power, even the power of democratically elected authorities in a majoritarian system, to law. The rule of law separates powers, or distributes them among different organs, and establishes how they should be exercised, delimiting the spaces that power must respect, providing individuals – and minorities – with an armour of inalienable basic rights which are also resistant to the majority principle.[45] Unfortunately, not even law and rights work perfectly, or are definitively protected from abuse of power on the part of the majority and by a democratically elected power.

For some time now a lively supranational debate has been taking place and has produced a broad consensus that conditions and often constrains single states, at least in the West. The rule of law is now considered an essential precondition when attesting to the democratic nature of a political regime.[46] Some recognise the regime constructed around constitutions and rights, the so-called 'constitutional democracy',[47] as the version of democracy most suitable for contemporary Western societies. Yet, although the prerogatives that the democratic state – and now also the international community – recognises for human beings, can be solemnly consecrated and denominated as rights, giving them more dignity by referring

---

45 For an in-depth review see Pietro Costa and Danilo Zolo (eds.), *The Rule of Law: History, Theory and Criticism* (Dordrecht, Springer, 2007). For a realistic perspective see José M. Maravall, Adam Przeworski (eds.), *Democracy and the Rule of Law* (Cambridge, Cambridge University Press, 2003). The starting point is that, insofar as it is a technique to make the exercise of power perdictable, 'Rule of law can prevail only when the relation of political forces is such that those who are most powerful find that the law is on their side, or, to put it the other way around, when the law is the preferred tool of the powerful'. This does not mean that the latter are the only ones to benefit, because once the principle is established, it generates automatisms that the balances of power can modify, but that do exist. In any case, 'When law rules, it is not because it antecedes political actions.... law cannot be separated from politics': see Maravall, Przeworski, 'Introduction', pp. 5, 15. One can then conclude that the rule of law, now internationally prescribed as a democratic obligation, is also a political technique to depoliticise issues: the certainty of rules opposed to the will of politics. On this point see Béatrice Hibou, *Anatomie politique de la domination* (Paris, La Découverte, 2011, pp. 109–114).

46 Even to attest its 'quality'. See, for example, Larry Diamond and Leonardo Morlino (eds.), *Assessing the Quality of Democracy. Theory and Empirical Analysis* (Baltimore, Johns Hopkins University Press, 2005).

47 Luigi Ferrajoli, *Principia juris. Teoria del diritto e della democrazia 1* (Bari, Laterza, vol. II, 2009, pp. 13–18).

to them as 'natural', 'human', 'fundamental' and 'universal', or crediting them with an ethical foundation antecedent to every other political order, we should nevertheless, remember that rights remain the object of incessant struggles and negotiations. Rights are a historical fact, a perishable fruit which grows in a specific cultural and political climate, and of the historically contingent majority that introduced them into the democratic order, and thus at the mercy of the competition for power.[48]

Despite their symbolic value, the purpose of rights is to reduce the discretionality of politics and to impose obligations on the latter. In the last instance, however, rights depend on the majority principle and on political struggle. Rights are subject to the rules of the democratic game which has consecrated them and cannot be definitively immunised against competition between political actors, between constitutional organs, and between organised and non-organised interests.[49]

Indeed, the courtly appearance of rights conceals historically contingent consolidations of interests, values and power. The label 'rights' only means providing a particular legitimacy to help perpetuate these interests, values and forms of power. Even the modest freedom of thought is a splinter of power. No-one recognises and protects rights out of spontaneous generosity, and no-one obtains them without effort. Moreover, rights are texts which have to be interpreted and which are therefore the potential object of interpretational conflicts, which are in turn conflicts of power.

The interpretation and application of rights are continually being renewed in the light of the cultural trends and the political expedience of the day. Even the idea of 'subject', protected by rights, turns out to be contingent. Finally, rights, and their interpretation, can also be in conflict with one another: think of the complicated nature of the relationship between the two rights generally held to be fundamental – freedom and equality.

The answer is not to rely on the judges' power. The judiciary safeguards rights, and in a constitutional democracy, which is strongly influenced by the American tradition, is now placed on the same level as legislative power. But even if the judiciary is declared to be a neutral and impartial third power, what judges exercise remains a power, disputed with other elected and non-elected authorities, never definitively fixed, and conditioned by the competition for power. The support for, or aversion to, the decisions made by judges are very evident proof of this, in the same way as the conflicts, that every so often flare up in public between the judiciary and politics.

Judges, of course, take part in the complicated game of power in their own way and with their own instruments. However this does not mean that this participation has to be traced back to competition between the parties, as is sometimes claimed

---

48 Norberto Bobbio, *The Age of Rights* (Cambridge, Polity Press, 1996).

49 This issue is raised by Michel Foucault in *Naissance de la biopolitique. Cours au Collège de France. 1978–1979* (Paris, Gallimard-Seuil, 2004, pp. 40–42).

by partisan politics when the work of the judges displeases them. But we must recognise that judges' work is inevitably political, even if rarely coherent, and is also due to their social, cultural and political heterogeneity. Whether judges are considered to be, to use Montesquieu's formula, '*la bouche de la lois*', who apply the norms aseptically and nothing else, or whether their task is to implement the rights that precede legislation, recognising in interpretation their professional specificity, the judges are bearers of politically relevant values and interests. These values and interests are always controversial and belong to the time in which they operate.[50] This is particularly relevant today, considering the growing importance that law has in collective life.[51]

For these reasons, rights, the rule of law and the work of the judiciary, often collide with democratic legitimation; that is, with the authority of the sovereign people and the majority that embodies it. The theory – invoked by anyone: the judiciary, the political opposition, so-called public opinion, civil society – can argue that power in democracy is limited, that rights are untouchable and that the autonomy of judges must be respected. It can also sustain that the popular will in all its authority is only expressed through constitutional norms and that ordinary legislation is subject to these norms. In reality, the theory too – in this case academic legal professionals[52] – takes sides, according to political criteria, but above

---

50 For a synthetic and convincing review of the historical expansion of the spheres of social life in which politics is prohibited to intervene, and as a consequence entrusted to the care of the judiciary, see Alessandro Pizzorno, *Il potere dei giudici. Stato democratico and controllo della virtù* (Rome/Bari, Laterza, 1998). Welfare first, and then the role taken on by rights, have increased the competition between the power of the judiciary and that of the elected authority. Having been placed before the rights of the constitution, constitutional democracy not only enlarges the spaces of action of the judiciary, but reinforces its political character, both intrinsic, and extrinsic. The phenomenon is also accentuated thanks to the transformation of the representative regimes, that have removed competences from partisan politics. A similar idea is supported by Marcel Gauchet, *La révolution des pouvoirs. La souveraineté, le peuple et la représentation. 1789–1799* (Paris, Gallimard, 1999, pp. 7–51, 259–286). On the growing competition between politicians and magistrates see also Carlo Guarnieri, *Courts as an Instrument of Horizontal Accountability: the Case of Latin Europe* and John Ferejohn, Pasquale Pasquino, 'Rule of Democracy and Rule of Law', in Maravall, Przeworski, *Democracy and the Rule of Law*. For a historical and sociological recognition on the theme see Jacques Commaille, Martine Kaluszynski (eds.), *La fonction politique de la justice* (Paris, La Découverte, 2007). Benjamin Ginsberg and Martin Shefter also stress the growing importance of judicial power, and classify it with a striking title: *Politics by Other Means: The Declining Importance of Elections in America* (New York, Basic Books, 1990).

51 For an introductory reconnaissance see Lars Ch. Blichner, Anders Molander, 'Mapping Juridification', *European Law Journal* 14(1), 2008, 36–54.

52 On the division of interpretative work between the theory and practice of law see Pierre Bourdieu, 'La force du droit. Éléments pour une sociologie du champ juridique', *Actes de la recherche en sciences sociales* 64, 1986, 3–19.

all it has also to work hard to contrast the powerful legitimation of whoever is backed by an electoral majority.

Like it or not, the majority constituted by the election, enjoys ample leeway in which to reinterpret and rewrite the norms. A majority – reinforced as required by the constitutional rules in some countries – is also allowed to review constitutional norms and rights. In this way the majority could even condition the physiognomy of judicial power and the composition and direction taken by the supreme courts that examine the constitutionality of the norms, and whose role therefore, evolves over time and according to political circumstances.

Neither should we forget that the majority principle has a formidable evocative potential, reinforced by the prestige conferred to numbers by modern science. This prestige does not seems to be reduced even when faced with the fact that the numbers often spring from an accounting strategy envisaged by electoral legislation. Unfortunately with numbers, even virtual numbers, one can do much. Sometimes too much.

For this reason, Kelsen, beyond circumscribing the power of the majority more rigorously through the justice of the constitutional courts, tried to weaken it at its base, through a partial and controlled delegitimisation of its foundations. Kelsen observed that it was not a foregone conclusion that a majority decision is preferable *per se* to any other. The majority principle is only a pragmatic expedient, which substitutes unanimity – unanimity being the most appropriate solution for democracy, understood as self-government. Unanimity, however, is by nature unobtainable, or almost, and may confer an unacceptable power of veto on single actors.[53] Moreover, even were unanimity obtained, its outcomes would not be fully reliable: who says that unanimity guarantees the quality of the choices adopted any more than the majority?

This, too, is a controversial point of view. There are arguments according to which the decisions of the majority are in actual fact superior to those of the minority. Once the full and equal dignity of the will of each has been recognised, it is accepted that the majority enjoys epistemic reliability on the theme being discussed, which is superior to that of the minority. Such an argument raises doubts, however, for who is convinced not only of the limits of the competences of electors, but also of the limits of the competences of the elected. But there is also someone who shares them and can make them count democratically. It is certainly debatable whether today's majority has the right to constrain that of tomorrow.[54] In any case, the only real antidote to the majority is to replace it with another majority, i.e. relying on politics. This conclusion is not very different from the one reached by Kelsen himself, when he distinguished the majority principle from the sovereignty of the majority.

---

53 Kelsen, 'On the Essence and Value of Democracy', p. 86.

54 Jeremy Waldron, *The Dignity of Legislation*, (Cambridge, Cambridge University Press, 1999). For a counterargument see, for example, Ronald Dworkin, *Is Democracy Possible Here? Principles for a New Political Debate* (Princeton NJ, Princeton University Press, 2006).

Pointing to the majority principle as a practical rule, Kelsen wanted to persuade, whoever applied it, to caution and for a reason that was primarily political: a majority decision favours some and is normally hostile to others, but in a democratic regime the more decisions are shared, the better things are. If conflict is inevitable, it is better not to exacerbate it, because the parts may sooner or later be inverted. Elections are unpredictable and a minority can become a majority, and, if it holds sentiments of revenge towards the previous majority, this is a risk for the democratic regime.

Nevertheless, minorities are not necessarily at the mercy of whoever claims the support of the majority. The effectiveness of rights, and of the authorities who apply them, is not absolute, but democratic procedures are more than just the majority principle. For example, before the majority decides, the democratic regimes expect that there will be a debate in the elected assembly. In the debate that precedes the vote the parts have the opportunity to be heard, to present their arguments, to persuade each other reciprocally or to negotiate compromises which satisfy, albeit to varying degrees, all actors involved. For Kelsen this is the essence of parliamentarism, and what he considered the definitive component of all democratic regimes.

Unfortunately nothing stops the practice of going in a totally different direction where it suits the actors involved. In parliament opposing parties can manage to talk to each other and to reconcile different points of view, but the opposite also occurs. Thousands of times parliaments have been used for dialogue, and thousands of times they have been the seat of very bitter contrasts. In spite of this, their existence constitutes an invitation to open a debate and the opportunity to do so. But it is by no means certain that the majority will accept the invitation.

This is the reason why theory – here Kelsen comes in again – and politics attempt to set limits to the exercise of power also in the collective conscience and culture. In a democratic regime the different parts should not consider each other as enemies and should enjoy mutual respect. In Kelsen's opinion democracy presupposes an atmosphere in which the majority does not pass itself off as the whole, and where it practices tolerance and is careful not to violate or unilaterally rewrite the rules of the game. Kelsen thus attributes also a symbolic value added to compromise. But in the same way as the surplus value of the numerical principle, this also depends on circumstances.

This means that a culture of compromise will not always be consolidated, or that democratic competition for power will not always respect this culture. Kelsen recognised a necessary relation between democracy and relativism so that value absolutism would be rejected.[55] However, culture aside, if the majority wants it, and has the power – or has generated sufficient consensus, or does not meet with sufficient dissent within or outside the perimeter of the elective institutions – there is no lack of instruments for overcoming all legal and institutional barriers.

---

55 Kelsen, *On the Essence and Value of Democracy*, p. 108.

Kelsen's concerns were dictated by dramatic circumstances. When these circumstances changed, the lessons of experience, although terrible, were softened and democratic culture was modified, as seems to be the case at the moment. In the first place the tenet according to which pluralism must be respected, and political confrontation must be carried out in a civil fashion, is easily contradicted by political competition: for politics, verbal exasperation is, alas, a non-secondary resource. Furthermore, if circumstances become less dramatic, it is more likely that whoever considers themselves legitimated by the majority will refuse – democratically – any invitation to caution and compromise, and will be content to offer minorities the protection of rights and constitutional rules and the reversibility of the majority.

The latter is an idea that has had so much success today that it even established another, symmetrical, idea as regards the redundant multiplication and sacredness of rights, and the expansion of the competences of the non-elected authorities and the judiciary. In the name of political stability and decisional efficiency, the aforementioned electoral rules that transform an electoral minority into a political majority, or that attempt to make a majority from a heap of disparate minorities, appear completely legitimate. Similar strategies should induce additional caution, but this is not the rule.

With such artificially constructed majorities, nothing, at least for some more sensitive matters, prevents the adoption of more elaborate and more decision-making techniques that are respectful of an articulated configuration of opinions and interests. The ongoing debate on so-called 'deliberative democracy', held to relegitimate and represent these techniques, *in primis* discussion, condemns the inadequacy of current decision-making procedures, because for some time, and in the name of efficiency,[56] it has been deemed opportune to curb these procedures. However, this does not seem to be the prevailing mood at the moment.

Today the only certainty seems to be that the majority cannot abolish the rules of the game, the right to vote, the majority principle and electoral competition, because in so doing, it would abolish the minimum conditions for democracy. It cannot even abolish the principles that are the premises of these minimum preconditions. But, as we know, the margins of application of rules and principles are large: too large for it not to occur to someone to profit from them. Majorities have sometimes rewritten the electoral rules in their favour, to reduce (or broaden) the options open to electors and to hinder their substitution. Thus, not only does

---

56 Indeed, but what do we know about the performance of democracies and of their decision-making procedures? Lijphart, has carried out a great deal of research on this issue, comparing the so-called majoritarian and consensual democracies. According to him the theory which considers the first as less representative, but more efficient, is unreliable. See Arendt Lijphart, 'Democracies: Forms, Performance and Constitutional Engineering', *European Journal of Political Research* 25(1), 1994, 1–17, and Lijphart and Manfred G. Schmidt, 'Dimensions of Democracies', *European Journal of Political Research* 31(1–2), 1997, 193–204.

the evocative power of the majority principle continually risk collision with constraints prepared by theory, rights, culture and politics, but in practice the majority in office enjoys many advantages which it can make, debatably, use of.

Placing ourselves in the shoes of the majority we can see that it may want to impose itself because this suits its interests, but it may also be because it is, in good faith, persuaded, or pretends to be persuaded, that seeking compromise may mean a paralysis of decision-making, or because it holds some of its convictions to be inalienable and for the good of the collectivity. In the last instance, the limits to democratic decision-making, and hence the limits to power, and the protection of minorities and individuals, remain a perennially disputed stake of political competition, albeit not always explicit.

Recently, difficult ethical questions have arisen more and more frequently, where different moral principles and their different interpretations are in conflict. In these cases there are actors who sustain that democracy protects rights and the dignity of the individual no matter what, and prescribes the basic freedom of each to choose their life, so that the majority principle is no longer applicable. In support of this argument they will invoke the authority of some illustrious assembly, national or international, that, has written down the constitution or sanctioned rights. Nevertheless, there will always be those who invoke reasons which are not in the least discreditable, such as collective responsibility, or the protection of some value or right, which is, in their opinion, more fundamental and more sacred, e.g. the right to life, than individual freedom, and that will want to apply the majority principle. Which of the two contenders is right? Unfortunately neither democracy nor democratic theory give any clear directions. Although both are constitutive elements of the democratic regime, between the majority principle and its limitations in the shape of rights, the rule of law and the separation of powers, the risk of abuse is perennially lying in wait.

In the last instance what weakens minorities is inertia and a scarce ability to rebel.[57] Minorities protest, democracy is the regime of voice and any voice is legitimate, but rebellion is expensive, and whoever suggests it is regarded with suspicion, and the intensity of dissent is rarely distributed homogeneously. If it wants to abuse the majority principle, a minimally aware majority will do so on issues where the parliamentary and electoral minorities are not unanimous. In any case, it will avoid coagulating all the minorities, to make them a compact body which is conscious that it shares the same preferences and is politically constituted.[58]

---

57 Paul Veyne gives a brilliant illustration of the difficulty in rebelling in *Le quotidien et l'intéressant, entretiens* with Catherine Darbo-Peschanski (Paris, Hachette, 2006, p. 99), and *When Our World Became Christian: 312–394* (Cambridge, Polity Press, 2010, pp. 124–126).

58 Another way for majorities, and also minorities, to act prudently, is to delegate some of the more difficult decisions to others. The US Congress has left the task of settling the abortion issue to the Supreme Court. Today the tendency to delegate difficult decisions to non-elected authorities such as the judiciary, supranational institutions, or even the sovereign people through referendum, is

Not only, but also, consensus is not a flux that moves from the bottom upwards. The legitimacy of power does not only consist of symbols, images, discourse and easily manipulable beliefs.[59] It is also empirically based on solid plans of expedience and interests between the governors and the governed, which are hard to upset and that always envelop political authority and whoever holds it. Those who govern always fabricate solidarity and connivance both with the governed, even when they oppress them, and with relevant interests. If ordinary citizens have problems rebelling, what about the actors who are involved in 'collusive transactions' with those who govern, who establish power, and who are with difficulty persuaded to forego certain advantages in favour of other absolutely uncertain advantages?[60]

In the last instance it follows that the most certain defence against the abuse of power by the majority is always politics, or the strength of the opponents. Laws and norms should certainly not be scorned, but it is those who take part in democratic competition who have the burden of preparing themselves, seeing that it is political struggle that establishes, albeit provisionally, where the boundaries to the majority's power lie and eventually the means to make it respected.

The latter also seems to be Kelsen's most profoundly held conviction. Not only did he recognise the political origin of the 'basic norm' which is the presupposition of the entire legal order,[61] but he wanted to reserve the production of law for parliament without the hindrance of too many rights and of a constitution anchored in the idea of the common good, whose unanimous condivision is always improbable and historically contingent. Conscious of the fragility of similar defences, Kelsen suggested a political remedy. He invited individuals to come out of isolation, to organise themselves and to make their voices heard, even in the formulation of law.[62] At the time and place in which it was pronounced, Europe in the early 1920s, the invitation was clearly aimed at the working class, so that that it would organise in parties, whose mobilising potential, electoral and otherwise, could slow down their opponents. The conclusion, however, is that it is impossible to entrust the burdens and responsibilities of politics to democratic regimes, which depend on

---

being reinforced.

59 On the multiple beliefs of legitimacy with which power maintains and reinforces the submission of the governed, see Jacques Lagroye, 'La légitimation', in Jean Leca, Madeleine Grawitz (eds.), *Traité de science politique* (Paris, Presses de la Fondation nationale des sciences politiques, vol. 1, 1985).

60 Michel Dobry, 'Legitimité and calcul rationnel. Remarques sur quelques "complications" de la sociologie de Max Weber' in Pierre Favre, Jack Hayward, Yves Schemeil (eds.), *Etre gouverné Études en l'honneur de Jean Leca* (Paris, Presses de SciencesPo, 2003). For the concept of 'collusive transactions', see Dobry, *Sociologie des crises politiques* (Paris, Presses de la Fondation nationale des sciences politiques, 1986).

61 Kelsen, *General Theory*, pp. 115–117.

62 Kelsen, 'On the Essence and Value of Democracy', pp. 91–92.

its relations of power and balances. It is therefore politics that is responsible for defending the democratic regime.

It is politically legitimate to want to make democracy coincide with rights and with the rule of law and this bodes well for the health of democracy. Even this, however, is a political move and should be realistically treated as such. Democracy cultivates noble principles. Its rules of the game are not without meaning, and without these principles democracy would become arbitrary. But like all things human, democracy is imperfect and if it handles its principles democratically, it is even defenceless.[63]

But only up to a point. The pluralistic configuration on which democratic society stands is a reasonably good antidote to the risks of abuse of power. It is too, an imperfect antidote, but the pluralism that democracy recognises even while it circumscribes it, is quite a resistant obstacle to any form of power. This is why, despite its imperfections, it is better to keep democracy. Experience shows that pluralism can be repressed, but in the long run it has always re-emerged, unless late modernity has, at last, developed sufficiently refined instruments as to render it innocuous.

Cohabitation and hybridisation

The mix between popular sovereignty and power is unstable and requires careful management. If the people are a problem, then the same can be said for the name: nothing is more risky than the rhetoric of the people, whose increasingly insistent use has recently been responsible for the exhumation of the debatable concept of populism. In pronouncing the name of the people, democracy has done as much against its fortune as for it. It has served to legitimate itself and to depersonalise power. The genetic code of democratic regimes registers a generic and emancipating, but undeniable, ambition, together with ambitious plans of social redemption, supported by popular mobilisation. Nevertheless, the people can be also rallied for less noble ends. Enriched by a new actor, albeit virtual, political competition has in any case, gained a new and formidable weapon and a new stake in the power struggle: the faculty to speak legitimately on behalf of the people.

A first difficulty is based on the fact that the expression of democratic ambition involving the people is contradicted by the need for power and government and the practices of their institutions. The democratic institutions, which inevitably

---

63 The scandalous – or celebrated – thesis of Ernst-Wolfgang Böckenförde, for which 'the liberal and secular state lives on assumptions that it is unable to guarantee. This is the big risk that it took on for love of freedom', is well-founded. See 'Die Entstehung des Staates als Vorgang der Säkularisation', now published in Böckenförde, *Recht, Staat, Freiheit* (Frankfurt A. M. Suhrkamp, [1967] 1991, p. 112).

cohabit with non-democratic institutions, will never be sufficiently democratic, or will never appear to be so. As far as we know, power will never be exercised directly by the people. Despite this, whoever is able to earn some advantage by doing it, will be ready to claim that power is not exercised enough to the people's advantage. Therefore, the risk that the people are instrumentally enrolled, even against their best interests, is intrinsic to democratic regimes.

Will the governors chosen by the majority of the electors, real or artificial, always withstand the temptation to evoke the popular mandate in order to impose their will? Can their competitors withstand the inverse temptation of claiming to be the authentic interpreters of the will of the people, in contrast to those in office who are betraying its will?

These are questions that we would do well to keep in mind, perhaps reflecting on the condition of contemporary democratic regimes, where the claims made by the spokespersons of the people have now mushroomed out of all proportion. In addition to the official and unofficial representatives of the people, we now have civil society, social movements, so-called populist parties, and the media, each brandishing their opinion polls with which the people has dictated its will in real time.

This is not a problem that can be ignored and goes to show how much democratic regimes are imperfect and difficult to run. Democracy has imperfections that raise doubts as to whether it is realisable. Perhaps it survives exactly because it is imperfect. Had it been perfectly realised, it could have disrupted collective life unbearably, not only for whoever holds power, but also for ordinary human beings. One can live with imperfection, and one can also die of perfection. In any case, democracy is not only imperfect, it is also incomplete.

Democratic regimes are hybrids and this may increasingly be the case. So much so that someone has asked whether the traditional classification of regimes is not obsolete: a number of heterogeneous regimes cohabit within the same boundaries, depending on the policy spheres, and can also be functional among them.[64] Total democratisation is a pledge made by democracy, but never kept, and there are quite broad spheres of social life that are unresponsive to all attempts to subject them to rules or even to democratic principles.

Even if religious authority is often instrumentalised by democratic rulers in political competition and by government action, it is difficult to understand, for example, how it can be democratised. Until now little has been done to subject the state apparatus – bureaucracies, the armed forces, courts, prisons, schools, universities and hospitals – to democratic rules. Naturally, there is no shortage of critics who invoke democracy in order to polemicise about the functioning of the public administration. The recruitment of senior civil servants can be made

---

64 Michel Camau, Gilles Massardier, 'Revisiter les régimes politiques', in Camau and Massardier (eds.), *Démocraties et autoritarismes. Fragmentation et hybridation des régimes* (Paris, Karthala, 2009).

more democratic or less socially selective, decisional processes can be made more transparent, and the less well-off social strata can be offered greater opportunities for access to education. Key offices can be made elective, or the control over administrative positions by the elective authority can be expanded. It is in any case intriguing that after the limited success enjoyed by attempts to expand the spaces of democratic participation, especially in the 1970s, the following decade, a rather different technology of power, that is, the market, was applied, or was simulated, the New Public Management, or competition applied to research and teaching institutions, are excellent examples.

Now we come to the most complicated theme – the market. Democracy has always had problematic and, to say the least, paradoxical, relations with the market. Historically the representative regime took its first steps when the new social strata, which emerged thanks to the market, expected to be recognised, to the detriment of pre-existing social hierarchies. At the same time, since the origins of representative regimes, a consistent part of the government of collective life has been assigned to the market. The artificial and hierarchical coordination through the state was accompanied by the market, pretending to be a spontaneous instrument of coordination. Its rhetoric demanded that the behaviour of actors was dictated not from above by a superior power, but by self-regulated exchange where each is master of himself and of his own choices. What is better then than to flank the market to the government of the people?

Karl Polanyi argued once that market mechanisms are neither natural, nor spontaneous and autonomous,[65] and no-one can deny that the market has always generated rigid and persistent inequalities. It reproduces inequalities from one generation to another and is intolerant of any attempt to reduce them. However, if some consider inequalities to be collectively virtuous, it is not surprising that, in the name of democracy, political actors very often appear who denounce these inequalities, recognising democracy as a useful instrument to reduce them, or rather distinguishing it precisely for its ability to promote such a reduction. Obviously, while it is legitimate to consider that this is not the specific task of democracy, the criticisms democratically directed at the market are always legitimate, so that the market and democracy are always potentially in conflict.[66]

In any case it is an indisputable fact that on a historical level democracy has always been accompanied by the market. Some scholars therefore postulate a synergy of values between the two, where political freedom and market freedom support each other reciprocally.[67] When the authoritarian regimes in Europe collapsed, their liberal critics acknowledged the restoration of the free market as the most

---

65 Karl Polanyi, *The Great Transformation* (Boston, Beacon Press, [1944] 2001).

66 Norberto Bobbio, 'La democrazia realistica di Giovanni Sartori', *Teoria Politica* 4(1), 1988, 149–158.

67 Giovanni Sartori, 'Mercato', in Sartori, *Elementi di teoria politica* (Bologna, Il Mulino, 1995).

effective antidote to authoritarianism.[68] This argument resurfaced with the fall of franchism and following the collapse of the socialist regimes in Eastern Europe after 1989, and is now proposed on a planetary scale. However, this sort of synergy has been questioned by the market itself, in the not rare cases where the latter, or its protagonists, fiercely oppose the rules of the democratic game. Most probably, the idea that political freedom can exist without market freedom needs still to be proved. But it certainly proved that market freedom does not necessarily mean political freedom. It is not enough for a policy measure to be adopted in conformity with democratic rules for it to be accepted by the market. More than once the market has had a non-democratic reaction to democratically adopted – but unwelcome – measures. The memory of the 1973 military *coup d'etat* in Chile, when the Allende government was working democratically and legally to introduce socialist reforms, still rankles. The *coup* that led to its fall, was first of all backed by the big landowners and businessmen, together with their not disinterested international democratic sponsors.

The economic *milieux* can of course, use more peaceful instruments to get their way, but it is legitimate to doubt their democratic nature. How democratic is a peaceful strike of investments? How peaceful is the flight of capital or the relocation of a firm when government action is not up to the expectations of managers and investors? How democratically acceptable is a peaceful media offensive orchestrated to discredit democratic institutions and rules? Finally, what about the *diktats* of international rating agencies and of international financial institutions on Western and non-Western governments? Their actions are formally compatible with democracy, but they can inflict very serious damage.

No one can rule out that someday economy-governing instruments will be discovered which are more coherent with the rules of the democratic game. Rivers of ink have been used to demonstrate the compatibility of democracy with a socialist economy. Supporters of socialism even say that democracy can only be fully realised when the inequalities created by the market have been removed. Naturally, there is always the question of understanding what democracy means. For all we know, the socialist planned economies that concentrate the management of the economy in the hands of the few, have compressed freedom with effects incompatible with democracy, in addition to exposing themselves as inefficient. Socialist economies that adopted the principle of workers' self-management, were no less inefficient, and no more democratic. In the long run, and perhaps due to the important economic and social changes that have taken place, both abdicated to the market. What has not yet occurred could, however, occur in the future.

What is quite sure is that democratic principles and rules have always been established wherever the market is, while they seem to benefit from economic growth and development. The theory, or a key part of it, has long deduced that this

---

68 See Foucault's account of the reawakening of German liberalism in the postwar period as an antidote to nazism in Foucault, *Naissance de la biopolitique*.

is a precondition of democracy.[69] It reduces inequalities, improves the standard of living, reduces the grounds for social conflict, and thus increases the probability of a peaceful and well-ordered democratic life. Being suspicious, we could suspect that by improving living standards, development reduces the likelihood, and embarrassment, for the market that someone will be interested in becoming a spokesperson for these inequalities and discontent, provoking unwelcome political demands.

Some go so far as to argue that we should not indulge in too much hair-splitting on how development is achieved, given its importance as a precondition for democracy. This means that non-democratic means are also acceptable, given that what is at stake is 'modernisation'.[70] This too is a theory to reflect on, even if recently it seems that it has been abandoned in favour of another theory.

According to this new theory, democracy benefits society, and the market, to such an extent that it is always better to adopt its rules and institutions. We must always understand what sort of democracy we are dealing with. The famous Report of the Trilateral Commission in the mid-1970s specified that an excess of democracy was bad for democracy itself, and accurately defined its limits, proposing a diet that democratic regimes have generally followed.[71] We can presume that this is the democracy deemed compatible with the market and healthy for it. The fact is that recently democratic rhetoric has become ubiquitous and indisputable, and that democracy has really become a precondition for development, which must immediately be coupled with the market.

After a long period of indifference, or almost, the United Nations and the big agencies that defend the global economy, enlightened by 'transitological theory', together promoted democratic institutions and, in fact, made them a criterion of political 'conditionality': no democracy, no aid.[72] It is enough to take a look at the official websites of these agencies to gain access to a mountain of official documentation that prescribe the importance of democratic institutions and rules.[73] Not

---

69 A classic work is Seymour M. Lipset, *Political Man. The Social Bases of Politics* (New York, Doubleday, 1960).

70 A famous example of indifference is given by Samuel P. Huntington, *Political Order in Changing Societies* (New Haven CT, Yale University Press, 1968), for whom democracy in what was then called the Third World, was not even desirable. On this and other developments of the theory, see N. Gilman, *Mandarins of the Future: Modernization Theory in Cold War America* (Baltimore, Johns Hopkins University Press, 2007).

71 Michel Crozier, Samuel P. Huntington, Jôji Watanuki (eds.), *The Crisis of Democracy. Report on the Governability of Democracies to the Trilateral Commission* (New York, New York University Press, 1975).

72 On 'transitology' see the critical account by Michel Dobry, 'Les voies incertaines de la transitologie: choix stratégiques, séquences historiques, bifurcations et processus de path dependence', *Revue française de science politique* 50(4–5), 2000, 585–614.

73 See Edward Newman, Roland Rich, *The UN Role in Promoting Democracy: Between Ideals and*

only, but they also stipulate that these should be socially and culturally rooted. Together with the liberalisation of the economy, these websites publicise a mixed package of policies promoting democracy, made of local government, civil society, associations or 'social capital'.[74] In so doing citizens are pushed to institute relations of reciprocal trust amongst themselves. Once democracy is established, and these furnishings have been added, development will follow.

In the old top-down approach the state was responsible for promoting economic development directly, while the task of supranational institutions and the richest states was to sustain this promotional action financially and technically. In comparison, the bottom-up approach is not a secondary innovation. But has this innovation only been successful because practically no-one now, in the name of democracy, dares to doubt the self-regulationary virtues of the market? Or because communism is now dead and buried, and competition between the blocs has been exhausted, while none of the rich countries either needs, or wants to invest considerable financial resources, in less-developed countries? Instead, rich countries make a saving and prescribe massive doses of low-cost ingredients, whose democratic virtuosity no-one dares to doubt. Or is it not the case, to remain suspicious, that similar ingredients – of so-called 'good governance' – keep the partisan struggle at a distance and help conceal a good dose of anti-political technocracy, together with the persistence of reassuring oligarchic set-ups?[75] Finally, by encouraging non-Western societies to practice do-it-yourself democracy, rather than subjecting them to the brutality of authoritarian regimes, aren't we trying to obtain docile behaviour on the part of populations, and avoid the dissipation of resources that authoritarianism inevitably demands?

Reality (Tokyo, United Nations University Press, 2004).

74 On the concept of social capital, its progress and applications, see Dario Castiglione, Jan W. van Deth, Guglielmo Wolleb (eds.), *The Handbook of Social Capital* (Oxford, Oxford University Press, 2008).

75 With some reason, there is recognition that in the exportation of civil society, there is a solid technocratic and anti-political component. See Kanishka Jayasuriya, Kevin Hewison, 'The Antipolitics of Good Governance', *Critical Asian Studies* 36(4), 2004, 571–590. To inaugurate the use of the concept of anti-politics with reference to assuming political responsibility by the bureaucracy and technicians of development, and when civil society was still not part of the most recommended remedies, see James Ferguson, *The Anti-politics Machine: Development, Depoliticization, and Bureaucratic Power in Lesotho* (Cambridge, Cambridge University Press, 1990). On ways to export democracy, and the not too liberal democracies promoted by the West and the USA, see Vedi R. Hadiz, 'The Rise of Neo-Third Worldism? The Indonesian Trajectory and the Consolidation of Illiberal Democracy', *Third World Quarterly* 25(1), 2004, 55–71. For a general reflection see Jean-Michel Severino, 'Refonder l'aide au développement au XXIe siècle', *Critique internationale* 1(10), 2001, 75–99. See also Béatrice Hibou, *Anatomie politique,* 2011, pp. 134–137.

Other reasons cannot be ruled out. Exporting democracy, also in its particulars, is also a way to 'assimilate the other, to do away with an exterior alterity'.[76] Resembling each other, democratic regimes appear to recognise each other better and thus have less reason to be at war with one another.[77] For every non-democratic regime that disappears, the degree of unexpectedness and uncertainty of the world around democratic regimes is reduced, or so it seems. Perhaps this is not true and the future will refute this hypothesis. Perhaps the term 'democratic' is becoming so broad that the uncertainty will remain. After all, what is being exported is not Western democracy, with the meanings that history has gradually attributed to it. And it is one thing to export and import institutions, but quite another to interpret and apply them.

In any case, it is always convenient for Western democratic regimes to vaunt the beneficial effects of democracy and to establish a norm, monitered by international agencies that manoeuvre the weapon of debt-and-aid and dictate the policies to adopt, also through the charitable involvement of NGOs. At the same time even war can be reclassified as a benevolent operation in the export of democracy. If not precisely compatible with it, democracy is such a holy cause that even the extermination of civil populations, illegal imprisonment and torture, can become forms of tolerable collateral damage!

---

76 Tzvetan Todorov, *The Conquest of America: the Question of the Other* (New York, Harper & Row, 1984, p. 247).

77 This is the 'democratic peace theory'. For an exposition and critical discussion of the theory see Michael E. Brown, Sean M. Lynn-Jones and Steven E. Miller (eds.), *Debating the Democratic Peace* (Cambridge MA, MIT Press, 1996).

chapter three | dispersion

From one form of capitalism to another

Once upon a time there was 'organised capitalism'.[1] Indeed, all capitalisms are organised insofar as each has protagonists and secondary actors, hierarchies that are more or less stable, and an organisation that is more or less visible. Among the protagonists the presence of what in a rather simplistic way we are used to call the state is a constant. In the tormented history of relations between democracy and the market, there has nevertheless been a period in which the market, in addition to being partly organised by the state, openly recognised that this was the case. This is the period following the era of liberal capitalism that had come to an end with the Wall Street crash.

Organised capitalism was a model of social organisation and industrial relations, characterised by the centrality of large enterprises and powerful trade union organisations. These established an agreement which gradually became more official, and which was supervised by the regulative, integrative and redistributive intervention of the state. The relations between these private and public actors gradually stabilised and – without ruling out tensions and conflicts, at times serious – were consolidated through forms of programming and planning arranged by the state, and even more through the unofficial institutions of government referred to collectively under the label of 'neo-corporatism'.[2]

The Gramscian-flavoured concept of 'Fordism'[3] allows us to draw a slightly more detailed picture showing a specific form of the productive process and organisation of work. On the one hand, this rested on mass production, the assembly line and the use of unskilled labour. On the other hand, it was placed within a much

---

1 Scott Lash, John Urry, *The End of Organized Capitalism* (Cambridge, Polity Press, 1988).

2 The concept of corporatism, taken from political catholic and fascist culture, to describe the coordinating practices between the public and private sector in Western democratic regimes in the postwar period, was first reproposed by Andrew Shonfield, *Modern Capitalism, The Changing Balance of Public and Private Power* (London, Oxford University Press, 1965, p. 231). Years later the concept will be reproposed again by Philippe C. Schmitter in 'Still the Century of Corporatism?', *The Review of Politics* 36(1), 1974, 85–131. (Neo)corporatism will be one of the most thoroughly analysed questions by scholars of political issues for a decade. For all see Gerhard Lehmbruch, Philippe C. Schmitter (eds.), *Trends Toward Corporatist Intermediation* (London, Sage, 1979).

3 Ash Amin (ed.), *Post-Fordism. A Reader* (Oxford, Blackwell, 1994).

broader socio-political framework. As a model of growth, Fordism was based on the presumption of full employment and the constant increase of productivity, thanks to economies of scale. In turn, the growth of productivity was the motor that drove increases in income, expenditure, consumption, profits and investments. The task of regulating the entire mechanism fell to the state. In addition to its normal tasks of external defence and internal maintenance of public order, it intervened in production, supported employment and incomes, promoted public and private consumption, and supplied a considerable bulk of public services in order to reduce social inequalities. This complied with the principles of justice, more shared at that moment, and helped prevent and control social conflict. In short, according to the Fordist approach, a very large part of collective life is governed through the state.[4]

The outcomes and equilibria generated by Fordism and organised capitalism differed from one country to another as did the balance between primary, secondary and tertiary sectors, and between small, medium and large enterprises. In some cases flexible specialisation maintained very relevant spaces. The levels of technological development also differed as did industrial relations, welfare models and the efficiency of the public administration. Not all the industrial sector was subject to Fordist discipline, and in many countries there were marked geographical disparities, with many forms of Fordism (and organised capitalism) in Germany, Italy, France and Britain. The performance of the model varied from one context to another, and was judged in different ways, given that there was no shortage of discontent and criticism. It is, however, a commonly held belief that Fordism was widespread in all Western societies. It is also commonly held that at the end of the 1970s Fordism was progressively shelved throughout the West, unexpectedly ushering in a new era,[5] that of 'disorganised capitalism',[6] or post-Fordism.

As always, formulae simplify things, but no-one denies that between the 1970s and 1980s a difficult and epochal changeover occurred: a change of phase, or cycle, and even the transition from one capitalism to another, and from one model of economics and society to another. What were the grounds for this striking transition which marked the beginning of what appears to be a new and absolutely different era from the previous one? What emptied the industrial plants, transforming the luckier part of them into shopping centres, museums of industrial archaeology and other things, luxurious lofts, hotels and so forth? What has upset the economic and social context in which the industrial plants were situated, together with its representations?

---

4   Bob Jessop, 'Post-Fordism and the State', in Amin (ed.), *Post-Fordism*.

5   It is enough to leaf through the book edited by Charles S. Maier, *Changing Boundaries of the Political* (Cambridge, Cambridge University Press, 1987). See, in particular, the essay by a highly esteemed scholar like John H. Goldthorpe, 'Problems of Political Economy after the Postwar Period', which then still stressed the precarious nature of neo-liberal policies and the, apparently weak, trade union and political resistance to them.

6   Claus Offe, *Disorganized Capitalism: Contemporary Transformations of Work and Politics* (Cambridge, MIT Press, 1985).

There are many explanations of this process of transition which started alongside the recurrent critical episodes suffered by Western economies in the 1970s, with the consequent halt, or almost, of growth. One of the many scholars who tried to reorganise these explanations has identified the three main ones: the 'regulation approach'; the 'neo-Schumpeterian approach'; and the 'flexible specialisation approach'.[7]

The 'regulation approach' stresses the slowed rate of productivity, attributed to the intrinsic limits of mass production, to full employment and to the rigidity of the labour force, caused by trade-union mobilisation. Secondly, while mass production favoured the internationalisation of the economy, at the same time it may have reduced the ability of the national authorities to govern it. A third critical element consists of the growth of demand – and supply – of public services, and hence of public expenditure, feeding heavy inflationary pressures and serious distributional conflicts. A fourth and final element is the inability of conventional mass production to satisfy a new, and more diversified, demand for consumer goods.

The 'neo-Schumpeterian' approach stresses the pull exercised by innovation. That is, by the introduction of new productive practices and forms of labour-saving organisation, for the most part thanks to informatics, and in line with the evolution of consumption and demand. The downward trend in the costs of transport and communication, in turn, marked the beginning of a massive delocalisation of the industrial plants. Firms began to look for more promising conditions in terms of labour costs and training, fiscal pressure, infrastructure and less onerous regulatory conditions.

The third approach, that of 'flexible specialisation', identifies two models of industrial production: mass and flexible. These two productive paradigms alternate and one or other prevails depending on the preferences and choices of firms and governments, national or local. At the time of Fordism, Keynesian policies sustained aggregate demand and mass consumption. The slump in demand was caused by the recession of the 1970s, and the qualitative evolution from a demand for mass goods to a demand for higher quality, non-standard goods, together with the introduction of new technologies and new methods of production, which encouraged the success of flexible specialisation.

Each of these approaches has its own political implications. It is one thing to stress the importance of technological innovation, accepting it as inevitable, and its consequences as unavoidable. It is quite another thing to insist on the defects of regulation. Leaving this aside, the debate surrounding the shift away from Fordism also corresponds to three main events. The first is what we can call 'globalisation'. In reality this is a process of convergence and hybridisation which has always affected human societies, but which has recently accelerated and assumed a preeminently economic meaning: the world was to become a single market thanks to

---

7   Amin, 'Post-Fordism: Models, Fantasies and Phantoms of Transition', in Amin, *Post-Fordism*, pp. 6–16.

the liberalisation of capital movements, the financialisation of the economy, the exponential increase of commercial exchanges, productive delocalisation and the entry of new and aggressive protagonists to the world economy.[8] The second event is the decline of the regulatory, organising and ordering action of the state. The third event is the break with the preceding model of industrial relations and the mutation, also sociological, of dependent employment.

Under Fordism blue-collar and white-collar dependent work was concentrated in large factories, big service enterprises such as banks and insurance and powerful public bureaucracies. Trade unions, usually backed by socialist parties, represented dependent labour and, from a Fordist horizon, had taken on governmental responsibility, sitting side by side with entrepreneurial representatives at the neo-corporatist negotiating table. The advent of post-Fordism dispersed employment, operating not only on the organisational level and on working conditions and income, but also on the cultural and political level. Together with the process of financialisation, all this induced firms to make employment a variable, manoeuvrable exclusively according to the benefit of management and shareholders. In the space of twenty years, the chaotic and unsteady universe of atypical, interim, temporary, flexible, para-subordinate and part-time work, has replaced stable employment not only in the factories, but also in services and even in public administration.[9] As if this were not enough, dependent work has been subject to a striking process of delegitimation. In postwar culture, work was considered a value, but thirty years later the modest job security that had been attained, has been theoretically and politically portrayed as a constraint to growth and an unjust condition of privilege.

Post-Fordist society, and the social transformations that characterise it, have stimulated a display of nostalgic sentiment. We should not forget, however, that in spite of welfare, which was only fully activated in the 1960s, the factory nevertheless remained a theatre of tension and dramatic alienation. The problems that arose, although in different forms, in factories and in the large public and private bureaucracies, were no less relevant and the benefits of Fordism did not stop the workers' condition from remaining the subject of lively critical discussion and conflict. By way of compensation, however, since the nineteenth century the factory had become the place where interdependencies, solidarity, a collective sense of belonging, and very intense forms of mobilisation, were built up.

The process of differentiation and fragmentation which hit the world of employment at the end of the millennium has had the opposite effect. The substantial use of what are euphemistically called social shock absorbers, pre-pensioning, and familial strategies, have certainly slowed down the drop in income for the social categories concerned. Nevertheless, the general deterioration in employment conditions lies at the root of the suffering, humiliation and discouragement

---

8   Danilo Zolo, *Globalization: An Overview* (Colchester, ECPR Press, 2007).

9   Luciano Gallino, *Il costo umano della flessibilità* (Rome/Bari, Laterza, 2001).

widespread in large segments of society, and has the effect of undermining its potential for collective action and hence political involvement.[10] How political and trade union representatives reacted to the challenge of this change in the world of work is a crucial issue which should be discussed. In any case, the shift away from Fordism coincided with the social and cultural dispersion of the main component of the constituency that had promoted the welfare state – the working class.

The promoters of welfare were not exclusively the working classes through their political and trade-union representatives. A determining contribution was also made by the establishment, keen to reduce the grounds for social conflict. Welfare policies served to sharpen the technology of power. An impressive government apparatus was created to apply these policies – including the public services. The actions of this apparatus have penetrated the lives of the governed, and stepped up the disciplining and reorganisation of collective life, initiated by modernity under the absolute monarchies, out of all proportion.[11] In addition to benefiting the governed, symbolically and materially, the welfare state has also reshaped them, and reshaped their existence. For the popular and socialist parties the expected return on welfare policies was a more just society. For nearly all political parties – liberal and conservative included, among other things, the return was to a more well-ordered society, with a consequent decline in conflicts and eccentric, deviant or unpredictable behaviour generated by excessive inequality.

That we are dealing with a technology of power is demonstrated by the fact that the provisions designed to alleviate inequalities and to reduce the risks of conflict came well before the birth of the welfare state. The latter, we should not forget, received crucial support also from the middle classes, who made their own welfare demands, and who are major consumers of public services, knowing how to use them – starting with the educational system – much more shrewdly and intensely than the working class.[12]

In any case, the transition to post-Fordism took place in a much more gradual and less visible way than what the models interiorised by commonly shared opinion suggest, and which rationalised an uncertain, tortuous and for a long time even open-ended course. The decline of Fordism was characterised by 'stagflation' and a marked drop in employment. But first of all it seemed resistant to the Keynesian treatment popular at the time, although according to some observers this was

---

10 On the French situation, although the data can be in large part generalised, see Stéphane Beaud, Michel Pialoux, *Retour sur la condition ouvrière* (Paris, Fayard, 1999).

11 On the issue of the disciplinary action of the modern State, very different authors come to mind. Two classical contributions are those of Norbert Elias and Michel Foucault. Dennis Smith proposes a contrast in 'The Civilizing Process and The History of Sexuality: Comparing Norbert Elias and Michel Foucault', *Theory and Society* 28, 1999, 79–100.

12 According to Gøsta Esping-Andersen there was a genuine coalition between the working classes and middle classes (*The Three Worlds of Welfare Capitalism*, Cambridge, Polity Press, 1990).

not applied properly and in the correct doses.[13] The extent of the difficulties at the time, however, meant that the situation was defined publicly as critical, presenting the different conditions of Western countries as if they were similar, and providing valuable fuel for the cultural and political offensive spearheaded by Reagan and Thatcher.[14] It was these two figures, with the support of an aggressive intellectual 'neo-liberal' *milieux*,[15] who pulled through and legitimated a stream of new public policies and encouraged a counter offensive by the entrepreneurial world.

In the light of a no less disruptive crisis that hit Western society and the entire planet at the end of the first decade of the new millennium, the trajectory taken may appear clearer. The thirty years of post-Fordism were marked by a fundamental political manoeuvre. On the one hand, the state started reducing welfare expenditure and stopped defending public and private employment and the public services, to the benefit of economic growth and enterprise profits. On the other hand, and with the full consensus of the national and supranational political authorities, entrepreneurial profits, but also the savings of families and pension funds, have been diverted in the whirlpool of global financial speculation. It is unlikely that the actors were aware of the risks they were taking. It is also unlikely that significant reductions in public expenditure were really obtained because other needs had arisen in the meantime. In any case, only the wealthier strata benefited from the reduction of fiscal pressure, while the cost of public services has generally increased. At this point, a dramatic contrast opened up between financial activities and productive activities, to the advantage of the former. Investments and employment were damaged, not to mention the well-being of citizens and of collective life itself.[16]

---

13   Colin Hay, 'Whatever Happened to Thatcherism?', *Political Studies Review* 5(2), 2007, 183–201.

14   On the ideological nature of Reaganism, see William C. Berman, *America's Right Turn: From Nixon to Clinton* (Baltimore MD, Johns Hopkins University Press, 1998, 85–118). On Thatcherism see Dennis Kavanagh, *Thatcherism and British Politics. The End of Consensus* (Oxford, Oxford University Press, 1990).

15   For a definition, and a reconstruction of neo-liberalism, see David Harvey, *A Brief History of Neoliberalism* (New York, Oxford University Press, 2005). Harvey's book deals with the events of the last forty years, but the history of neo-liberalism is older, even if liberalism cannot be reduced to neo-liberalism: see Richard Cockett, *Thinking the Unthinkable. Think-Tanks and the Economic Counter-Revolution, 1931–1983* (London, Harper & Collins, 1995) and François Denord, 'Le prophète, le pèlerin et le missionnaire. La circulation internationale du néo-libéralisme et ses acteurs', *Actes de la recherche en sciences sociales* 5(145), 2002, 9–20. Neo-liberalism dates back to the years of the 1929 crisis, when we witness the reconstruction of an international network of intellectuals and above all, liberal economists who reacted to the success of Keynesianism and increased State intervention. But the fundamental contribution is Michel Foucault, Naissance de la biopolitique. Cours au Collège de France, 1978–1979 (Paris, Gallimard-Seuil, 2004).

16   Luciano Gallino, *Finanzcapitalismo. La civiltà del denaro in crisi* (Turin, Einaudi, 2011).

Post-materialism?

By all available accounts the epicentre of the earthquake was the industrial sector, whose transformation had already been on the cards for some time. At end of the 1960s, a famous cultural sociologist, Daniel Bell, and a no less famous industrial sociologist, Alain Touraine, coined the term 'post-industrial society'.[17] In a society based on knowledge, information, research and advanced services the one recognised a promising change, the other new forms of power and new sources of potential conflict. Both were democratically risky. Nonetheless, both agreed in predicting profound changes, carried out following multiple and anything but linear paths, making it difficult to understand the immediate course of events.

The contraction of industrial production in Western societies was decisive, but the course taken by the transformation has not always been the same. The change is not always initiated in the industrial sector. In many local situations the use of the territory has begun to change, such as the deployment of urban spaces and the transport networks. Elsewhere, and in many spheres of society, the change first hit culture, mentality and lifestyles. In other cases it involved forms of political organisation and the practices of government. Curiously, if one considers the cultural aspects, even if it is not easy to distinguish them, some are attributable to the end of Fordism, but others appear to have been at work for at least a decade.

There were more than a few culturally relevant consequences of development – thanks to full employment, welfare measures, increasing private and public consumption, growth in living standards, and mass education. In the long run this had favoured striking upheavals in behaviour and lifestyles. The great mobilisation for civil rights which exploded at the end of the 1960s, lasting nearly ten years, is the most visible political testimony of this impact. In the social sciences among those who recorded these changes was an American scholar, Ronald Inglehart. Starting in the early 1970s, he applied large-scale comparative survey techniques and examined the new cultural orientations, designating them as, 'post-materialistic values',[18] one of the many 'post-something' that will enrich our lexicon.

Beginning with the younger generations and the middle classes, the population of advanced societies was, according to Inglehart, reappraising and refining its

17 Daniel Bell, *The Coming of Post-industrial Society: a Venture in Social Forecasting* (New York, Basic Books, 1973) and Alaine Touraine, *The Post-Industrial Society. Tomorrow's Social History: Classes, Conflicts and Culture in the Programmed Society* (New York, Random House, [1969] 1971). The two authors disputed the paternity of the term although Bell had used it in an essay in 1967, then included in the book.

18 In a first version Ronald Inglehart actually spoke of 'post-bourgeois values'. See, 'The Silent Revolution in Europe. Intergenerational Change in Post-industrial Societies', *American Political Science Review* 65(4), 1971, 991–1017. The concept of post-materialism will be made explicit in *The Silent Revolution: Changing Values and Political Styles Among Western Publics* (Princeton NJ, Princeton University Press, 1977).

value preferences. Once basic needs had been satisfied, traditional acquisitive orientations declined and part of the citizenship renovated their priorities and their values, which became personal freedom, creativity, self-expression, self-realisation and active participation in politics, flanked by new forms of cultural consumption.

Although widely criticised, Inglehart's thesis had no lack of arguments. The idea of the pre-eminence of post-materialist values over material needs is excessive, yet it is not surprising that, thanks to economic development, and in the protective shadow of welfare, Western society had become not only more prosperous, but also more mobile, more varied, more educated and more informed. The welfare state had only eased, but not removed, inequalities and poverty, as shown by the bitter social conflicts of the 1970s. It is no wonder that greater economic security and mass consumption had eroded the constraints of religion, family, hierarchies and conventional sexual roles, etc., and stimulated a vigorous flourishing of new demands. Some of these were individualistic and libertarian, whilst others were sectoral, local or occasional, and all were sustained by forms of unconventional collective mobilisation. In any case the decline of forms of mobilisation that had previously supported the demands to intensify (and extend) democracy, thus found an other point of reference. In the meantime parties and forms of political representation were also being transformed, and once again in such a way as to discourage political participation and collective action.

What is unquestionable is the ability of the conservative and moderate political leadership, reanimated by the determination and successes of Ronald Reagan and Margaret Thatcher, to culturally exploit both neo-liberal theories, and the cultural fruits of Fordism, and the democratic period that accompanied it.

Neo-liberal economists headed by Hayek and Friedman had always questioned Keynesian orthodoxy, but in the mid-1970s they finally had a breakthrough. In the USA the task was easier. Tax revolt, embodied by Ronald Reagan,[19] had been a recurrent grounds for debate in the USA, now accompanied by, at times very complex theoretical formulations.

It would be incorrect to reduce the renewal of economic theory to the dealings of the Mont Pèlerin Society, but examining what took place in what was one of the most venerated temples of liberalism, which had initially taken a solemn stand against communism and even social democracy, will help us understand what happened.[20] Initially, that authoritative circle was rather condescending towards state

---

19 Remember that in 1978 in California, where Reagan had been governor, a referendum approved *Proposition 13* that amended the constitution abolishing all forms of taxation on property.

20 On the Mont Pèlerin affair see Richard Cockett, *Thinking the Unthinkable*, 1995. See also Yves Steiner, 'Ce marché qui rassemble et qui divise: les Firsthand dealers in ideas de la Mont Pèlerin Society', in Guy Bensimon, Jean-Pierre Potier (eds.), *Histoire des représentations du marché* (Paris, Houdiard, 2005) and Yves Steiner, Bernhard Walpen, 'L'apport de l'ordolibéralisme au renouveau libéral, puis son éclipse', *Carnets de bord* 11, 2006, 94–104. For an account of

intervention. After all it included figures such as Ludwig Erhard, who had invented the 'social market economy' in West Germany. But at the end of the 1960s, when Milton Friedman became president,[21] the Mont Pèlerin Society converted to more radical ideas. These ideas were to become very popular beyond the normal conservative circles, on account of the economic misfortunes of the following decade. The neo-liberal turn was consecrated by two Nobel laureates – Hayek in 1974 and Friedman two years later[22] – and not only offered a convincing interpretation of those misfortunes, but became the inspiring doctrine of the offensive against the interventionist policies adopted from the 1930s onwards in the USA and Europe.[23]

It is a paradox. On the one hand, the economic difficulties and social tensions of the 1970s opened an unexpected window of opportunity to similar ideas. On the other hand, the issues raised by the cultural change, produced by wealth, were also used to overturn the pro-welfare constituency and to promote the transition to post-Fordism. Some political, entrepreneurial and intellectual *milieux* have specifically drawn on these themes, in particular to represent a widespread intolerance of all forms of institutions, including the welfare state. Nothing is less credible than this intolerance. Except for cases such as the Scandinavian countries, welfare was a long way from offering full and satisfying coverage of life's risks. At the same time it was in all probability, much less opaque, invasive and oppressive than the critical anti-state rhetoric pretended: but the neo-liberal critique of welfare succeeded in accentuating the antagonistic demands of the new left and obscured the solidaristic ones. This in any case led to a political discourse promoting the autonomy and self-sufficiency of individuals and delegitimating collective action. We should not forget that the basic grounds for visibility and political success had become inviting media attention. This was more inclined to focus on post-materialist preferences, libertarian demands, the recognition of differences, *in primis* gender differences, but also of local cultures, than on traditional conflict.

---

the success of neo-liberalism on a planetary scale see Dieter Plehwe, Bernhard Walpen, Gisela Neunhoffer (eds.), *Neoliberal Hegemony: A Global Critique* (London, Routledge, 2006).

21 In the 1960s the Mont Pèlerin Society is Americanised and radicalised in a neo-liberal and anti-statist sense, while in the 1950s and 1960s liberal ideas were contaminated with those of the advocates of a moderate statist interventionism: see François Denord, 'Le prophète, le pèlerin et le missionnaire'.

22 A confirmation of the uncertainties of the time, Friedrich Hayek won the Nobel in 1974 together with Gunnar Myrdal, an economist with a social-democratic background. In 1976 Milton Friedman was instead on his own.

23 On Britain, see Keith Dixon, *Les évangélistes du marché. Les intellectuels britanniques et le néo-libéralisme* (Paris, Raisons d'agir, 2008). Nothing is really new, either on the grounds of theory or on that of politics. In 1964 Barry Goldwater was the presidential candidate standing against Lyndon B. Johnson and presented a programme to cancel progressive taxation and to establish full market freedom. In 1970, let us remember, Edward Heath won the British elections with a liberalist programme.

It would be absurd to underestimate the importance of the technological change that brought about a revolution in the organisation of work and production. But since this sort of change does not come about by chance, we must also ask ourselves what directed it along the course that it took historically. The fact remains that politics has been the decisive motor also in the new transformation. It was politics that symbolically revoked the former primacy of full employment, that delegitimised public expenditure, backed the growth and control of inflation, and collided with the trade-union movement.

The unwinding of political dealings is not irrelevant. What the cases of Reaganism and Thatcherism show is that it was politics, stimulated by the neo-liberal doctrine, that promoted the recovery of the business and entrepreneurial world against the state, civil servants and trade unions, relieving the former of all responsibility for the alleged economic decline and saddling the latter, together with old-fashioned politics, with this responsibility.[24]

Finally, the change was also oriented by the way in which it was narrated and interpreted while in full swing. Neo-liberalism, insofar as it is a proposal of innovative government and supply-side economics and an alternative to Keynesianism, was used by conservative and moderate parties to discredit not only welfare and the state, but also the very idea of society, and the prevailing notions of common good and general interest, legitimating and encouraging the egoistic instinct of individuals. Political leadership, and its intellectual spheres of reference, in fact persuaded the entrepreneurial class to denounce the practice of neo-corporate concertation, which had to date governed development together with the trade unions and the state.

The dramatisation of the economic and social scenario, the rhetoric of unavoidable change, the use of concepts such as crisis and decline, all helped – in addition to highlighting the responsibilities of the world of work and the state – to revolutionise the political agenda.[25] For their part, the socialist and leftist parties,

---

24 It was the clash between the government and the miners in 1984–1985 – sought and won by Margaret Thatcher – that ratified this symbolic transformation. The British Prime Minister, who had come to power with a programme which broke with the previous party line, had shown great determination in renewing the running of the country. Until then the results had been modest, and usually as a result of restrictive moves in public spending, but above all fiscal measures to the benefit of higher-income groups. The unexpected victory in the Falklands War opened the road to Mrs. Thatcher's electoral victory in 1983, and reversed her previously negative standing in the opinion polls. In *Thatcherism and British Politics* (pp. 123–150) Dennis Kavanagh stresses the driving action that politics exercised on the entrepreneurial world. In fact, politics had taken the initiative in grand style with Reagan's reaction to the flight controllers' strike in 1981 – he fired them all.

25 Was the British economy really in decline? In *English Culture and the Decline of the Industrial Spirit, 1850–1980* (Cambridge, Cambridge University Press, 1981) Martin J. Wiener describes the decline as age-old. But not everyone agrees with this image, shared and promoted by Thatcher,

and trade unions, demonstrated a rather limited resistance. They may have un-derestimated the centrifugal tensions generated by modernity and may have been too uncritical in their compliance with the season of civil rights, underestimating its political and cultural implications.[26] Perhaps they were simply exhausted and disoriented by the appearance of strong social movements that hit them directly, questioning their representative function and, in particular, their monopoly of rep-resentation of demands for social change. In much the same way, it is likely that leftist forces undervalued the opportunities for redistribution of the resources of power that would become available to the entrepreneurial and financial *milieux* to the cost of their constituencies, and in the last instance, themselves. The fact is that even the leftist parties have often married the rhetoric of inevitability, only seeking marginal adjustments.

In the mid-1940s, the Hungarian anthropologist Karl Polanyi proposed a fasci-nating interpretation of the developments taking place in the economy and market society, and sketched a first ambitious theory of the welfare state. An essential element of his reasoning was the artificiality of market mechanisms. In response to the claim that these were naturally occurring mechanisms, Polanyi argued that the self-regulating market was a political artifice promoted by a *laissez-faire* con-ception of society and that as an artifice, it was in turn, the cause of dramatic shortcomings. In his words market society 'could not exist for any length of time without annihilating the human and natural substance of society; it would have physically destroyed man and transformed his surroundings into a wilderness'.[27] Polanyi's conclusion was that the New Deal and fascism had been two different forms of state protection of society against the market, the first virtuous, the sec-ond perverse.

Polanyi's ideas were not a common patrimony of the postwar ruling or intel-lectual classes, and in this sense the ideas of Keynes had much more success, but one can consider them a sound rationalisation of a perspective long shared by the main political actors, especially of the big popular parties. Remembering the disorder of the immediate first postwar period and the Wall Street crash, on the regulatory and ordering action of the state, and the recognised priority of full em-ployment, liberal thought and politics also agreed, and they played an important role in the postwar reconstruction. It was the socialist and popular parties which supported the more sympathetic conceptions of the welfare state: the universalistic

---

and instead presents Britain as a country that has always enjoyed regular growth, albeit slower than other European countries, and which was only interrupted in 1973 with the oil crisis (Dennis Kavanagh, *Thatcherism and British Politics*, pp. 17–18).

26 For a criticism of the individualistic drift inherent to the use of rights to the detriment of the universalistic principle of republican solidarity see Marcel Gauchet, *La Révolution des droits de l'homme*, Paris, Gallimard, 1989. See also the in-depth work by Colette Bec, *De l'Etat social à l'Etat des droits de l'homme?* (Rennes, Presses universitaires de Rennes, 2007).

27 Karl Polanyi, *The Great Transformation* (Boston, Beacon Press, [1944] 2001, p. 3).

principle of solidarity on which it was to be based sought nothing less than to promote a form of society which would allow each individual to exploit their own freedom fully.[28] At that moment, even if the liberals appreciated the market, finding in economic freedom a precious antidote to authoritarianism, that had been economically *dirigiste*, they nevertheless recognised the centrality of the state: the 'social market economy' was their invention.[29] The break produced by neo-liberalist ideas and policies, not by chance also defined as 'anarchic', therefore lies in having recanted both points of view, legitimating the market as the new and natural basis of collective life.

The construction of a new commonly held opinion owes a great deal to the theory, especially to economic science. The latter employed all its authority to make dependent work and its excessive costs and excessive fiscal pressure responsible for the drop in investments and the growth of unemployment. It claimed that the rigidity of the labour force was attributable to the action of trade unions which slowed down progress and the spread of new technologies. Once again it was economic science that legitimised the extension of the competitive principle beyond its traditional limits, towards previously unimagined spheres, which had until now been firmly defended by the state. Thus, as *homo oeconomicus* became the archetypal human being, so economic science became the exclusive science of how he functioned. The objective has not been fully realised, but a substantial revision of the categories and concepts used by the social sciences, by theory and hence by common sense, has indeed taken place.

In the light of this theory, the impressive cultural and political rehabilitation of the business sector and of private initiatives made by politics, has released them from any element of social responsibility. On the contrary, once work had been struck off the list of basic rights, unemployment – previously indicated as one of the reasons for the success of fascism in the 1920s – could be reduced to a secondary cause of public disorder and, if anything, a problem of electoral consent.

The end of social classes?

The great political-cultural revision that accompanied the transition to post-Fordism is well illustrated by the destiny of one of the basic ingredients of the previous representation of society, that of social classes. This was not the only category used by the theory to describe social stratification, but it has long been the most widespread and politically the most used.

However old and venerable the concept, classes do not exist in nature, where at most, we find individuals occupying similar or adjoining social positions in the division of labour and the distribution of income, prestige, power and culture, or

28 Bec, *De l'Etat social à l'Etat des droits de l'homme?*.
29 See the reconstruction by Michel Foucault in Naissance de la biopolitique, pp. 77-103.

who share the same living standards. The concept of class groups and 'classifies' individuals in terms of division of labour, equality and inequalities of income, living conditions and life opportunities, and draws a map of society that helps explain how it functions and its transformations.[30] Even if it did not invent classes, Marxism made them a key interpretative category and above all, in the case of the working class, and thanks to socialist parties, key political actors.

Sociology – Weberian sociology, for example – has tried to strip the concept of class of its political meaning, but this was not enough to make its sociological use universal. American sociology sometimes refered to classes, but generally used other categories to represent a social stratification deemed more mobile and complex than its European equivalent, and politically less exploited. One question which merits more attention is whether the characteristics of society in the USA and Europe were so dissimilar as to require the use of different interpretative categories, or whether the difference lay in politics.[31] What is nevertheless typical of Europe, and that occurs much less in the USA, is that politics has long presented to classes, particularly to the working classes, a specific supply of representation and recognition – in Pizzorno's sense of the term[32] – promoting them as collective bodies and as historical subjects, competing with other similar collective bodies, also united by feelings of belonging and a desire for common political objectives.[33]

In Europe classes are thus one of the significant inventions that have accompanied modernity, industrialisation and urbanisation. Where we find, at times, a traumatic, erosion of solidarity and traditional forms of deference (local,

---

30 For a re-examination of the use of the class concept by the social sciences, but also the way that social stratification is represented today, as well as today's debate on the utility of the concept to understand society, see Arnaldo Bagnasco, *Prima lezione di sociologia* (Rome/Bari, Laterza, 2007, pp. 61–76). For a more detailed analysis see in 'Introduzione a una questione complicata', in Bagnasco (ed.), *Ceto medio. Perché e come occuparsene* (Bologna, Il Mulino, 2008).

31 For a good example of the conceptual instruments used by the social sciences in the USA see Reinhard Bendix, Seymour M. Lipset (eds.), *Class, Status And Power A Reader in Social Stratification* (Glencoe, The Free Press, 1954). One often asks why it went like this. Indirectly the theme is raised in at least two famous contributions. The first is by Werner Sombart, *Warum gibt es in den Vereinigten Staaten keinen Sozialismus* (Tübingen, Mohr, 1906), for which the opportunities offered by US society and the character, let's say, inter-classist of the two big parties impede socialism taking root, and that, at a distance of a century, of Seymour M. Lipset, Garry Marks, *It Didn't Happen Here: Why Socialism Failed in the United States* (New York, Norton & Co., 2000). Lipset and Marks point out political factors, such as the electoral system and the structure of political competition, but also the individualistic culture and the ethnic, religious and cultural heterogeneity of the working classes.

32 See Pizzorno's elaboration of this concept in *Il velo della diversità. Studi su razionalità e riconoscimento* (Milan, Feltrinelli, 2009).

33 On classes as social constructions see Pierre Bourdieu, 'Social Space and Genesis of "Classes"', in Bourdieu, *Language and Symbolic Power* (Cambridge MA, Harvard University Press, 1991).

family, clientelistic, religious), thanks to classes, we find new divisions and new inequalities, but also a tool to reconstitute society politically and culturally. The constraints that – thanks to socialist parties and labour unions – classes instituted, such as solidaristic behaviour, shared culture, the effects of imitation among its members, became basic instruments of the government of collective life for at least a century. In this task classes intersected and accompanied the nation, which not only unified the people symbolically, but was also largely used to compensate for the decline of pre-existing solidarities, as well as the inequalities created by the market, and not only. [34]

In order to establish classes as political actors, as well as to establish nations, impressive organisational and cultural mechanisms were introduced. Classes and nations compete against one another to establish symbolic equality and solidarity,[35] but the trajectories taken by the two concepts, in the last quarter of a century, appear to be particularly divergent. Worn out by the disasters of nationalism and decolonisation, nations and national identity had undergone a prolonged period of eclipse. Unexpectedly, while the exhaustion of the Fordist model together with globalisation have marginalised classes from representation in society, elaborated both by politics and social theory,[36] the destiny of the nation has been quite different thanks to politics, which has returned to invest considerable resources within it.[37]

We can suppose that inequalities and tensions emphasised by a representation of society stratified in classes are currently deemed more politically problematic and harder to manage, than those that stimulate a sense of belonging and national identity. The egalitarian demands of the working classes appear more disturbing and more costly, than episodes of intolerance towards immigrants. In addition, national identity may help legitimate aggressive exploits beyond national boundaries. It is nonetheless difficult to deny that the profound transformations involving social structure and stratification for more than half a century have weakened a category inherited from the nineteenth century. There are many reasons why the lines that

---

34 On the political use of the two concepts see Peter Wagner, *A Sociology of Modernity: Liberty and Discipline* (New York, Routledge, 1994).

35 See Alessandro Pizzorno's analysis, reproposed in *Il velo della diversità*.

36 On the political and theoretical setting, in particular the concepts, and also the working class see Luc Boltanski, Eve Chiappello, *Le nouvel ésprit du capitalisme* (Paris, Gallimard, 1999, pp. 376–392). See also, Luc Boltanski, *Rendre la société inacceptable* (Paris, Raisons d'agir, 2010).

37 Regarding a sub-national sense of belonging one can cite the cases of Spain, Britain, Belgium and Italy. The latter is perhaps the most interesting case, since the other countries have historically represented themselves as a summation of different nationalities, whereas in Italy there is a municipal culture, but historically differentiated nationalities have never been recognised. Catalonia and Scotland have always existed, Padania is a very recent invention. This witnesses that such inventions are always possible, even if not necessarily enduring over time. See M. Machiavelli (M. Avanza), 'La Ligue du Nord. et l'invention du "Padan"', *Critique Internationale* 10, 2001, 129–142.

cut through today's society appear uncertain, broken, unstable and often indistinct, and this explains why the social sciences and politics have engaged in a massive drive of rethinking. But perhaps the political reasons for this are pre-eminent.

At the time of the big postwar development, classes were a widely accepted interpretative tool, even accepted by those political forces that refused the idea of class conflict, but instead preached interclassism. Progressively material wealth, the expansion of public and private services, mass education, the gradual convergence of incomes and consumption patterns of the working classes with those of the so-called middle classes, the development of welfare and its bureaucracies, have all challenged the imagined and conflictual, dichotomy, proposed by Marxism.[38] Despite this, the concept of class, if only to stress its increasingly problematic nature, continued to be widely used until the end of the 1970s.

Urged on by development, the socialist parties extended their supply of representation to the middle classes, and also the social sciences started to pay more attention. The expansion of these classes appeared to be the sign of renewed social stratification. This obliged even Marxist scholars to take on the arduous task of reconciling the Marxist dichotomy with the new articulations of the social structure.[39] Despite this, the idea of a society basically structured in classes prevailed, also in the political sphere, where it was officially sanctioned by neo-corporative pacts.

As mentioned, the moderate and conservative parties also used the social classes lexicon: the middle classes have always been an inalienable component of their political support base. It is to them that these parties always directed themselves, even if through more articulated strategies of attraction, and not through an appeal intended to promote strong identity and horizontal constraints. A first strategy was symbolic mobilisation: if nationalism was an old pre-war tool, in the years of the postwar boom, anti-communism, anti-collectivism and anti-labour provided movement, with religion itself as an important catalyst. A second strategy was based on articulated offers of representation and protection, often stigmatised by political competitors, as corporatist, backward and socially pernicious.[40]

This old classist scenario has been capsized by the restructuring promoted by post-Fordism and globalisation. The progressive contraction of industrial employment for both blue-collar workers and white-collar employees, and the fragmentation and generalised flexibility of employment, have loosened the political interdependencies between employers and the working classes. Restructuring has also made a representation of society in terms of big social blocs

---

38 Ralf Dahrendorf, *Class and Class Conflict in Industrial Society* (Stanford, Stanford University Press, 1959).

39 A good example is Nicos Poulantzas, *Les classes sociales dans le capitalisme aujourd'hui* (Paris, Seuil, 1974).

40 Alessandro Pizzorno, 'The Individualistic Mobilization of Europe', *Daedalus* XIIIC(1), 1964, 199–224.

aggregated around common interests and common political plans more uncertain. In response, new interpretative categories have been created. Hence individuals replace classes,[41] and social exclusion replaces working-class poverty,[42] even if there is a stubborn minority of scholars who, in view of the persistence and exacerbation of inequalities and their relentless intergenerational transmission, hold that the concept of class, albeit revised, still remains a useful tool.[43]

What has certainly relinquished the representation of society structured in relatively coherent blocs are politics and the actors that condition it most: the media and entrepreneurs. Politics is much more determined and inclined to simplify than the social sciences.[44] Therefore, with the help of broad sectors of social theory and communication experts, it has ousted classes from their discourses and adopted a new representation of society, characterised by the primacy of the individual.

The individual, no longer oppressed by need, impatient of the discipline and hierarchies of the Fordist factory, and of any institution - public bureaucracies, parties, trade unions, churches, family, and especially the 'paternalistic' and bureaucratic protection of the welfare state - reluctant to accept solidaristic constraints and to express public commitment, and riding on the crest of neo-liberal discourse, has become the protagonist of the new society. After all, what is more alluring that to represent not a hierarchical, statist power, that works painstakingly to put collective life in order, but a condition of spontaneous order, where more educated and informed individuals, craving authenticity and self-affirmation, cultivate their own preferences, interests, lifestyles and patterns of consumption? Together with responsibility for their own destiny, individuals are represented as willing to take on the risks incumbent on their lives, without any need to cooperate with others in order to resolve common problems.[45]

---

41 For a good example of how the concept of class is set aside to the benefit of the individual (and of the individualisation of social risks!) see Ulrich Beck, *Risk Society: Towards a New Modernity* (Sage, London, 1992).

42 Boltanski, *Rendre la société inacceptable.*

43 For a contrasting reflection, see Gøsta Esping-Andersen, who considers a political recomposition of inequalities to be plausible: 'Politics Without Class: Postindustrial Cleavage in America and Europe', in H. Kitschelt, P. Lange, G. Marks, J. D. Stephens (eds.), *Continuity and Change in Contemporary Capitalism* (Cambridge, Cambridge University Press, 1999). See also see Erik Olin Wright (ed.), *Approaches to Class Analysis* (Cambridge, Cambridge University Press, 2005).

44 This is also because the economic inequalities are a variable much less used by the social sciences to decipher the behaviour of social actors. *Eurobarometer* surveys prefer the formula of socio-demographic groups, putting together sex, age, employment, etc.

45 For an in-depth brilliant reflection on the individualisation of risk, see Giuseppe Di Palma, *Viaggio nelle modernità. Rischio sociale e solidarietà dall'assolutismo al neoliberalismo e oltre* (Soveria Mannelli, Rubbettino, 2011).

How deeply the rhetoric of the autonomous individual, stretched to the point of narcissism,[46] has penetrated common sense remains to be seen. Enormous efforts of persuasion, backed also by the social sciences, have been carried out to rewrite social norms in favour of competition, subjectivity and self-realisation and the spirit of initiative, and to negate sociality. Similar efforts have been made to replace the obligation of reciprocal solidarity guaranteed by the state, and perhaps even constitutionally sanctioned, with the spontaneous charitable impulses of civil society, or with the liberality of the better-off social strata. The naturalisation of inequalities by those who suffer them is an other very old resource used by the powerful, as is the naturalisation of egoism. The neo-liberal promotion of individualism, however, wanted to legitimate a new way of governing collective life and a new way of constituting social hierarchies, intending to do away with the welfare state's recognition of an individual's right to enjoy basic protection against life's risks.

To conclude. According to neo-liberal individualism, a person's living standards depend on their ability to compete on the market, also in spheres – statist, for example – where the principle of competition has been transplanted. But this does not mean that the interiorisation of the new values and norms has successfully achieved all its desired aims. There is no shortage of critical representations of the processes of individualisation highlighting the disastrous effects for social cohesion.[47] The individualisation of risk in globalised society is still widely thought to be a reason for precariousness and uncertainty. The latter does not even save social strata previously considered protected, such as the middle classes. Reactions are, however, largely contradictory. On the one hand, there are the difficulties that many encounter when trying to conform to both the principles of autonomy and individual self-sufficiency and to public policies that inspired them, beginning with those in the sectors of education and employment.[48] On the other hand, we find associational reactions that develop spontaneously, even if not systematically, to counter the dissociative effects produced by social change, making the actual condition of individuals more supportable. Until now reactions have been short-term, sectoral and local, with limited political effects, but they demonstrate that the course taken by collective life could also go in the opposite direction.

The individualistic rhetoric, however, has not even prevented politics, and not only politics, from reproposing the concept of class, albeit selectively and in a new perspective. On closer examination we find a double rhetoric. On the one hand, it extends the middle class, on the other, it places it again at the centre of collective

---

46 See the critical observation of Christopher Lasch, *The Culture of Narcissism. American Life in an Age of Diminishing Expectations* (London, W. W. Norton, 1978).

47 Richard Sennett, *The Erosion of Character: The Personal Consequences of Work in the New Capitalism* (New York, Norton, 1998). On the individual *qua* social construction, see the classical work of Norbert Elias, *The Society of Individuals* (Oxford, Blackwell, 1987).

48 Fabrizio Cantelli, Jean-Louis Genard (eds.), *Action publique et subjectivité* (Paris, Librairie Générale Droit et Jurisprudence, 2007).

life. In Fordist society, the rhetoric of the middle class was politically positive in the sense that it was a point of social arrival, accepted not only by conservative parties, but also by socialist parties. In the most recent rhetoric the middle class, which is a very difficult to define social strata, has become virtuous, hard-working, risk-taking savers with business acumen, and averse to futile and raucous trade union and political protest. In spite of all it merits, it is persecuted by fiscal pressure and over-regulation, and besieged by both the upper classes and the working class.

The symbolic and political value of this move is abundantly clear. Solidaristic behaviour or shared political plans are not expected from the autonomous middle classes, even if this expectation does not exclude protest actions and forms of collective mobilisation. This has not stopped them becoming a symbolic constituency, and even the 'silent majority' – initially evoked by Nixon against strident American minorities – lionised by Margaret Thatcher, formulating a model successively replicated by all liberal-conservative parties.[49] Shopkeepers, small entrepreneurs, professionals, experts, upper management, specialised workers in private firms, but also small investors and the property-owning segments of the working classes, have been promoted as a lever of renewal, and enticed with promises of tax cuts, privatisation and containment of trade-union power.

Thirty years on from that attempt to mobilise them, the parties still evoke the virtues of the middle class and make it their offer of representation, but the main problem is that the condition of the middle class has become anything but idyllic. Sociologists testify how meanwhile instability and the individualised risk of post-Fordist society have not spared the middle class, and early on, placed hardship on their research agenda[50] – and politics has taken this into account. In reality, even if we reason in restrictive terms, the condition of the middle class is highly differentiated. There are segments of the middle class, such as executive management, the professions and entrepreneurs of sectors in expansion that have earned considerable benefits from neo-liberal policies, but there are many others that have been strongly penalised. Revenues decline and downward mobility have hit not only the dependent middle class, but also a part of the autonomous middle class, e.g. shopkeepers threatened by large-scale distribution, artisans and small entrepreneurs operating in sectors most exposed to global competition. Politics and policies, whether symbolic or not, have also had an impact on the destiny of these social groups, and we can observe its effects in the long run, not only in terms of social unease, but also as regards political mobilisation and protest. The new parties of the extreme right, the so-called populists, have found a privileged audience

---

49 Kavanagh, *Thatcherism and British Politics*, pp. 303–306.

50 See: Jean Ruhlmann, *Ni bourgeois ni prolétaires. La défense des classes moyennes en France au XXe siècle* (Paris, Seuil, 2001); Oliver Zunz, Leonard J. Schoppa, Nobuhiro Hiwatari (eds.), *Social Contract Under Stress: the Middle Classes of America, Europe and Japan at the Turn of the Century* (New York, Russel Sage Foundation, 2002); Louis Chauvel, *Les classes moyennes à la derive* (Paris, Seuil, 2006); Bagnasco (ed.), *Ceto medio*, 2008.

in this segment of society and managed to radicalise a part of them. But there are also political moves in the opposite direction, such as Barack Obama, who made the decline of the middle class an issue from his first election campaign onwards.

In any case, there are plenty of reasons to consider the dispersion of social classes first of an effect of the changed representations of the individual and society – sometimes particularly official, such as those of the national statistical services – and of the rejection of the practices of collective action formerly carried out by politics. This hypothesis is confirmed by the fact that, concerned about more serious damage, in the long run politics has rediscovered the importance of solidaristic behaviour, with the help of theory. In the last part of the millennium, thanks to the 'third way', promoted by New Labour in Britain, and the concurrent policies carried out by President Clinton in the USA, concepts such as civil society, social capital, networks and so forth have enjoyed a surprising degree of success.[51] The re-evaluation of similar forms of sociality, witnesses that other narratives of change were possible. Perhaps social change could have been pointed in a different direction and towards other outcomes. The individual *qua* principle is inscribed in the genetic code of modernity and market society, based on private profit, and even in Fordist society the individual is a rather taken-for-granted protagonist. Parties and trade unions based the need for the welfare state on the excesses of individualism which they contested. We should ask ourselves whether the welfare state could have continued and whether the narrative of post-Fordism could have turned out differently.

Politically-speaking, perhaps making labour relations precarious in the extreme was not altogether unavoidable. Flexibility is understandable in enterprises which are more subject to the challenge of technological adjustment or competition from emerging economies, but in cases such as the public sector or big service enterprises flexibility has merely increased profit margins. This also means that the state has still to contain the political and social disadvantages of the operation through expensive social shock absorbers.

The persistence of profound, and interconnected, differences and inequalities in culture and living standards, adding new or newly-salient inequalities, such as gender inequality, could have marked the starting point for different interpretations of society, which exist, but have remained minoritarian. Above all, we should ask whether society could have profited differently from the new productive technologies and energies unleashed by the higher levels of education and information and from post-materialist values. What prevented the new technologies from being used to make work activity less onerous? Why did the higher levels of education not encourage more solidaristic behaviour? Individualist egoism is no more natural than solidarity, and surely post-materialist values announced a growing, rather than a declining, demand, albeit different, for participation and cooperative behaviour.

---

51 Anthony Giddens, *The Third Way. The Renewal of Social Democracy* (Cambridge, Polity Press, 1998).

chapter four | a tale of two democracies

Democratic paradigm and post-democratic paradigm

Not only does society appear to have undergone a profound transformation between Fordism and post-Fordism, but the way in which it is described and interpreted has also changed. It is difficult to understand which came first. In parallel, profound changes have also affected politics, starting with the way in which it is represented, and beginning with political and social theory. In defining the term *ex quo*, an effective concept is 'postwar consensus', used in Britain to describe the period of significant policy convergence between the Tories and the Labour Party that began in 1945.[1]

The cultural and political differences between the two parties were not entirely cancelled and the political struggle between them remained bitter, respecting the tradition of British bipartisanship. But for around thirty years there was a significant convergence as regards policies. This was not total convergence: there were not two different *équipes* for the same policy, but the conservatives had adopted an inter-class perspective, and Labour had watered down its original socialist design. Notwithstanding the diversity of values, conceptions of the world and of represented interests, a sort of a common paradigm emerged, roughly consisting of Keynesianism and the Beveridge Report. Each party applied policies in its own way, but there was some syntony. It was when it abandoned these shared themes that the Thatcherite revolution succeeded in breaking the postwar consensus.

Postwar consensus did not only apply to British politics. In the same period we witnessed an analogous convergence between conservative, confessional and moderate parties, and socialist parties which united the governing classes of all the continental democratic regimes. Even in Italy, where the local government was run by the Communist Party in large areas of the country, their style of government was characteristically welfarist.

---

1   The first to discuss this was Dennis Kavanagh in *Thatcherism and British Politics. The End of Consensus* (Oxford, Oxford University Press, 1990), and with Peter Morris, *Consensus Politics from Attlee to Thatcher* (Oxford, Blackwell, 1989), and again Kavanagh's 'The Postwar Consensus', *Twentieth Century British History* 3(2) 1992, 175–190. In the lively debate that followed see, Anthony Seldon, 'Consensus. A Debate Too Long?', *Parliamentary Affairs* 47(4), 1994, 501–514; Duncan Fraser, 'The Postwar Consensus: a Debate Not Long Enough?', *Parliamentary Affairs* 53(2), 2000, 347–362; Richard Heffernan, 'The Possible as the Art of Politics: Understanding Consensus Politics', *Political Studies* 50(4), 2002, 742–760; and Colin Hay, 'Whatever Happened to Thatcherism?', *Political Studies Review* 5(2), 2007, 183–201.

In the academic debate in continental Europe scholars preferred to talk of 'social democratic' consensus, or compromise.[2] The only problem is that this label gives social democratic parties a pre-eminence that is not confirmed by the facts. In the postwar reconstructions in France, Germany and Italy it was catholic or liberal experts and politicians who were in the front line of reform more than those with a social democratic background. Furthermore, in the years of growth the social democratic parties were only in power for limited periods, while the measures inspired by the postwar consensus were generally adopted by parties of another political colour.[3]

Even if there was an intense process of reciprocal learning, every democratic regime interpreted the postwar consensus in its own way. In Britain, France and Scandinavia the point of theoretical convergence was Keynesian interventionism. In Germany it was the formula of the 'social market economy', which was nearer to the liberalism, that prevailed. Italy oscillated between these two poles. A preference for liberal economic measures often thrived in the central banks, in the senior management of the public sector and, obviously, in the private sector. Social democratic parties preferred expansive and redistributive measures, whereas moderate and conservative parties backed more restrictive measures. The former were in favour of a mixed economy, whereas the latter were more uncertain. In Germany the *Große Koalition* between CDU and SPD in 1969 marked an important turning point. In Italy, this was ratified by the centre-left governments: from the early 1960s, policies previously carried out tentatively were systematically pursued by governments that included socialist ministers.

In the background, beyond ideological divisions, electoral conflict and political moves, there was a shared atmosphere. This can be attributed not only to the sphere of economic policies and social policies, but also to the practice of democratic regimes. Democracy was reborn as formal democracy, but was accompanied by welfare policies. In tune with practice – or rather with the imposing presence of parties and mass organisations in collective life, and with the concentration among the most powerful organised interests behind the scenes of official government institutions – political democracy was not reduced to elections and to the use of the majority principle. It was also considered a useful technique to promote political participation. The task of the parties and trade unions was to involve the governed in the running of collective life and to maintain a counterweight to the economy. The

---

2   Wolfgang C. Müller, 'Political Traditions and the Role of the State', in Wolfgang C. Müller, Vincent Wright (eds.), *The State in Western Europe. Retreat or Redefinition* (London, Routledge, 1994).

3   In Britain Labour governed in the periods 1945–1951, 1964–1970, 1976–1979. In France the socialists took part in various ministries in the Fourth Republic, but were excluded from government from 1958 to 1981. In Germany the SPD were in power in the period 1966–1982. In Italy the Socialist Party first took part in the centre-left government in 1963, but in a minority position.

latter was the task of the state, but parties and trade unions provided the necessary support. The preferred techniques used to resolve conflicts were mediation and prevention. The public institutions, official and unofficial – parliament, the executive, organs of economic planning, neo-corporatist negotiating tables and so forth – were intent on producing compromises among contrasting interests and between different ideas on the desired order of things.

In this story the theory recited a crucial part in its own sense. For democracy and democratic politics more or less the same happened as occurred for economic policies. That is, there was a democratic paradigm which was not unitary, but was in large part shared.

If we look at the unfolding of events, in the 1970s we can see a double window of opportunity. In addition to the window for economic neo-liberal theory, a window was also opened for political theory and for the intellectual circles sceptical of democracy. The auspicious conditions allowed the latter to give a different interpretation of democracy from that prevailing at the time. The economic instability of the 1970s, in the wake of the oil shock, corresponds to the rehabilitation of the critics' ideas of how democracy should be realised and subjected the intellectual conceptions of democracy to a merciless critical review, which led to the formulation of a new meaning for the word democracy. A new 'post-democratic' paradigm overturned the generally shared perspective in effect until then and favoured an energetic reorientation of democratic practice.

If we want to represent quite simply this turnover of paradigms, an easy way is to compare the idea of democracy promoted by Hans Kelsen, who influenced all the constitutional charters drafted in Europe after World War II, with that of Joseph A. Schumpeter, spokesman of an opposed position which has conquered the theoretical scene in the late twentieth century.

It is a curious twinning that brings these two protagonists of twentieth-century democratic theory together. One was born in Prague, the other in Triesch, Moravia, and both were subjects of the Austro-Hungarian Empire. After having completed their studies in law in Vienna, both held public office for a brief period in the Austrian Republic. Kelsen helped draft the new Austrian constitution, and was then a constitutional judge for a short time; Schumpeter was minister of finance. Later both moved to Weimar Germany and finally the USA, where they taught at Harvard: Schumpeter definitively, Kelsen provisionally, his last teaching post being Berkeley.

Kelsen was a specialist in public law and Schumpeter was an economist. Both happened to write about democracy almost by chance: Kelsen in an essay written in the early 1920s, subsequently reformulated a number of times; Schumpeter in some tens of pages of a long and caustic pamphlet on quite another argument, that is, the inarrestable decline of property-based capitalism in favour of managerial capitalism and then socialism.

First we need to clarify that both Kelsen and Schumpeter kept themselves rigorously within the limits of a procedural notion of democracy. The difference lies in the way in which they read proceduralism. The scenarios in which their reflections took place help us to understand this diversity. Kelsen, who in his autobiography does not disown his social-democratic inclinations,[4] formulated his theory in Austria and Germany during a tormented period of history. By contrast, the backdrop to Schumpeter's thought was the much less dramatic scenario of America, now out of the Great Depression. It is no coincidence that in Kelsen's theoretical thought the prescriptive component prevails and with Schumpeter it is the descriptive component.

There are two essential arguments in Kelsen's thought. The first takes it that the opportunity to realise the democratic ideal, based on the principle of individual autonomy, can only be realised by approximation. Therefore, if democracy is to be realised, for Kelsen it means that direct democracy needs to be rejected in favour of representative democracy. This means also a rejection of the principle of unanimity, which would be the perfect form of self-government, in favour of majority government.[5] It is the conformation of modern society that counterposes itself to direct democracy and that imposes the extension of the principle of the division of labour to the political sphere. Representation is the application of this principle, whereby we entrust a minority of elected with the task of taking collective choices. It is also a 'fiction', given that in reality 'no legal relation of proxy or representation exists' between electors and elected.[6]

Kelsen does not place a great deal of trust in ordinary citizens, who he describes as 'the undiscerning crowd of those unreflectively accepting the influence of others',[7] and who constitute by far the majority. Nevertheless, he does not believe that citizens must necessarily play a merely marginal and passive role. If they associate together, he stresses, on the basis of common interests, they can avoid the condition of impotence to which their isolation would otherwise condemn them. In his view, this type of association is even a condition of democracy, as democracy can only exist where 'collective entities uniting the similar wills of individuals as political parties have to insert themselves between the individual and the state'.[8] As a theorist of procedural democracy, but not indifferent to social justice and to egalitarian policies, although not recognising them as a constituent component of democracy, Kelsen was concerned that all citizens could effectively exercise their political rights.

This is what parties are for. If the citizen remains isolated, Kelsen argued, he is condemned to have 'no real political existence whatsoever, because he can gain

---

4   Although Kelsen did not belong to any political party he recognised his political sympathies, see *Autobiographie*, now published in Kelsen, *Werke: Band 1: Veröffentlichte Schriften 1905–1910 und Selbstzeugnisse* (Tübingen, Mohr, [1947] 2007, p. 59).

5   Hans Kelsen, 'On the Essence and Value of Democracy' in Arthur Jacobson, Bernhard Schlink (eds.), *Weimar. A Jurisprudence of Crisis* (Berkeley, University of California Press, [1929] 2000), and *General Theory of Law and State* (Cambridge MA, Harvard University Press, 1945, p. 285).

6   Kelsen, *General Theory of Law and State*, p. 291

7   Kelsen, 'On the Essence and Value of Democracy', p. 91.

8   Kelsen, 'On the Essence and Value of Democracy', p. 92.

no actual influence on forming the will of the state'.[9] The reasoning is allusive, as suits an author who intends to neutralise his own political preferences, but it is not obscure. The virtue of democracy lies in the incentives that its rules offer citizens, enabling them to join together to exploit the potential of the 'big numbers'. That is, democratic rules are an incentive to set up parties that organise citizens, mobilise their interests and aspirations, in order to contrast the privileged condition of those who enjoy extrapolitical resources of power.[10]

The second line of Kelsen's democratic theory lies in the already mentioned concern for the risk of conflict that overshadows it and the consequent appreciation of compromise. If democracy recognises the pluralism of interests and values, then it is vital that actors are oriented to compromise in order to avoid conflict. This helps prevent minorities from feeling extraneous to decisions taken by the majority. A democratic regime must be institutionally equipped to favour compromise. Parliament is the institution best suited to promoting the cohabitation of the multiple and heterogeneous parts that make up society, recognising the existence of each one, but reconciling it with all others.[11] Once Kelsen had formulated his diagnosis of the difficulties and contradictions in which democracy flounders, he did his pragmatic best to protect and strengthen it.

Schumpeter's attitude is completely different and has a paradoxical destiny. He is a relentless critic of democracy, who was nevertheless later transformed into a venerated icon of democratic thought. For Schumpeter citizens are unreliable. They are able to look after their private interests, but unable to take on board public interests and even to confer a mandate on their own representatives. As a result democracy is only a debateable and demagogic – albeit obligatory —— lip service to the spirit of the time and a method to select the governing class. It is 'that institutional arrangement for arriving at political decisions in which individuals acquire the power to decide by means of a competitive struggle for the people's vote'.[12]

For Schumpeter competition is thus a constitutive element of democracy and its recognition is the basic legacy of his theory. In reality he does not attribute any of the merits attributed to economic competition to electoral competition. Contrary to what some of his later imitators claim, for Schumpeter competition

---

9   Kelsen, 'On the Essence and Value of Democracy', p. 92.

10 This point of view is not too different from that of an author well known by Kelsen: Robert Michels. According to Michels, 'organization is the weapon of the week in their struggle with the strong': see, *Political Parties: A Sociological Study of the Oligarchical Tendencies of Modern Democracy* (New York, Free Press, [1911] 1962, p. 61).

11 Kelsen, 'On the Essence and Value of Democracy', pp. 95–100 and also 'Das Problem des Parlamentarismus', in *Soziologie und Sozialphilosophie. Schriften der Soziologischen Gesellschaft in Wien*, H. III (Vienna/Leipzig, W. Braumüller, 1925).

12 Joseph A. Schumpeter, *Capitalism, Socialism and Democracy* (New York/London, Harper & Brothers, 1942, p. 242).

does not improve the quality of the ruling classes or public policies, but only causes damage.[13] As democracy is primarily competition for power, whoever enters politics is guided exclusively by their own ambitions of electoral and political success, so that the political market is not driven by the citizens' demands, but by the advantage of politicians. Thus, 'the democratic method', writes Schumpeter, 'produces legislation and administration as by-products of the struggle for political office',[14] while the 'social function' of democratic politics 'is fullfilled, as it were, incidentally – in the same sense as production is incidental to making profits'.[15]

It is easy to understand why, in a subsequent chapter entitled 'Conditions for the Success of the Democratic Method', Schumpeter completed his critical reflection with a catalogue of corrective measures that are specifically non-democratic, non-competitive and not particularly pluralistic: a quality ruling class within which to select the elected; competent bureaucracies to flank them and guide them; severe restrictions on the range of political decision-making; the willingness of citizens to forego exercising pressure on the elected between one election and another, and tolerance for the opinions of others.[16]

Yet, however severe and sarcastic his critique, Schumpeter made an extraordinary contribution to democratic theory. This contribution was not immediately recognised, in spite of the fact that its author was a well-known economist. The critical review which appeared in the *American Political Science Review* in 1943 is emblematic. It concluded rather impatiently that 'a system in which the most important duty of a politician is to guess whether particular decisions will be successful is not likely to be democratic'.[17] But by the mid-1950s Schumpeter will, nevertheless, find a first-rate audience and, by virtue of a surprising reversal of his thought, no democratic theorist will ever again fail to cite him.[18]

---

13 This issue is frequently raised today, but for a long time democratic theory counted little in the competition among elites, and hence on the electoral choice of voters. For Dahl, for example, the only merit of competition is that it protects minorities from abuse by the majority. See Robert A. Dahl, *A Preface to Democratic Theory* (Chicago IL, University of Chicago Press, 1956, p. 132).

14 Schumpeter, *Capitalism, Socialism and Democracy*, p. 286.

15 Schumpeter, *Capitalism, Socialism and Democracy*, p. 282.

16 Schumpeter, *Capitalism, Socialism and Democracy*, pp. 290–295.

17 See the review of 'Capitalism, Socialism and Democracy', by William Seal Carpenter in *American Political Science Review* 36(3), 1943, 523–524.

18 One of those citing it, ten years after the publication of his book, is Kelsen in *Foundations of Democracy*, in Kelsen, *Verteidigung der Demokratie: Abhandlungen zur Demokratietheorie* (Tübingen, Mohr Siebeck, [1955] 2006, pp. 349–350).

Politics as science

There is a radical difference between Kelsen and Schumpeter. Kelsen is moved by a normative ideal and wants to adapt it to the real world. The democratic ideal of government, is precisely this, he says, and it can be realised, at least partly, in this way. By contrast, Schumpeter wants to give a realistic representation of the real world with a total ban on illusions. This is democracy in the real world, even if it is not very valuable, and we can only work to limit its shortcomings. Despite this, Schumpeter's epigones managed to make an ideal out of this description. According to them, democracy as market is a valuable model of government, just as market is valuable as a mechanism for the production and distribution of resources and the organisation of collective life.

Based on the unreserved acceptance of pluralism, and, according to his perspective, of compromise, Kelsen's theory of the feasible involvement of citizens in political life is an exemplary illustration of the democratic paradigm of the mid-1900s, that considered democracy as a realisable goal and a perfectionable instrument.[19] A quarter of a century and some delusions later, this conception was set aside and *Capitalism, Socialism and Democracy* instead satisfied the needs of realistic, but also prescriptive, theory-making. As a result its author became the principle initiator of the post-democratic paradigm in vogue at the end of the twentieth century. With some non-secondary variation, the assimilation of democracy to the market – and market competition – took root and the elitism and dry proceduralism inspired by Schumpeter and his American experience, could be used to confute any expansive claim of democracy. After some initial perplexity, his elitism provided sociologists, economists and political scientists with a powerful interpretative and normative instrument.

In these circumstances a particularly important role was played by political science and its empirical approach. This is not to say that in Europe the study of politics was empirically indifferent. In France Tocqueville had left more than a few traces. In Britain in the 1920s, Lord Bryce compared the working of the main democratic regimes, thirty years after having carried out an in-depth inquiry of American democracy, focused on public opinion and political parties.[20] In Italy elitists like Mosca and Pareto witnessed another realistic analysis of parliamentary regimes. In Germany a more systematic style of empirical observation was

---

19 In Britain, the *patria* of adversary politics and of the so-called majoritarian democracy, examples showing that it was once possible to find similar positions. Another good example is Bernard Crick's, *In Defence of Politics* (Chicago IL, University of Chicago Press, 1962). Crick increases the recognition of pluralism and diversity, and considers caution, the spirit of conciliation and compromise to be absolutely vital and puts us on our guard against the abuse of the majority principle in democracy.

20 Lord James Bryce, *Modern Democracies* (New York, Macmillan 1921) and Bryce, *The American Commonwealth* (New York, Cosimo, [1888] 2007).

developed by Robert Michels' research on the Social Democratic Party,[21] and in France by André Siegfried's empirical study of electoral behaviour.[22] In the early 1950s Maurice Duverger will draft an impressive analysis of political parties.[23] But American political science has had the good fortune to operate in quite another context: it was not tied to the monumental image of the continental European state, and to the equally monumental theoretical construction built up around it, nor conditioned by powerful corporations of jurists, and it was consequently more predisposed to apply new research methodologies.

Since the early twentieth century American political science substituted the state as the basic unit of analysis with the concept of group.[24] It was the start of a pluralist representation of democratic politics which did not intend to be normative, but empirical. Between the 1920s and 1930s the discipline had also been accredited with the task of making an empirical study of mass politics, especially in its urban dimension. As in economy and sociology, we meet with a pioneering and productive Chicago School, that has brought political science and sociology closer together. In the 1950s, political science was renovated thanks to the concept of political system (or subsystem),[25] understood as a device which converts inputs – demand and support – into outputs, sharing structural-functionalist ideas such as values, norms and roles in order to regulate the action of actors, with sociology.

The new disciplinary canon therefore ratified an inductive vocation according to the model of the natural sciences, that abjured every normative claim, and progressively accumulated a new conceptual and theoretical apparatus.[26] The

---

21 Michels, *Political Parties*.

22 André Siegfried, *Tableau politique de la France de l'ouest sous la troisième république* (Paris, Colin, 1913).

23 Maurice Duverger, *Political Parties: their Organization and Activity in the Modern State* (New York, Wiley, [1951] 1964).

24 Arthur F. Bentley, *The Process of Government. A Study of Social Pressures* (Chicago IL, University of Chicago Press, 1908).

25 What is more coherent than a similar model with the rhetoric of democracy, that places governors at the service of the governed? See David Easton, *The Political System: An Inquiry into the State of Political Science* (New York, Knopf, 1953).

26 For a critical point of view of the discipline see, Robert Adcock, Mark Bevir, Shannon Stimson, 'A History of Political Science. How? What, Why?', in Adcock, Bevir, Stimson (eds.), *Modern Political Science*, 2007, pp. 9–10. See also Mark Bevir, Rod A. W. Rhodes, *The State as Cultural Practice* (Oxford, Oxford University Press, 2010) and Mark Bevir, *Democratic Governance* (Princeton NJ, Princeton University Press, 2010). For an example of French style criticism see Antoine Cohen, Bernard Lacroix, Philippe Riutort (eds.), *Nouveau manuel de science politique* (Paris, La Découverte, 2009). American political science is also not lacking in critical and auto-critical reflections: explosive in expressing the intrinsic politicity of the discipline – Theodore J. Lowi's presidential address at the annual congress of American political scientists: see 'The State in Political Science: How We Become What We Study', *American Political Science Review* 86(1),

study of politics officially became a science in the positivist sense, that it searches for regularity and causal explanations, in order to make universal assertions on the basis of empirical facts.[27] Economics maps out economic life, sociology draws pictures of society, its actors and social stratification, and political science draws up maps of politics. Numbers, rates, samples, statistical inferences all helped place it on the same level as other sciences, social and otherwise, and helped legitimate it in public discourse. Insofar as it is a rigorously evaluative, apolitical and neutral science that establishes laws and makes forecasts, political science aspired to nothing less than a representative function competing not only with the professionals of representation who sit in the elective assemblies, but also with public opinion and the media, eager to protect democracy against the incompetence of politicians and the peculiarities and unpredictability of the popular will.

Research techniques have also contributed to shaping theory. The tendency to quantify, and the aptitude to select some empirical information rather than others, has favoured the objects which are easiest to observe using its new methods. This may have also induced political scientists to raise what they discovered to the status of optimal standard, which could conform with: that is, the pluralistic distribution of power and the increasingly pluralist interaction of interests,[28] or civic and participative culture discovered through surveys carried out in the USA and Britain and that appeared to be the secret of success of these democratic regimes.[29]

It would be unjust to reduce the enormous contribution of this often very high-quality empirical research by political science to just this. But over time the normative inspiration of political science has developed, albeit unintentionally, consolidating a bias favouring the American meaning and practice of democracy. The point is that this bias not only encouraged further research, but made the discipline a powerful instrument for exporting the American way of life as applied to the democratic polity.[30] This was even more the case when political science

---

1992, 1–7.

27 I suggest a re-reading of Gabriel A. Almond's essay, which was for a while considered of programmatic and founding value for the discipline: 'Comparative Political Systems', *Journal of Politics* 18(3), 1956, 391–409. Almond classifies political systems in four categories: consensual (Anglo-Saxon), fragmented (European), totalitarian (communist and fascist) and pre-industrial. The classification implies a hierarchy and, a model to imitate. Fragmented political systems, for example, were for Almond condemned to immobilism.

28 This is the theory of Robert A. Dahl confirmed by the research on New Haven. See, *Who Governs? Democracy and Power in an American City* (New Haven CT, Yale University Press, 1961).

29 See Gabriel A. Almond and Sidney Verba's classic work, *The Civic Culture. Political Attitudes and Democracy in Five Nations* (Boston, Little, Brown & Co., 1965).

30 The coincidence between pluralism, in the technical sense of Bentley and Dahl, and 'democratic' elitism, and the fact that neither is too interested in the participation of citizens, is stressed by Geraint Parry in *Political Elites* (London, Allen & Unwin, 1969, pp. 141–53).

became comparative and started to classify political regimes, not solely according to their formal institutional structures (authoritarian, democratic, presidential, parliamentary, etc.), but by the degree of differentiation of political structures and the type of political culture, values and behaviour shared by elites and the population.[31] Being able to distinguish backward and unstable regimes from modern, stable and virtuous ones, where virtue is associated with the Anglo-Saxon countries, it was only a short step from making the latter the norm.

With the generous, but not disinterested, support of the big American foundations, mostly from prestigious universities or the government agencies that used political science expertise,[32] transatlantic scholars were stimulated by genuine cognitive curiosity when they studied Europe and the rest of the world. Understandably many of them were convinced of the preferability of the American democratic model, in much the same way as much anthropological research is characterised by a Westernist bias.

Fierce debates and different theoretical and methodological perspectives always competed within political science. The attempts to compare and represent American democracy were not entirely unequivocal and self-celebratory. There was no shortage of scholars of political change wary of instituting hierarchies of virtue,[33] while for at least a decade, empirical research on power centred on a fierce debate on its distribution: there were scholars who were more inclined to criticism and whose research depicted power as being concentrated in the hands of an elite, whilst others described it as being spread between several groups and an elite in competition with each other.[34] Nevertheless, in the last instance it was the American representation of democracy, as a pluralistic dispersion of power, with competition among groups and a tempered elitism, that prevailed, even if not deemed democratically virtuous by all.[35] At the same time the solid associative habits of Americans became the optimal and desirable final step in a evolutionary process, also defined in particularly aseptic terms such as 'modernisation' and 'political development'.[36]

---

31 Gabriel A. Almond, George B. Powell Jr., *Comparative Politics: A Developmental Approach* (Boston, Little & Brown, 1966).

32 There is now a fairly good body of literature on the cultural hegemomy of the big American foundations. See, for example, Inderjeet Parmar, 'American Foundations and the Development of International Knowledge Networks', *Global Networks* 2(1), 2002, 13–30.

33 See for example, David E. Apter, *The Politics of Modernization* (Chicago IL, University of Chicago Press, 1965) and Barrington Moore Jr., *Social Origins of Dictatorship and Democracy: Lord and Peasant in the Making of the Modern World* (Boston, Beacon Press, 1967).

34 Among the anti-pluralists, see Charles W. Mills (*The Power Elite*, Oxford, Oxford University Press, 1956), and George W. Domhoff (*Who Rules America? Power Politics and Social Change* (New York, McGraw Hill, 1967).

35 Robert A. Dahl, *Dilemmas of Pluralist Democracy: Autonomy vs. Control* (New Haven CT, Yale University Press, 1982).

36 For a critical rereading, see Nils Gilman, *Mandarins of the Future* (Baltimore MD, Johns Hopkins University Press, 2003). See also, Michael E. Latham, *Modernization as Ideology: American Social Science and Nation Building in the Kennedy Era* (Chapel Hill, University of North Carolina

Transatlantic democracy claimed the merit of having absorbed the impact of mass politics without any damage. By contrast, many democratic European regimes had suffered, and still risked suffering, the trauma of dictatorship, and all of them had suffered the consequences of dictatorship and still lived with the threat of communism. Raising American democracy to a model was reasonable, as it was reasonable to investigate European regimes, together with Asian or African former colonies that had become independent.

On the other hand, in Europe there was no lack of reasons, and also incentives, for taking lessons from America. The theoretical exchanges and research experience between the two sides of the Atlantic had been intensified by European intellectual emigration in the 1930s and deepened even further, in the postwar period and during reconstruction. The reconstruction of European democratic regimes had come about with the expertise of jurists, who were at that particular moment of time considered the main specialists in politics. The new science imported from the other side of the Atlantic at the end of the 1950s, promoted a substantial renewal of the study of politics, together with the acceptance of its implicit normative guidelines. Jurists were, after all, bound to the traditional notion of the state – the sovereign state – that had proved so disastrous in the preceding fifty years. They appeared much less well-equipped to study the new interventionist state and party-based democracies, whereas political science was instead the science of democracy, formulated in the reassuring shadow of the most renowned democratic regime on the planet.

Once in Europe, American scholars, who had already studied, at home, public opinion, elections, parties, bureaucracies, urban politics and interest groups, were welcomed by the local specialists of all things political (jurists, philosophers, historians, sociologists). They won the attention of some of them, intrigued the youngest, diffused their research techniques and contributed to establish a new disciplinary field. This field immediately expanded according to the dynamics typically at work within the academic world, and claimed its own 'scientific' superiority with respect to the other disciplines that had previously monopolised the study of things political. This in turn led to lively forms of communication and well-grounded attempts to emulate American political science horizontally across Europe, where home-grown political scientists, who had often studied or trained at American universities, began to constitute a scientific community on a continental scale and often competed to promote the American democratic regime as a model. The model turned out to have advantages not only for politics, but also for the media. Both realised that the new discipline promised to decipher obscure or little studied phenomena, such as voting behaviour and the moods of public opinion. Some politicians or media professionals were also keen to use the transatlantic norm, partly present in Europe through the British experience, as a political weapon in the form of an objective to achieve – adapting what is not normal to the norm – and consequently adapting the democratic rules.[37]

Press, 2000).

37 While there is not yet a history of the transmigration of political science in Europe, a contribution

A three-sided relationship

Political scientists were not the only ones to transfer expertise and political culture from America to Europe. In the postwar period politicians also made the transatlantic crossing, while the European media broadcast the American electoral campaigns and the political style of its politicians. In the 1960s European leaders and parties hired American media consultants and experts in electoral propaganda, convinced of getting their hands on a more sophisticated and efficient technique for obtaining consensus. But, above all, it was the research tradition in political science – well-known and widely institutionalised in America and being institutionalised elsewhere – that is behind what is perhaps the most important indication of the change about to hit democratic theory, and the meaning of the word democracy, in the mid-1970s, together with the opinions on it shared within the ruling classes of the more advanced countries. This indication was the famous Report on the state, or rather, the crisis of democracy, prepared by the Trilateral Commission and published in 1975.[38]

If we examine the academic literature of that time we can find other indications,[39] but few were as widely broadcast or enjoyed such media and political audience as that Report, produced by one of the most influential lobbies on the planet. Key figures from the world of politics, business, public sector and academia from both sides of the Atlantic and Japan sat side by side in the Trilateral Commission, with the initial task of outlining a scenario different from Nixonian unilateralism in foreign policy. The Commission can be legitimately defined as one of the many agencies – in this case of a very high level – that presented the American democratic and economic model to the world, defining itself as 'free', but that this time invited the free world to close ranks and to become more coherent and homogeneous in methods of government.[40]

---

considering the interaction between the United States and Britain, is Adcock, Bevir, Stimson (eds.) *Modern Political Science*, 2007. For France see Loïc Blondiaux, 'Pour une histoire sociale de la science politique', in Déloye and Voutat (eds.), *Faire de la science politique* pp. 45–63. For a unique guide to the international panorama see G. Sola, *Storia della scienza politica. Teorie, ricerce e paradigmi contemporanei* (Rome, Nuova Italia Scientifica, 1996).

38 Michael Crozier, Samuel P. Huntington, Jôji Watanuki (eds.), *The Crisis of Democracy. Report on the Governability of Democracies to the Trilateral Commission* (New York, New York University Press, 1975).

39 See, for example, the impressive theoretical construction of Niklas Luhmann and his theory of procedural legitimation in *Legitimation durch Verfahren* (Neuwied/Berlin, Luchterhand, 1969), and *Political Theory in the Welfare State* (Berlin, de Gruyter [1981] 1990).

40 On the Trilateral Commission, see Holly Sklar (ed.), *Trilateralism: The Trilateral Commission and Elite Planning for World Management* (Boston, South End Press, 1980). See, in particular, the chapter by Alan Wolfe, 'Capitalism Shows its Face: Giving Up on Democracy'. On the international action of the Trilateral Commission, see Stephen Gill, *American Hegemony and the Trilateral Commission* (Cambridge, Cambridge University Press, 1990).

The Report was drafted by academics, but was not specifically directed at them, but at the political, business and media *milieux*, as it revealed the growing concerns of some circles in the West. In essence, it proposed a rigorous transnational and convergent diagnosis – though there are differences across its chapters – that popularised some political science perspectives, once carefully stripped of critical entreaties that were certainly not lacking within the discipline.

The Report was written by two political scientists and a sociologist. It was presented by a political scientist and specialist in international relations, Zbygniew Brzezinski.[41] He was the director of the Trilateral Commission and the driving force behind the Report, soon to become National Security Advisor to Jimmy Carter in the footsteps of Henry Kissinger, who was also a political scientist, specialist in international relations.

The choice of authors had been very thoroughly carried out. Samuel P. Huntington was chosen for the chapter on the USA. He was a Harvard political scientist known for his work on military regimes and for a polemical book published in 1968, questioning the prevailing theory according to which the economic and cultural factors in countries, then defined as 'developing', should be privileged over other factors. On the contrary, Huntington firmly maintained the absolute priority of order and the authority of the state, even to the detriment of democracy.[42] Later, in the early 1990s Huntington will become the alarmed theorist of the 'clash of civilizations'.[43] The author of the chapter on Japan, Jôji Watanuki, was a Japanese political scientist with intense contacts in the USA. Finally, Michel Crozier, who wrote the chapter on Europe, was a sociologist from France, a country where the institutionalisation of political science was just beginning. But he was well known, above all, for a severe investigation of French bureaucracy, that criticised its excesses of centralism and legalism.[44]

The laborious aftermath of the mid-1970s was characterised by what were considered extremely serious economic problems. In addition, there was the humiliation of the biggest power on the planet, in the Far East and the Watergate scandal that engulfed the Nixon administration. Furthermore, throughout the

---

41 Zbygniew Brzezinski was also the author of a brilliant and influential work on the incipient information revolution in *Between Two Ages: America's Role in the Technetronic Era* (New York, Viking Press, 1970).

42 Samuel P. Huntington, *Political Order in Changing Societies* (New Haven CT, Yale University Press, 1968). See also, the essay, published slightly before the Report of the Trilateral, 'Postindustrial Politics: How Benign Will It Be?', *Comparative Politics* 6(2), 1974, 163–191, whose diagnosis already concluded, ordering the recovery of a more robust authority in advanced democracies.

43 Samuel P. Huntington, *The Clash of Civilizations and the Remaking of World Order* (New York, Simon & Schuster, 1996).

44 Michael Crozier, *Le phénomène bureaucratique* (Paris, Seuil, 1963). Several years later Crozier wrote a polemical work where he called for radical liberalising reforms. See, *La société bloquée* (Paris, Seuil, 1970).

West there were the after-effects of nearly a decade of insubordination: protest against the war in Vietnam, student demonstrations and strikes together with dramatic episodes of political violence. After the successes of Fordism, organised capitalism, the postwar consensus and *détente*, something simply snapped. The war, as is often the case, had revitalised the patriotic and conservative mood in the USA. In similar conditions a rethinking of democracy comes as no surprise.

The economic and political difficulties that formed the background to the Report have largely obscured the memory of the intense and broader cultural and political activity that was interwoven around surmounting the class cleavage in the 1960s. The cleavage had opened up with the industrial revolution and had remained engraved, through opposition among socialist, moderate or conservative parties, in the architecture of European societies. Thanks to the great postwar growth it nevertheless seemed to have been healed. The very propitious formula for which we are indebted to Daniel Bell and Alain Touraine – the post-industrial society – recapitulates, but does not exhaust, the sense of the change taking place. This sense was not exhausted either by another successful expression coined by Bell with 'the end of ideology'.[45] These were just two of many ways that the arrival of a new model of industrial production, and a new model of society, was greeted between the 1960s and 1970s.

Taking the institutionalisation of social conflict as given, together with the erosion of inequalities, the broadening of the middle class, also thanks to the inclusion of a sizeable part of the working class, and the advent of a service society, there were scholars and pundits who imagined a more mature democracy, free of the complex reconciliation that the postwar consensus predicted between political and social forces. With the success of the postwar consensus there was hope for a new post-conflictual, post-ideological period, entrusted to science and to the inarrestable nature of progress. This would offer better chances of power for the experts and technocrats who manoeuvred the levers of organised capitalism, the public economy and the new welfare bureaucracies.[46] While they anticipated a reform of the state, experts, technocrats, top civil servants, scholars and even some politicians, revealed the uncertainties, intrigues, incompetence of the elected leadership, and also tried to write a new chapter of the ever resurgent struggle for representation. Already the application of the neo-corporate pacts, with which many advanced societies were governed, had given these actors crucial spaces in which to operate, but what they openly aspired to was to take on an official government role. Considering themselves as legitimate representatives of society as a whole and

---

45 Daniel Bell, *The End of Ideology: on the Exhaustion of Political Ideas in the Fifties* (Glencoe, The Free Press, 1960).

46 The French case is that in which similar discourses make themselves heard more clearly. Outlined in real time, or almost, this intellectual affair in, Pierre Bourdieu and Luc Boltanski, 'La production de l'idéologie dominante', *Actes de la recherche en sciences sociales* 2(2/3), 1976, 4–73. See also the more recent observations of Mark Bevir, *Democratic Governance*, pp. 25–27.

not of its single parts, why should they not govern it too? By way of compensation, citizens and local communities would be granted an enlarged participatory space.[47]

This perspective belongs to the rosy scenarios of the 1960s and was clearly statist and certainly different from the more pro-market perspective of the authors of the Report. But the authors of the latter certainly did not not ignore it, and neither did they ignore the contemporary post-Marxist considerations, being in particular harmony with many of their own. Thanks to development and welfare, according to authors like Jürgen Habermas, Claus Offe and James O'Connor,[48] western societies, reclassified as advanced, post-industrial, neo-capitalist or late-capitalist, had overcome the contradiction between capital and labour, but had to face a new and no less serious challenge. The successful marriage between capitalism and democracy had saddled the state with two incompatible democratic tasks: capital accumulation, or support for the capitalist economy, and legitimation, that is, the search for mass loyalty. This transferred the grounds for the crisis from the economy to politics, putting the management of the economy on a collision course with the commitment to guarantee legitimation and to avoid social conflict. What responsible ruling class would have dared break the relative social peace that had been consolidated to adopt unpopular policies that might have relaunched the economy, rehabilitating its privatistic nature? Who would have run the risk of provoking a much-feared crisis of legitimation? According to these authors, the only outcome that one could expect would be 'stagflation'. The cross between stagnation and inflation, would become chronic.

Without using the same terms, the Trilateral Commission shared the diagnosis of the fiscal crisis and the crisis of legitimacy and also shifted its attention to the political sphere. The entrepreneurial world was apparently under siege and conventional political forces were exhausted and discouraged. The Report had the capacity not only of tracing the state of democratic regimes in alarmed, but not catastrophic, tones, but above all it prescribed treatment and hence, a political line of action. What really made the Report credible and accepted beyond its sheer media impact – or what its sponsors managed to stimulate – were some well-targeted interpretative moves.

There were many different reasons for the stalemate of democratic regimes and the evolution of the crisis differed from one country to another. But the first, and perhaps the most successful, move of the Report was the peremptory unification of the Western world and Japan through a diagnosis that evoked a multiplicity of factors present everywhere. It was not a case of one or other country having a sick democracy, but that democratic regimes, as such, were sick.

---

47 Bourdieu and Boltanski cite the pamphlet by Pierre Mendés-France, *La république moderne* (Paris, Gallimard, 1966) and his proposals to 'modernise' society and French institutions inspired by American sociology.

48 Jürgen Habermas, *Legitimation Crisis* (Boston, Beacon Press, 1975); James O'Connor, *The Fiscal Crisis of the State* (New York, St. Martin's Press, 1973); Claus Offe, *Strukturprobleme der kapitalistischen Staates: Aufsatze zur politischen Soziologie* (Frankfurt a.M., Suhrkamp, 1975).

Following the formulation of a unitary diagnosis, the second winning move was to avoid re-proposing both the defence of order *tout court* and hierarchy, as previous conservative critics of democracy used to do, who never resigned and were still active in elaborating their prescriptions. On the contrary, the Report defended democracy and its preface cited no less than the most prestigious exponent of postwar European social-democracy, and one of the few Germans to have resisted nazism arms in hand, Willy Brandt. This stand won it a very large audience. From the perspective of traditional conservative critics, it would have been possible to argue that the Report re-proposed arguments that were not in the least original, but in this way it still managed also to offer some solid evidence to the progressive spheres. Democracy was up for debate, but it had to be protected against the woodworm that was eating into it, in tending to it in a more sober way than what had been done until now.

The analysis contained in the relatively few, but very densely written pages of the Report, did not present innovative comparative research or even exceptional theoretical statements. What it contained, in strongly simplified tones, was an outline of a diagnosis which was plausible, not too difficult to digest and based on two fundamental concepts: 'overload' and 'ungovernability'. The first reason for the malaise of democratic regimes was the widespread mistrust of all sorts of authority, public and private, secular and religious, provoked by the diffusion of values of equality and individualism. Second, everywhere, too much participation overloaded the work of government, multiplied its interventions and caused inflationary tensions. Third, serious responsibilities were imputed to too much political competition, disaggregated interests and weakened parties, while the susceptibility of governments to electoral pressures was accused of encouraging coarse nationalistic behaviour.[49]

In the first place, the Report obtained important effects of redefinition and reclassification. Until then, crisis had been diagnosed as an economic crisis, whereas in the Report it was reclassified as a political crisis and a crisis of democratic authority. Economic stagnation, the combination of unemployment and inflation that corroded the most advanced economies, was no longer imputed *in primis* to the economy, and only secondarily to politics, but directly to politics: to the insubordination of the younger generations, workers, intellectuals, ordinary citizens, organised interests, and thus to the state of democratic regimes and their institutions. Political science had already prepared a similar explanation. If

---

49 For the concepts of 'overload' and 'ungovernability', see Crozier, Huntington, Watanuki (eds.), *The Crisis of Democracy*. The same year in Britain, Anthony King published 'Overload: Problems of Governing in the 1970s', *Political Studies* 23(22–23), 1975, 162–74. The concept of overload, however, comes from David Easton's theory of the political system, indicating the excess of claims made by the environment. See *A Systems Analysis of Political Life* (New York, Wiley, 1965, pp. 58–59).

development and economic wealth were preconditions of democracy,[50] once this most perfect form of government imaginable had been attained, wasn't it obvious to saddle it with responsibility for the economic crisis?

At the same time, what had, until then on the political side, been considered a crisis of legitimacy was reclassified as a crisis of authority. It is true that there was a lack of trust in politics, but this was because authority was missing. Put in these terms, the Report exhumed also a very old, and recurrent, accusation made against democracy. Democratic regimes suffered the intrinsic tendency of democracy to resort to demagogy to the detriment of the governed. A similar reasoning opened the way to the reclassification and democratic rehabilitation of those who had always been hostile to, or at least sceptical of, democracy. The latter were promoted to standard bearers of true democracy, which needed to be freed from bureaucratic, party and participatory fetters. This was the premise of the imminent reclassification of the sceptics towards democracy as innovators and reformers, whereas those who had previously fought for democracy, and still wanted to safeguard the welfare state, would have been relabelled – and discredited – as conservative. This effect persists, and has meant the semantic reversal of the word 'reform'. If for one century the term has indicated policies which were more generous towards the large mass of the population, more recently it has been associated with measures that take back what was previously given. Using the same word to indicate reforms by subtraction and those by addition is clearly suspect.[51]

By pointing to the responsibility of the elites, the Report, far from being fatalist, was also indicating also a way out. After a decade of social and political turmoil, the constraint of consensus, especially electoral consensus, had to be loosened, freeing leadership and allowing it to exercise its authority and meet its responsibilities.[52] A revision of representation, with a restored, vigorous and credible authority recognised by citizens, was necessary. To this end the power of the executive and the local authorities had to be reinforced, parliamentary control had to be better exploited, the public administration had to be reformed to make it more transparent and dynamic, the role of experts – this was the era of scientific progress – needed to be recognised, and the organisation of work needed to be reviewed so as to frustrate the blackmailing potential of trade-union organisations. While public powers needed to be protected from manipulation by the mass media, criticisms and proposals did not save the parties. Their reputation had begun to deteriorate in the late 1960s, under pressure from social movements and nascent civil society, and interest groups had staked a very serious claim on their activities. Therefore they had to be reformed.

---

50 For example, Seymour M. Lipset, *Political Man. The Social Bases of Politics* (New York, Doubleday, 1960).

51 Luc Boltansky, *Rendre la société inacceptable* (Paris, Raisons d'agir, 2010).

52 Crozier, Huntington, Watanuki (eds.) *The Crisis of Democracy*, pp. 150–51.

The Report of the Trilateral Commission raised the question, especially in the chapters on the USA and Japan, because in the chapter on Europe, the problem was above all the persistent influence of the communist parties. At the discussion of the Report by the assembly of the Commission, one of the themes raised was thus the 'reinvigoration of political parties'.[53] Without too much explicit emphasis, the Report did not want the end of parties, but a renewed model of party: no longer a vector of interests and political demands, but as a rigid filter. If parties previously 'focused on material benefits such as jobs, patronage, and social insurance', the time had come to dedicate much more effort into supplying 'knowledge': more ideas and less services.[54]

Without saying it in so many words, a basic constraint to be removed, or at least loosened, was democratic participation. Pluralism had overflowed the conventional channels, and had to be driven out of the political sphere, putting things back in their correct place. Is it too much to assume that the Trilateral Commission invited democratic regimes to take a well-measured dose of non-democracy? All things considered, the question is not so bizarre.

Certainly the Report was, among other things, liberating. It liberalised the criticism of democracy so that reservations about democracy would no longer be considered with suspicion or even as detrimentally hostile. Choosing its words extremely shrewdly, the Report confirmed the age-old liberal diffidence with regard to mass democracy,[55] but it did so by referring only to its 'excess'.[56] On its guard against claiming too much from it, democracy was invited to be a bit less accommodating towards citizens. The similarity with neo-liberal formulas, that had not yet dominated the scene, was not immediately evident. But anticipating these formulas, and perhaps facilitating their future application, the Report invited a review and a restrictive reinterpretation of the rules of the democratic game. At the same time, another authoritative political scientist Robert A. Dahl, who had in his time codified the rules of the game meticulously, suggested how to enrich its content. In the 1980s Dahl defined equality as a precondition of democracy and went so far as to suggest restrictions on property rights.[57] But Dahl's recommendations were ignored.

53 *Appendixes*, in Crozier, Huntington, Watanuki (eds.), *The Crisis of Democracy*, p. 178.

54 Crozier, Huntington, Watanuki (eds.), *The Crisis of Democracy*.

55 A good example is Giovanni Sartori, *Democratic Theory* (Detroit, Wayne University Press, 1962), Another example is Raymond Aron, *Démocratie et totalitarisme* (Paris, Gallimard, 1965).

56 Samuel P. Huntington, 'United States', in Crozier, Huntington, Watanuki (eds.) *The Crisis of Democracy*, p. 113.

57 After pleading for more participation – see *After the Revolution? Authority in a Good Society* (New Haven CT, Yale University Press, 1970) – Robert A. Dahl went so far as to plead for a workplace democracy. See *A Preface to Economic Democracy* (Berkeley, University of California Press, 1986).

Setting aside Dahl's revisionism, as well as the critics of Dahl himself and others, who – in line with a persistent American tradition – hoped for an evolution of democratic regimes in a participatory sense,[58] the Report championed a movement in the opposite direction: the transition from the Kelsenian democratic paradigm to a post-democratic paradigm, of which Schumpeter is the basic, albeit partly betrayed, inspirer. Now that class conflict had become a memory, what counted was the performance of the govenors, that had to be immunised against democracy itself, electoral competition and the partisan dialectic.

The ambitions of scientific politics

The recommendations of the Trilateral Report were influenced not only on Schumpeter's competitive elitism, but also, and in perhaps greater measure, on another recently consolidated theory, that of 'rational choice' (or 'social', 'public', 'collective' choice). Applying the basic axiom of his original discipline, i.e., economic science, according to which to dictate the behaviour of the individual or collective actors is to aim to maximise their utility, since the mid-1950s, the advocates of this approach had invaded political science, becoming one of its most fertile and recognised components in the space of twenty years.

This invasion offered sharpened conceptual tools to examine and interpret political facts, but it also formulated a point of view regarding democracy where the relationship with the 'political market' was much closer than what Schumpeter originally intended, and that led to different prescriptive conclusions.[59] Schumpeter adopted the market as a metaphor in a critical description of the mediocre functioning of democratic regimes. Starting with the work by Anthony Downs,

---

58 American political science has never denied, and continually revisits, its Tocquevillian inspiration. Besides Dahl, and waiting for the success of social capital and deliberation, another well known author asking for more participation, and citizens' inclusion in policy-making, is Benjamin Barber in *Strong Democracy. Participatory Politics for a New Age* (Berkeley, University of California Press, 1984).

59 Anthony Downs, *The Economic Theory of Democracy* (New York, Harper & Row, 1957), as well as two other influential rational choice theorists like James M. Buchanan and Gordon Tullock's *The Calculus of Consent: Logical Foundations of Constitutional Democracy* (Ann Arbor, University of Michigan Press, 1962) all cite Schumpeter in passing. On the complicated relation between Schumpeter and the theory of rational choice, see William C. Mitchell, 'Schumpeter and Public Choice, Part I: Precursor to Public Choice?', *Public Choice* 42(1), 1984, 73–88 and 'Schumpeter and Public Choice, Part II: Democracy and the Demise of Capitalism: The Missing Chapter in Schumpeter', *Public Choice* 47(3), 1984, 161–74. For a critical appraisal of rational choice and of the political context political see Sonja M. Amadae, *Rationalizing Capitalist Democracy. The Cold War Origins of Rational Choice Liberalism*, (Chicago-London, The University of Chicago Press, 2003).

which is significantly entitled *The Economic Theory of Democracy*, and applying the neo-utilitarian perspective to politics, rational choice assimilated democracy fully to the market and considered it based on economic rationality.[60]

In doing so rational choice formulated four basic theorems: the theorem 'of analogy', where the analogy with the market is vital in order to understand how democracy functions; the theorem 'of necessity', where, as a system of dispersed power the market, both political and economic, is a necessary precondition of democracy; the theorem 'of superiority', where the market places the autonomy and rationality of individuals at the centre and is even more democratic than democracy; and the theorem 'of disability', where democracy distorts the market, or puts the functioning of the economic market at risk.[61]

With respect to Schumpeter, rational choice means a double theoretical upheaval. Not only is the democratic market deemed virtuous, but it is where the individual is fully rehabilitated. For Schumpeter, as soon as the individual starts to be involved in politics his ability to reason and his judgement regresses and he cannot be relied on. On the contrary, rational choice, that once accused public administrations and parties of being exclusively guided by their ambitions for power and their need for self-maintenance, argued that individuals are able to cultivate their own preferences even in terms of political choices. Therefore its concerns are concentrated on what distorts the free play of such preferences: public bureaucracies, trade unions, interest groups and, above all, parties and elected politicians, that act exclusively on the basis of their own electoral advantages.

Rational choice takes little interest in the mediation of interests, but only in their thorough hierarchisation. Thus, by applying the accounting logic of costs and benefits, it highlights the progress made by the economy, or rather by entrepreneurial profit, even to the detriment of principles like social justice and widespread issues like wages, salaries, public services, the standard of living of the population and so forth. At the end of the 1970s a similar interpretation proved convincing. It would be a mistake to classify all the advocates of rational choice as conservatives. Downs, for example, was a valued consultant on urban planning in the Johnson administration. Nevertheless, the rhetoric of the virtues of the market has caused a radical rethinking not only of where to place the citizen in democracy, but of democracy itself, against which rational choice has raised one insuperable objection.

Democracy's task is analogous to the market's task. It is supposed to aggregate the preferences of self-interested actors (including political leadership), but elections remain a much more inadequate tool than prices to aggregate the individuals' preferences. Irrespective of the rationality of electors, collective choices run into insoluble paradoxes, an idea that dates back to Condorcet and that is confirmed by rational choice. William Riker argues that the sheer ambiguity of election results drains elections of any meaning. Whoever believes that they

---

60 Downs, *The Economic Theory of Democracy*.
61 David Beetham, 'Four Theorems about the Market and Democracy', *European Journal of Political Research* 23, 1993, 187–201.

reveal the popular will commits the mortal sin of 'populism', which in turn masks manipulation by the elites. Thus, also according to the rational choice theory, democracy only serves to select leadership and is an antidote to despotism.[62]

Until the reawakening of the so-called 'practical reason',[63] rational choice worked to reconcile democracy with neo-liberalism and to provide it with a new and successful theory.[64] Yet, political science is more than this. It is a prestigious academic discipline with thousands of scholars world-wide, articulated in a plurality of heterogeneous approaches, research networks, politico-cultural orientations, some critical and others heterodox.[65] Among them, one approach that has recently become particularly important is that of institutions.

Both behaviouralist and systemic political science, and rational choice, had underestimated the way in which institutions condition electors, parties, organised interests and policy-making. Rational choice came up against insuperable *impasses*: the best known being self-interested behaviour. If everyone pursues their own interests, who will produce public goods?[66] From the 1990s, neo-institutionalism has been the perspective that rediscovered what was always known: that institutions count, and count a great deal. When political science had carried out its empiricist revolution, old-style institutionalism was accused of formalism and legalism: too much focus on norms that regulate the public administration, parliaments, parties, judiciary, and little on the effects. Its close link with legal science was evident. Political science had discovered behaviour. Through neo-institutionalism, which also crossed brilliantly with rational choice, political science goes back on its steps, broadening the use of the concept of institution. In addition to the institutions of government and formal rules, there are norms, values and shared aims, markets, welfare systems, past history, civil society and so forth. This has given rise to an impressive flow of research and theories, culminating, in a wave of self-promoting pride, in convincing some political scientists of the prospect of manoeuvring institutions at will.[67]

---

62 William H. Riker, *Liberalism against Populism: A Confrontation between the Theory of Democracy and the Theory of Social Choice* (San Francisco, W. H. Freeman, 1982).

63 John Rawls stands out among the protagonists for the return of normative political philosophy. See John Rawls in his *A Theory of Justice* (Cambridge MA, Harvard University Press, 1972).

64 On the effects of rational choice on democratic common sense see Colin Hay, *Why We Hate Politics* (Cambridge, Polity Press, 2007) and Bevir, *Democratic Governance*.

65 Apart from the famous email sent on 17 October 2000 to APSA signed by Mr. Perestroika (www. psci.unt.edu/enterline/mrperestroika.pdf) for a more in-depth analysis of this critical perspective see Sanford F. Schram, Brian Caterino (eds.), *Making Political Science Matter. Debating Knowledge, Research, and Method* (New York, New York University Press, 2006).

66 This is defined as 'the tragedy of the commons', and has given rise to a rich and passionate debate in which rational choice has been quick to propose intriguing solutions. For a critical appraisal see Bevir, *Democratic Governance*, pp. 43–44.

67 Adcock, Bevir, Stimson, 'Historicizing the New Instituzionalism(s)' and Bevir, 'Institutionalism

Social and political engineering are an intrinsic ambition of the social sciences. Their ideas have always stimulated policies, including those relating to institutions, but the formulas of the theory are one thing and their application is another. After Britain invented parliamentary government, it was a critic of French absolutism, Montesquieu, who perfected Locke's theory and established parliamentary government as a scientific truth by the canons of the day, in terms of good government and as a standard destined to be widely used. But the British parliamentary regime is one thing, the formalisation of that regime by Montesquieu, or by his readers, is another, and the representative regimes introduced around the planet, in the last two centuries, are yet other thing.

Even the postwar consensus spread in this way and it is not surprising that the same happened to the post-democratic paradigm arriving from the USA. This time political science was a protagonist. Once political science had accredited it as the new standard, it became an imperative in virtue of its internationally legitimated scientific reputation, yet often forgetting that institutions are hard to transplant.[68] Users experience institutions in rather different ways, they furnish them in their own way and according to the will and mood of the moment. Different social strata and populations experience democracy differently and stubbornly resist any demand for standardisation. The hybrids that result from the more or less voluntary importation of standards, function obstinately in their own way, conditioned by ideas, history, behaviour of whoever inhabits them.[69]

To use another metaphor: the manipulation of institutions bears some resemblance to conversion from one religion to another. From non-democracy one can convert to democracy, and from one democratic model one can convert to another. But the converted have a heavy baggage to carry. Syncretism is the rule for both religion and for politics.[70] This is not to say that reforms are useless, and however they are called, they will be introduced just the same. They are public policies like any other. It is enough that some political actors recognise them as suitable and advantageous. It can also be often a good idea to introduce them. Even the adoption of standards is an obvious practice. When different worlds communicate, learn from each other reciprocally and contaminate each other: if an instrument functions, especially if its functioning is scientifically certified, why not adopt it? The rhetorical over-investments that are an integral part of what are defined reform policies, are not surprising either. Nor should we scorn, on

---

and the Third Way', in Adcock, Bevir, Stimson (eds.), *Modern Political Science*.

68 Yet, a part of the theory is very well informed. One sees the observations on the risks entailed by institutional transplants by Claus Offe, 'Designing Institutions in East European Transitions', in R. Goodin (ed.), *The Theory of Institutional Design* (Cambridge, Cambridge University Press, 1996).

69 Michel de Certeau suggests the metaphor in *The Practice of Everyday Life* (Berkeley, University of California Press, 1988, p. 30).

70 On religious hybridization see Tzvetan Todorov, *The Conquest of America: the Question of the Other* (New York, Harper & Row, 1984, pp. 202–218).

principle, the hybrids produced in various ways, that often turn out to be lucky. It is only a question of observing the peremptoriness with which standards are now dictated, the excessive trust placed in them and the very active role that an honoured academic discipline has decided to play.

Where socially redistributive policies were once promoted, the remedy for success is now institution-building: devising new institutions, adjusting existing ones, reforming the state, reviewing electoral norms, promoting good governance, stimulating social capital and civil society and so forth. At the height of its institutionalisation, political science was thus enrolled as indispensable expertise in the service of whoever wishes to propagate democracy: Western governments, international institutions, NGOs, foundations.[71] The action of 'democracy assistance', that favours the homologation of democratic regimes, and the democratisation of non-democratic ones, can even be considered a benign action. Reconversions roughly promoted by CIA intervention, by other occult powers, or by financing parties, lobbies or the media, have been much more devastating. At the same time, however, when diversities held to be incomprehensible and unpredictable are reduced, conversions and standardisation may not only have unforeseen effects, but may turn out to be another technique of power. What have been the benefits for regimes and citizens subject to similar conversions and from standards imposed on them with such zeal? It is an interesting research question.

One indisputable outcome is the lexical revolution that accompanied the transition from one democratic paradigm to another. An entire dictionary of words and concepts has fallen into misuse: class, state, solidarity, equality, collective, public, general interest, common good, party, work, compromise. In their place we find individual, market, business, governability, profit, merit and leadership. More recently, when the inefficiency of the market, and the shortcomings of the new democratic order started to become apparent to the omnipresent concept of civil society, identity, social capital, network transparency, accountability, subsidiarity, governance, sustainability, conditionality, non-profit, third sector were added. There is enough to fill a dictionary.[72]

---

71 On political science as democracy expertise, that has now accumulated a discrete service record, initiated with the Cold War, see Nicolas Guilhot, *The Democracy Makers: Human Rights and International Order* (New York, Columbia University Press, 2005).

72 For a brilliant and polemical catalogue of the neo-language see Eric Hazan, *LQR, la propagande du quotidien* (Paris, Raisons d'agir, 2006). More academic, and not limited to the neo-language, but still very useful, is Mark Bevir (ed.), *Encyclopaedia of Governance* (London, Sage, 2007). For an interesting reflection on the neo-language, on its 'magic' virtues which can condition the research agendas of the social sciences see Christopher Pollitt, Peter Hupe, 'Talking About Government', *Public Management Review* 13(5), 2011, 641–58.

chapter five | making the state by other means

On the alleged decline of the state

Once there was organised capitalism, just as once there was also 'organised democracy'. The repetition may seem gratuitous, because democracy, in so far as it is a technology of power, serves to organise collective life and disorganised democracies do not exist, just as disorganised capitalism does not exist. What we want to indicate, however, is once again a form of particularly stringent organisation. In line with the democratic paradigm formulated by the political theorists, organised democracy entailed impressive institutions, such as the state and parties, as well as the interest organisations – entrepreneurial associations and trade unions – which were often unofficially involved in decision-making through neo-corporate concertation behind the scenes.

A long cycle, governed thanks to these institutions, opened with the adoption of interventionist measures to combat the Depression of the 1930s. It effected democratic and authoritarian regimes alike, and continued well into the postwar period. But from the end of the 1970s we witnessed the start of a new Depression. This time it was a political Depression, marked by the decline of the earlier institutions typical of the democratic regime. This brought the market economy back into fashion and has progressively redesigned democratic institutions.

One of the important narratives of the last thirty years is, therefore, the retreat of the state from the economy and from society. What we need to examine, however, is whether the state has really retreated, or whether it has simply assumed a different, and perhaps not totally unprecedented, form. Historical research confirms how relations between state and non-state have always been up and down and how it has not even been a zero-sum game: the growth of the one does not necessarily take place to the detriment of the other.

Towards the end of the 1970s, Michel Foucault introduced the concept of 'governmentality'. Oversimplifying his point of view: the state is not a unique tool to govern human beings, which are subject to many other regulation and control techniques, while the state does not have an unique essence and a unique way to operate.[1] This was a real conceptual revolution, but it might be interesting to

---

1   Michel Foucault, 'Governmentality', in Graham Burchell, Colin Gordon and Peter Miller (eds.), *The Foucault Effect: Studies in Governmentality* (Chicago IL, University of Chicago Press, 1991) and *Naissance de la biopolitique. Cours au Collège de France. 1978–1979* (Paris, Gallimard-Seuil, 2004).

observe that more than ten years earlier, within comparative political science, John P. Nettl already felt the need to revisit the concept of state, then rather unpopular within the discipline, putting forward the concept of 'stateness' in an influential essay.[2] His objective was to indicate to what extent the state was a complex phenomenon still worthy of being considered, even if not reducible to Hobbesian sovereignty or to the Weberian ideal-type.

Up to that moment sociology and political science, shaped by history and by the traditional American democratic rhetoric, had in general, refused the image of the state formulated in Europe by political and legal theory, and by sociology, and above all by the Weberian matrix. Anglo-Saxon political science preferred to use the concept of government, and later on the concept of the political system,[3] in which it placed public administrations, representative institutions, parties, interest groups, as well as culture and politics. On the contrary, Nettl rehabilitated the state through the concept of 'stateness', and invited political science to consider its various forms and meanings in different historical contexts and warned against all oversimplified representations of it. This would have facilitated the comparison between cultural and historical experiences which were very different in the West, and then to take into account the broad diffusion of the model of the state outside its original Western catchment area. This diffusion, juridically sanctioned by admission to the UN, stimulated a rough *rapprochement* of political entities that had little to do with the Western tradition of the state, such as those that emerged from processes of decolonisation, or in the experience of socialist countries, raising significant problems of adaptation and comparison.

The multidimensionality and sheer range of the state were not exactly new. For two centuries the dilemma between state and nation, juxtaposes, albeit schematically, the coercive and organisational apparatus of the state to the symbolic and cultural space circumscribed by it.[4] The merit of the concept of stateness is that it explicitly made the state a variable. This allows us to extend – in the light of the historical, organisational and cultural specificity of each case – the opportunities for the application and articulation of the concept of state, to take into account the extension of the state following from the postwar policies of intervention in the economy and welfare, or to consider the more recent developments, usually described, in a way loaded with political meanings, with terms such as 'crisis', 'retreat', 'decline' and 'reform'. In other words, if the state is a variable, before decreeing its decline or end, it would be better to consider that the state can always be made by other means and represented by other words.

In the thirty years of postwar consensus, European political culture had had an easy time confirming the old idea of state as an axle of collective life. After all, it had democratised the nineteenth-century official rhetoric, and the official principle

---

2   John P. Nettl, 'The State as a Conceptual Variable', *World Politics* 20(4), 1968, 559–592.

3   See David Easton, *The Political System: An Inquiry into the State of Political Science* (New York, Knopf, 1953).

4   Joe Painter, 'Prosaic Geographies of Stateness', *Political Geography* 25(7), 2006, 752–774.

according to which the state embodies the destiny and general interests of the social body on which it is built. Certainly, the idea of the state emerged from the conflict rather battered. The version of the state advocated by fascist dictatorships – an offspring of the ambitions of power transmitted by the nineteenth-century state to the twentieth-century state – was necessarily rejected. Germany therefore did redraw the state through federalism. Italy imagined a state diluted by regional and local autonomies. In respect of a national tradition, France set out to 'technicise' the state by founding the *École National d'Adminstration* (ENA).

At the same time, everywhere the state was subjected to party government.[5] Those that had long been considered its most feared adversaries, the parties, not only took the lead, but were officially given the task of organising and governing large segments of society and of legitimating and competing to realise public policies.[6] In this way, in addition to becoming a welfare state, the state managed to give itself a new reputation, becoming, in its current academic and political representations, 'society's turn-key', which 'regulates economic life and takes on, the needs of society', making it 'guarantor of collective well-being'.[7]

The state guaranteed the full use of individual freedoms, the functionality of the market and a well-ordered collective life. Symbolically and practically, the state was awarded the task of removing the more lacerating grounds for social tension and providing for the well-being of citizens. Even Marxist scholars had adapted to this rhetoric. Once the image of the state as a 'committee for managing the affairs of the ruling class' had been archived, some of them recognised the state's autonomy from the dominant classes, together with the ability to satisfy the interests of the dominated classes, so as to constitute 'the factor of cohesion between the levels of a social formation'.[8]

Even American political science, which had now come into closer contact with the European experience, was in favour of a reappraisal and adopted the concept of the state. Curiously enough, this reappraisal, and the start of intense empirical examination of the state's actual and past forms, took place precisely on the eve, or at the start of, the striking cultural and political upheaval that was to put aside the postwar consensus and the centrality which it attributed to the state.[9]

---

5   For a definition, see Elmer E. Schattschneider, *Party Government* (New York, Holt, Rinehart & Winston, 1942) and Martin Shefter, *Political Parties and the State: The American Historical Experience* (Princeton NJ, Princeton University Press, 1994).

6   The image of the parties as organs of the state has been re-examined by Ingrid van Biezen in 'Political Parties as Public Utilities', *Party Politics* 6(10), 2004, 701–22. But in the 1960s this was anticipated by the future theorist of the empire and of the multitude: see Antonio Negri, *Alcune riflessioni sullo Stato dei partiti*, 1964, now published in *La forma Stato* (Milan, Feltrinelli, 1977).

7   Jacques Chevallier, *L'Etat post-moderne* (Paris, LGDJ, 2003, p. 25).

8   Nicos Poulantzas, *Political Power and Social Classes* (London, NLB. [1967] 1975, p. 44). Some years later another author expressed himself in much the same way, by crossing Marxism with functionalism: see Claus Offe, *Strukturprobleme des kapitalistischen Staates: Aufsatze zur politischen Soziologie* (Frankfurt a.M., Suhrkamp, 1975).

9   It is interesting to consider the timing of the theoretical revision made by political science and

Classical liberalism had often criticised the shortcomings of bureaucracy, but without condemning the state. On the contrary, it harboured statist currents itself. Liberal and conservative leaderships which governed in the postwar era had no particular prejudices against state intervention, and had also favoured the growth of the public sector.[10] The innovation introduced by neo-liberalism consisted in reactivating and exacerbating recurrent irritation with public intervention in American political culture, something that was not even cancelled by the success of the New Deal and the ambitious interventionist policies passed in the 1960s by Kennedy and Johnson. Let us not forget that in 1964 Barry Goldwater stood as Republican candidate for the presidency by opposing such policies with a fiercely liberalist and anti-centralist programme. Once the irritation was reactivated, Europe too became contaminated. A decisive point of transition was Britain, which had often considered itself a stateless society,[11] and where between the last decades of 1800 and the first ones of 1900 the dispersion of stateness had been openly pointed out by the pluralistic and anti-statist doctrine of authors such as, G. D. H. Cole, J. N. Figgis and H. J. Laski.[12]

sociology, which can be considered a largely integrated scientific community on the international level from the late 1970s. A year after the publication of Nettl's article, a Weberian sociologist, Reinhard Bendix, published *Nation-Building and Citizenship: Studies of Our Changing Social Order* (Berkeley, University of California Press, 1969). Ten years later, combining David Easton's concept of political system, and Carl Schmitt's concept of the political (*The Concept of the Political*, Chicago IL, University of Chicago Press, [1932] 1995), it was an Italian sociologist Gianfranco Poggi, then teaching in Britain, who published another successful book, *The Development of the Modern State: A Sociological Introduction* (Stanford, Stanford University Press, 1978). Immediately afterwards in France Bertrand Badie and Pierre Birnbaum published *The Sociology of the State* (Chicago IL, University of Chicago Press, [1979] 1983). Soon after American political scientists Peter B. Evans, Dietrich Rueschemeyer, Theda Skocpol, restored the state to its status as an autonomous actor under a rather provocative title, *Bringing the State Back In* (Cambridge, Cambridge University Press, 1985).

10 As regards timing, it is worth rereading the comparative assessment of public intervention (USA, Canada, Britain, Germany and France) made by a British scholar. See Anthony King, 'Ideas, Institutions and the Policy of Governments: A Comparative Analysis: Part I and II', *British Journal of Political Science* 3(3), 1973, 291–313. King completes his reflection in 'Ideas, Institutions and the Policy of Governments: A Comparative Analysis: Part III', *British Journal of Political Science* 3(4), 1973, 409–423. In his opinion the variable that explains the important differences between the USA and Europe is political culture. Not the widespread culture that King then witnessed in America, quite willing to enlarge the spaces for intervention by the state, but the political culture of policy-makers. King subsequently published the essay, 'Overload: Problems of Governing in the 1970s', in *Political Studies* 23(22–23), 1975, 162–174.

11 Nettl, 'The State as a Conceptual Variable'.

12 On this tradition see Paul Q. Hirst, *The Pluralist Theory of the State: Selected Writings of G. D. H Cole, J. N. Figgis and H. J. Laski* (London, Routledge, 1989) and the reconstruction by David

It was the theory of 'overload' and 'ungovernability' which sparked criticism of the state of the postwar consensus, accused of inadequacy in the mid-1970s. This was the start of a newly emerging and commonly held conviction according to which the state was no longer able to meet the expectations of a society that had become too complex and too demanding. The increasing costs of policy hindered investments and growth, while the unbounded multiplication of public administrations and their competences created serious problems of coordination.[13] Government had not yet become a malaise *per se*, or 'the problem', as Ronald Reagan would soon claim, but was already considered a solution not adapted to the challenges created by the social change that it had stimulated.

However, it was the economic theory critical of Keynesianism that supplied a complex critical argumentation, that the state was to become a commonly shared belief, helped by rational choice theory. For the latter, the image of the state was reduced to the image of public bureaucracies, defined, no differently from the electoral political leaderships, as unrepentant rent-seekers, inclined to waste and corruption. The expansion of the state in the postwar period was not the effect of the growing demand for collective goods, but only of the vocation of public bureaucracies to enlarge their policy supply in order to extend their influence. To this end, the bureaucracies committed two inexcusable errors: inciting interest groups to mobilise in order to satisfy claims, but to their own advantage, thanks to the state; and pushing political actors, keen to maximise electoral consensus, to carry out the demands of organised interests and electors, with no concern for the consequent damage for public finance and economic growth.[14]

But it was politics that finally popularised and loaded similar theories with *pathos*, exploiting their persuasive capacity and adopting their therapeutic

---

Runciman, *Pluralism and the Personality of the State* (Cambridge, Cambridge University Press, 1997).

13 The discussion on overload and ungovernability, started by the Trilateral Commission's Report, immediately caught on in Britain, then at the peak of a prolonged economic decline. At the same time the concept of 'overload' was used by Anthony King in 'Overload'. Soon after, the concept of ungovernability was reproposed by Richard Rose, 'Ungovernability: Is There Fire Behind the Smoke?', *Political Studies* 23(2–3), 1979, 351–370. For a reflection on the conceptual instruments used to analyse the British situation see Anthony H. Birch, 'Overload, Ungovernability and Delegitimation: The Theories and the British Case', *British Journal of Political Science* 14(2), 1984, 135–160.

14 See James M. Buchanan, Gordon Tullock, *The Calculus of Consent*, 1962, and James M. Buchanan, Richard E. Wagner, *Democracy in Deficit: The Political Legacy of Lord Keynes* (New York, Academic Press, 1977), where Keynesianism was accused of having legitimated the violation by the democratic leaderships of the principle of balancing the budget, consequently condemning the economy for electoral reasons to a burdensome public deficit that inhibited growth. The restoral of the principle, at the expense of the welfare state, tying the hands of political management, was the only realistic solution.

proposals, at the same time representing the condition of Western economies as dramatically critical. Political actors made the neo-liberal criticism of 'big government' popular and the thesis, whereby a system of prices set by private actors competing on the market, is a due tribute to modernity, which would allow a more efficient and less expensive supply of public services.

A similar line of reasoning was first shared by conservative and moderate parties, but subsequently was adopted also, even if with corrections, by socialist parties. In any case, all the parties were persuaded not to oppose a particularly striking flow of neo-liberal reform policies of the state. There has been no shortage of opposition, but was it so unreasonable to imagine the state, not as a protagonist, but as a less awkward 'regulator' of collective life, mitigating the very high costs of the inefficiency of public administration?[15] There is no politician who would not be happy to concede tax cuts. Why defend obsolete industrial sectors to the detriment of public budgets when free enterprise allows us to set up new ones? And if transport, energy and pensions can be guaranteed at a lower cost by entrusting their running to the private sector, why pass up the opportunity?

All things considered, the polemic against big government was as fierce as the policies hostile to it were usually cautious and graduated. In particular, the cuts imposed on welfare had to take into account the popularity of many of its services and so have normally been carried out selectively and with care.[16] Moreover, these cuts have always been masked as part of the unavoidable – and easily popular – fight against unproductive waste or the parasitic dependency caused by some welfare policies. Guided by New Labour, around which an important theoretical school of thought had developed with links to the British pluralistic and stateless tradition,[17] parties and social-democratic governments later placed greater emphasis on social justice and social cohesion, set against the harshness

---

15 Giandomenico Majone, 'The Rise of the Regulatory State in Europe', *West European Politics* 17(3), 1994, 77–101. A sort of manifesto of this reconversion is David Osborne, Ted Gaebler, *Reinventing Government* (Reading, Addison Wesley, 1992). The processes of reconversion are many and diverse. For a detailed reconstruction of reconversion in the French case see Bruno Théret, 'Néo-libéralisme, inégalités sociales et politiques fiscales de droite et de gauche dans la France des années 1980. Identité et différences, pratiques et doctrines', *Revue française de science politique* 41(2), 1991, 342–381. Mark Bevir reconstructs the mix of political advantage and intellectual formulations for the case of New Labour in Britain in *Institutionalism and the Third Way* (Princeton NJ, Princeton University Press, 2007).

16 The popularity of welfare varies from one context to another, depending on political balances, institutions and procedures, public opinion and political culture, type of welfare state and the services offered, and is confirmed by practically all the research. See, for example, Clem Brooks, Jeff Manza, *Why Welfare States Persist. The Importance of Public Opinion in Democracies* (Chicago IL, University of Chicago Press, 2007), who use survey data to analyse the direction taken by public opinion.

17 See, in particular, Anthony Giddens, *The Third Way* (Cambridge, Polity Press, 1998).

of conservative governments, whilst carefully avoiding the rehabilitation of state intervention and always recognising the merits of the market and free enterprise.

In any case, reform policies that have transformed the state more than a little are one thing, but the decline of the state is quite another. The state still concentrates a remarkable load of resources and dictates the rules that support collective life. But the image and *modus operandi* of stateness have been radically reconfigured. This has been done by ceding of some of its competences, sovereign or not, to private operators, with the introduction of new instruments of public action – the reform of public bureaucracies through New Public Management – the creation of independent regulatory agencies, devolution and deregulation, as well as through the concertation of governance. There is also good reason to believe that the direct and indirect interventions of public powers – to use a generic formula – on society and the economy, have even grown.[18] To mention just one case, who are markets saddling with the expenses of damage-limitation caused by the economic crisis which exploded in 2008, and the cost of the future prospects for recovery?

A recent typology has attempted to reorganise the mass of instruments currently used by the state, clarifying things at the same time. The instruments of public action have always been numerous and differentiated. Recently, however, conventional 'legislative', 'regulatory', 'economic' and 'fiscal' instruments are flanked by other instruments which are based on 'agreements', 'incentives', 'information' and 'communication'.[19] These instruments are often used jointly, but each is supported by a theory of the relations between governors and the governed, and impacts in its own way on the condition of policies, their reception and their effect. The conclusion is not that society is less governed by the state and self-governs more, but only that it is governed differently, as the use of unconventional instruments has overwhelmed the use of the conventional ones.

On the other hand, policies in the fields of defence, public order and international relations have always been carried out by invoking the national interest, but on account of their economic relapses and by favouring specific private interests. The last innovation is that the state's official mission has become to encourage private profits and to promote the opportunity to obtain them. The state legitimates itself without reserve as a service structure for private interests. It is in the light of

---

18 Peter Evans, 'The Eclipse of the State? Reflections on Stateness in an Era of Globalization', *World Politics* 50(1), 1997, 62–87. According to Evans, the most successful cases of growth in the new globalised economy – in the Far East for example – were those where the public powers turned out better able to support society and local economies. See, for example, also the doubts raised and the observations made by Wolfgang C. Müller, Vincent Wright (eds.) *The State in Western Europe: Retreat or Redefinition?* (London, Frank Cass, 1994).

19 Pierre Lascoumes, Patrick Le Galés, 'Introduction: Understanding Public Policy through Its Instruments. From the Nature of Instruments to the Sociology of Public Policy Instrumentation', *Governance: An International Journal of Policy, Administration, and Institutions* 20(1), 2007, 1–21.

this official mission that we must interpret the conferral, albeit partial, in addition to the running of transport, healthcare, territory, environment and so on, even of some of the state's sovereign functions to private operators. Why privatise prisons, use contractors in war zones, private security agencies to protect banks, shopping centres and wealthy residential areas, and the many forms of private conciliation, if not to make profitable all spheres of state action previously defined as unproductive?

At the same time, the privatisation of public services has not prevented their strengthening. The labour market has been liberalised and the state no longer supports employment. But when workfare substitutes welfare, calling on the unemployed to stop being unemployed can be rather more demanding than providing previous forms of income maintenance. Workfare requires committed state measures and very substantial organisational and financial investments to prepare adequate social shock absorbers, or to reconcile the offer of labour with the needs of enterprises, or to retrain workers to cope with technological development.

We should not forget also that in recent decades the prison population has grown out of all proportion, and that public expenditure on security has also increased enormously. Replacing a sizeable quota of the welfare state with the 'police state', even if the latter is privatised, is not necessarily a low-cost solution.[20]

Yet, another accusation directed at the welfare state was that it invaded the lives of its citizens by tying them up in red tape and by forcing an uninterrupted series of inroads into institutions – from maternity wards, to schools, hospitals, the workplace, chambers of commerce, and so forth – each ratified by certificates, performance reports, medical prescriptions, licences, authorisations, fines, salaries, taxes and pensions. None of this has been cancelled, and we should note the renewed vigour of a very old instrument like law.

Law is asked to regulate the most disparate issues, consequently multiplying the apparatus and procedures of application of norms and control: from car production to the manufacture of dairy products, from traffic to the installation of domestic electrical plants, from the freedom to smoke in public places to the display of products on supermarket shelves, from the prescription and sale of medicines to waste disposal, from fire prevention to the co-ownership of housing. The list is very long. The state regulates the protection of privacy, the right to exhibit religious symbols and even death and dying in meticulous detail, the latter despite the fact that it is publicly acknowledged that each person should be free to dispose of their end-of-life as they choose.

---

20 On the US obsession with security and its European imitations, see Loïc Wacquant, *Les prisons de la misère* (Paris, Raisons d'agir, 1999, and *Punishing the Poor: The Neoliberal Government of Social Insecurity* (Durham, Duke University Press, 2009). Wacquant proposes an effective dilemma (untranslatable without losing the assonance), l'*état pénitence* against l'*état providence*. A classic work is David Garland's, *The Culture of Control: Crime and Social Order in Contemporary Society* (Chicago IL, University of Chicago Press, 2001).

The regulative redrawing of stateness is thus accompanied by a striking inflation in the number of rules and in the expansion of judicial intervention. 'Juridification' is the offspring of 'constitutional democracy' and basic rights, but also depends on other factors.[21] Granted that in many cases juridification corresponds to a symmetrical phenomena of de-juridification, albeit more contained, neither are imaginable without the state. The pyramid of the state may have lost its exclusive right to emit norms, the latter are no longer hierarchically ordered and now spring from a pluralistic and gridlike constellation of public and private normative sources, but similar developments still occur under the *aegis* of the state.[22]

The regulatory agencies, that define the standards, certify quality, attribute ratings, draw up statistics, classifications and percentages have often a purely privatistic nature. But their mandate to operate is dictated by state authority. Thus, it is always the latter that indicates the objectives of public policies and orders courses of action.[23] In reality, what we call the state also intervenes when it contracts out, and also intervenes a great deal when it decides to refrain. Finally, we should not forget that the norms that it enacted in its mythical and sovereign past were also systematically negotiated. The state has always operated in terms of 'command and control' much less than what the rhetoric of sovereignty would claim.[24]

Today another and very well advertised instrument of 'indirect government', beside the market, is so-called civil society. To what extent should we consider it an entity totally independent of the state, especially when it takes the form of 'no-profit', 'third sector', or 'associations'? How much is it just a way of making the state by other means, including welfare, where the state makes provision for the regulation, organisation and the supply of financial support through its most traditional instruments?[25]

---

21 In 'Mapping Juridification', *European Journal of Law* 14(1), 2008, 36–54, Lars Ch. Blichner and Anders Molander distinguish five dimensions of 'juridification'. The first dimension is where there is a multiplication of constitutional type norms. The second dimension consists of the expansion and differentiation of legislation. The third is increased conflict solving through legislation. The fourth is the growth of judicial power. The fifth, and last dimension, consists of the growing tendency of social actors, individuals and groups, to understand themselves and their relations from a legal perspective. Where politics once wove common identities there now appear holders of rights, who aim to protect themselves through those same rights.

22 François Ost, Michel van de Kerchove, *De la pyramide au réseau ? Pour une théorie dialectique du droit* (Bruxelles, Publication des Facultés universitaires Saint-Louis, 2002).

23 For a comparative review of this argument see the essay in Béatrice Hibou (ed.), *Privatizing the State* (New York, Columbia University Press, 2004).

24 Donald F. Kettl, 'The Transformation of Governance: Globalization, Devolution, and the Role of Government', *Public Administration Review* 60(6), 2000, 488–497. See also Béatrice Hibou, *Privatizing the State*. See in particular the essay by the editor: 'From Privatizing the Economy to Privatizing the State: An Analysis of the Continual Formation of the State'.

25 The subtle critical notes, in the framework of a broader and persuasive reflection on welfare and

Furthermore, the supranational institutions of government that would have expropriated the state stick to the revised model of stateness. They do not always manage, owing to the 'egoism' of the individual states. But the EU aims to replicate the features elaborated by Western stateness of the last two centuries. The democratic legitimacy that upholds the EU government institutions is modest, and it lacks representative institutions comparable to the national equivalents. The EU however has a central bank and in various decision-making spheres disposes of a normative power able to bind its member states, enterprises and the life of its citizens.[26] The fact that one of the major themes of the moment, and a very lucrative research topic for social scientists, is how to rouse a shared identity among the citizens of the EU – comparable to national identity – is certainly not insignificant.

The reforms of the state *ab initio* were not by chance accompanied by a revival of the symbolic dimension of stateness. It was Thatcherism that proclaimed and sparked off the inversion of the trend. Thatcherism accompanied policies of state reform with a massive symbolic and cultural offensive, intended to valorise not only the individual and the market, but also discipline, the family and traditional values, public authority, the nation and national pride.[27] The same can be said of Reagan. Not only family, faith, work and freedom were the values he proclaimed, but the meaning of the battle he engaged against the 'empire of evil' was congruent with these values. The phenomenon has been accentuated over time. Are we sure that there isn't any relation between the current rather vigorous revival of the old national and nationalist symbolism, and the pretended retreat of the state?

In conclusion, the scope of state activities has not shrunk, but has even become broader, even if we lack the synthetic indicators to measure stateness and to compare its progress in the various national contexts. If we limit ourselves to considering the state as government apparatus, the most reliable indicator, albeit rather approximate, is public expenditure. In recent decades it has not been reduced, but has stabilised and been redirected.[28] It is not much, but it is something to confirm how the withdrawal of the state and the discovery of the non-state – be

---

its transformations, of Ota De Leonardis, *In un diverso welfare: sogni e incubi* (Milan, Feltrinelli, 1998). David Runciman raises the point in the conclusions to his book, *Pluralism and the Personality of the State.*

26 Richard Bellamy, 'Still in Deficit: Rights, Regulation, and Democracy in the EU', *European Law Review* 12(6), 2006, 725–742. See also the peremptory observations of Luigi Ferrajoli in 'Past and Future of Rule of Law', in Pietro Costa, Danilo Zolo (eds.), *The Rule of Law: History, Theory and Criticism* (Dordrecht, Springer, 2007, pp. 338–341).

27 Andrew Gamble, *The Free Economy and the Strong State: The Politics of Thatcherism* (Durham, Duke University Press, 1988).

28 Among the first is Richard Rose, *Understanding Big Government: The Programme Approach* (London, Sage, 1984). See also Clem Brooks, Jeff Manza, *Why Welfare States Persist*, pp. 68–73. For a comparative reading stressing restructuring rather than reorganisation, also in terms of costs, see François-Xavier Merrien, Raphaël Parchet, Antoine Kernen, *L'Etat social: une perspective internationale* (Paris, Colin, 2005).

it market, civil society, governance, etc. – conceals, together with a lot of rhetoric, a great deal of method and even more government, organisation and rules than is generally admitted.

Depoliticisation and de-democratisation

Withdrawal or not, what has certainly changed is the way in which, in the light of conflicts and political struggles that have flared up around its action, the state is perceived and represented, and how it perceives and represents itself. The competition among political actors has among other things exhumed the old liberal bias against the interference of parties and has delegitimised, together with the state, what was for some decades its orientative principle, that is party government. The management of ever wider policy spheres has therefore been redistributed among agencies and non-partisan institutions and removed from elected institutions. Other competences have been pushed upwards, towards the supranational institutions. Yet others have been pushed towards the bottom, towards local government, or assigned to civil society. In turn, the implementation of the doctrine of New Public Management has installed managers where there were once bureaucrats, with the promise of an autonomous public administration, free of partisan interferences.

Defining the innovations in question with the term 'depoliticisation' is appropriate, albeit impressionistic.[29] Despite efforts to disguise it, the caustic criticisms of the state that prepared the readjustment of the stateness are still very vigorous and loaded with political meanings and effects. state reforms are policies in their own right, and have their own political value, as do the different dosages of the instruments of government, the privatisation of public services and the new hierarchies instituted in democratic polities between the executive and the legislative power. In the same way the ceding of important competences to the supranational authorities has major political effects. This is particularly evident in the case of policies transferred to the EU institutions by its member states.

In order to circumvent their inability to take unpopular decisions, the national authorities encourage public opinion to see them with their hands tied. Thus, on the one hand, the national authorities attribute responsibility for these decisions to the European authorities. On the other hand, even in the anti-European reactions of national public opinion, they find supplementary resources to negotiate with the other states and with the authorities of the EU.[30]

The measures to readjust public expenditure, the reorganisation of the welfare state, the privatisation of public firms and public services, and the deregulation of the labour market, have found incontrovertible arguments in the need for

---

29 Colin Hay, *Why We Hate Politics?* (Cambridge, Polity Press, 2007, p. 82).

30 Klaus Dieter Wolf, 'The New Raison d'Etat, as a Problem for Democracy in World Society', *European Journal of International Relations* 5(3), 1999, 333–363.

greater efficiency and cost-reduction, and in the recommendations from time to time given by authorities, all well immunised against electoral consensus, such as the European Commission, but also the World Bank, the IMF and private rating agencies.

The same script contains a second move, the multiplication of non-representative regulatory agencies, not bound by the majority principle. Previously, the basic and politically neutral authorities were the central banks and the judiciary. More recently a line-up of new non-majoritarian institutions, or unelected bodies, has gained a footing in all democratic regimes and operates above them, carrying out tasks of regulation, vigilance and policy-making. Once again, the superiority of the technical competence of these institutions is considered preferable to the incompetence and bad habits of elected politicians. The intent is to renew the separation of powers by making a clear distinction between 'professional judgements based on knowledge' and 'political judgements that bring to bear outside values and principles on that knowledge'.[31]

A third, and no less committed move, has been the depoliticisation of the functioning of public administrations. Promising to reduce waste and to recuperate otherwise unobtainable efficiency, states have made recourse to the brand-new doctrine of New Public Management. This doctrine is in line with the neo-liberal critique of the public sector, and its aim is to introduce market values, to simulate competitive instruments and to apply private efficiency criteria to the running of public administrations.[32]

Based on rational choice and on the theory that the chief aim of bureaucrats is to maximise their own utility,[33] the first element of New Public Management has been to dismember administrations and services which had remained public and to convert them into a conglomerate of competing agencies, making their heads responsible for the delivery of services. As the latter become managers, the administration is freed from having to respect the bureaucratic rules, but is now bound to produce results. Citizens have been re-baptised users, and taxpayers, who support the financial burden of the public services, are therefore called to evaluate their performance.

---

31 Frank Vibert, *The Rise of the Unelected. Democracy and the New Separation of Powers* (Cambridge, Cambridge University Press, 2007, p. 199). See also, Mark Thatcher and Alec Stone Sweet, 'Theory and Practice of Delegation to Non-Majoritarian Institutions', *West European Politics* 25(1), 2002, 1–22. The issue is dedicated to this argument. For a general review see Fabrizio Gilardi, *Delegation in the Regulatory State: Independent Regulatory Agencies in Western Europe* (Cheltenham, Edward Elgar, 2008).

32 Among the first to illustrate the new doctrine were David Osborne and Ted Gaebler, *Reinventing Government: How the Entrepreneurial Spirit is Transforming the Public Sector*.

33 Even if rational choice has not always shared this point of view, an influential work was that of William A. Niskanen, *Bureaucracy and Representative Government* (Chicago IL, Aldine Atherton, 1971).

According to the theory, this would automatically cut any link of dependency between the public administration and politics. Elected politicians keep the task of setting objectives and providing budget lines to managers, while 'scientific' techniques to measure costs and evaluate results and user satisfaction would replace the precedent and inadequate forms of political and legal control.[34]

New Public Management is applied differently across countries, but to what extent have the reforms inspired by this doctrine delivered their promised effects? The ambition of those promoting the reforms was to reduce costs and to streamline, simplify and update the central and peripheral bureaucracies. But are the outcomes convincing? The reforms have totally discredited and humiliated the public administration and its personnel, among other things destabilising employment relations. This is a problem because the prevalent organisational form is still the public bureaucracy, and the functionality of the public sector still depends on this. Moreover, the issue of cost-cutting is extremely controversial.

In third place, the declared decoupling of the public administrations from partisan politics does not seem to have been maintained, granted that the idea of a depoliticised administration only implies a different form of political direction. If we consider the relations with the politico-electoral sphere, even with substantial national differences, what we observe is instead a complex movement – depoliticisation and repoliticisation at the same time.

In one of his best known works Weber states that '[I]n a modern state, real rule, which becomes effective in everyday life neither through parliamentary speeches, nor through the proclamations of monarchs, but through the day-to-day management of the administration, necessarily and inevitably lies in the hands of officialdom, both military and civilian'.[35] Specialised training, hierarchy of authority, calculable rules and impersonality, but also *ésprit de corps*, are the devices that made the public administration a *de facto*, but crucial, political actor. It was not known as such, but nevertheless it did stand in the front line, in spite of the conditioning which it suffered at the hands of elected politicians with colonising claims. The dimensional growth and functional articulation connected to the advent of welfare had changed stateness, but not weakened the public administration as a political actor. Even if partisan politics were used to boost their influence, not only had the competence of bureaucracy grown, but also the army of public-sector employees had become electorally relevant.

Thanks to the New Public Management, to deprive the public administration of its intrinsic Weberian political role, managerial logic, budgetary endowments,

---

34 For a general presentation that focuses on the non-secondary national variants in the application of the theory see Christopher Pollitt, Geert Bouckaert, *Public Management Reform: A Comparative Analysis* (Oxford, Oxford University Press, 2004).

35 Max Weber, 'Parliament and Government in Germany Under a New Political Order', in Peter Lassmann and Ronald Speirs (eds.), *Max Weber: Political Writings* (Cambridge, Cambridge University Press, [1918] 1994, p. 145).

objectives and delivery standards have been introduced, freeing it at the same time from the interference of parliament and parties. This step has nevertheless been balanced by a second one of surreptitious re-politicisation. The political role of Weberian bureaucracy has been negated, but in compensation it is now the executive power that dictates management objectives, that recruits according to criteria based on trust, and that monitors the results, projecting its own political orientations.[36]

Moreover, once public administration had been removed from the influence of a great part of the elected politicians, the area where political pressures had originated was tightened up. But this even helped to strengthen such pressures by breaking down old barriers – the monopoly of procedures and respect for the norms – that protected, albeit imperfectly, the old Weberian bureaucracies. On the one hand, public administration managers are often recruited in the private sector, also because this helps political authorities deal with one or other specific organised interest. On the other hand, the contextual weakening of party government finally deprived public administration of a precious counterweight to such interests.[37]

Reducing wastage and boosting efficiency is a commendable ambition, but the most certain impact of the reforms that hit the public administration has been the dismissal or subjection of top bureaucrats most linked to the welfare state, and the progressive erosion of another component of the pro-welfare constituency, that is, the public sector employees. Stripped of all prestige, it has been dismembered among different agencies and between a huge multiplicity of contractual, and often precarious, figures.

It is not even certain that substituting the principle of legality with the principle of results has guaranteed appreciable earnings in terms of efficiency. In the same way, it is not certain that the radical delegitimation and removal of public interests to the benefit of typical market efficiency has produced advantages. Historical research confirms that bureaucracies have never been the 'universal class' imagined by Hegel and have always been conditioned by external pressures. At the

---

36 An authoritative scholar of American politics recalls that the constitution of a professional bureaucracy, able to wield power and expertise and with an *ésprit de corps* to counter the discretionality of politics, has been long considered a vital instrument in combating administrative and political corruption and moralising public life and electoral competition in the USA. See Martin Shefter, *Political Parties and the State*. Today it seems to be obvious, exactly the opposite. Public bureaucracies are no longer a restraint, but stimulate politics to increase public spending and no longer exert a moralising influence. That is why it is better to disperse bureaucracies and to substitute them with New Public Management.

37 For a comparative review of the reforms of the public administration, which analyses the ambiguous political implications and stresses the substantial national specificity, see Ezra N. Suleiman in *Dismantling Democratic States* (Princeton NJ, Princeton University Press, 2003). See also the general remarks in Philippe Bézes, 'Construire des bureaucraties wébériennes à l'ère du New Public Management?', *Critique internationale* 35(2), 2007, 9–29.

same time, even the most reputable traditional public administrations were much less rational, efficient and centralist than the Weberian ideal-type. Nevertheless, the *milieux* from which civil servants came, or were trained were not without influence, and the values which circulated in them and their self-representation as a public service, were a discrete resource to spend against political and non-political interference. Some bureaucracies were more conscious and more resistant than others, but in any case their consciousness and resistance has been discredited among other things by assessment procedures whose fundamental concern is the number of practices dealt with in the briefest possible time and the reduction of costs.

The entrepreneurial turn has meant a frenetic activity of defining objectives, drawing up programmes, collecting data and information, drafting strategic reports and white papers, planning, accounts, codes of conduct, as well as the meticulous regulation of user rights and relations with the public. There is a continual setting up and streamlining, with quality standards, benchmarks and 'good practices' to respect. National and international rankings have become very fashionable. Health systems, legal systems, secondary and tertiary education,[38] research institutions and local administrations are all measured and ranked, and each ranking corresponds to an evaluation, often preceded by a protracted process of certification.

This does not always correspond to the goal. Moreover, certifying and ranking require new, bureaucratic and costly agencies and complex procedures.[39] Now an enormous, tentacled and expensive bureaucracy of professional training, consultancy, inspection, transparency, is inextricably wound around the public administration. In part it developed within it, and in part it helps feed a vigorous and costly sphere of external entrepreneurial initiative.[40]

The depoliticisation of stateness is not limited to this. Another very important manoeuvre is so-called devolution. Inspired theoretically by Hayek and other neo-liberal economists, 'New Federalism' was launched in great style by Reaganism. It

---

38 A careful examination on these procedures applied to research and university teaching in Isabelle Bruno, *À vos marques, prêts cherchez ! La stratégie européenne de Lisbonne, vers un marché de la recherche* (Bellecombe-en-Bauges, Éditions du Croquant, 2008). For a reflection on measurement procedures applied to courts and on the philosophy inspiring them, see instead Antoine Garapon, *La raison du moindre État. Le néolibéralisme et la justice* (Paris, Jacob, 2010).

39 On the costly and uncertain control of performance procedures, see the brilliant reflection of Béatrice Hibou, *La bureaucratisation du monde à l'ère néolibérale* (Paris, La Découverte, 2012)..

40 It is not at all certain whether the competition among services – and freedom of choice for users – have produced satisfying results for customers. Take the case of education where only a limited part of the clientele is free to choose schools or universities that offer the best service. Primarily, because they are unable to evaluate the service offered, or because only circumscribed and privileged segments of the population manage to transfer their children from one school to another. Instead, the large part has been denied the right to enjoy an equally qualified service, apart from its territorial origins and social extraction.

predicted the inability of central administrations to adapt policies to local conditions and invited a strengthening of decentralised institutions of government, promising to draw governors closer to the governed and the supply of public services to the preferences and demands of citizens and enterprises. The new federalism stated that local government must become a responsible entrepreneur for itself in the same way that individuals must become responsible entrepreneurs of themselves. This was the official account and it only just concealed a less visible, but politically more salient intention: to dismember the bureaucracies created in the wake of Kennedy's and Johnson's ambitious welfare programmes, and which constituted a powerful electoral weapon for the Democratic Party.[41]

In reality by the late 1960s local movements had begun to raise the theme of local identity: from Quebec to Scotland, from Corsica to Giura, and from Flanders to Catalonia. Fifteen years later, when the theme of globalisation began to condition the representations of stateness, the federalist perspective was placed enthusiastically on the agenda in Europe.[42] The *patria* of democracy, the USA, is federal, the ultra democratic Switzerland is federal, Germany is federal and Spain, reborn to democracy, is almost federal. How can we negate the valuable democratic meaning of federalism, that incidentally proved useful in relieving the political leadership of its committed and burdensome responsibilities, apart from encouraging the territories to take advantage of each other by offering appealing conditions to economic operators?

The finishing touch for federalism was the triumphant reception of the 'subsidiarity' principle.[43] This held that decentralised institutions of government, firms, associations, families and religious communities are, for some mysterious reason, less artificial than the state. Therefore it encourages them to take action wherever they are able to do so. The direct intervention of the state is thus only legitimate in case they are unable to function, and such an intervention would only be a complement, that is, subsidiary. If anything, the state is responsible for promoting the competence of these agencies, spurring them on to collaborate among themselves and to become involved in the concertation and self-government

---

41 See Matthew Crenson, Benjamin Ginsberg, *Downsizing Democracy: How America Sidelined its Citizens and Privatized its Public* (Baltimore MD, Johns Hopkins University Press, 2002, pp. 84–89). See also Timothy Conlan, *From New Federalism to Devolution: Twenty-Five Years of Intergovernmental Reform* (Washington, Brookings Institution Press, 1988).

42 Reaganism and Thatcherism differ in this respect. The latter was rigorously centralist. In fact, this followed the weakening of local government, whose rehabilitation is later promoted by New Labour, whose communitarianism helped legitimate the policies of devolution in Scotland and Wales.

43 The principle of subsidiarity has also been hosted with all the honours in a document with a constitutional breadth, the Lisbon Treaty of 13 December 2007. For a synthetic presentation see Antoine Mégie, 'Subsidiarity', in Mark Bevir (ed.), *Encyclopedia of Governance* (London, Sage, 2007).

practices among the public and private interests that constitute 'governance'. What is certain is that subsidiarity and privatisation are strictly related concepts and policies.

An additional advantage of such a rehabilitation of the local sphere seems to be its ability to soften partisan opposition.[44] With some assistance it also awakens traditions and community identity. It is rather approximate, but it appears that even this may function as a remedy against the disorientation attributed to the most feared challenger – globalisation.[45]

The promises are generous, but once again it remains to be seen how much these are maintained in practice. Federalist reforms have strengthened local government – together with many related discourses – and have helped carve out new social aggregations. Classes have been discarded and in their place we find territories, localisms, dialects. Village festivals, music, dance and customs, presumed popular, now replace party meetings and party gatherings. But there is a shortage of reliable evaluations of costs and the efficiency of such a change,[46] while there is no shortage of the accounts reporting not only that stateness has been dismembered, but that the way it functions has become increasingly complicated, and more permeable to private interests.

One of the unconfessed objectives of the greater decisional autonomy conceded to the local electoral authority is to limit it, contextually with the accompanying new fiscal responsibility. In a period when taxation has been undermined by a massive delegitimising offensive, moving fiscal choices nearer to citizens reduces the tax-raising capacity of local authorities, damaging the delivery of public services. How many local policy-makers are ready to introduce new taxes to be paid by their electors with whom they have more direct contact, and how many simply prefer to drop the services previously offered? It is difficult to establish. In any case, if federalism was invented a long time ago to overcome differences, it has recently become an instrument to divide: for istance the more prosperous and the more disadvantaged areas.

Finally, to what degree is decentralisation real and to what degree is it merely apparent? How much are local powers interested in decentralisation and how much do they maintain tight relations, perhaps not visible, with the national political authorities and central public administrations which may consider it expedient to interfere with the local sphere? There are also cases where decentralisation and

---

44 On such effects in the case of the USA, see Harry C. Boyte, 'Reframing Democracy: Governance, Civic Agency, and Politics', *Public Administration Review* 65(5), 2005, 536–546.

45 For a strong criticism of the redundant rhetoric of globalisation, its misinterpretation and its political instrumentalisation, see Jean-François Bayart, *Global Subjects. A Political Critique of Globalization* (Cambridge, Polity Press, 2007).

46 For a comparative balance see Norbert Kersting, Angelika Vetter (eds.), *Reforming Local Government in Europe. Closing the Gap between Democracy and Efficiency* (Opladen, Leske-Budrich, 2003).

the symbolism that accompanies it, make the governed more exigent and prompts them to present new claims, also towards the centre. In the local sphere the resistance of the governed may at times enjoy a degree of success that is denied at the national level, giving rise to new conflicts. This confirms how constraints and incentives do not operate unequivocally to the benefit of whoever institutes them.[47]

The governance against the state?

The other innovation that has redrawn stateness is what we now call 'governance'. It is not easy to say what governance is, although there is no shortage of explanations.[48] The confusion is first of all caused by the fact that the part absorbs the whole, especially in public discourse. The phoenix of governance having arisen from the ashes of the state and government, seems to take on the entire body of reforms considered until now, together with the last – to which the term is more precisely applied – that consists of the use of concerted, contractual and inclusive policy-making procedures.[49] Let us stick to this.

From both a descriptive and a normative viewpoint, governance promises to substitute the vertical authority of the sovereign state with the horizontal coordination among involved policy actors. Given the pluralist dispersion of

---

47 See the general remarks of Patrick Le Galès, *European Cities: Social Conflicts and Governance* (Oxford, Oxford University Press, 2002, pp. 186–195).

48 It would be interesting to reconstruct a genealogy of the concept. For a long time the term was used generically: in the Anglophone world 'governance' is not very different from 'government', although it tends to apply to traditional societies. A specific and frequent use is made with reference to schools, universities and public sector in general. There is much talk of governance for welfare services and local government. At the same time, the language of management and enterprises has used the concept 'corporate governance' with growing intensity from the 1980s. Hence governance began to substitute government in the literature on ungovernability and overload, but in a sporadic way until the mid-1990s. The same occurs in international relations, where the push was provided by Clinton's multilateral foreign policy, while in internal policy the propellant was New Labour's 'third way'.

49 For a general presentation, critical of the changes introduced through governance in democratic regimes, see Mark Bevir, *Democratic Governance* (Princeton NJ, Princeton University Press, 2010), and *Encyclopedia of Governance*. On the problems faced by the concept see also Bruno Jobert, 'Le mythe de la gouvernance dépolitisée', in Pierre Favre, Jack Hayward, Yves Schemeil (eds.), *Être gouverné, Études en l'honneur de Jean Leca* (Paris, Presses de Sciences Po, 2003); Silvano Belligni, 'Mrs Governance, I Presume', *Meridiana* 50–51, 2004, 181–209, Guy Hermet, 'Un régime à pluralisme limité? À propos de la gouvernance démocratique', *Revue française de science politique* 54(1), 2004, 159–178 and the reader by Guy Hermet, Ali Kazancigil, Jean-François Prud'homme (eds.), *La gouvernance. Un concept et ses applications*, Paris, Karthala, 2005; Claus Offe, 'Governance: An "Empty Signifier"?', *Constellations* 16(4), 2009, 550–562.

post-modern societies and polities, the vertical image of the state was considered obsolete,[50] as well as the aggregative and integrative action of political parties regarding interests. The remedy adopted is to rely on the strategic behaviour of actors, extending its application, through privatisation, marketisation and New Public Management, to running the public services. But all these solutions also have their drawbacks, so that, rather than unearthing big government with its bureaucratic hierarchies, governance is entrusted to networks, constituted by public administrations, private firms, entrepreneurial organisations, trade unions, professional and other associations, local committees, groups of experts and so forth. This last adjustment imposed on stateness is willing to involve also the policy recipients in the formulation and implementation of policy.[51]

Governance provides for the symbolic streamlining of public institutions, that combines with the organisational dispersion of New Public Management. On closer examination, however, the public authorities have always operated in a much more contractual mode than is claimed by the rhetoric of sovereignty. The practice of negotiation between the public sector and private actors is no less antique. Sovereignty is a symbol which immediately dissolves on contact with the practical articulations of state power and with a pluralism of interests. As to the technique of government by contract, it was already unofficial in the second half of the twentieth century through neo-corporate agreements, that flanked the representative and the decisional circuit, hinged on the citizens–parties–parliament–executive linkage. These agreements had a triangular character and were stipulated at the national level, conferring a prominent role on the public partner. Governance has innovated by extending and officialising the technique of consultation and negotiation, multiplying partners and placing public and private on the same level, and allowing citizens, as 'stakeholders', or bearers of interests and users of public services, or consumers, to have their say.[52] But here too, it is also a question of making the state by other means.

Governance has its own prestigious ancestors, in the shape of pluralistic theory in general – normative theory in the British tradition and the empirical theory of American political science. But currently governance is an idea and a practice that has been legitimated in a special way by the European Union. After having relinquished any federalist ambition, the EU limits itself to putting its policies to work in a form negotiated between the member states. In this way it tries to circumvent resistance by making a legitimate interlocutor out of every willing public and private agency. To this end a Commission White Paper has codified the principles and purpose of governance – civil society, dialogue, participation,

50 Oliver Williamson, *The Economic Institutions of Capitalism: Firms, Markets, Relational Contracting* (New York, Free Press, 1985).

51 Bevir, *Democratic Governance*.

52 Jean-Pierre Gaudin, *Gouverner par contrat. L'action publique en question* (Paris, Presses de SciencesPo, 1999).

empowerment, consensus, accountability, efficiency and coherence – thus elevating multi-level bargaining to a normative ideal.[53]

Governance is another term giving off a subtle democratic aroma, knowingly mixed with the efficiency-based language of management. Governance even functions well at the international level. In addition to the European Union, UN, World Bank, WTO, the regional associations among states and NGOs, all expect their reciprocal relations to be inspired by governance and insistently recommend its instruments to the governments of non-Western countries. Yet, governance has had no shortage of drawbacks or criticism.

Governance consists of networks of partners who negotiate and share their objectives and are open to stakeholders, or to whoever has interests at stake. But who decides which interests should be promoted? Can all those with a potential interest to protect be part of the concertation of governance? And how credible is the idea that all stakeholders are on a level of parity, or is it true that some count *a priori* more than others? Abundantly irrigated by the rhetoric of empowerment of citizenship and inclusivity, there is more than one reason to suspect that behind the friendly face of governance lurks a new and more subtle form of exclusion. Not only are citizens not all stakeholders, but there are also serious asymmetries of information and power among those that are. The institutions of governance are non-majoritarian and hence independent of any electoral mandate. Governance is therefore strongly suspected of being yet another complicated and underhand technique to reduce political pluralism and to increase depoliticisation,[54] paradoxically subject to politics. This is because it is political authorities that set up the negotiating tables, and it is political authorities that decide the issues to be negotiated and that recognise the partners of the negotiation, and we need to see how much the political authorities are absent from negotiations, case by case.

Understanding what happens in the real world is always difficult and requires empirical investigation. But in any case the concept of governance represents a way of conducting collective life which openly collides with the traditional unified and hierarchical image of the state, and with values such as public, or general, interest and the common good transcending particularistic interests. The general interest, we know, is a noble normative principle, but that each part evokes it always to its own advantage.[55] Nevertheless, by officially legitimating the fact

---

53 EU Commission, *European Governance. A White Paper* (Bruxelles, COM, 2001). For a detailed analysis see Didier Georgakakis, Marina de Lassalle (eds.), *La 'nouvelle gouvernance européenne': Genèses et usages politiques d'un livre blanc* (Strasbourg, Presses universitaires de Strasbourg, 2008).

54 Guy Hermet in 'Un régime à pluralisme limité', *Revue française de science politique* 54(1), 2004, 159–178, actually refers to governance as an instrument of a new 'liberal semi-authoritarianism'.

55 According to Hans Kelsen, the general interest is just a 'metaphysical, or even better, a metapolitical illusion', obscurely veined with organicism. See 'On the Essence and Value of Democracy' in Arthur Jacobson, Bernhard Schlink (eds.), *Weimar. A Jurisprudence of Crisis* (Berkeley, University of California Press, [1929] 2000, p. 93).

that partners only pursue their private interests, and that agencies that constitute the state are partners on the same level as others, governance risks sanctioning a symbolic and substantive re-feudalisation of collective life.

To conclude. Since all public policy is a power game, as are the reforms to reorganise and depoliticise stateness, there is a rather complicated headache to resolve: who wins and who loses from the reforms of stateness? There are many innovations and many actors, and it is not always easy to identify the line-ups in the field, also because they change depending on circumstances. There are professional politicians, entrepreneurs, public bureaucracies, trade union organisations, interest groups, elected local leaderships and others. The lines of division are not clear and we find professional politicians on both sides, entrepreneurs and intellectual advocates of restrictive or extensive interpretations, as well as there are public bureaucracies hostile to reforms and others that are keen to reconvert.[56]

We do not even know if, and to what degree, the promises to favour a more efficient allocation of resources to improve the quality of services, and to reward interests defined as more noble than others, have been kept: those of entrepreneurs, users, consumers, savers and taxpayers. It is quite evident that economic interests have certainly gained, and that their margins of discretion – and profit – have grown. However, not all entrepreneurs have profited, only some, for instance if we look at the Italian experience, not those operating in technologically more advanced sectors, but those who benefit more from the state's and politics' support. Finally, things have not gone too well for a large part of public service users either, with a very long line-up of losers.

There are also constellations of interests for which the attribution of advantages and disadvantages is less visible and more uncertain. This is the case of politicians as a professional category. Stateness has been realigned in order to remove broad portions of power from the state and from elected politicians and to transfer them to another sort of depoliticised politics: the politics of the independent regulatory agencies, central banks, experts, governance and market actors. This made way for a bitter – and crucial – game played between politicians, between those for whom new hierarchies and a new organisation of work have been instituted. It is this issue that will be dealt with in the next chapter.

---

56 For example, Bruno Théret sustains that the top echelons of the French administration have been ready to reconvert for at least three reasons. First because of the ideas circulating in the environments where people are trained (ENA and the Institut d'Etudes Politiques in Paris). Second, because the welfare state was often perceived more as a limit to state action than as a resource. Third, because deregulation is understood as an opportunity to set new rules. See Théret, 'Néo-libéralisme, inégalités sociales et politiques fiscales de droite et de gauche dans la France des années 1980. Identité et différences, pratiques et doctrines'. See also Théret 'Rhétorique économique et action politique. Le néo-libéralisme comme fracture entre la finance et le social', in Pascal Perrineau (ed.), *L'engagement politique. Déclin ou mutation* (Paris, Presses de la Fondation nationale des sciences politiques, 1994).

chapter six | on political parties

From mass-integration parties to catch-all parties

Organised democracy has also counted on a second basic pillar – political parties. Primarily, this meant representative institutions. Parties were collective agents, which symbolically and materially aggregated parts of the population around shared values and interests. In doing so, parties represented the parts they had aggregated, substituting the individual relations, typical of representation of the liberal age. This was one of the many serious reservations that liberalism had about parties.

A second argument at the time was that parties caused divisions which were prejudicial to the unity of the state and the broader collectivity.[1] A third argument instead was what Weber defined as the 'patronage of office'.[2] If the notables of the liberal age disposed of personal political capital, based on their personal prestige and wealth and by virtue of which they competed for elective office, the collective political capital of parties was accumulated and consolidated, among other things, by occupying public office and exploiting it to their own advantage. Understood as grounds for clientelistic practices and corruption, this is a polemical theme from which parties are not yet free.[3]

These criticisms were already directed at parties of notables, but the grounds for bias against mass parties is rather more serious. The socialist parties represented social groups, and pursued values, alien to the liberal regime. Moreover, if the socialists came to power, they would be accompanied by political recruits deemed incompatible with the established order. What made them particularly feared was the unknown weapon that they had introduced into the political struggle: the mobilisation of the big numbers, in the light of a common expectation on the future

---

1   This was one of Carl Schmitt's arguments: see *The Crisis of Parliamentary Democracy* (Cambridge MA, MIT Press, [1923] 1985).

2   Max Weber, 'Parliament and Government in Germany Under a New Political Order' in Peter Lassmann and Ronald Speirs (eds.), *Max Weber: Political Writings* (Cambridge, Cambridge University Press, [1918] 1994).

3   Naturally, the phenomenon appears in different forms. Martin Shefter's hypothesis is that what makes the difference is the existence or absence of professionalised public bureaucracies before the advent of parties, able to contrast the expectations of patronage and public office. See *Political Parties and the State: the American Historical Experience* (Princeton NJ, Princeton University Press, 1994, pp. 21–60).

state of the world. This was no longer a question of the blind violence of the great revolutions, but it was the formidable and organised threat of big numbers which could be used as an intimidating weapon in the political struggle, giving the opportunity, that mass demonstrations symbolised, to paralyse key aspects of collective life.

We have to wait for the end of World War II when politics – and theory – agreed with Max Weber's thesis. A quarter of a century earlier he had recognised in parties not a threat to social and political order, but a valuable instrument to reinforce and to constitute that order, by disciplining conflict and neutralising its effects. According to Weber, parties were the instrument best suited to avoid the much-feared 'street democracy'.[4] After the storm that had hit the nation-state in many countries, parties became the new protagonists of political life. It is true that although collective action had been cleansed of its violent component, the potential for disobedience held by parties, called into question the monopoly of force claimed by the state. But the experience of single party regimes, as well as the contribution in many European countries of parties to the resistance movements, had legitimated them as well as their pluralism, inviting their recognition as prized intermediate bodies, and even as a precious tool in restoring the authority of the state.[5]

Another serious indictment against parties had been that they challenged not only individual representation, but also the role of representative assemblies as the legitimate arena of political decision-making.[6] Yet, in Germany, Italy, France and Spain, parties and party government were recognised by postwar constitutions, and were also legitimated through the theory of representation.[7] If parties conditioned official political representation concentrated in parliament, one has to admit that they updated the forms of representation.[8] Here too the indictment was archived.

---

4 Max Weber, 'Parliament and Government in Germany Under a New Political Order'.

5 Maurice Duverger was among the first to sanction this development theoretically in *Political Parties: Their Organization and Activity in the Modern State* (New York, Wiley, [1951] 1964).

6 Once again Carl Schmitt, *The Crisis of Parliamentary Democracy.*

7 A good example is that of the German jurist, Gerhard Leibholz, who, in the period immediately following the end of World War I had taken a critical position on parties similar to that of his teacher, Carl Schmitt, and then in the period following World War II, he became a member of the Constitutional Court in Bonn, ruled in favour of the constitutional recognition of parties, claiming that 'they only reunite the electors in groups capable of acting politically .... Without their acting as intermediaries the people would not be absolutely able to exercise a political influence on state affairs, and would not manage then to realise themselves in the political sphere', making democracy unrealisable. See *Das Wesen der Repräsentation und der Gestaltwandel der Demokratie im 20. Jahrhundert* (Berlin, de Gruyter, 1960, p. 225).

8 Didier Mineur, *Archéologie de la représentation politique : Structure et fondement d'une crise* (Paris, Presses de SciencesPo, 2010, pp. 186–198).

Thanks to political parties, representation was stabilised. Not only had they helped to confer political unity to heterogeneous territorial situations and interests, but representation's time limit became much longer than the elective mandate. Parties created long-lasting affiliations for both their political personnel and for electors and the latter, even if incompetent, were credited with a stable opinion over time. It is true that mass parties divided up society, but they also recomposed large segments of it, whose juxtaposition also had a stabilising effect – the construction of classes was largely their work. Finally, by instigating and reorganising opinions and interests on a vast scale, parties helped direct public debate and offered powerful legitimating support to policies adopted by parliament and the executive.

In conclusion, parties were powerful instruments of government. It was the sectors of society least well provided with extra political resources, hence the popular classes, which benefited in a special way from the representative action of parties, and in relation to which, parties also produced effects of sociological aggregation and social integration.[9] We can argue that, being parties political enterprises, the mobilisation of the popular classes served the ambitions of power for their leaders. But at the same time this occurred by educating, informing and protecting individuals, compensating for their political incompetence, stimulating bonds of horizontal solidarity among them and accompanying them into the labyrinth of universal suffrage. Mass parties even invented the first forms of social protection. From the perspective of the government of society the contribution of parties was decisive.

As if this were not enough, parties ran election campaigns, directed government programmes and recruited candidates and elected personnel: if the interchangeable nature of governors and governed is one of the fundamental promises of democracy, it is not irrelevant that parties provided aspiring politicians with a collective political capital, that was competitive with respect to wealth and social prestige.[10]

Mass parties counted millions of members, revitalised society with their machines, offered robust ideological reassurances to their own base, provided reliable associative services, and even aspired to include all of society. Parties worked in different ways, conditioned by electoral regimes, the institutional architecture, the form of the state and their political and cultural options, but they aimed to coordinate all other forms of associationism. First, the trade unions, with which socialist

---

9   Günther Roth, *The Social Democrats in Imperial Germany. A Study in Working-Class Isolation and National Integration* (Totowa, Bedminster Press, 1963).

10 On the concept of political capital, see Pierre Bourdieu, 'Political Representation. Elements of a Theory of the Political Field', in Bourdieu, *Language and Symbolic Power* (Cambridge MA, Harvard University Press, 1991). On collective political capital as an alternative to personal political capital, see Daniel Gaxie, *La démocratie représentative* (Paris, Montchretien, 2004), and Michel Offerlé, *Les partis politiques* (Paris, Puf, 2002).

and communist parties often set up a complex yet efficient division of labour, but then, also, cooperatives, sporting societies and specialised organisations for women, young people, pensioners and leisure, etc. Beyond this, little else remained: churches and religious associations – which nevertheless had robust links with the confessional parties – and entrepreneurial organisations, whose links with parties were weaker and more discontinuous, but not inexistent.

In the mid-1950s it was a veteran of the Weimar period, who in the 1920s was a member of the Social Democratic Party and who had spent the years of nazism overseas and experienced the practice of American parties, who first announced the changes taking place in European parties. In Otto Kirchheimer's reconstruction, economic development not only levelled out the most strident inequalities in society, but also corroded the social background of socialist parties. Thanks to the growth of the public and private tertiary sector, the middle classes expanded by attracting the more professionally qualified parts of the working classes. Equally relevant changes occurred at the level of political culture, as the secularisation produced by material well-being eroded ideologies. Once the long-standing prejudices against them were declining, the socialist parties could make access to government a priority. This had several consequences: they renewed their programmes; recognised the market economy, tempered by the presence of the welfare state; and deactivated their collective mobilisation potential to compete with moderate, conservative and confessional parties on purely electoral grounds.

According to Kirchheimer, it was also the recently discovered technologies, such as television, that encouraged parties to renew themselves and to extend their supply of representation beyond their traditional reference *milieux*.[11] For all these reasons, parties, or what another political scientist and Weimar emigré to America, Sigmund Neumann, had called 'mass-integration' parties,[12] became 'catch-all parties' for Kirchheimer in an essay published in the late 1960s.[13] The term has caused some misunderstanding, alien to the idea of its inventor. For Kirchheimer 'catch-all' did not mean that parties moved around the political market without restrictions. Indeed, no party had abandoned its original electoral catchment area, or acquired a new one to replace it. At most, parties worked to extend it. With the

11 Otto Kirchheimer, 'Party Structure and Mass Democracy in Europe', now in Frederic S. Burin, Kurt Shell (eds.), *Politics, Law and Social Change: Selected Essays of Otto Kirchheimer* (New York, Columbia University Press 1969). A presentation of Kirchheimer's complex formulation, which lasted over a decade, is in Andre Krouwel, 'Otto Kirchheimer and the Catch-All Party', *West European Politics* 26(2), 2003, 23–40.

12 Siegmund Neumann, 'Toward a Comparative Study of Political Parties', in Neumann, (ed.), *Modern Political Parties: Approaches to Comparative Politics* (Chicago IL, University of Chicago Press, 1956).

13 Otto Kirchheimer, 'The Transformation of the Western European Party System', now in Frederic S. Burin, Kurt Shell (eds.), *Politics, Law and Social Change: Selected Essays of Otto Kirchheimer* (New York, Columbia University Press 1969).

toning down of the social and political landscape, if anything, parties had made attempts to get segments of the electorate located at their edges, between themselves and competing parties. At the same time Kirchheimer stressed how parties were doing without the now superfluous integrative action and renewed their programmatic bid. Above all, the socialist parties tried to reassure the private sector and public bureaucracies of their intentions should they come to power.

According to Kirchheimer, the consequence was a major organisational and operational change. For socialist parties, redefining their own image meant doing without big numbers' active mobilisation to make themselves heard. When they finally reached the executive levels of national and local government, socialist parties profited from the resources offered by the public office occupied by them. But it was a rather less sudden revolution than what social science typologies suggest.

Among other things, while membership dropped and the party machine became more professionalised and narrowed, the decisional echelon of the parties was relocated within the national electoral representation, in parliament and, in case of electoral success, in government and its ministries. Once the role of the basic organs, the party machine, congresses and rites which cemented the collective sense of belonging, had been narrowed down, it was obvious that the weight of the elected would increase. At the same time, once their presence in the institutions had been reinforced, to the detriment of their presence in society, it was obvious that those elected nationally and locally would become the backbone of the party.

Finally, Kirchheimer argued that, on the symbolic level, leadership figures were becoming increasingly important. In many senses this personalisation is intrinsic to democratic regimes and is indeed the most elementary way to represent power. The modern state has made a great effort to free itself of personalisation, but without ever managing fully, and the life of parties has always been characterised by the figures of their leaders. Again in Weber's terms, parties are also born as machines to select political leaders.[14] In addition to overshadowing programmes and ideologies, another original characteristic of the catch-all party is that the national leadership figure became the pre-eminent instrument to mark the party's bid on the electoral market.

Parties as public utilities

One of Kirchheimer's basic concerns was the decline of political competition and the decline of the opposition, which he considered as a depoliticising effect dangerous for democracy's health.[15] This risk should have reassured the old

---

14 Weber actually described parties as places where plebiscitary, charismatic and demagogic leadership was created, and which he believed balanced out the rigidity of the 'iron cage' of bureaucracy. See 'Parliament and Government', pp. 230–231.

15 See, in particular, Otto Kirchheimer, 'The Waning of Opposition in Parliamentary Regimes', 1957,

adversaries of parties. Nevertheless, at the end of the 1950s, anti-party arguments took on new life, starting from Italy and France and recuperating classical themes from the pre-war critique.[16] The times and forms in which the controversy will manifest itself will differ from one country to another, as did the party systems and their relations with the state. The dispute has been long-lasting, aggressive or submissive by turns, but continues to this day. The themes invoked, albeit with different emphasis, were political stability, efficient government action and the morality of public life. In particular, there is the question of the intrusion of parties with regard to the public sector. Another controversial target were the parties themselves, which since then, have always been accused of too little internal transparency, oligarchic tendencies, scarce internal democracy, and closure towards the outside. It is in this context, but for other reasons, that in the 1970s, once the catch-all model was consolidated,[17] the introduction of public financing for political parties finally matured, on the initiative of the parties themselves.[18] The state funding of political parties was first proposed in the USA in the early twentieth century. Among the advanced European democracies, it was introduced in Germany in 1959 and soon after in Austria. It spread widely in the early 1970s.

There are two ways to tell this story. In the first, strong in the positions of advantage acquired alongside the state, parties agreed among themselves to draw the necessary financial resources from public budgets. This was a necessary adaptation to social change and to the change of the political struggle, but also a way to democratise and moralise public life. Organising ordinary citizens and convincing them to participate permanently in party life had become more difficult. In turn, this had reduced both the financial support offered by party members, and the free voluntary work of its militants. Public financing was also a remedy to the problem of illegal financing and the not disinterested support of lobbies and pressure groups.[19]

---

and 'Germany. The Vanishing Opposition', 1966, both now in Burin, Shell (eds.), *Politics, Law and Social Change,* 1969.

16   Two interesting examples are an Italian jurist and columnist who coined the term 'partitocracy': see Giuseppe Maranini, *Miti e realtà della democrazia* (Turin, Comunità, 1958), and in France, a good example of anti-party polemic is Michel Debré, *grand commis,* gaullist and long-standing figure in the political life of the Fifth Republic, in *Ces princes qui nous gouvernent* (Paris, Plon, 1957).

17   At that time Angelo Panebianco revisits Kirchheimer's themes in depth in *Political Parties: Organization and Power* (Cambridge, Cambridge University Press, 1988).

18   For an overview of the different forms of public financing of politics see Kevin Casas-Zamora, *Paying for Democracy: Political Finance and State Funding for Parties* (Colchester, ECPR Press, 2005).

19   This is, for example, the opinion of John Rawls in *Justice as Fairness: A Restatement* (Cambridge MA/London, Harvard University Press, 2001, p. 149).

According to the second narrative, the unconfessed intention of public financing was to guarantee, the already installed political actors, a comfortable survival protected from election outcomes and to make it more difficult for new political entries to the electoral market. Public financing would also be an instrument to reinforce the party leaderships to the detriment of the machine, making its action, as a collector of economic and organisational resources offered by militants and membership alike, superfluous. The two narratives are not mutually exclusive. Whatever the case, public financing induced changes suggesting a theoretical tune-up, provided by Richard Katz and Peter Mair, to whom political science is indebted for another successful party model, that of the 'cartel party'. This announces the accentuation of transformations described by Kirchheimer,[20] attributing them to public financing. Among other things public financing demolishes the incentives that induce parties to mobilise and take care of electors.[21]

Such a model is not without political importance. The mass parties emerged to challenge the state. When they reached maturity, not only party government took its reins, but it did not take too much time for the governing parties, and for their acknowledged opponents, to discourage new challengers, even instituting a new stake in the game. In addition to winning elections, today's parties compete to maintain their public financing. The theory of the cartel party, as with catch-all parties, reveals some regret by the parties that once proudly challenged the state and mobilized citizens.

We should obviously ask whether public financing was the only possible solution, and if in adopting it, parties have not given up other methods more in line with their own past. The fact is that, although parties have contracted their representative role, and of government of collective life, and are transformed into vote-seeker and office-seeker agencies, they still dominate the scene. Their evolution is comparable to, and synchronised with, that of large enterprises. In the transition from Fordism to post-Fordism, labour-intensive enterprises became capital-intensive and labour-saving enterprises. In the long run parties have become capital-intensive, thanks to their increased financial resources, and also leadership-intensive instead of membership-intensive.[22] Parties have even borrowed the technique of

---

20 Richard S. Katz, Peter Mair, (eds.), *How Parties Organize: Change and Adaptation in Party Organization in Western Democracies* (London, Sage, 1994) and Richard S. Katz, Peter Mair, 'Changing Models of Party Organization and Party Democracy', *Party Politics* 1(1) 1995, 5–28.

21 In reality this effect was long anticipated by the competition of public bureaucracies with parties. The more efficient they are, the less space remains for patronage, and hence for looking after electors. See Shefter, *Political Parties and the State*.

22 One of the characteristics of the cartel party is the decline of the party 'on the ground' and the pre-eminence of the party 'in public office': see Richard S. Katz and Peter Mair, 'The Ascendancy of the Party in Public Office: Party Organisational Change in Twentieth Century Democracies', in Richard P. Gunther, José R. Montero, Juan J. Linz (eds.), *Political Parties: Old Concepts and New Challenges* (Oxford, Oxford University Press, 2002, pp. 113–135). On declining membership, see

outsourcing from the post-Fordist enterprise. The activities of information-gathering, communication and propaganda are often assigned to professionals outside the party or to agencies specialised in electoral marketing. Moreover, the adoption of a managerial-style organisation, inspired by New Public Management and centred on leadership, is the rule in most of today's parties.[23] Parties seem also to withdraw from their traditional representative function. Policy-making depends always more from experts and policy control has been parcelled out to a plethora of agencies of certification and evaluation. In coherence with such premises, the latest metamorphosis of political parties seems to be the party 'in franchising'.[24]

There are two paradoxical effects that can be attributed to public financing. The first is that when democratic regimes enthusiastically offer sacrifices to the gods of competition, not only parties have been recognised as 'public utilities',[25] but even the most zealous parties officiating such sacrifices have protected themselves thanks to public financial support. The second paradox is that where public financing ratifies the definitive legitimation of parties – democratic regimes need parties so much that they transform them in public utilities – at the same time it creates the conditions of an aggravated delegitimation. Even if it is a policy measure intended to moralise public life, living at the cost of the state and on the backs of taxpayers has not improved the reputation of parties a great deal.

---

the data and arguments of Richard S. Katz, Peter Mair *et al.*, 'The Membership of Political Parties in European Democracies, 1960–1990', *European Journal of Political Research* 22(3), 1992, 329–345; Peter Mair, Ingrid van Biezen, 'Party Membership in Twenty European Democracies, 1980–2000', *Party Politics* 7(1), 2001, 5–21; Susan E. Scarrow, 'Parties without Members? Party Organization in a Changing Electoral Environment,' in Russell J. Dalton, Martin Wattenberg (eds.), *Parties without Partisans: Political Change in Advanced Industrial Democracies* (Oxford, Oxford University Press, 2000); Ingrid van Biezen, Peter Mair, Thomas Poguntke, 'Going, Going, . . . Gone? The Decline of Party Membership in Contemporary Europe', *European Journal of Political Research* 51(1) 2012, 24–56. For his part, Daniel Gaxie stresses and analyses the loss of attractiveness for militants of the causes pursued by parties and the correlative growth of interests for material benefits in 'Rétributions du militantisme et paradoxes de l'action collective', *Swiss Political Science Review* 11(1), 2005, 157–188.

23 Anne-Sophie Petitfils, 'L'institution partisane à l'épreuve du management. Rhétorique et pratiques managériales dans le recrutement des "nouveaux adhérents" de l'UMP', *Politix* 79(3), 2007, 53–76, and Philippe Aldrin, 'Si près, si loin du politique. L'univers professionnel des permanents socialistes à l'épreuve de la managérialisation', *Politix* 79(3), 2007, 25–52. See also, Florence Faucher-King, 'La "modernisation" du parti travailliste, 1994–2007. Succès et difficultés de l'importation du modèle entrepreneurial dans un parti politique', *Politix* 81(21), 2008, 125–150.

24 Kenneth R. Carty, 'Parties as Franchise Systems. The Stratarchical Organizational Imperative', *Party Politics'* 10, 2004, 5–24.

25 Ingrid van Biezen also offers empirical evidence in 'Political Parties as Public Utilities', *Party Politics* 10, 2004, 701–722.

The close relations established between parties and the state was first denounced by the critical left in the 1960s,[26] but recently the fact that they have evolved into public utilities, has become quite a persistent issue in public debate, albeit once again in rather paradoxical terms. On the one hand, parties are accused of being a very rigid filter in opposition to citizens, that is, they represent them too little, suffocating the will and voice of their principal. On the other hand, parties are still accused of representing citizens too much. Their electoral opportunism makes them disproportionately compliant towards the demands of electors and organised interests.

Can we in any case deny that parties have managed to have an almost total monopoly of public offices, to the detriment of other actors, such as firms, universities, interest organisations and associations? It follows that parties are also extremely vulnerable to the accusation of penalising merit and competence, and restraining the spontaneity and will of civil society. But let us be honest. From big organisations such as parties, how realistic is it to expect more democracy than what is required from other institutions? Yet, the lack of democracy in parties is a ritually repeated reproach, since at least the works of Ostrogorski and Michels at the turn of the twentieth century.[27]

Traditional mass parties were certainly based on a rather approximate practice of representative, or rather, delegated, democracy. In the territorial sections the membership used to interact with each other continuously and took part in party life, even if their influence was limited. Delegates were elected to congresses, but under the *aegis* of the party machine. Nevertheless party congresses were the scene of bitter discussions and clashes. Finally congresses elected a national assembly which was convened between one congress and another and nominated – and conditioned – a collegial party leadership. As a model of democracy this was certainly not perfect, even if it was not totally ineffective. But it is equally doubtful, that after its most recent changes, party democracy has really improved.

Not all parties have adopted the schema of the cartel party. The label is telling and suggests that we consider state funding policies and their implications. But each party adapted to these policies in its own way. If some appeared readier to free themselves of their past, others remained more attached to the schema of the conventional mass party, or at least tried to maintain it. There are still parties that provide services to citizens, perhaps indirectly, and it is not incidental that the competition to occupy public office in local government is so fierce. In addition to satisfying the demand for public office, local governments can be an excellent substitutive instrument of the old party machine, helping to root the parties in collective life.[28] What has been however upset, is the representative function of parties.

---

26 Antonio Negri, *Alcune riflessioni sullo "stato dei partiti"* (Milan, Feltrinelli, [1964] 1977).

27 Moises Ostrogorski, *Democracy and the Organization of Political Parties* (Garden City NY, Doubleday, [1902] 1964) and Robert Michels, *Political Parties: A Sociological Study of the Oligarchical Tendencies of Modern Democracy* (Cromwell-Collier Publishing Company, [1911] 1962).

28 Frédéric Sawicki, *Les réseaux du parti socialiste* (Paris, Belin, 1997). However, local government

Mass parties used to constitute their own electorate, and to take on its representation, aggregating composite constellations of interests, some directly represented by them, others with their own spokesperson, co-opted by parties. The more recent transformations of parties have meant even exhuming individualised forms of representation. Electors are no longer enrolled within a collective body that presents a request for representation. Instead, they are attracted individually, via the media, leaving policy-makers freer to negotiate with organised interests, preferring those with greater financial resources or more media visibility. On the other hand, this does not rule out the substantial revival of clientelistic and neo-patrimonial practices, encouraged by the opportunity for access to public offices.[29]

We said before that from the point of view of the electors the traditional mass parties presented themselves as associational spaces which could be collectively exploited. Section meetings, congresses, electoral manifestations, party celebrations were all occasions to interweave solidarity, and not just political solidarity. Combining the individualised mediatic appeal to vote with the effects of differentiation, induced by post-Fordism and postmaterialist culture, pluralism and associational life now tend to be rejected in the archipelago of civil society outside of parties. Nevertheless, from time to time, because subject to the pressures of their numerous critics and in homage to the rhetoric of citizens' empowerment, parties seem to be rethinking things. Promising greater transparency, they carry out campaigns to recruit members, organise meetings to collect sympathisers or primary elections, or activate some deliberative conference or promise to do so.[30] But, however frequent, it is a question of episodes, whose democratic effectiveness is extremely uncertain.

During the age of Progressivism in America, in the name of political morality, the destiny of parties was consigned to the primaries and to whoever financed them. In Europe this has not yet occurred, because primaries are rare and perhaps because European parties have not yet learnt how to use them effectively. But

---

is not the only instrument that parties use to establish their roots within society. For an exploration, raising interesting research questions, see the special issue on 'Ancrages politiques', *Politix* 92(23), 2011.

29 For confirmation of this see Simona Piattoni (ed.), *Clientelism, Interests and Democratic Representation. The European Experience in Historical and Comparative Perspective* (Cambridge, Cambridge University Press, 2001). See also Günther Roth, *Politische Herrschaft und persönliche Freiheit: Heidelberger Max Weber-Vorlesungen 1983* (Frankfurt a.M., Suhrkamp, 1987).

30 On these attempts see Jonathan Hopkin, 'Bringing the Members Back In? Democratizing Candidate Selection in Britain and Spain', *Party Politics* 7(3), 2001, 343–361. See also Patrick Seyd, 'New Parties/New Politics? A Case Study of the British Labour Party', *Party Politics* 5(3), 1999, 383–405. Still on Labour, see Patrick Seyd, Paul Whiteley, *New Labour's Grassroots: The Transformation of the Labour Party Membership* (New York, Palgrave, 2002). On the French case see Frédéric Sawicki, 'Les partis politiques comme entreprises culturelles', in Daniel Cefai (ed.), *Cultures politiques* (Paris, Puf, 2001).

if primaries, and other assimilable techniques, constitute homage to the rhetoric of democracy and transparency, it is doubtful that they are really conducive to involving electors and/or causing a permanent and robust reconciliation between them and parties. In Europe primaries are just an instrument used by party hierarchies and internal factions to get out of situations of *impasse*. The constellation of competing factions within the party cannot reach an agreement on leadership? Then primaries are a way to free the leadership of the bother, even if they are not enough to contrast the bad reputation of parties.

Nor has the reputation of parties been improved by the last transmigration of the public debate. In its time the public debate transmigrated from parliaments to parties, not without causing some scandal. The last transmigration of public debate seems to be to the 'infotainment' and talk-shows, where it has taken on a theatrical form.[31] But this cannot hide the fact that the debate continues in expert commissions, think-tanks, study centres and foundations, inside and outside the parties, where politicians may find a way to devise policies and foster relations with the organised interests in a much more confidential way.[32]

Media logic and personalisation

We cannot fully understand the striking changes that took place in political parties without considering another very important innovation, that is, the role of the media, and television in particular. In the USA a very attentive Kirchheimer saw the influence exercised by television well in advance. However, these were only early warnings. Since the end of the 1950s the role of television and the media evolved, expanding quantitatively and qualitatively. Before, parties used to interact with a minority of politically active citizens. Thanks to them, they tested the needs and moods of their potential voters and worked to shape a functional public opinion sympathetic to their objectives. In recent decades the media have supplanted them in this activity, competing to produce effects that it would however be wrong to attribute to them as such.

More than newspapers and radio, television communication is now the ordinary citizen's main source of information on politics and the state of the world in

---

31 Bernard Manin, *The Principles of Representative Government* (Cambridge, Cambridge University Press, 1995).

32 Foundations and study centres are often set up by politicians themselves, and is one of the first signs of leadership ambitions. See the case of Sarkozy in Joseph Confavreux, Jade Lindgaard, 'L'hémisphère droit. Comment la droite est devenue intelligente', *Mouvements* 4/52, 2007, 13–34. The experience of New Labour is also interesting: see Mark Wickham-Jones, 'Communautés épistémiques et évolution de la stratégie économique du Parti travailliste britannique', in Michel Camau, Gilles Massardier (eds.), *Democraties and autoritarismes: fragmentation et hybridation des regimes* (Aix-en-Provence, Karthala, 2009, pp. 305–528).

general. Thanks to television, politics has become much more visible. The drawback is the constant drive to increase the audience – especially in the case of commercial television which does not receive any support from the state. It is audience that pulls in the advertising, on which the budget and the destiny of the media depends. Because of the audience, politics is then subjected to entertainment constraints, urging the star-system consecration of political figures and making a show of all their actions. Sport, art and religion have changed, why cannot media logic change politics?[33]

In short, media logic expects politics to become a spellbinding show for its audience. To this end the media accelerate the rhythm of events, dictate a continuous stream of new issues, expect rapid responses in the form of simple and understandable summaries, pretend images that print themselves on the spectator's mind, as well as political personalities able to represent political competition and catch audience attention. The narrative of political life is thus permeated by tough gladiatorial stances, fights to the death, host of individual protagonists, spectacular scandals. Electoral campaign has even become 'permanent' and the electoral contest has become a 'horse race'. Candidate-centred competition occupies the scene and risks obscuring other, more relevant, elements, beginning with programmes, policy issues and interests, of which the current leaders and potential leaders are interpreters or spokespersons.

For a long time leaders have had to earn the trust and respect of their equals: other eminent figures in their own party, in allied parties or opponent parties. This trust was normally based on the leader's ability to persuade, mediate and organise consensus around himself. The trademark used was the party, with its vision of the world, its symbols, its programme, its history and the collegial image offered by its executive group. Thanks to television, the object to be persuaded is now the public directly, and it is to the public that the leader must orient himself. This is the personalisation of politics. To this end the leader has to stimulate and maintain media attention, to make himself recognisable among the other contenders, and above all, to make himself popular. In turn, the media press him, investigate and exhibit his private life, anticipate his political moves while urging parties to invest in political marketing, to concentrate on the personality of contenders, their supposed decision-making ability, their morality and their innovative potential.[34]

---

33   Ralph M. Negrine, *The Transformation of Political Communication: Continuities and Changes in Media and Politics* (Basingstoke, Palgrave Macmillan, 2008). See also Franca Roncarolo, *Leader e media. Campagna permanente e trasformazioni della politica in Italia* (Milan, Guerini, 2008). On media logic, see David L. Altheide, 'Media Logic and Political Communication', *Political Communication* 21(3), 2004, 293–296.

34   The phenomenon of personalisation was already being discussed in the 1960s: see Albert Mabileau, 'La personnalisation du pouvoir dans les gouvernements démocratiques', *Revue française de science politique* 10(1), 1960, 39–65. For a general review see Ian McAllister, 'The Personalization of Politics', in Russell J. Dalton, Hans-Dieter Klingemann (eds.), *The Oxford Handbook of*

According to Bernard Manin, the opinion polls are a valuable opportunity offered to citizens to express their own preferences.[35] We may have our doubts about this statement, but it is often the opinion polls, corroborated by their scientific and democratic reputation, and promptly publicised by the media, that finally dictate a leader's destiny.[36]

It remains to be seen how much this representation responds to reality. Certainly, the media are very influential. It is the media that generally communicate the actions and discourses of politicians. Media professionals take a very active part in political competition, represent it publicly, elaborate it and make their own politically relevant discourses, and even put forward opinions in competition with official politics. Once attention is placed on the candidates, the media condition his image and dictate the political agenda, often deciding which issues are salient and which are not. In addition to ensuring a favourable climate of opinion for one or other competitor, opinion poll, often commissioned by the media itself, are anxious to certify their results publicly. Yet, despite this, the media are not the exclusive protagonists of political life today.

Electors are less volatile than they seem[37] and, after all, their choice of vote still matures much more in local contexts, in the sphere of the family, in friendship networks, neighbourhood relations, and workplaces rather than in front of the television screen.[38] Parties and politicians know this and take it into account, paying significant attention to the context in which electors make their choice. Nevertheless, the centrality of the media is a narrative that suits many and is therefore extremely successful. It is better for the media and media professionals, who acquire influence with political actors. It is better for the opinion polls professionals who

Political Behavior (Oxford, Oxford University Press, 2007). For a broad comparative analysis see Jean Blondel, Jean-Louis Thibault, *Parties and Citizens. The Personalisation of Leadership* (London, Routledge, 2009). For the British case see Ana I. Langer, 'A Historical Exploration of the Personalisation of Politics in the Media: The British Prime Ministers 1945–1999', *Parliamentary Affairs* 60(3), 2007, 371–387.

35 Manin, *The Principles of Representative Government.*

36 On the presumed 'scientificity' of opinion polls see Pierre Bourdieu in *Distinction. A Social Critique of the Judgment of Taste* (Cambridge MA, Harvard University Press, 1984, pp. 397–465), and Patrick Champagne, *Faire l'opinion. Le nouveau jeu politique* (Paris, Éditions de Minuit, 1990) and Loïc Blondiaux, *La Fabrique de l'Opinion. Une histoire sociale des sondages* (Paris, Seuil, 1998).

37 Margaret Scammell, 'Citizen Consumers: Towards a New Marketing of Politics?' in John Corner, Dick Pels (eds.), *The Re-styling of Politics* (London, Sage, 2003). For an account based on research data see Lawrence R. Jacobs, Robert Y. Shapiro, *Politicians Don't Pander. Political Manipulation and the Loss of Democratic Responsiveness* (Chicago IL, Chicago University Press, 2000).

38 The theme of contextual effects is widely developed, analysing a vast range of experiences of research, by Céline Braconnier, *Une autre sociologie du vote. Les électeurs dans leurs contextes. Bilan critique et perspectives* (Cergy-Pontoise, Lextenso Éditions, 2010).

sell their merchandise to the media and to politicians. It is even better for civil society which profits from the exhibitions of its morality that the media set against the immorality of politics. But it suits politicians too.

Faced with the media, politics and politicians are not as vulnerable as is sometimes claimed. The media use them, but in return politicians have learnt to use the media too, as well as they use opinion polls, which allow them too not only to monitor, but also to orient, public opinion. The media appear before politicians armed with a formidable persuasive capacity and also help keep down the costs – organisational costs *in primis* – of popular mobilisation. Through the tribune of television, leaders can speak directly to electors, and only sporadically pay the price of appealing directly to the street, or some crowded assembly, whose political value is also determined by the media audience it manages to stir up.

A second reason why politicians have come to terms with media logic is the rhetoric of the elector–customer who chooses, depending on the political supply dear to the post-democratic paradigm, and which also conditions the behaviour of politicians. But even calculations of a more strictly political nature persuade politicians. Mediatised parties are the more than legitimate offspring of the preceding form of party, with its organisational difficulties and internal conflicts. In addressing the public directly, leaders downgrade and oppose the party machine, keep the circles of local notables at bay, and counter competing factions.

Indeed, media logic even conditions marginal actors, such as social movements and civil society. These mainly use other techniques, but if they are not exhibited in a mediatised manner then they are condemned to exclusion.[39] What politicians may not have foreseen were the implications of the personalisation of leadership, so convenient to the media. Politicians legitimated personalisation by amplifying the theme of leader's personal responsibility *vis-à-vis* membership, electors, the entire country. But personalisation, in addition to revolutionising the forms of political competition, might have questioned the entire equilibrium and functioning of democratic regimes. Procedural democracy has recently undergone some important revisions. Could it not be the way in which parties adapted to the media logic and, above all, to their preference for personal duels, that accounts for such a revision?

The constitutional rules have remained more or less unaltered, but have been often radically reinterpreted. Since the post-democratic paradigm recommended that democratic rules should guarantee more adequate governability, this was achieved not by changing the rules, but by silently renewing first of all the *modus operandi* of parties and the forms of competition among them, particularly thanks to new modes of communication. The media allowed the updating of the methods of leader investiture and was the driving force behind the renewal in the way in which it was exercised. Here again, the break was marked by Margaret Thatcher, with her interpretation of premiership and, before that, her interpretation of the role of party leader.

---

39 On the techniques used to mobilise consensus, and specially on the media's role, see Erik Neveu, *Sociologie des mouvements sociaux* (Paris, La Découverte, 2005, 102 – 107).

Mrs Thatcher reached the top echelon of a party which was in serious difficulty, in a situation which was considered socially and economically critical. A shrewd mediatic organisation presented Thatcher as an out-of-the-ordinary personality for British politics, on the grounds of gender and social background, with a strongly personalised leadership style. In contrast to the usual image of the party leader, pre-eminent, but within a collegial executive, the 'Iron Lady' was represented as a solitary protagonist in contrast with her own party and the traditional institutions of the country. In the end, this symbolic redesign conditioned the running of the executive, and had an impact on the entire democratic regime, with important implications for relations between the executive, parliament and parties, delineating a model that gained new ground.

The time was very probably right. Since then, forms of personal leadership have appeared everywhere and almost all parties have transformed themselves symbolically using the personal accessories of their leader, or almost. To all appearances, once a leader has been chosen, with the added factor of their media appeal, all responsibility of command is conferred to them. [40] Indeed, if we examine the facts more carefully, we find that 'personal parties' do not exist.[41] Parties are always collective undertakings, that involve heterogeneous actors, moved by different aims. No leader can free himself definitively of the party executive, of past leadership contenders, aspiring successors, second-level leaders who have become popular in the institutions of local government. Furthermore, even the most authoritative leader needs deputies, assistants, an electoral machine and a personal following which can be displayed. The leader needs a retinue that has invested in him, that trusts him and that is ready to mobilise for him.

The model of personal party, which is anything but personal, is not even exclusive. There are still parties which are collegially-led and, if we consider them carefully, all parties are run collegially. Yet, this has not stopped the personalisation of party leadership, in coherence with the media-style management of electoral campaigns, ready to produce the image of an equally personal government and even to redefine the equilibria among institutions. The head of government appears to dominate the executive and the executive to dominate the elective assembly. The origins of this change are not particularly recent,[42] but only recently it has been

---

40 In 1994 Tony Blair took precedence over the more experienced Gordon Brown, mainly for mediatic reasons, and in 1998 Schröder was preferred to Lafontaine who was also secretary of the SPD. Fort the same reasons, Sarkozy held out over other hopefuls in the UMP and Ségolène Royal over those of the PS. See Peter Mair's observations in *The Challenge to Party Government*, EUI-SPS Working Paper 2007/09.

41 Mauro Calise, 'Presidentialization, Italian Style', in Thomas Poguntke, Paul Webb (eds.), *The Presidentialization of Politics. A Comparative Study of Modern Democracies* (Oxford, Oxford University Press, 2005, p. 98).

42 Its roots are in the hypotheses of 'rationalisation of parliamentarianism' in the late-1950s. See Georges Vedel, 'Rapport général sur le problème des rapports du législatif et de l'exécutif présenté

represented and emphasised through the formula of the 'presidentialisation' of parliamentary regimes.[43]

The presidentialisation of parliamentary regimes has in fact occurred in many different ways, and is more or less accentuated. Moreover, if presidentialisation is meant to evoke the American model of today, it does in a rather approximate way. To begin with, in Europe the executives remain, in the greater part of cases, responsible to parliament. What the formula signals, however, is the increasingly personalised nature of the competition between candidate leaders and its effects on the institutional structures. These evolved in a monocratic perspective, even if rather differently from the American model. In Europe, demanding that electors make *de facto* the choice of who will head the executive, has meant replacing parliament as the basic receiver of the representative mandate, even if the executive formally depends on parliamentary trust. In the USA, by contrast, the Congress receives its own representative mandate and the relations between the Congress and the President remains relatively balanced with a lively dialectic between the two institutions.[44]

If there has been a convergence between continental European politics and the American model, it has above all been a convergence in the candidate-centred style of electoral contests. In both cases this has been promoted by the performance-related needs of the media. In regimes such as the British parliamentary model or the Fifth Republic in France, the pre-eminence of the executive and the binary simplification of the electoral contest, have been consolidated over time: nearly two centuries in the case of Britain. Nevertheless, until parties managed to maintain their associative physiognomy, and their collegial management, they heavily conditioned the functioning of government. *Vice versa*, once the candidate leader has been subject to the protracted examination of a television electoral campaign, and has been solemnly consecrated, how can he tranquilly return to the rank-and-file after the duel is won and necessarily continues to be at the centre of media attention?[45]

---

au Congrès de l'Association internationale de science politique', *Revue française de science politique* 8(2), 1958, 755–781. The most well-known application of the principle of rationalisation, penalising the representation and rewarding public technocracies and senior civil servants, under the charismatic cover of Gaullism, is the French Fifth Republic. See Bastien François, *Misère de la Ve République* (Paris, La Découverte, 2001).

43 Anthony Mughan, *Media and the Presidentialization of Parliamentary Elections* (New York, Palgrave, 2000). See also, Poguntke, Webb (eds.), *The Presidentialization of Politics*. For a note of caution in Britain see Anthony King, *The British Constitution* (Oxford, Oxford University Press, 2007, pp. 318–322).

44 The two branches of Congress can make life extremely difficult for the President and easily deny him a majority even when he has a politically coherent majority. A minority of forty-one senators out of one hundred is enough to block any important legislative proposal.

45 Marc Abélès, 'La mise en représentation du politique', in Marc Abélès, Heny-Pierre Jeudy (eds.), *Anthropologie du politique* (Paris, Colin, 1999, pp. 258–270).

Nevertheless, mediatic symbols and needs mask a more complex practice. There is no less reliable myth than that of the solitary, and even heroic, decision-maker, on whose initiative and on whose impulse all political choices depend. Recently, the exasperated electoral duels that characterise presidential regimes have even aggravated the dependence of the elected on their electoral constituencies and on the coalitions of interests that sustain them financially. The mythology of leadership is certainly not enough to reduce this dependence, neither is it enough to isolate opposition parties in a generic function of control and accusation. New forms of opposition, such as media opposition, are ready to take their place. The consequent weakness of democratic leadership, even for those more inclined to flex their muscles, is not a mystery.

What appears more probable is an effect of the de-institutionalisation of democratic regimes. Procedures and institutions are dominated by the 'horse-race' rhetoric and that of popular investiture, and pass into second position. What counts are the context, circumstances, personality and style of leader, whose words and actions obscure the parliament, parties and even the executive itself. Therefore, between one election and another, the credibility and authority of the institutions are symbolically conditioned by fluctuations in the popularity of the leader in office, depending on the media and the opinion polls' fluctuations. The leader has the difficult task of denying them using techniques corresponding to the audience needs of the media, and at times heterodox. This clearly raises other problems, which have often questionable effects on the image of democratic regimes.

Politics by other means?

Some years ago one of the most influential political scientist of the present generation, Robert D. Putnam, opened up a very successful line of research on the preconditions of a healthy democratic regime. Coining a formula destined to success, that is 'social capital', he recognised these preconditions in a mix of trust, reciprocity, civic engagement, willingness to cooperate and associative life.[46] In the 1980s, Putnam concentrated his research on Italian regions. Comparing the regional governments of the Centre-North to those of the South, he explained their different performances in terms of the different endowment of social capital of the two parts of the country.[47] When Putnam turned his attention to the USA some years later, he used the same concept and imputed the unhappy state of the

---

46 In last instance social capital broadens and revisits the concept of political culture. See, Filippo Sabetti, 'Democracy and Civic Culture', in Carles Boix and Susan Stokes (eds.), *The Oxford Handbook of Comparative Politics* (New York/London/Oxford University Press, 2007, pp. 340–362).

47 Robert D. Putnam, Robert Leonardi, Raffaella Y. Nanetti, *Making Democracy Work: Civic Traditions in Modern Italy* (Princeton NJ, Princeton University Press, 1993).

democracy to the decline of social capital registered in the last decades.[48] What would have worn out the associative habits that since Tocqueville's times were held to give life to democracy in America? For Putnam it is generational change, the growth of women's employment and over-exposure to television.

The criticisms were not slow in arriving. Why should television not inform citizens more and better than in the past? Why should work not involve women more intensely in democratic life? Instead, why not establish a link between the decline of social capital and factors such as the increasingly precarious forms of employment, the relative drop in wages and salaries and increased working hours? Why not call into question the much-preached values and models of today's individualistic behaviour which run counter to civic behaviour and sociality?

Yet, despite the criticisms, Putnam's considerations stress a point well worth examining. Democracy owes its vitality to the presence of institutions able to involve and mobilise citizens. The doubt raised by some of Putnam's critics is whether the instrument best-suited to the objective are, as he claims, local associative networks, or whether what is needed are broader promotional agencies. On this point, another prestigious political scientist, Sidney Tarrow, discussing the survey on Italy, recalled attention to political parties. His thesis is that mass parties, organised nationally and branching out at the local associative level, make the difference between the two parts of the peninsula. Parties have long been decisive in stimulating the growth of social capital. In some regions they managed and in others they did not.[49]

The research findings of other American scholars are in this line of reasoning. They have recognised the roots of the decline of the American democratic regime not in local associations, but in what can be defined as the privatisation of political demands. For several decades the big national associative structures, including parties, that spread in a capillary way and attracted a socially mixed mass membership, which put forward collective demands, have been deactivated. Citizens, on the other hand, have become holders of rights, asserted individually or through professional and highly specialised associations. This is the interpretation proposed by a renowned specialist of the state and welfare like Theda Skocpol.[50]

Skocpol argues that the current state of American democracy depends on the

48 Robert D. Putnam, *Bowling Alone: the Collapse and Revival of American Community* (New York, Simon & Schuster, 2000).

49 Sidney Tarrow, 'Making Social Science Work Across Space and Time: A Critical Reflection on Robert Putnam's Making Democracy Work', *American Political Science Review* 90(2), 1996, 389–397.

50 Theda Skocpol, *Diminished Democracy: From Membership to Management in American Civic Life* (Norman, University of Oklahoma Press, 2003). A discussion of the same argument is presented in Theda Skocpol, 'Government Activism and the Reorganization of American Civic Democracy', in Paul Pierson, Theda Skocpol (eds.), *The Transformation of American Politics: Activist Government and the Rise of Conservatism* (Princeton NJ, Princeton University Press, 2007).

decline of wide-ranging associations and parties, and of the civic involvement that they implied. This has been the undesired effect of protection agreed by the federal institutions to the civil rights movement in the 1960s, and of the expansion of government intervention in new spheres of social and economic life, not only in terms of welfare.

This body of measures has obtained some key successes in terms of rights in general, and racial equality in particular. But they have generated a new claims-based associative model, which fragments representation and discourages participation. The traditional national associations based on, and financed by, membership and with a remarkable organisational apparatus, have been replaced by a myriad of organisations dedicated to specific issues. These are based in Washington or New York, ready to defend their members' interests in court, financially supported by large private foundations and managed by highly professionalised managers and media and fundraising professionals, all ready to transmigrate from one to the other.

There are at least three consequences of the transition from membership to mailing lists, and from activism to professional advocacy. The first, as mentioned, is the discouragement of collective mobilisation. The second is the downsizing of the opportunities to be heard, especially for the less well-off and less educated, who are contextually dispossessed of vital instruments of democratic education and of important occasions to interact with others and hence sociality. The third effect is that, while the membership obliged the leadership to pay them some attention, the mailing lists frees it from this burden. Leaders of national associations had once to harmonise with the most varied social ambits, to listen to people's needs, to construct shared languages and to interact with them continually in order to mobilise membership. The most that mailing lists provide are impersonal protest messages.

Benjamin Ginsberg and Matthew A. Crenson came to similar conclusions, but broadened the premises.[51] According to them, to defend the country, to provide it with public services, to finance the state's activities and to administer locally, the American elite had traditionally used the consensus and collaboration of citizens. To this end suffrage was progressively extended, people were given the opportunity to be represented and received substantial material benefits. This continued until the elite discovered that so much generosity was superfluous. The armed forces were professionalised, tax collection was automatised and local government was reformed. It now costs less and produces better results to persuade citizens that they do not need so many public services and that the market is much better qualified to organise their healthcare, supply them with education, and guarantee their old age.

As already stressed by Skocpol, the transformation of American democracy

---

51 Matthew Crenson and Benjamin Ginsberg, *Downsizing Democracy: How America Sidelined its Citizens and Privatized its Public* (Baltimore MD, Johns Hopkins University Press, 2002). The book is a sequel to the work by Benjamin Ginsberg, Martin Shefter, *Politics by Other Means* (New York, Norton, 1990).

also means the opportunity conceded to ordinary citizens, from the season of civil rights onwards, to have direct individual access to the courts, regulatory authorities and the public administration. However, it is the middle and upper classes who are more able to use a host of organisations in Washington that supply citizens their services of advocacy – from the protection of civil rights to the protection of the environment, to consumer protection – without asking any committed form of civic activism in exchange.

In this way the figure of the political customer re-emerges: no longer a theoretical invention, but a practice-driven reality. According to Crenson and Ginsberg, the citizen is always less a member of a political collectivity, holder and end-user of public services, who mobilizes with others to pursue common ends. Once revised, the rhetoric of citizenship, is now where the citizen becomes a customer who privately asserts rights to which he or she is entitled.

This does not necessarily mean that citizens have become egocentric and are educated to be so. Once American students were taught self-government: they voted to elect representatives in class, in institutes and even in sports teams, and were invited to discuss their common problems. Today community service is included in study programmes. The practice of voluntary work is still widespread, even among adults, and involves cultural goods, the environment and the disadvantaged. But even if community service is a form of participation, there has been a radical change of perspective. Collective action to protect common interests has been replaced by humanitarian initiatives carried out by individuals or small groups, which help produce services formerly supplied by the state, and which have the effect of dispersing democratic citizenship.

Another important factor is the evolution of political competition. If the non-elites have less reasons to act together, then the elites will have less reasons to mobilise them. For whoever wants to influence public policies, or whoever has ambitions of political power, it is more profitable to act through lobbies, the media and think-tanks, instead of through the tiresome task of mobilising electors.

According to Crenson and Ginsberg, the demobilisation of the latter is in fact a cyclical phenomenon in American politics. It first occurred in the so-called age of Progressivism, between the nineteenth and twentieth century. The Progressives were exponents of the upper classes, critical of the corrosive effects of machine politics and bossism on public morality, and who worked to reform political parties and electoral rules.[52] Previously, political struggle had been based on

---

52 See Martin Shefter's reconstruction in *Political Parties and the State* where he speaks of constituency for bureaucratic autonomy (or universalism) intending a coalition to reinforce public authority to the detriment of sectoral interests and parties. Taken together, American parties anticipated the evolution that would take place in Europe. But even in the 1950s some authoritative theorists stood firmly in support of the European party model. Elmer E. Schattschneider, for example, argued that democracy would be unthinkable without parties, since only parties were able to compensate inequalities favoured by political struggle, delegated solely to interest groups:

the ability to persuade ordinary citizens to vote, to become members of parties and to act collectively. A first tough blow to American parties was dealt by the professionalisation of the public administration promoted by the Progressives to contrast patronage and the spoils system. The legal obligation to register on electoral lists, which in turn favoured the non-vote, instead distanced immigrants and the working class from parties. Finally, the institutionalisation of the primaries removed the selection of candidates from the party machine. The official justification was to encourage electors to participate, but the result was the transferral of this task of selection to whoever finances the campaigns of the candidates.

A new mobilisation took place in the 1930s under the Roosevelt administration, albeit more through the unions than through the parties, and lasted until the mid-1960s. The New Deal invested impressive public resources, distributed by the Democrats together with the trade unions and through the creation of special agencies. In doing so, electors were mobilised, to the disadvantage of the Republicans controlling the top echelons of public bureaucracies and courts. After more than thirty years of awakening, which at the time of Johnson's 'Great Society' also involved the coloured population, a new demobilisation occurred. This was provoked first of all by the opportunity to give life to new associative forms of involvement, able to transmit the demands of citizens without demanding any form of durable commitment from them. From that moment onwards politics – and representation – would take place with totally different means and in totally different forms. Pluralism was rejected below the threshold of political representation. In the so called constitutional democracy, individuals and associations find an audience with public authority through different channels, *in primis* law courts.[53]

---

see *The Semi-Sovereign People: A Realist's View of Democracy in America* (Chicago, Holt, Rinehart & Winston, 1960). Ten years earlier nothing less than a committee set up by the American Political Science Association, led by Schattschneider, had stressed this point: see 'Toward a More Responsible Two-Party System', *American Political Science Review* 44(3), 1950, supplement, 15–36. Looking at European parties with this in mind is Joseph La Palombara and Myron Weiner in editing another well-known contribution: *Political Parties and Political Development* (Princeton NJ, Princeton University Press, 1966).

53 Yet, we must admit that the interpretation of Crenson and Ginsberg is not uncontroversial. Others believed that reinforcing the presidency at the time of Wilson and above all, of Roosevelt – and the federal administration – marked a plebiscitary turn, which emancipated the president from being conditioned by parties and has suppressed these as autonomous political actors, demolishing the capacity of mobilisation. See Sidney M. Milkis, Jesse H. Rhodes, 'George W. Bush, the Republican Party, and the "New" American Party System', *Perspectives on Politics* 5(3), 2007, 461–88. For Andrea L. Campbell the phenomenon is more recent. From the 1960s onwards parties have mobilised less and when they do, it is selectively. See, 'Parties, Electoral Participation, and Shifting Voting Blocks', in Paul Pierson, Theda Skocpol (eds.), *The Transformation of American Politics: Activist Government and the Rise of Conservatism* (Princeton NJ, Princeton University Press, 2007). Where there is agreement is that the decline of parties, whatever the reason, is

Once again it is a paradoxical and unexpected effect. One of the most frequent accusations directed at parties is that they only transmit partial interests. If taken seriously, and presuming that a general interest does not exist or is impossible to pursue, we cannot deny that mass parties were able to represent widespread interests and to mobilise the big numbers. Had this not been the case, it would have been other much more circumscribed interests which would have obtained a predominant audience, those of economic spheres, which is exactly what occurs today. Naturally, it is not just economic interests that make their weight felt, but the interests of the big numbers are nevertheless penalised, not only in the USA, but also in Europe, where too, though with some differences, politics is nowadays carried out in another way.

In Europe, as we have said, parties have long provided a valuable linkage between politics and citizens.[54] As intermediary bodies, they constructed bonds locally and recomposed them at the national level. For some time now, European parties have been persuaded that it is no longer up to them to satisfy the needs of linkage, counting instead on interest groups or welfare systems. But this does not mean that this is the only possible future. It is precisely American politics that could herald a turning point for parties on both sides of the Atlantic.

There are those, for example, who hold that George W. Bush revived and re-mobilised the Republican Party and did this by tracing new and clear ideological divisions, and using the party to accredit his values and programmes. Strengthening the party machine also at a decentralised level, Bush constituted a pole of attraction and a collective spokesperson for conservative organisations, also of a religious strain. These are often very active locally, and their action, partly disproving Crenson and Ginsberg, is also be felt at the national level. In this way, in the presidential campaign of 2004, over 1,200,000 volunteers were involved by the Republican Party, bringing turnouts up to 1968 levels. It seems that a symmetrical reawakening occurred in the Democratic Party during the electoral campaign of Barack Obama in 2008.[55]

Therefore we cannot rule out that sooner or later parties will return to being powerful vehicles of mobilisation and representation, electoral and otherwise. This is even suggested by the experience of the new so-called populist parties. In addition to promoting forms of active militancy, they invest conspicuous organisational energies on the ground and in assisting electors.[56] The scale is reduced and

---

responsible for the drop in participation, including electoral participation.

54 Kay Lawson, *Political Parties and Linkage* (New Haven CT, Yale University Press, 1980).

55 Sidney M. Milkis, Jesse H. Rhodes, 'George W. Bush, the Republican Party, and the "New" American Party System', *Perspectives on Politics* 5(3), 2007, 461–488. See also Sidney M. Milkis, Jesse H. Rhodes, 'Barack Obama, the Democratic Party, and the Future of the "New American Party System"', *The Forum* 7(1), 2009.

56 Virginie Martin, Gilles Ivaldi, Grégory Lespinasse, 'Le Front national, entre clientélisme et recherche d'un enracinement social', *Critique internationale* 4, 1999, 169–181 and Roberto

the segment of citizenship involved is limited, although is tending to consolidate and broaden. Therefore, we do not know whether the model is replicable, and applicable to themes different from those raised by populist parties. We only know that meanwhile, conventional parties seem to be imprisoned by the narrative of citizens who despise politics. At most, citizens are invited to take part in primaries and in some innocuous deliberative consultation, generously sprinkled with promises of empowerment and participation.[57] Unfortunately, not even the parties seem to believe too much in the results.

Biorcio, *La rinvincita del Nord. La Lega dalla contestazione al governo* (Rome/Bari, Laterza, 2010, pp. 98–111).

57 Rémi Lefebvre, Antoine Roger (eds.), *Les partis politiques à l'épreuve des procédures délibératives* (Rennes, Presses universitaires de Rennes, 2009).

chapter | the democracy of our discontent
seven |

A success story

How have those who are in principle the key actors in democratic life, that is citizens, reacted to the great, many, exacting changes that have reshaped the economy, society and politics? According to one of the more successful accounts of contemporary democracy, there is a widespread mood of discontent and impatience with politics circulating among the governed. This feeling is transnational, well-established, touches all political institutions and is indifferent to political and ideological divisions.[1] Not only is public approval of politics low, but it is tending to decline even further.

As an account it is disturbing. Democratic regimes have multiplied, are relatively stable and generally considered to offer the governed conditions of life preferable to those offered by non-democratic regimes. In spite of this, and taking the title of an outstanding book, backed up by an abundance of data and persuasive arguments, why do people hate politics?[2]

The term 'hate' is so scandalous that we have to ask, first of all, whether it is used with a particular purpose. The same question could be asked about the rich repertoire of synonyms – indifference, discontent, mistrust, scepticism, delusion, resentment, cynicism, disenchantment, antipolitics and yet others – used to describe what is considered to be the obscure disease currently affecting democratic regimes.

Although less numerous and less convincing – perhaps because less dramatic and less spectacular – there is no shortage of rebuttals. Not everything is for the best, say some authoritative scholars, but neither is it for the worst.[3] Yet, are the accusations and denials by any chance unconsciously conditioned by the political preferences of whoever formulates them?

---

1 Mattei Dogan, 'The Erosion of Confidence in Thirty European Democracies', in Dogan (ed.), *Political Mistrust and the Discrediting of Politicians* (Leiden/Boston, Brill, 2005).

2 Colin Hay, *Why We Hate Politics* (Cambridge, Polity Press, 2007) and Eugen J. Dionne, *Why Americans Hate Politics: The Death of the Democratic Process* (New York, Simon & Schuster, 1991). There is a vast bibliography on this issue. For general reviews on the issue see Peter Mair, 'Ruling the Void. The Hollowing of Western Democracies', *New Left Review* 42, 2006, 25–51 and Michael Hogan in 'Anti-political Sentiment in Contemporary Liberal Democracies', *Australian Review of Public Affairs* 8(1), 2007, 1–18.

3 Pippa Norris (ed.), *Critical Citizens: Global Support for Democratic Government* (Oxford, Oxford University Press, 1999).

The narrative – or, rather, the many narratives – of the citizens' malaise lend themselves to the most varied and contradictory uses. They are welcomed by the media, since tensions and conflicts create audience: those between politicians and citizens not less than those between politicians. They also suit the media because they are in competition with politics. The story of malaise also suits the political forces in opposition, but also the incumbents, as citizens' mistrust is a good reason to demand another sort of politics, or of all sorts of reform. The narrative suits civil society even more, because it can pretend to be a different, and healthier, sort of politics, and it suits all those actors who claim that there is too much politics and that, if politicians counted less, the government of democratic society would be more moral and more efficient.

One can sustain that the governed are dissatisfied because democracy is not sufficiently democratic, or because current policies do not satisfy everyone. Politics may also be unpopular because it does not involve ordinary citizens enough, or because it excludes them from decisive choices, so that democratic procedures need to be radically renewed. This narrative can also be re-proposed merely in order to deny it. We can argue that it is the fruit of unreliable or instrumental dramatisations, and serves to delegitimate actual forms of democracy and subject them to debatable manipulation. In any case, the zeal with which scholars, the media, politicians and all sorts of observers crowd around the supposed divide that separates governors from the governed, raises suspicions.

In reality the idea of widespread dissatisfaction with politics is by no means new. Concepts such as apathy, depoliticisation, political alienation, dissatisfaction and indifference, have been in circulation since the 1950s and 1960s.[4] Charles W. Mills' accusation of the political indifference of his co-nationals dates to 1951,[5] but was soon matched by less dramatic analyses. According to, for instance Seymour M. Lipset, participation is generally, but not always, desirable in democratic regimes insofar as an excess of participation by socially and economically disadvantaged groups may tend towards extremism.[6]

---

4   For an interesting example of concern in former times about the discontent of citizens and on abstentionism, critical of gaullism and its intolerance of parties, see France, Georges Vedel (ed.), *La dépolitisation: mythe ou realite?* (Paris, Colin, 1962), where – how strange – we find terms like 'apolitics' and 'antipolitics'. See, in particular, Marcel Merle, 'Inventaire des apolitismes en France', in Geoge Vedel (ed.), *La dépolitisation: mythe ou réalité* (Paris, Armand Colin, 1962). For a contemporary and reassuring picture of political alienation in America in that period see instead Robert Lane, *Political Ideology* (New York, The Free Press, 1962).

5   Charles W. Mills was drastic. *In White Collar: The American Middle Classes* (Oxford, Oxford University Press, 1951, p. 328), he wrote: 'If we accept the Greek's definition of the idiot as a privatized man, then we must conclude that the US citizenry is largely composed of idiots'.

6   Seymour M. Lipset, *Political Man: The Social Bases of Politics* (New York, Doubleday, 1960, pp. 226–229).

But it was their well-known comparative study of the attitudes of citizens towards the political system, carried out by Gabriel Almond and Sidney Verba, that presented data, and an interpretation, which were very reassuring. In some countries, such as Germany, Italy and Mexico, disinterest, detachment and feelings of impotence had been prevalent. But this was not the case in Anglo-Saxon countries, where citizens felt sufficiently involved in political life and considered that they had a good chance of being heard. According to Almond and Verba, what made the difference was the 'civic culture' found in the USA and Britain, which was then promoted both as a certificate and a condition of a virtuous democracy.[7]

It is a pity that the reassurance did not last long. In the mid-1970s one of the most interesting findings of the Report of the Trilateral Commission was the discovery of a generalised mood of discredit, which appeared to have hit all political leaderships in advanced democracies.[8] From then on the discontent of citizens, and the alarm surrounding this discontent, became an unavoidable issue, despite the fact that available empirical evidence is far less unanimous than is generally affirmed. First of all, it may be precisely this contradiction that needs to be stressed in order to propose not an alternative account, but a more animated one, beginning with what is normally deemed to be the symptom of symptoms, that is, the dramatic drop in electoral participation.

The alarmists stress that from the 1970s to the current day turnout in Europe at national elections has dropped everywhere (and even more at local elections, not to speak of European elections). In Italy, the Netherlands and Germany non-voters rose from 10 per cent to around 20 per cent. In Austria from 8 per cent to 16 per cent. In Britain from 25 per cent to 40 per cent. In France from 19 per cent to over 35 per cent, to which we should add the 10 per cent of the electorate who do not even register.

The data appear dramatic. If we consider that today majoritarian electoral regimes prevail, and that governments with a broad parliamentary and electoral following are the exception, the rule is that Western governments enjoy the explicit support — but not necessarily conscious or informed — of slightly over one third of those entitled to vote. The rest desert the polls, not forgetting those who spoil the ballot or return a blank ballot, which are also unrepresented in parliament, while those who prefer opposition, thanks to the electoral system, are often underrepresented.

Yet, although the data are disturbing, there is no shortage of theories that minimise the phenomenon. Some scholars recognise the non-vote as a form of tacit consent and even a sign of success of the democratic regime: if the elector

---

7   Gabriel A. Almond, Sidney Verba, *The Civic Culture. Political Attitudes and Democracy in Five Nations* (Boston, Little, Brown & Co., 1965).

8   Michel Crozier, Samuel P. Huntington, Jôji Watanuki (eds.), *The Crisis of Democracy. Report on the Governability of Democracies to the Trilateral Commission* (New York, New York University Press, 1975).

abstains, so goes the argument, this is a sign that major differences of opinions are absent, that whoever governed would be acceptable and that the democratic regime is in excellent health. An excess of mobilisation would make the political temperature dangerously high.[9]

The argument of tacit consent has been re-proposed half a century later,[10] and has even been historicised, defining as anomalous not current low turnouts, but the high turnouts of the first twenty-five years of the postwar period. Today's decline thus indicates a return to the norm, while the high postwar turnouts were the offspring of a unrepeatable period, where democracy was still new or taking root. When it becomes routine, it is understandable that electors are likely to be less zealous about going to the polls.[11]

Rational choice theory instead prefers to highlight the paradox of the vote. In a world populated by strategic actors, non-voting is more rational than voting: the elector knows that his vote is costly in terms of time and information, and that it is more or less irrelevant. Despite this, a large share of citizens do vote, a fact that rational choice has some difficulty explaining without radically modifying its assumptions.[12]

The most reassuring argument, however, is that the trend is more uncertain than is often claimed. This kind of comparison is always problematic, because each country has different forms of political life and different institutional rules. But, although the comparison is questionable, we can observe that elections where turnout picks up have become indisputably more frequent in the last decade. In 2004 in Spain the challenge between Aznar and Zapatero (together with the public feeling caused by the attacks on Madrid) brought 8 per cent more electors to the polls, reaching 76 per cent. This then fell to 74 per cent in 2008 and 69 per cent in 2011. At the first round of French presidential elections in 2007 turnout was 84 per cent, twelve points more than in 2002, while in 2012 it dropped again four points. In two countries known for low turnouts, Britain and the United States, more re-

---

9   Starting from the assumption that it would be unhealthy for democracy if people placed too many expectations in politics, see William H. Morris-Jones, 'In Defense of Apathy. Some Doubts on the Duty to Vote', *Political Studies* 2(1), 1954, 25–37.

10 See, for example, Russell Hardin,'Do We Want Trust in Government?', in Mark Warren (ed.), *Democracy and Trust* (Cambridge, Cambridge University Press, 1999, pp. 31-32).

11 Étienne Schweisgut, 'La dépolitisation en question', in Gérard Grunberg, Nonna Mayer, Paul M. Sniderman (eds.), *La démocratie à l'épreuve: une nouvelle approche de l'opinion des Français* (Paris, Presses de SciencesPo, 2002, pp. 53–55).

12 On the paradox of the vote see Anthony Downs, *An Economic Theory of Democracy* (New York, Harper and Brothers, 1957, pp. 265–268). A now classic critique is Alessandro Pizzorno, 'On Rationality and Democratic Choice', in Pierre Birnbaum, Jean Leca (eds.), *Individualism: Theories and Methods* (Oxford, Clarendon Press, 1990). Among many others see also Patrick Lehingue, 'L'analyse économique des choix électoraux, I', *Politix* 10(40), 1997, 88–112, and 'L'analyse économique des choix électoraux, II', *Politix* 11(41), 1997, 82–122.

cent elections have seen an inversion of the trend. In America between 1996 and 2008 turnouts increased by nothing less than 10 per cent, reaching 62 per cent of eligible voters (that is, registered or not on electoral lists) and coming close to the 1968 level, when Nixon beat Humphrey. In 2010 in Britain, nearly 4 per cent more electors voted in contrast with five years earlier.

Another relevant event is that some countries reported a relatively high level of turnout for the referendum consultations on the European Convention. Moreover, the popular mobilisation around these referenda has often been very active, as for example in the French case.

Has the long trend of declining turnout been interrupted? Waiting to discover what the future holds, we can be content to observe the erratic, and perhaps cyclical, nature of non-voting. This might not be a good thing in itself, but there are elections when turnout falls and others when it grows. There are also significant variations at the individual level. Non-voting can be systematic or intermittent.[13] For some time now there has been particular growth – around half – in the share of intermittent non-voting. The two obviously do not have the same meaning. Intermittence, far from being an indication of rejection or alienation, may be interpreted as a warning consciously sent to politicians, who, for instance, may have reduced or changed their political supply. For instance, when electoral competition is restricted to a binary choice, voters who are dissatisfied with both candidates can be motivated not to vote at all.

This consideration invites us to consider the meaning of non-voting also in relation to the electoral system. It is one thing to abstain in a proportional regime, where electors have more of a chance of receiving a supply of representation in line with their preferences, and it is another thing in a majority system. In a uninominal system, electors of uncontested electoral constituencies, where the winner is known beforehand, are much less motivated to vote than those in marginal constituencies, where parties invest more in terms of candidature, propaganda and financial resources. These differences disappear in international comparisons.[14]

A confirmation of the changeable meaning of non-voting is the altered social composition of non-voters. If the latter once prevalently came from the less well-off and less educated strata, non-voting has now become widespread even among those who are interested in and informed about politics, with high levels of income and education. In the case of the less educated and less affluent social strata, low turnout probably certified the existence of a hidden – and democratically debatable

---

13 For the French case of the intermittent vote, see François Héran, 'Voter toujours, parfois... ou jamais', in Bruno Cautrès, Nonna Mayer (eds.), *Le nouveau désordre électoral. Les leçons du 21 avril 2002* (Paris, Presses de SciencesPo, 2004). According to François Clanché, the intermittent vote has grown and the systemic vote has dropped a little. See 'La participation électorale au printemps 2002 : de plus en plus de votants intermittents', in *Insee première*; 877, 2003.

14 Laura Morales, *Joining Political Organisations: Institutions, Mobilisation and Participation in Western Democracies* (Colchester, ECPR Press, 2009).

– census threshold.[15] On the contrary, when turnout declines among the more well-off and educated electors it is possible to assume that they do so not since they hate politics, but in order to warn or reproach politicians.[16]

Finally, are we sure that electoral participation is *per se* reliable proof of support for democracy? In particular, should the vote for so-called 'anti-system parties',[17] as communist and neo-fascist parties have long been defined, be considered as such? This too is electoral participation, even if it lends itself to a double evaluation and has once again become topical. For the last twenty years the old anti-system parties have been replaced by a hardened bunch of new generation rightist parties, radical in tone and style and often defined – faute de mieux – as populist.[18] The label is debatable, but the political supply made by these parties is certainly problematic, being generally racist and centred on the accusation of politicians' vices. Nevertheless, if the vote attracted by populist parties can be defined as a radical protest vote, and despite the fact that it is often reviewed as one of many symptoms of citizens' dissatisfaction, what is the meaning of this vote? Is it a proof of approval or disapproval for politics and democracy? The forms of politics are updated, the grounds for conflict and the ways it is expressed evolve. As with the vote for old anti-system parties, perhaps in the vote for so-called populist parties we should recognise not a refusal of politics tout court, but the approval of a political perspective which is democratically eccentric. Indeed, this type of vote is often accompanied by lively demonstrations of activism. If it witnesses discontent, it is not toward politics *per se*, but only towards a part of it.

Another symptom of dissatisfaction cited by alarmists, is growing electoral volatility.[19] Until the 1960s the average elector voted and re-voted the same party,

---

15 This is the theme of Daniel Gaxie's book, *Le cens caché. Inégalités culturelles et ségrégation politique* (Paris, Seuil, 1978).

16 On the multiple meanings of abstentionism, see Anne Muxel, 'La poussée des abstentions: protestation, malaise, sanction', in Pascal Perrineau, Colette Ysmal (eds.), *Le vote de tous les refus. Les élections présidentielles et législatives de 2002* (Paris, Presses de Sciences Po, 2003), and Muxel, 'L'abstention: déficit démocratique ou vitalité politique?', *Pouvoirs* 1(120), 2007, 43–55. Fortunately, one can distinguish between 'out-of-game' abstentionism and 'in-game' abstentionism.

17 Giovanni Sartori, *Parties and Party Systems: A Framework for Analysis* (New York, Cambridge University Press, 1976, p. 133).

18 We will return to this theme in Chapter 8.

19 For a comparative analysis of the phenomenon see Russell J. Dalton, Martin P. Wattenberg, 'Partisan Change and the Democratic Process', in Dalton, Wattenberg (eds.), *Parties Without Partisans: Political Change in Advanced Industrial Democracies* (Oxford, Oxford University Press, 2000). On France see Jérôme Jaffré, Jean Chiche, 'Mobilité, volatilité, perplexité', in Daniel Boy, Nonna Mayer (eds.), *L'électeur a ses raisons* (Paris, Presses de SciencesPo, 1997), and Marc Swyngedouw, Daniel Boy, Nonna Mayer, 'La volatilité électorale en France (1993–1997)', *Revue française de science politique* 50(3), 2000, 489–514.

from one election to another. Since the 1970s electors have become impatient and increasingly seem to mature their preferences on the eve of elections. But even this symptom, as the weakening of party identification revealed by surveys,[20] is not entirely unequivocal. The thesis of volatility creates suspense, and suits the media and political marketing experts alike. But electoral sociology shows how the volatility is not only reversible, but also occurs prevalently between contiguous parties.[21] In local elections, where the political supply attempts to depoliticise candidates and issues and where personal relations – especially in small municipalities – have greater weight, it is easier to change sides. Moreover, all the so-called second-order elections give voters the opportunity to send warnings to their own party of reference. But it is still a question of a provisional and reversible way out.

As regards the uncertainty of electors on the eve of elections, reported by the polls – often taken as another proof of discontent – why is it excluded that it might be a conscious or unconscious inclination for interviewees to mislead opinion polls or to use them to send signals to politicians? There are many cases where an electoral result has contradicted the polls. Electors may be more uncertain than in the past, but this does not mean that they are flippant or impulsive.[22]

Once reassured on this aspect, the narrative of discontent recognises another symptom in the conspicuous drop in membership for conventional parties in recent decades.[23] Even if it was only a limited share of the electorate, after World War

---

20 Russell J. Dalton, 'The Decline of Party Identification', in Russell J. Dalton, Martin P. Wattenberg, *Parties Without Partisans: Political Change in Advanced Industrial Democracies* (Oxford, Oxford University Press, 2000).

21 Peter Mair, *Party System Change. Approaches and Interpretations* (Oxford, Oxford University Press, 1998, pp. 27–31, 79–81), and Donald Green, Bradley Palmquist, Eric Schickler, *Partisan Hearts and Minds: Political Parties and the Social Identity of Voters* (New Haven CT, Yale University Press, 2002, pp. 14–20, 82–84).

22 Electors on the extreme right tend not to declare a preference which is publicly stigmatised. See Annie Collovald, *Le 'populisme du Fn': un dangereux contresens* (Broissieux, Éditions du Crocquant, 2004, pp. 138–146). For an interesting approach to the issue, see Robert E. Goodin and James M. Rice, 'Waking Up in the Poll Booth', *Perspectives on Politics* 7(4), 2009, 901–910. Analysing data on the USA, Australia and Britain, Goodin and Rice observe that during the electoral campaign opinion polls register much broader shifts than those effectively verified. There are two hypotheses: in the poll booth electoral electors take the vote more seriously and are not led by temporary impressions; or when electors are more uncertain they simply do not vote.

23 Peter Mair, Ingrid van Biezen, 'Party Membership in Twenty European Democracies, 1980–2000', *Party Politics* 7(1), 2001, 5–21; Susan E. Scarrow, 'Parties Without Members? Party Organization in a Changing Electoral Environment,' in Russell J. Dalton, Martin Wattenberg (eds.), *Parties Without Partisans*; Ingrid van Biezen, Peter Mair, Thomas Poguntke, 'Going, Going, . . . Gone? The Decline of Party Membership in Contemporary Europe', *European Journal of Political Research* 51(1), 2012, 24–56. For a longer time span see Richard S. Katz, Peter Mair *et al.*, '*The Membership of Political Parties in European Democracies, 1960–1990*', *European Journal of*

II party membership was in the millions and often very active. The available data are not very recent, but still give a good idea of the trend. In 1960 nearly 13 per cent of Italian electors were members of a party, this fell to 4 per cent at the end of the millennium. In Sweden in the same period, membership fell from 22 per cent to about 5 per cent, and in Britain from 9 per cent to 2 per cent. In France in 1999 membership was less than one third in comparison to the end of the 1970s, when it neared 5 per cent of those entitled to vote. Finally, in Germany in 1960 membership was nearly 5 per cent of the electorate, but twenty years later this had fallen by a fourth of the previous share.

Yet, variations in membership are not excluded. Sometimes parties even declare an increase in membership, despite the fact that the degree of the members' activism, where this can be measured, would be presumably lower than in the past, apart from those with ambitions for a political career. But two provisos should also be made as regards membership. The first is that parties have stopped systematically encouraging it. The second is that every time parties try to mobilise members and sympathisers for one reason or another, they still manage to get a response. In 2005 the Italian primaries, called by the centre-left to choose the candidate premier for the next elections, saw four million and half electors queue up to declare their consensus for a pre-selected candidate. In 2009 three million took part in the primaries to choose the new leader of the *Partito Democratico*. In France over two and a half million voters took part at the primaries held by the Socialist Party to designate the presidential candidate for 2012. This was a great success, in a country traditionally little inclined to participation.

Parties, trade unions and movements have filled the streets of Spain, Italy, France and elsewhere many times over. In the last French presidential campaigns parties convened surprisingly crowded meetings. Barack Obama did the same in 2008, and his success was preceded by a thriving civic mobilisation that made innovative use of new technologies and the new social media. Electoral meetings are always prepared with care, as they help construct the image of a candidate who is esteemed and popular. But if politicians manage to assemble a large public, then this public must exist somewhere, and the issue is simply how to mobilise it properly.

Despite these assurances, another grounds for alarm is provided especially by cyclical surveys where data is collected on representative samples to scan and measure the mood of the electorate.[24] For some decades the data have testified to

---

Political Research 22(3), 1992, 329–345.

24 Using mainly survey data, Pascal Perrineau (ed.), *L'engagement politique. Déclin ou mutation L'engagement politique. Déclin ou mutation* (Paris, Presses de la Fondation nationale des Sciences Politiques, 1994); Thomas Poguntke, Susan E. Scarrow (eds.), 'The Politics of Anti-Party Sentiment', special issue *European Journal of Political Research* 25(4), 1996; Daniel Boy, Nonna Mayer, *L'électeur a ses raisons* (Paris, Presses de SciencesPo, 1997); Pippa Norris (eds.), *Critical Citizens* (1999); Susan J. Pharr, Robert D. Putnam (eds.), *Disaffected Democracies* (Princeton NJ,

a widespread feeling of mistrust in politics, political institutions and, above all, politicians themselves. Yet, however worrying the results, the same surveys indicate that ordinary citizens are resolutely in favour of democracy and unwilling to exchange it for non-democratic forms of government.[25]

Unfortunately no-one knows with any certainty what meaning citizens give to the term democracy, or what they expect from it. Given the times in which we live, who would dare to admit to being non-democratic? However, this does not offset the mistrust that politicians seem to attract, the discontent with what they do, or the actions of the main political institutions and parties. This doubt is exacerbated by the fact that surveys also report a low interest in politics. Italy is considered an extreme case because only four electors out of ten feel 'very' or 'somewhat' involved in politics. But is there any reason to rejoice if in what is considered to be a more fortunate democratic regime such as the German one, the electors interested in politics are six out of ten?

Fortunately, the theorists of post-materialist values and cognitive mobilisation give a hand to rule out a dramatic condition of detachment. For them it is higher levels of information and education which make individuals more critical and demanding, less conditioned by party, associative or religious ties and more inclined to give their opinion on candidates and single issues, or to abstain, to protest, to change party or to declare their dissatisfaction to opinion polls.[26] Once traditional political loyalties have been exhausted, and the most urgent material needs satisfied, citizens' tastes become more sophisticated. Consequently, we should not read too much into either declining turnouts, or all the presumed indicators of dissatisfaction.

Princeton University Press, 2000); Gérard Grunberg, Nonna Mayer, Paul M. Sniderman (eds.), *La démocratie à l'épreuve* (Paris, Presses de SciencesPo, 2002); Russell J. Dalton, *Participation, Democratic Choices, Democratic Challenges: The Erosion of Political Support in Advanced Industrial Democracies* (Oxford, Oxford University Press, 2004); Mattei Dogan (ed.), Political *Mistrust and the Discrediting of Politicians* (2005); José R. Montero, Mariano Torcal (eds.), *Political Disaffection in Contemporary Democracies Social Capital, Institutions and Politics* (London, Routledge, 2006); Marco Maraffi (ed.), *Gli italiani e la politica* (Bologna, Il Mulino, 2007).

25 Lipset anticipated this interpretation in 'The Decline of Confidence in American Institutions', Political Science Quarterly 98(3), 1982, 370–402.

26 Ronald Inglehart, *The Silent Revolution: Changing Values and Political Styles Among Western Publics* (Princeton NJ, Princeton University Press, 1977). This is re-proposed by Russell J. Dalton, 'Political Cleavages, Issues, and Electoral Change', in Lawrence LeDuc, Richard G. Niemi, Pippa Norris (eds.), *Comparing Democracies: Elections and Voting in Global Perspective* (Thousand Oaks, Sage, 1996), and more fully in *Citizen Politics: Public Opinion and Political Parties in Advanced Industrial Democracies* (New York, Chatham House, 2002). See also Russell J. Dalton, 'The Social Transformation of Trust in Government', *International Review of Sociology* 15(1), 2005, 133–154 and Norris, *Critical Citizens*.

Indeed, according to this theory, instead of worrying about the delusion of citizens with the performance of politicians, it is better to appreciate the critical spirit that feeds it and the transfer of citizens' expectations from material needs, to culture, the environment, the quality of life, the status of women and so forth. It is doubtful that post-materialist needs have taken precedence over material needs. Surveys report that employment still comes top of the list of citizens' needs, followed by economic well-being, healthcare and education. There is no evidence to show that post-materialist needs are higher up on the list. But another post-materialist argument, according to which citizens always maintain a broad willingness to cooperate with their fellow beings, is not in the least irrelevant. They are electorally more uneasy and desert conventional forms of participation, but do not scorn non-conventional and extra-political forms of involvement. The space where participation has expanded is the area of social movements, or the multicoloured associative universe today reassembled under the label of civil society, which, as we know, benefits from a bias of virtuousness.[27] Citizens witness a greater tendency to criticism and dissent. For their part democracies have to learn to live with it, without charging it with too much polemical significance.

Other signs

The evidence provided by electoral and other statistical data or by surveys, is therefore contradictory,[28] or at least, the glass is either half empty or half full. Luckily, some additional light on citizens' feelings can be obtained from qualitative research, which adopts instruments like discursive interviews or focus groups. It is a well-known fact that in surveys, even the most professional and reliable ones, the interviewee is taken by surprise by a remote telephone interviewer on generally delicate questions, where they may not be competent to reply. Without having much time to reflect, the interviewee must select an option from a list of items predefined by experts, who are in turn unavoidably conditioned by their opinions on the state of the world.[29]

---

27 Pippa Norris re-examines the explanations for malaise from a post-materialist perspective and defends the reasons of the virtuously critical citizen in *Democratic Phoenix: Reinventing Political Activism* (Cambridge, Cambridge University Press, 2002, pp. 35–57).

28 In the case of surveys such World Values Survey or Eurobarometer, it is uncertain whether there is any sense in putting the same question to electors in different countries, where the history and characteristics of political life, electoral competition, actors, rules of the game, meaning of the words, all differ.

29 For a critique of opinion polls and surveys see Patrick Champagne, *Faire l'opinion. Le nouveau jeu politique* (Paris, Éditions de Minuit, 1990). See also, Pierre Bourdieu in *Distinction. A Social Critique of the Judgment of Taste* (Cambridge MA, Harvard University Press, 1984, pp. 397–465), and Loïc Blondiaux, *La Fabrique de l'Opinion. Une histoire sociale des sondages* (Paris, Seuil, 1998).

On the contrary, qualitative interviews are designed to replicate a natural conversation. Whether they manage is of course very unlikely. After all, a qualitative interview carried out by a professional interviewer obliges respondents to 'speak in public' and may have distorting effects. If interviewees are given the freedom to interpret the questions, without being forced to choose between pre-fixed responses, they will still feel obliged to show that they are up to it, and will try to disguise any lack of competence. Despite this, the closer relation between the interviewer and the respondent normally allows interviewees to reflect on what they are being asked, and to choose the terminology to structure their responses. In focus groups participants can even formulate responses interactively among them.

Qualitative interviews cannot be carried out on statistically representative samples. What can be done, however, is to delineate ideal-types that simplify the concrete situations revealed by interviews. While quantitative analysis allows us to make large-scale maps of broad portions of territory to explore, qualitative research is however useful when it comes to examining the details and differences on smaller areas, and to retrace in a more particularised way, the opinions of individuals.

We shall cite here a research project carried out by the author of this book. The results are limited to Italy,[30] but converge with those of similar, but more robust, studies carried out in France, on the same themes.[31] Apparently banal, but rich in implications for our theme, the first issue that these enquiries confirm and give depth to is that not all citizens are, carefully informed and interested as the democratic ideal would like. Before complaining about the mistrust and growing discontent with politics, we need to explore the relations that ordinary citizens have with it. Politics does not mean the same thing, have the same relevance, let alone provoke the same intolerance, for all. In the light of our interviews, we distinguished three main types of citizen: 'remote', 'detached' and 'involved'. The distinction is certainly schematic and does not exhaust all possibilities, but is a useful approximation.

---

30 The research was carried out with the students of the MA course in political sociology at the University of Turin. My thanks go to them for having carried out around a hundred in-depth interviews with citizens from a highly differentiated sample in terms of social and cultural backgrounds, and selected on the basis of four main variables: sex, age, level of education and socio-professional status.

31 Daniel Gaxie, 'Le vote désinvesti. Quelques éléments d'analyse des rapports au vote', *Politix* 6(22), 1993, 138–164; 'Les critiques profanes de la politique. Enchantements, désenchantements, ré-enchantement', in Jean-Louis Briquet, Philippe Garraud (eds.), *Juger la politique: entreprises et entrepreneurs critiques de la politique* (Rennes, Presses universitaires de Rennes, 2002); 'Sur l'humeur politique maussade des démocraties représentatives', in Oscar Mazzoleni (ed.), *La politica allo specchio* (Lugano, Casagrande, 2001); 'Appréhensions du politique et mobilisations des expériences sociales', *Revue française de science politique* 52(2/3), 2002, 145–178. For some methodological clarifications see Daniel Gaxie, Jay Rowell, 'Methodology of the Project', in Daniel Gaxie, Nicolas Hubé, Jay Rowell (eds.), *Perceptions of Europe. A Comparative Sociology of European Attitudes* (Colchester, ECPR Press, 2011).

Let us start from the ideal-type of 'remote citizen', characterised by a reluctance to talk about political issues, a vague knowledge of them and a pre-emptive admission of inadequacy and incompetence. 'I don't have any education', declares an old pensioner from Fiat, who had only completed the second year of elementary school, 'and when certain things come up I just stop'. Not too differently, in the words of a housewife, 'I don't feel up to talking about politics, perhaps because I don't think I can express myself well. [...] I don't know [...] I've never taken an interest in politics and I don't feel ready to talk about it'. This does not mean that the 'remote citizen' has no opinion at all about politics, or refuses to be aligned one way or another. He may often have very clear sympathies, but the modest cultural capital at their disposal, and their limited degree of information, conditions their opinions. The 'remote citizen' distinguishes between right and left only roughly and expresses approximate evaluations, tending to a generic moralism in line with current stereotypes. He may report an appreciation for political figures who are very different, but who are brought closer by their media success. When 'remote citizens' have no direct experience of politics they consciously or unconsciously rely on the media's more visible displays of political debate.

The 'remote citizen' does not judge his own vote as very efficient, and reports 'understanding nothing', or feeling irrelevant and consequently not voting, or voting sporadically, often after being prompted to do so by a relative, friend, acquaintance or political intermediary. This type of citizen does not have contacts with politicians, rarely reads newspapers and seldom talks about politics. Their vision of politics is blurred, based on television, which is watched without paying much attention. But the electoral campaign acts as a wake-up call, and ends up focussing the attention of the 'remote citizen' on some key figure made more visible by the media (and his/her provocative actions), or on some particularly important event. In the words of our pensioner quoted above: 'There they [politicians] are, arguing. [...] They talk and talk but in the end they don't do anything, they never finish anything [...] look at them all, arguing about nothing'. Or, in the words of a female blue collar worker and leftist voter, according to family tradition, and now a pensioner: 'What's the use of politics? I've never understood it. It doesn't interest me because it's something that [...] what's the use of politics?'

It would be absurd to affirm that the vote preference of the 'remote citizen' is hetero-directed or casual. This choice is backed up by arguments, even if not abstracted from personal experience and mainly based on widespread stereotypes. Nevertheless, the 'remote citizen' still has an idea of personal utility and understands who promises to satisfy it and declares a political orientation accordingly. This does not always mean that vote preferences are coherent over time, but at least it circumscribes them. The 'remote citizen' is quite receptive to simplifying images and discourses, and is also more likely to change his/her own vote preference depending on the mood of the moment, or to media appeals. But on the whole their relation with politics fluctuates between indifference, resignation, scepticism and diffidence, not without some trace of resentment and anger.

Our second ideal-type is the 'detached citizen', who has a good level of education and some familiarity with political affairs, reads newspapers, follows television information programmes, has some contact with politics and public policies as a user of services or due to local initiatives, or involvement in some episode of political or civic mobilisation. In contrast to the 'remote citizen', the 'detached citizen' keeps up-to-date with public debate and is able to formulate evaluations which are often accurate. At first sight, this type of citizen appears likely to repeat the usual critical stereotypes, but when asked to give a personal experience can express opinions, and indicate grounds for inefficiency, and even suggest improvements.

The 'detached citizen' does not formulate unequivocal judgements on politicians and their performance, which indicates a capacity to distinguish. This ideal-type may have had the opportunity to meet specific political figures, and be willing to recognise their merits, and to ascertain their limitations, expressing less hasty verdicts. A local politician can enjoy the appraisal and comprehension denied to national politicians, and with regard to the latter, the 'detached citizen' is able to sketch a scale of credibility, at least on the basis of their television appearances. This type of citizens often reports having other things to do, for professional or other reasons, other than getting involved in politics. Yet, they appreciate political or social commitment. A forty-year-old worker, much involved with family and home, declared that 'taking part in democracy means living [...] committing yourself so that democracy works', but at the same time adds that: 'right now [I'm] just too busy surviving, [...] we just haven't got time to be involved [...]'.

Despite everything, the 'detached citizen' takes politics seriously: values it, criticises it, justifies it, talks about it with friends and acquaintances, and distinguishes between the work of one government – national or local – and another. The 'detached citizen' also has different expectations of different political parties and declares a political orientation. This can change over time for reasons that the citizen is ready to declare. 'Detached citizens' are sufficiently sceptical, and also vote, albeit irregularly, and justify their choice of vote, and do not rule out the option of abstention or a protest vote.

Finally, the third ideal-type is the 'involved citizen', who is informed, follows political affairs closely, has quite an exigent idea of politics, who reads newspapers and watches political programmes on television, who votes regularly and does not rule out some form of civil or other activism, and declares a willingness to mobilise or be mobilised. The 'involved citizen' discusses politics with friends and colleagues and makes complex value judgements. 'Involved citizens' also take the reasons of others seriously, or say they do. 'I don't have a closed mind,' reported a political science student, a little over twenty years of age, politically active in a populist party (*Lega Nord*), 'in the sense that I like to listen to other people's ideas. I'm critical of my political party when it makes mistakes, and I'm ready to listen to the ideas of others when these are reasonable and right'. The familiarity of the 'involved' with things political is correlated with level of education, but political and trade union activism, also in the past, is an excellent surrogate.

The 'involved citizen' may be discontent with how politics functions, nostalgic for better times, resigned and with a sense of impotence, but always maintains a critical approach, and can also have faith in a future improvement of politics. Moreover, the impatience of the 'involved citizen' leads to discrimination. He/she expresses impatience on some grounds, but satisfaction on others, and is ready to express very critical opinions of the behaviour of ordinary citizens: in the words of a fifty-year-old worker, with a long history of political militancy on the left,'people who talk badly about politics just don't want to go into it deeply. It's easy to make a good impression by saying 'they're all thieves, they're earning'. You need to see who they all voted for […] in Italy […] the percentage of people who go and vote is greater than in any other country […] if everyone says: 'God, what rubbish' […] then why do they all go and vote?'.

The 'involved citizen' distinguishes clearly between right and left, and even stresses the decline of traditional distinctions. Politically the 'involved citizen' may declare a specific location, or none at all, but in any case gives reasons for this. If this citizen cites a political family tradition, adhesion or detachment to it will be explained, just as the convergence of political supply from the different parties will be critically discussed, and evaluations formulated about the incumbents and the opposition. Sometimes 'involved citizens' accuse the opposition of being remissive, and sometimes they place their hopes in it. When the 'involved citizen' does not vote, his/her refusal is active, and politically motivated: to protest or to testify a sense of impotence, as a refusal to recognise what has been supplied by the parties. The conduct and style of politicians are grounds not of generic unrest, but of reasoned criticism. The 'involved citizen' emphasises the impunity of politicians, their widespread corruption, and their inability to respect the principles they claim to inspire, or also their electoral promises.

Obviously, we knew from the outset that the range of relations that citizens have with politics is wide, but these three types give us an idea of their variety. In any case, from our interviews, even when interviewees openly agree that politics is of little use and may actually be damaging, it is always a high point in their landscape. They may have little familiarity with politics, feel inept, lack the instruments to understand it or speak about it, ignore it or despise it, but broadly speaking, the words that politicians pronounce, and that citizens hear, fill the atmosphere. Not everyone listens to their words in the same way, but few manage not to listen to them at all.

In second place, relations with politics and personal feelings about it are influenced by many factors: sex, age, upbringing, education, employment, trade union activity, associative activism, religious affiliation, political inclination, reference milieux and so forth. Not all are equally familiar with politics and its language and not all use the political discourse.[32] The meaning of the words changes from one person to another, depending on personal experiences, the context of life and work, and political inclination. On closer examination these attitudes to politics

---

32 On the concept of political competence see Gaxie, *Le cens caché*, and 'Appréhensions du politique'.

appear very articulated and even contradictory. Those who are unequivocally and coherently critical of politics are the exception, even among those who declare that they abstain because they are sickened with politics.

It is quite realistic to conclude that a great number of human beings share a limited understanding of the problems and language of politics, and have a rather limited interest in it.[33] They think more about getting to the end of the month, the family or, when they can, holidays or what to do at the weekend.[34] Electoral campaigns push them to take a position, but they may not do so. A dramatic event, a critical situation, a war, or a scandal may raise their level of attention, but critical attitudes are normally uncertain. There are those who argue politically, but there are also those who repeat the commonplaces in circulation. In any case we can conclude that the judgements of citizens are generally less drastic than what one may deduce from a simplified examination of low turnout levels, electoral volatility or the discontent revealed by survey data.

Customer satisfaction or something else?

Not all citizens have the same expectations, not all are discontent with politics, and not all are discontent about the same things, to the same degree or for the same reasons. Indifference is not discontent. There is persisting discontent and the temporary gesture of exasperation. There is the dissatisfaction of those who see their political adversary in power, and who are discontented, irrespective of whoever is in government. Once the ritual tribute has been made by all, or nearly all, to the rhetoric of discontent, the account of the, by now, congenital mistrust – and the dramatic crisis of legitimacy that has hit democratic regimes – seems, to say the least, be overrated. We should also remember that what people say is one thing and what they do another is another. In their behaviour citizens show more respect for politics than they admit, and it is no surprise that non-voters remain a minority, albeit sometimes quite large.

At this point we should perhaps raise the question: is a non-secondary reason for the alarm surrounding the democratic malaise the same interpretative key currently used to understand the declarations and conduct of citizens, which could have a substantial impact on the meaning indirectly attributed to them? Is the reputation of malaise, and the malaise itself, by any chance the effect of an interpretation that treats citizens' declarations as a competent verdict on the performance of politicians and democracy itself?[35]

---

33 Robert A. Dahl, *Modern Political Analysis* (Englewood Cliffs, Prentice Hall, 1963, pp. 55–58).

34 Paul Veyne gives a brilliant explanation in *Le pain et le cirque. Sociologie historique d'un pluralisme politique* (Paris, Seuil, 1995, pp. 93–98).

35 Pierre Bourdieu, *Distinction*, and Patrick Lehingue, 'L'objectivation statistique des électorats: que savons-nous des électeurs du Front national?', in Jacques Lagroye (ed.), *La politisation* (Paris, Belin, 2003).

Let us take electoral choice. Democratic theory has long considered competition among alternatives just as an instrument with which to safeguard pluralism. As society is pluralistic, and legitimately split between different interests and values, it was obvious that representation should be pluralistic and that electors be offered more opportunities to choose. The theory did not consider that the choice of electors served to judge the performance – past or promised – of policy-makers and thus to improve its quality. By contrast, the current public discourse, and democratic theory, weave the eulogies of electoral competition and expect from the voter a judgement of satisfaction in the real sense. A reliable judgement of satisfaction is, as a consequence, traced together with voting behaviour, to electoral outcomes. The voter is supposed to be an informed and responsible consumer, who lingers in front of the shop windows of politics, weighs up what is on supply and looks for what best corresponds to his tastes, or that best promises to maximise personal utility, ready to move from one party to another, from one candidate to another, judging the promises or performance of government. But can we really liken the vote to customer choice?

The intriguing question is why not only politics, but also political theory, have appropriated the image of the competitive market and the elector-consumer. The most obvious hypothesis is that the market metaphor, and that of customer satisfaction, match the spirit of the times, characterised by the symbolic pre-eminence of the free market. Once the identification between the citizen, as a user of public services and as a consumer and tax-payer is recurrent in public debate, the obvious implication is to reduce the vote result to a verdict of customer satisfaction.

But other hypotheses can be proposed. It suits politicians to attribute a will to electors, and full capacity to judge the promises and performance of politicians, seeing that it ennobles the meaning of the vote and increases its legitimating value. The vote can be considered a judgement of approval for winners – their actions and programmes – and disapproval for losers. It reinforces the investiture of the first, who thus do not govern by chance, or because they have tricked the electors, but because this is the manifest will of the people.

The idea of politics as market competition also appeals to the media and electoral marketing experts, whose professional skills become more valuable as a consequence. The massive use of opinion polls is a determining factor in pulling along and reinforcing this meaning of the vote. Polls, whose authority is backed up by the media, have become one of the latter's most powerful weapons when competing with official politics. We must clearly distinguish between professional polls and improvised polls. Opinion polls commissioned by policy-makers or the media are different from surveys motivated by scientific reasons, and that use sophisticated and reliable sampling, selection and data processing techniques. Nevertheless, polls remain an instrument which has been imported from marketing to measure trends and consumer preferences, even giving the impression of declarations of will being made on the spot which are easily exploitable by whoever finds it expedient to do so.

But customer satisfaction applied to the performance of politics may also suit for another reason. Overshadowing the image of a pluralist society, grouped around different interests and different conceptions of the world, represented by politics, this analogy stresses another image, for which representation is guided from above, by the political supply. We can agree that this is effectively how things stand – according for instance to Schumpeter's theory. But it is significant that this interpretation of representation is quite simply raised to a norm, calmly ignoring the limits of the electors' ability to make judgements and consciously choose, denounced once again by Schumpeter.

Despite the reasons for caution, customer satisfaction applied to politics now carries great weight in the public debate. Many democratic regimes pay homage to it, and have promoted a majoritarian turn in their working rules, conferring the task of deciding the political colour of the executive, and its leader, directly to electors. Indeed, if citizens are the best judge of their own interests, why should democracy renounce such a worthy virtue?

The paradox is that the practices adopted by politicians, at the same time, deny the idea that it is possible to liken the voter to the consumer, ready to change choice of product according to its quality or the effectiveness of an advertising campaign. Politicians consider the stakes too high not to stimulate – and revive – lines of division, loyalties, choices of field, and not to propose beliefs, narratives, cognitive maps, common sense and so forth. Thanks to the media, only the techniques used to this end change, but this still remains one of the basic tasks of politicians.

Electoral sociology identifies a 'vote of opinion', by the strategic elector, who weighs up the alternatives and carefully judges the personality, actions and programmes of candidates.[36] But when it examines the reasons for the vote more deeply, electoral sociology also provides for other options. There is the 'belonging vote', when the vote confirms a person's support for a particular political cause or the affiliation to some associative, party or confessional circle.[37] There are people who vote as those around them vote and, finally, there is the 'exchange vote', when a vote is given in exchange for something. In reality, although clientelistic networks are not entirely a post-modern left-over,[38] the concept of exchange inappropriately simplifies, and stigmatises, more complex situations. Voters can

---

36 On the difference between an opinion vote, an exchange vote and a belonging vote see Arturo Parisi, Gianfranco Pasquino, 'Relazioni partiti-elettori e tipi di voto', in Parisi, Pasquino (eds.), *Continuità e mutamento elettorale* (Bologna, Il Mulino, 1977). For an analogous typology see Olivier Ihl, *Le vote* (Paris, Montchrestien, 2008). In general on the meanings of the vote see Daniel Gaxie (ed.), *L'explication du vote* (Paris, Presses de la Fondation nationale des Sciences politiques, 1989).

37 This was already observed by Robert A. Dahl in his research on New Haven. See *Who Governs? Democracy and Power in an American City* (New Haven CT, Yale University Press, 1961, p. 91).

38 Jean-Louis Briquet, Frédéric Sawicki (eds.), *Le clientélisme politique dans les sociétés contemporaines* (Paris, Puf, 1998), and Simona Piattoni (ed.), *Clientelism, Interests and Democratic Representation. The European Experience in Historical and Comparative Perspective* (Cambridge, Cambridge University Press, 2001).

vote for reasons of convenience, but also for deference towards some social authority they recognise, or due to direct or indirect personal relations with a candidate. Nothing prevents the motivations for the vote from being overlapping. In any case, and this needs to be repeated, political orientations – and vote preferences – are by no means accidental and are normally coherent with other opinions, *in primis*, religious opinions. In recent decades the social collocation of individuals has become more mobile, making it more difficult to arrive at unequivocal definitions, also weakening all forms of identification. The short range of electoral volatility nevertheless confirms how the choice of vote is rarely taken on the spot. What, in the last instance, decides electoral outcomes is the ability of contenders to reactivate the cognitive and value maps of their own electoral catchment area to their advantage. Where possible, they should avoid mobilising the electors of the adversary as a consequence, but it is first of all a question of diverting the distracted, the discontented and the uncertain, from non voting.[39]

Although they are not the same thing, individual political identification and orientations are not only coherent with religious feelings, but also enjoy some similarity with them. Normally they are 'inculcated' from childhood, assimilated in the family environment,[40] and successively conditioned as electors are collocated in a political, cultural, ideological context where they interact with and reciprocally recognise others. In spite of the modern rhetoric of the autonomous individual, political opinions, and hence electoral choices, develop socially and are confirmed or modified socially. They are, as stated, contextually conditioned by family, neighbourhood, work, religious practice, friendships and associative life and therefore also by participation in a party, trade union, association or movement.[41]

The rhetoric of the good democratic citizen legitimates any change in voter choice. Yet, the dissatisfaction narrative complains of excessive electoral volatility, which is, as just seen, less than is generally declared. In reality, for electors to review their own established political maps there needs to be an important biographical change such as a change of professional position, social status, reference milieu, or traumatic external events like an economic crisis,[42] or great historical processes. In their day industrialisation and urbanisation benefited socialist par-

---

39 The issue has been raised by, among others, Green, Palmquist, Schickler in their study of the USA. The problem for them is not how electors vote, but how democrats, republicans and independents vote, see Partisan Hearts and Minds, pp. 85–108.

40 Pierre Bourdieu, *Distinction*, pp. 437–440. See also Green, Palmquist, Schickler, *Partisan Hearts and Minds*, pp. 4–5.

41 For a broad analysis based on research data confirming this explanation, see Céline Braconnier, *Une autre sociologie du vote* (Cergy Pontoise, Université de Cergy Pontoise, LJEP, 2010).

42 Green, Palmquist, Schickler, *Partisan Hearts and Minds*, pp. 6–7. For a lively account of reconversion of moderate white-collar and blue-collar electors to the Republican fundamentalist right, see Thomas Frank, *What is the Matter with Kansas?* (New York, Macmillan, 2004).

ties, while the development of the welfare state has led public sector employees to prefer the parties of the left to those of right. Yet, the single elector tends to move within the political space to which he/she has always belonged or in its environs.

Together with the position of the 'opinion voter', who autonomously and strategically decides how to vote, we cannot rule out that the intense promotional action which focuses on the vote as customer satisfaction, has in the long run, reinforced the tendency to make this type of electoral choice, or non-vote, or protest vote. This is certainly encouraged by the poor moral reputation of politics in general, with its empty promises and disappointing actions. But the customers' expected attitude could also be a way for the individual elector to justify his/her choice of vote which is not in line with his/her own original preferences. Finally, electoral volatility also includes a share of electors who occasionally express a 'spite vote'.

Generally speaking, however, if the average elector is static, he/she is not necessarily irrational. Voters are rational in terms of their cognitive maps and values. Even if not inclined to change preferences radically, this does not mean that they do not notice the behaviour of the elected or listen to political discourse. In any case, we can safely conclude that electors cannot be reduced to strategic consumers, as well as, cannot at all be reduced to compact and growing negative judgements the multiple reasons for non voting, the vote for an unconventional party, the temporary switches of vote preference, or the declarations of discontent in opinion polls.[43]

There is another element to take into account, and that we have partly anticipated. It is difficult to speak of dissatisfaction and of growing political estrangement without considering the actual state of democratic regimes. We must also take into account the generally held feeling surrounding politics today, its reputation and the way in which it is cultivated. The same story of malaise is part of a circular movement that on the one hand shapes common sense, and on the other confirms it.

In this perspective many things have changed in the last sixty years. In the postwar period, democratic politics was rehabilitated after the failure of authoritarian regimes, and was a much valued activity. It was not valued by all, but certainly was by the political ruling classes. Citizens were strongly encouraged to vote and the vote was seen as both a right and a civil obligation: in Italy (now repealed), Belgium and Greece voting was compulsory. Non-voting was openly stigmatised, if not legally sanctioned. A significant trace of this remains in the fact that, at least until now, and apart from the account of generalised mistrust in politics, when interviewed personally, electors find it difficult to admit to non-voting.[44]

---

43 Opinion polls and international comparisons are all relatively recent. Who knows what the results would have been if had they been carried out regularly in the past?

44 Braconnier, *Une autre sociologie du vote*, pp. 28–31 and Mark Gray, Miki Caul, 'Declining Voter Turnout in Advanced Industrial Democracies, 1950–1997: The Effects of Declining Group

In the past citizens were also encouraged to belong to parties. Parties were recognised as privileged centres of participation and civil behaviour. On their side, parties were first of all powerful organisational machines designed to promote membership, to stimulate consensus towards the political personnel and to encourage electoral turnout.[45] This sort of party, that both integrated and mobilised, no longer exists. Finally, the capacity of opposition parties to drain off social unrest and dissatisfaction has also decreased. Once the opposition's job was to single out potential grounds for discontent and unrest, and to mobilise them together. Various reasons for discontent were reorganised around projects for a different sort of preferable future, thus making of them a political resource. Parties in office also drew advantage from this activity as well as the entire democratic regime. Contemporary parties operate uniquely on the electoral ground, do not associate citizens any more and use discontent just for short term objectives.[46]

Politicians are very pleased to evoke the people, but offer citizens only a simulated and episodic reception, arguing that the post-modern citizen agrees on the division of political labour and is, in the most favourable hypothesis, only interested in good government. These are contradictory and confusing messages, when from time to time there is also the reappearance of the rhetoric of the good citizen interested in politics on which their fate depends.

This type of citizen is a rarity. Politics is omnipresent and the media administer it in massive doses, but as with religious feeling, knowledge of, and interest and participation in politics, have to be encouraged and cultivated for the great majority of people on both the organisational and the symbolic level.[47] The fact that citizens are now on average more educated and better informed does not mean

---

Mobilization', *Comparative Political Studies* 33(9), 2000, 1091–122.

45 Citing Elmer E. Schattschneider, on the declining ability of parties to activate electors, see Martin P. Wattemberg, *Where Have all the Voters Gone?* (Cambridge MA, Harvard University Press, 2002). See also Braconnier, *Une autre sociologie du vote*, pp. 144–151, where ample use is made of research data that confirms this explanation.

46 On this point Kirchheimer was provident: see 'The Waning of Opposition in Parliamentary Regimes' *Social Research: An International Quarterly* 24(1), 1957, 127–156. At the end of the 1970s the differences among parties became a relatively popular research theme, beginning with Richard Rose, *Do Parties Make a Difference?* (London, Macmillan, 1980). It depends on what indicators are used, or what policies are examined. A study of fifteen Western countries shows how economic policies vary noticeably according to the party that is in power: see André Blais, Donald Blake, Stéphane Dion, 'Do Parties Make a Difference? A Reappraisal', *American Journal of Political Science* 40(2), 1996, 514–520. It remains to be seen what the range is, of the variation.

47 Carried out on in a cite of the Parisian banlieue, subject to a prolonged and close observation, the study by Céline Braconnier and Yves Dormagen, *La Démocratie de l'abstention. Aux origines de la démobilisation en milieu populaire* (Paris, Gallimard, 2007), explore in depth how much the environment counts, and how much the political environment in which individuals are inserted counts.

that they have any less need to be prompted.[48] They may even need more atten-tion, because there are reasons to suppose they have internalised the idea – so fre-quently confirmed by politicians – that in democracy citizens merit respect. It is an hypothesis that has been put forward by Margaret Canovan: how can the sovereign people resign himself to his own impotence and irrelevance and to the impotence of the regime that put him on the throne?[49] And yet there is no lack of proof that politics prefers to keep citizens at a distance. Is it citizens that hate politics or is it politics that hates citizens?

In overturning the current point of view we are not stating that discontent and mistrust do not exist. Let us put it this way: collective life, as has always been the case, has thousands of grounds for suffering and complaining, but this does not mean that these must necessarily and exclusively lead to discontent with politics. A closer examination of the situation shows that this is not the case. We read very dubious displays of dissatisfaction as democratic malaise, and the way in which this is interpreted, amplifies its political meaning disproportionately. Politicians are not without their faults. But we must ask: is it by any chance the way that democratic regimes have evolved, and the way they display themselves to the public, that has transformed politics into a tool which acts as a magnet for the ordinary sufferings of human beings, and which distracts them from other objects?

There is no need to imagine conscious management in a similar development, although undoubtedly neo-liberal criticisms of politics are now widely shared. The fact is, however, that we find many politicians, rather than deny it, actually compete to reveal democratic discontent, so that at times we suspect that they are reciting part of some collective rite. In this rite politics plays the role of scapegoat, which is obviously difficult to reconcile with that much older role of the benevo-lent tribune of the general interest.

Denigrating the powerful is a time-honoured custom. In medieval times, Car-nival was a subversive occasion that allowed the governed not only to mock the powerful, but even to live a second existence for a limited space of time, where normal life was suspended, social hierarchies turned upside down, thus creating a temporary condition of alternative equality to everyday inequality.[50] Is the repeated and amplified account of discontent nothing other than a way to exorcise and con-ceal reasons for social unrest, channelling them against politics and politicians, but leaving them politically under-represented?[51]

---

48 This point is also supported by qualitative research. See Gaxie, *Sur l'humeur politique maussade.*

49 This argument is raised by Margaret Canovan in 'Trust the People! Populism and the Two Faces of Democracy', *Political Studies*, 27(1) 1999, 2–16.

50 Mikhail M. Bachtin, *Rabelais and his World* (Bloomington, Indiana University Press, 1994, pp. 9–12). Pierre Bourdieu talks instead of an 'adolescent revolt' and of a primary inclination to an 'anti-institutional mood', which is particularly acute in some historical moments and among some social groups: see *Sur l'État. Cours au Collège de France* (1989–1992) (Paris, Seuil/Raisons d'agir, 2012, p. 17).

51 It is certainly a sign the fact that non-voting is in France is the most frequent choice among the

This might explain the critical, but also irreverent and even scornful, behaviour of politicians *vis-à-vis* politics. Competition among parties has been replaced with candidate-centred competition, and big political projects have been replaced by 'negative campaigning' where the opponent is denigrated. We cannot even count the number of discourses and antipolitical actions used by unconventional, but also by conventional politicians, to poison the atmosphere, each hoping to unload damage on their competitors. Even if this manoeuvre is partly successful, the problem is that no-one remains unharmed. Antipolitical discourses and actions damage politics in its whole. Perhaps this is a rather important issue that needs to be faced.

---

unemployed. See Emmanuel Pierru, 'Sur quelques faux problèmes et demi-vérités sur les relations entre chômage et vote', in Frédérique Matonti (ed.), *La démobilisation politique* (Paris, La Dispute, 2005).

chapter eight | antipolitics

Antipolitics from above

One of the many terms that have renewed the political lexicon is 'antipolitics'. It is not a new term and may even date back to the French Revolution,[1] but it has the drawback of being polysemic. In the mid-1950s, Stanley Hoffman recognised Poujadism and its mix of anti-tax revolt, anti-intellectualism, anti-parliamentarism and anti-elite protest as a form of antipolitics.[2] Not much later, in the early 1960s, the same word was used in France to label the attempts to redimension the elected ruling class in favour of the technocratic elites.[3] Both meanings of antipolitics are still in vogue,[4] but what really brought the concept of antipolitics back into mainline circulation with all the honours was the civil mobilisation against communist regimes in Eastern Europe in the years running up to the collapse of the Berlin wall.[5] If the communist regime was official politics, then its opponent was antipolitics.

The conditions prevailing in the two different parts of the continent were completely dissimilar. But this did not stop the term from being reimported into the West, standing for the many examples of civil society's protest against official politics from the 1980s on.[6] Initially, the intention was to exploit the virtuous reputation of the uprising against communist regimes. Hence the reimportation was deliberate. Yet, the positive meaning of the term was soon overturned. Today,

---

1   Luciano Monti, 'Antipolitica', in Roberto Esposito, Carlo Galli (ed.), *Enciclopedia del pensiero politico. Autori, concetti, dottrine* (Bari/Rome, Laterza, 2000).

2   Stanley Hoffmann, *Le Mouvement Poujade* (Paris, Colin, 1956).

3   Michel Merle, 'Inventaire des apolitismes en France', in George Vedel (ed.), *La dépolitisation : mythe ou réalité* (Paris, Armand Colin, 1962, pp. 43–60).

4   For the second meaning, considering the case of development agencies, see James Ferguson, *The Anti-Politics Machine: Development, Depoliticization, and Bureaucratic Power in Lesotho* (Cambridge, Cambridge University Press, 1990).

5   György Konrád, *Antipolitics: An Essay* (New York, Holt, 1984). At that moment, when nobody could expect the collapse of communist regimes, Konrad's idea was that of an alternative both to communism and to liberal democracy: politics from below, politics without power. See also Vaclav Havel, *The Power of the Powerless: Citizens Against the State in Central-Eastern Europe* (London, Hutchinson, 1985).

6   One of the first to use the term is Geoffrey J. Mulgan, *Politics in an Antipolitical Age* (Cambridge, Polity Press, 1994).

politicians and journalists polemically call antipolitics any manifestation of democratic malaise of which we spoke in Chapter 7. Not voting, electoral volatility, the protest vote or the vote for populist parties are all considered disturbing and disqualified by calling them antipolitics.

We will define this sort of antipolitics as 'antipolitics from below', but there is also a second, equally thriving version of antipolitics, made up of the immense repertoire of polemical discourses, gestures and actions regarding politics that fill public debate and electoral competition. This form of antipolitics – in particular, the theme of the morality or efficiency of politicians – is a move that has always been used by outsiders from the political field. But this dispute is not theirs exclusively. Quite the reverse. For around the last thirty years the most visible and noisy producers of antipolitics have been the so-called populist parties. As the last arrivals in the politico-electoral arena, they have been most damaged by the oligopolistic agreements typical of cartel parties. But antipolitical discourses are a move that even actors well rooted in that arena, or in its surroundings, and provided with impressive resources, resort to in various forms.

Many of these actors do not take part in electoral competition: this is the case of the mass media and the business *milieux*. As regards civil society, which has long since become a recognised political actor, it would contradict itself if it entered into direct competition with political parties. What is paradoxical is that conventional political actors, as well, are not sparing in their harsh criticisms of official politics, against which they supply a thriving antipolitical polemic, and not only during electoral campaigns. If all this can be defined as 'antipolitics from above',[7] it is reasonable to suppose that it contributes abundantly to exciting protest and 'antipolitics from below'. Once the atmosphere is permeated with antipolitical polemics stirred up by all sorts of actors, how can the ordinary citizen avoid being influenced?

Nothing, however, is more political than antipolitics, from above or below. Citizens' dissatisfaction and even indifference, as we could see, has a political meaning. *A fortiori* antipolitical discourses and actions are authentic politics, irrespective of who carries them out or makes them. Is it by any chance the blackout of other critical discourses, starting with the socialist discourse, dedicated to society and the economy, that has recently provoked so much congestion?

The rhetorical repertoire of antipolitics from above is particularly varied. Andreas Schedler has drawn up a meticulous inventory which identifies two main families of antipolitical rhetoric.[8] On the one hand, there are rhetorics where

---

7   For the distinction between 'antipolitics from below' and 'antipolitics from above', see Vittorio Mete, 'Four Types of Anti-politics: Insights from the Italian Case', *Modern Italy* 15(1), 2010, 37–61.

8   Andreas Schedler, 'Introduction: Antipolitics – Closing or Colonizing the Public Sphere', in Schedler (ed.), *The End of Politics? Explorations into Modern Antipolitics* (New York, St. Martin's Press, 1997). For an earlier catalogue of forms of antipolitics, see Bernard Crick, *In Defense of*

politics is superfluous, and to be suppressed or minimised. On the other hand, there are rhetorics where politics needs to succumb or to be radically renewed. The first family includes extreme individualistic doctrines, doctrines of spontaneous order, antipluralist doctrines and doctrines that state the impracticality of correcting the natural laws that support society or the creation of order through politics. The second includes technocratic rhetoric, the 'amoral' conception, according to which politics is merely the strategic pursuit of private ends, 'moral' antipolitics, i.e., religious fundamentalisms, and 'aesthetic' antipolitics, that denies any sort of politics that reduces it to mere spectacle.

At the heart of political competition similar rhetorics remain largely in the background. They help constitute the images of political actors, or feed the discussions of intellectuals, but only occasionally appear in the limelight as such. In that case they must be modified to one degree or another and require a consistent drive towards simplification. In the public debate more banal registers prevail. Complaints about the misdemeanours of politicians are more easily adaptable to the contingent needs of political struggle. But let us now see, starting from the media, how the actors use these registers.

It has long been known that the media participate actively in political competition, with politically autonomous aims, or with aims that benefit whoever controls them. Indeed, if the media are viewed as outsiders, given their collocation *vis-à-vis* political institutions, this does not mean that they have not become direct competitors of politicians, in the first place, regarding the political agenda.[9] What makes the media particularly fearful, and feared, is not only their degree of penetration, which has become so much more capillary in recent decades, especially in the world of television, but the way in which they currently communicate politics to citizens.

Media logic, the audience constraint that orients not only commercial television, but also its public counterpart, offers an additional incentive to contrast politics harshly and to make a spectacle of its rivalries, privileges, failures and misdemeanours. It is the audience that urges the media to offer a victimised representation of the condition of the governed with respect to those who govern. Thanks to the permanent display of wrongs suffered by the governed and their complaints, the media even lays claim to a representative function – of a tribunitial sort – competing with official political representation.

The media have always claimed, and carried out, a representative function. If representative and democratic regimes recognise the pre-eminence of public opinion, the media are considered the basic instrument through which public opinion emits its judgements. The new technologies offer an additional opportunity to recite this part. In homage to democratic rhetoric, what is more attractive than

---

Politics (Chicago IL, University of Chicago Press, 1962).

9   On journalists as agents of the political field see Pierre Bourdieu, *Propos sur le champ politique* (Lyon, Presses universitaires de Lyon, 2000, p. 37).

contesting politics with its simple sign on a ballot paper, or membership activism, with nothing less than the direct voice of the man on the street?

There is little reliable data, but radio and television promote a popular account of the voice of the ordinary citizen who criticises and denounces the insecurities of daily life, unemployment, inflation, the malfunctioning of public services and the tyranny of the bureaucracy and public office, and so on. The citizens to whom the media gives a voice are not representative of the population, and the electoral effects of their complaints are probably quite modest.[10] Protest and discontent, amplified in the name of the freedom of information, of the dutiful vigilance of public opinion, and of service made to citizens, nevertheless penetrate public opinion and compete to shape the image that citizens have of politics.

In addition, news of political events or policy measures are obscured by agitated gossip, rows, the sensation-seeking actions of politicians that the media mercilessly put on display, not without some paradoxical consequences. Since ideological politics ran out of steam, the media have reprojected an exacerbated version of the rivalries of politicians on the public, together with their multiple transgressions, committed to the detriment of public morality. Governors have always been expected to demonstrate morality and disinterest. Today the media have much more powerful instruments to unmask and expose transgressions and to create scandals, not without encouraging a mood of distrust among citizens. Let us not forget that most ordinary citizens have sporadic contact with politics and therefore have an image permeated by the flow of media-generated news, with effects that vary depending on the more or less aligned style of the media, on political circumstances, the presence of competing agencies, and their own level of cultural and political competence.

The disadvantage is not light, but it is inevitable. Political actors have learnt to live with the media and to use them, but so have other actors. Let us be realistic. The disappointing and deluding image that the media give of politics is a problem which politicians must get used to, just as they must get used to the advantages which their competitors gain from this image.

The second voice of antipolitics from above, consists of the business *milieux*. This is also a closed category which tends to reproduce itself. Moreover entrepreneurs and managers enjoy incomes and privileges which are well above those of politicians. These are even more difficult to measure against outcomes, and they are often indifferent to their failures. Yet, with the help of a general mood oriented

---

10 According to research carried out in the USA, this does not mean that who listens is not influenced in their opinions. They are directly and, above all, indirectly, influenced, see David Barker, *Rushed to Judgement: Talk Radio, Persuasion and American Political Behavior* (New York, Columbia University Press, 2002). See also Diana Owen, 'Talk Radio and Evaluations of President Clinton', *Political Communication* 14(3), 1997, 333–353 and Stephen E. Bennett, 'Americans' Exposure to Political Talk Radio and Their Knowledge of Public Affairs', *Journal of Broadcasting & Electronic Media* 46(1), 2002, 72–86.

in their favour, when the economic *milieux* intervene on the public scene, they are not deaf to the preachings of antipolitics. Pushed towards the centre of the public scene, not only by post-Fordism and globalisation, but also by neo-liberal ideology, the business *milieux* are keen to profit from the condition of weakness in which politicians now find themselves, and they do so by openly casting doubt on their morality and efficiency. Sometimes they adopt the technocratic register, but the market register is easier to apply, and by definition the market has become more efficient and more moral than politics.

Politicians' antipolitics

It is, however, in the heart of the political world that antipolitical discourses and actions are mainly produced. Public morality is the most obvious theme. On the one hand, this has become the subject of debate and of reciprocal accusations. On the other hand, due also to media logic, it has induced a transformation of the behaviour of political actors. The often voyeuristic attention that media professionals dedicate to politics has not only increased the focus on the issue of morality, but has pushed politicians to continually trade accusations of immorality, inefficiency, distance from ordinary people, and inability to deal properly with key questions. At the same time – and this is more surprising – media logic has induced politicians to divest themselves of the role of authority in order to fraternise with ordinary citizens in a continuous display of non-ritual discourse, informal language, irritated actions, tribunitial type emphasis, and even unexpected generosity and farcical behaviour.

Once politicians have abandoned their official theatrical space, they step down into the midst of the public and recite their part at street level.[11] Even the discontent of citizens has become a rich occasion to exploit and politicians do so in the most disparate forms: Margaret Canovan has defined this conduct as 'politicians' populism',[12] while Claus Offe prefers to speak of 'antipolitical politicians'.[13]

It is doubtful whether it is appropriate to use the concept of populism, even if Canovan, who is the author of one of the most valued contributions on the phenomenon, does so. In any case, what it indicates is an extension of personalised leadership and a style which is now much in vogue. The actor puts new blood into the personage of the leader and directs it in various ways against the institutional

---

11 Gianfanco Marrone, develops the argument in *Corpi sociali. Processi comunicativi e semiotica del testo* (Turin, Einaudi, 2001, pp. 215–285). On the theatrical metaphor see Eric Landowski in *La société réfléchie. Essais de socio-sémiotique* (Paris, Seuil, 1989).

12 Margaret Canovan, *Populism* (London/New York, Harcourt Brace Jovanovich, 1981, p. 351).

13 Claus Offe, 'Democracy, Disaffection and Institutions: Some Neo-Tocquevillean Speculation', in Mariano Torcal, José R. Montero (eds.), *Political Disaffection in Contemporary Democracies* (London/New York, Routledge, 2006, p. 37).

dimension of politics. In the past leaders presented themselves as the disinterested servants of a collective cause. By contrast, today's leaders stand out individually on the political horizon and are content to testify to their personal morality. They do this by displaying their extraneousness to the liturgies of conventional politics, even at the cost of confirming the account in question of its misdeeds. The reciprocal accusations that politicians direct against each other, each politician vindicating their own diversity. But the sum of these accusations reinforces the critical narrative of politics currently in circulation.

Jimmy Carter stands out among the examples cited by Canovan. Even if he had already been the Governor of Georgia, he stood for and won the presidential elections presenting himself as a peanut farmer and Baptist preacher. Above all, he publicly professed his faith and his religious commitment in a context where interest in religion was showing signs of a reawakening. Until then American politics had treated religion with caution, but Carter wanted to use it as a public pledge of morality, in contrast with the cynicism of professional politicians *à la* Nixon.

Since then the moral register has enjoyed an impressive boost in response to the upsurge of scandals. These have always been an object of media attention, and the media have always worked to stir them up, but in recent decades scandals seem to have multiplied. Together with the subsequent atoning actions, scandals provide plenty of material to draw up an antipolitical perspective for whoever is interested in it: political opponents, journalists, exponents of civil society or judges in search of notoriety.[14]

Calling to mind the old antiparliamentary polemics, the moral register hits the *politique politicienne* severely. The idea is that official politics is inherently corrupt, that professional politicians are contemptible characters, distant from ordinary people and their problems, and a privileged caste whose only concern is to look after its own affairs. A good example is Italy in the early 1990s, where the fierce campaign sewn up by key political figures and pushed into the limelight by the media against the practices in use in politics, and among those in charge – that is, Italy's top political management – was one of the decisive factors in the collapse of the so-called First Republic.[15] In 1994 this was the opportunity for Berlusconi to take up the challenge, making use of his background as a self-made man, his entrepreneurial merits and his promises to import the virtuous logic of the private sector into politics, to periodically mock the useless rites and the '*teatrino*' of politics.

But politicians can also return the accusation of immorality to the sender, by playing the part of the victim. When touched by the Clairstream scandal, Sarkozy reacted by thundering out against the political-business *combines* of the Fifth Republic. Scandals are also an opportunity for low-cost demagogic gestures. Dur-

---

14 Hervé Rayner, *Dynamique du scandale: de l'affaire Dreyfus à Clearstream* (Paris, Le Cavalier Bleu, 2007).

15 Alfio Mastropaolo, *Antipolitica. Alle origini della crisi italiana* (Naples, L'Ancora, 2000).

ing the 2007 electoral campaign Sarkozy's adversary, Ségolène Royal was busy putting citizens on the heels of deputies – not the President of the Republic – promising to set up, if elected, participatory monitoring of their activity.[16] Each one has his own arguments to exploit.

But it is not just a question of explicit polemics. There are also other more subtle and indirect forms of antipolitics. A good example is Tony Blair, who was extremely prolific in of all sorts of antipolitical moves.[17] For instance, in order to distance himself from conventional politics, he often used the hyper-democratic register. Blair did this when he introduced devolution in Scotland and Wales with a new referendum procedure. As regards the war in Iraq, decided in sharp contrast with public opinion, the British premier used instead the moral register: even if it was unpopular, the war against Saddam Hussein was a moral cause to be pursued. Finally Blair often declared himself a non-professional politician. Not casually, he also exploited his private-family sphere. After the birth of his youngest child, he took short paternity leave, casually changing nappies for the cameras. In a similar vein, at the start of her career as minister, Ségolène Royal made her maternity a media event. She too set a fashion.

In order to represent official politics as alien to the man on the street politicians not only use the ostentation of their private lives, but are also ready to reveal, with the help of the media, its most intimate aspects. Just to confirm that they are ordinary people, politicians are even ready to reveal the most titillating details, coming nearer to media stars portrayed in glossy weeklies.[18] Chirac let himself be photographed naked by the sea, Berlusconi boasted of his plastic surgery and his success with women, as well as his marital problems, the latter shared publicly with Nicolas Sarkozy.[19] What are the consequences of all this on the idea and credibility of politics?

And what about the mania for youthfulness so widespread in the public debate? In sharp contrast to the old politics, today's leaders must be young and the old ones scrapped. Those who are not young enough become young, update their wardrobe, smooth out their wrinkles, jog or cycle on the streets and surround themselves with young people. For centuries political leadership has embodied authority in the

---

16 Royal obtained also the support of the theory. See Loïc Blondiaux, 'La démocratie participative, sous conditions et malgré tout. Un plaidoyer paradoxal en faveur de l'innovation démocratique', *Mouvements* 2/50, IV, 2007, 118–129.

17 Peter Mair, 'Partyless Democracy. Solving the Paradox of New Labour?', *New Left Review* 2(2), 2000, 21–35.

18 In France Jamil Dakhlia has put forward the formula of 'peoplisation' in *Politique people* (Rosny-sous-Bois, Bréal, 2008).

19 The press was already prying into the private lives of politicians in the 1930s, but the phenomena is now accentuated and exaggerated. See the account of the developments in France by Christian Delporte, 'Quand la peopolisation des hommes politiques a-t-elle commencé? Le cas français', *Le temps des médias* 10(1), 2008, 27–52.

shape of a father figure. The traditional task of the leader was to protect, reassure and guide, making experience a condition of esteem. No-one was ever concerned about the age of Adenauer, de Gaulle or De Gasperi, while figures such as Brandt, Schmidt, Kohl, Heath, Nixon and Thatcher were, without anyone noticing, all around the same age as today's 'young' leaders. Nevertheless, if necessary, today youth can be surgically simulated, as an obligatory sign of the refusal of routine and officialness, as well as of a dynamism that politics is no longer able to offer, if not in this way.

There is even a heroic register and the rediscovery of charisma. It has become more modest, requires more banal virtues, but is sometimes re-proposed by politics.[20] This is a tried-and-tested mechanism. A sense of alarm is created, followed by the anticipation of dramatic events and, hence of a personality ready to adopt extra-ordinary solutions to deal with them. As always happens with the construction of charisma, the holder of the alleged charisma works with words and actions.[21] Meanwhile the circle of his collaborators recite their part, especially displaying the relations of deference and even submission they have with the leader. The media intervene to highlight personal accomplishments and actions, to narrate the leader's unstoppable rise to the top, destinies sealed in childhood, miraculous conversions, and at the same time publicly discrediting potential competitors as responsible for previous failures.

Charisma requires that a leader governs in solitude and shoulders responsibilities heroically,[22] harangues enthusiastic meetings, and if need be wear warlike garb, or meets his or her equals in impressive circumstances to decide the destiny of the world. The continuous state of stress required by charisma also helps to remove the holder from the grinding duty of day-to-day problems. Therefore, leaders must generate stress on their own, open up new conflicts, avoiding the rules, take unexpected actions and utter unexpected words. Being 'men of action'[23] their commitment is necessarily tireless and unceasing. Unfortunately, the risk that charisma, under the irreverent scrutiny of the media, turns out to be a caricature is very high.

---

20 On the artificial construction of charisma see Norbert Elias, *The Court Society* (Dublin, Dublin University Press, [1969] 2006). For a refined analysis of the construction of charisma, see Ian Kershaw, *The 'Hitler Myth'. Image and Reality in the Third Reich* (Oxford, Oxford University Press, 1987). For an interesting case see Brigitte Gaïti, *De Gaulle, prophète de la Cinquième République* (Paris, Presses de SciencesPo, 1998). The mediocrity of the contemporary replica is highlighted by Jean-Louis Briquet on Berlusconi: 'Le 'phénomène Berlusconi'. Crise et recomposition du jeu politique en Italie', in Fédérique Matonti (ed.), *Le désengagement politique* (Paris, La Dispute, 2005).

21 On George W. Bush's style, see Colleen S. Shogan, 'Anti-Intellectualism in the Modern Presidency: A Republican Populism', *Perspectives on Politics* 5(2), 2007, 295–303.

22 For some interesting arguments with a sociological analysis of heroic decision see the special issue of *Politix*, 2/82, 2008 on *Figures de la décision*.

23 Gianfranco Marrone, *Corpi sociali. Processi comunicativi e semiotica del testo*, p.260.

All this obviously corresponds to the media-logic requirements. The tendency to oust the classic parliamentary debate also corresponds to this logic. Once parliamentary debates were carried out in public, according to the severely codified rules of good manners, together with the oratory disputes of leaders on key issues of public interest and the negotiations that often surpassed party differences. Personal offence is no longer unusual and no longer publicly stigmatised. The noble tradition of parliamentary civility is showing very apparent signs of deterioration in several countries, presumably with some polarising effects on public opinion.[24]

Finally, in search of a low-cost surrogate of more valued and more taxing arguments, another example is the peacemaking and unifying vocation occasionally discovered by politicians. After his election in 2007, Nicolas Sarkozy brought together expertise in a rigorously non-partisan *Commission sur la libération de la croissance française.* This was presided over by a former Mitterrand advisor, superseding all political differences and referred to a mixed group of business executives, academics, senior civil servants and even foreign experts, to reassure citizens with an authoritative depoliticised diagnosis of the state of French society. A similar move was outlined, albeit more timidly, at the British elections in 2010, by Nick Clegg, leader of the Liberal Party, when he called for shared choices by all parties, at least on some issues. We can also cite the so-called 'technical governments' in Italy and Greece at the end of 2011. Political leaders step aside and leave government responsibility to experts, academics, senior civil servants and even bankers. Generally unpopular political decisions are taken under their supervision and with their agreement. This too is a variation of antipolitics. We will see if it is destined to have a future.

The return of the extreme right?

If denigration and antipolitical tones have become a commonplace in the staging of conventional politics, this is even more true for its opponents, i.e., for the outsiders. The most sensational innovation among the latter appeared unexpectedly precisely where political life has the reputation of having colder and more sober tones, that is, in Denmark and Norway. At the end of the 1960s, two new parties appeared in these countries loudly denouncing exorbitant taxes, welfare wastage and the inadequacy and immorality of conventional politics, and immediately had considerable success.[25]

---

24 See the special edition edited by Olivier Rozenberg and Pierre-Yves Baudot (eds.), 'Violence des échanges en milieu parlementair', *Parlement[s], Revue d'histoire politique* 14(8), 2010.

25 In 1972 a rich tax lawyer founded the Danish *Fremskidtspartiet.* In 1973 its anti-tax and anti-welfare programme won 16 per cent of the vote, making it the second party in Denmark. In 1973 in Norway, a journalist, Anders Lange, founded a similar party under his own name.

Were they rightist parties? There are good reasons to argue that they were. What such parties tried was to mobilise the protest – until now a near monopoly of the working class – of the middle classes, and to make this protest electorally exploitable.[26] Importing an American term during this period, in Europe there was often talk of 'silent majorities'. This was probably the start of a process of reciprocal learning. In 1972 the recipe was enriched with some nationalistic ingredients thanks to the setting up of Le Pen's *Front National*. In 1978 in Flanders, the *Vlaams Blok* (now *Vlaams Belang*) came into being. It had some fascist ancestors, and its programme contained a demand for Flemish independence from Belgium.

In Italy, in the early 1980s a constellation of regional parties appeared and finally federated in 1989 to become the *Lega Nord*, which quickly attracted a part of the electorate of the *Democrazia Cristiana* in the northern regions. Between 1992 and 1994 the collapse of the latter, and of the entire party system, allowed Berlusconi to create an explosive mixture of antipolitical provocation, neo-liberal declarations, cultural conservatism and mediatic seduction, successfully amalgamated thanks to an unexpectedly rapid access to government, named *Forza Italia*. Between the end of the 1980s and the beginning of the 1990s in Austria and Switzerland two small moderate parties, the UDC and the FPÖ, began to recycle similar themes, starting an extremely successful electoral ascent.

In the early 1980s the *Front National* was the first to exploit the theme of immigration, until then laboriously dealt with thanks to the policies of welfare integration. The discovery spread rapidly and combined with the rhetoric of the protection of national workers *vs.* immigrants, aided by the process of de-industrialisation, with security and the protection of cultural identity against the threat not only of immigration, but also of globalisation. Yet, this did not reduce the polemic against fiscal pressure and against the oligarchies of official politics, public bureaucracies, trade unions and parties. In the end a polemic against European institutions, considered too bureaucratic, too costly and too cosmopolitan, was added.

It is an apparently minor problem, but the appearance of such political parties not only destabilised party systems that had frozen in around the 1920s, but created problems for whoever wanted to classify them.[27] Given the tribunitial type

---

26 A successful but short-lived precedent was Pierre Poujade's *Union et fraternité française*. See Stanley Hoffmann, *Le Mouvement Poujade*.

27 On problems of classification raised by the new-generation right see Cas Mudde, 'The War of Words. Defining the Extreme Right Party Family', *West European Politics* 19(2), 1996, 225–248. There is those who talk of the 'radical right': see Peter H. Merkl, Leonard Weinberg (eds.), *Right-Wing Extremism in the Twenty-First Century* (London, Routledge, 2003). Others prefer the label of 'extreme right': see Martin Schain, Aristide Zolberg, Patrick Hossay (eds.), *Shadows over Europe: the Development and Impact of the Extreme Right in Western Europe* (New York, Palgrave Macmillan, 2002). Another label is that of 'anti-establishment parties': see Amir Abedi, *Anti-political Establishment Parties: A Comparative Analysis* (New York, Routledge, 2004). Finally, others talk of populism, with many variations: neo, national, ethnic, alpine, television, etc. See,

tones and popular rhetoric shared by these parties, the most frequent solution has been to recall to service the old, and approximative, label of populism. According to this rhetoric, on the one hand we have the people, a virtuous, wise and hard-working body of citizens, and on the other hand, we have its enemies, starting with the establishment, which threaten the hard-won wealth, the identity and the future of the people.[28] But is this label really appropriate? What if, on the contrary, it is nothing other than the return of the extreme right, that between the end of the twentieth century and the start of the new millennium has found the conditions for a new and unexpected renaissance in Europe and not only?

The extreme right is an old spatial classification that has long been used to identify fascist movements and regimes. As always happens in cases like this, it is a rather debatable classification and therefore difficult to use, and has been used to label rather different things, temporally and spatially. If we use the conservative right as a reference point, the extreme right in the nineteenth century corresponded to the anti-parliamentary discourse that sought to avoid or neutralise universal suffrage and mass democracy. This was an ultra-conservative right, conditioned by the memory of the *ancien régime*. Its end was perhaps marked by the Dreyfus affair in France, in which anti-parliamentary conservatism married anti-semitism and nationalism. A second epoch was that of fascism *stricto sensu*, when violence and extremism exploded and came to power in Italy and in Germany. What followed was a third, more obscure, season of postwar neo-fascism, strewn with episodes of violence: from the French OAS to the Italian '*stragismo*'.[29] What stops us from thinking that we are now in a fourth season, clearly different from the preceding ones?

What is the common denominator of the extreme right? And what is the rich repertory of issues on which these new parties can draw? According to Piero Ignazi,[30] a first characteristic is the rejection of the principle of equality. This brings

---

inter alia, Yves Mény, Yves Surel, *Democracies and the Populist Challenge* (New York, Palgrave Macmillan, 2002); Daniele Albertazzi, Duncan McDonnell (eds.), *Twenty-first Century Populism: the Spectre of Western European Democracy* (London, Palgrave Macmillan, 2007). Cas Mudde suggests a synthesis: *Populist Radical Right Parties in Europe* (Cambridge, Cambridge University Press, 2007).

28 Canovan extended the use of the concept of populism, but introduced accurate differences, however it was Ghita Ionescu and Ernest Gellner's *Populism: its Meaning and National Characteristics* (London, Weidenfeld & Nicolson, 1969), that extended it much further, in an attempt to classify phenomena hard to classify, phenomena such as third-world parties and regimes, which are neither fascist nor communist.

29 On the terrorist strategy of the extreme right in Italy in the 1970s see Anna Cento Bull, *Italian Neofascism: The Strategy of Tension and the Politics of Nonreconciliation* (New York, Berghahn Books, 2007).

30 Piero Ignazi, *Extreme Right Parties in Western Europe* (New York, Oxford University Press, 2003).

us to a organicistic and hierarchical conception of politics and social order and to racism. A second characteristic is the focus on traditional values – the family, religion, but also, always in an organicistic perspective, the 'nation' and the 'people'. Moreover, the extreme right has an inclination towards law-and-order policies, to intolerance in home affairs and aggressiveness towards the outside world. Finally, the extreme right is resolutely hostile to any political regime that recognises pluralism. According to its organicistic perspective, it always accused interests and parties of causing artificial and odious divisions within the national community.

On the contrary, neither state intervention in the economy nor its opposite are required preconditions of the extreme right. Sometimes this has led to statism in the economy, e.g. during the interwar periods, when state intervention became fashionable, whereas Italian fascism, for example, had a lively liberal season at the outset.

There are therefore good reasons to ask why the term 'populism', which was coined to classify phenomena quite different from those of today, has recently been preferred to that of 'extreme right', to label these new parties.[31] Classical populisms were quite different, beginning with their notion of the people. The people of Russian populism, the people of the American tradition, the people of Latin-American populisms from the 1920s, and the people of the populisms of former European colonies after the 1950s, were all the people of the popular classes. It may not always be the same class: in Russia it was the peasants, in America the farmers and the weakest parts of the middle classes of the Midwest and South, in the populisms of South America, like peronism, and the third world, like nasserism, it was the poor peasants or urban masses. Nevertheless, it was always the popular classes, for whom the populist parties when in power claimed, or offered, concrete redistributive measures.[32]

Today's audience of pseudo-populists is quite different, and certainly nearer to that of the conventional extreme right. A recurrent diagnosis recognises the electoral audience most suitable for them among 'modernization's losers'. These are the electors most penalised by socio-economic changes, who feel most at risk, and who may be the most likely to accept the protection and the gloomy promise of revenge that these parties offer.[33] According to other analyses, these electors

---

31 The controversy over the term 'populism' is particularly intense in France. Annie Collovald is severely critical of the use of the concept in Le "populisme du FN", un dangereux contresens (Bellecombe-en-Bauges, Éditions du Croquant, 2004).

32 Gino Germani, *Authoritarianism, Fascism, and National Populism* (New Brunswick NJ, Transaction Publishers, 1978). Germani argues that Southern-American populism should not be discredited, and claims that the links of the working class with populism are irrational. It is a technique of rudimentary inclusion, but for example, peronism supplied concrete benefits to the working classes and a sense of identity which was previously lacking.

33 The theme of fear – of unemployment or immigration – has been widely raised by French analyses of the success of the *Front National*. See Pascal Perrineau (ed.), *Les croisés de la société fermée. L'Europe des extrêmes droites* (Gémenos, Éditions de l'aube, 2001). It is a successful account. It

come from the independent middle classes and the more advantaged sectors of the dependent workforce: people who work in technologically more advanced firms with higher levels of productivity. In reality it is not clear whether the target of this sort of mobilisation really consists of social groups at more or less immediate of risk of decline, or groups ready to profit from the difficulties of others in order to increase their own slice of the resources cake. Yet, there is clear evidence that this section of the electorate, that scorns politics, despises bureaucracy and is intolerant of tax demands, is tenaciously attached to welfare. They are 'welfare-chauvinists', wanting to exclude immigrants, but who have no intention of foregoing the public health coverage, the school system, or pensions.[34]

Reliable data tell us that, among the electorate of pseudo-populist parties, men, young people, old people, independent and manual workers and the unemployed are overrepresented, that the level of religious participation is below average, and that the average level of education is low. We can add that the phenomenon tends to take root more in small and middle-sized towns and in the countryside than in large urban centres.[35] On the contrary, there is nothing to indicate that these parties profit from a steady electoral haemorrhage suffered by leftist parties. Considering that conventional conservative parties have always enjoyed a broad consensus among the middle classes and popular classes, the most reasonable hypothesis is that a part of these electors has been radicalised.[36] This does not mean that the pseudo-populist parties do not also focus successfully on the world of blue-collar workers in difficulty[37] – why not try to profit from the disorientation and problems of the leftist

suits the segments of the reformist left that have distanced themselves most from their traditional popular roots and that draw some justification from it. It suits the far left, that stresses the importance of this rooting and criticises the distancing of the social democratic left. It is welcomed by the right, especially the new-generation extreme right (e.g. *Lega Nord*), as this label gives it the opportunity to be accredited as the paladins of popular classes.

34 Herbert Kitschelt, Andrew J. McGann, *The Radical Right in Western Europe* (Ann Arbor, University of Mitchigan, 1995, pp. 22–24).

35 Marcel Lubbers, Merove Gijsberts, Peer Scheepers, 'Extreme Right-Wing Voting in Western Europe', *European Journal of Political Research* 41(3), 2002, 345–378. See also Kai Arzheimer, Elisabeth Carter, 'Political Opportunity Structures and Right-wing Extremist Party Success', *European Journal of Political Research* 45(3), 2006, 419–443.

36 Although limited to France, Patrick Lehingue suggests caution on the worker vote for the *Front National* in 'L'objectivation statistique des electorates : que savons nous des électeurs du Front National' in Jacques Lagroye (ed.), *La politisation* (Paris, Belin, 2003). But how much is approximative classification on the basis of employment, ignoring the relational context in which individuals are situated, fundamental: Norbert Elias, John L. Scotson, *The Established and the Outsiders* (London, Sage, 1994).

37 On the USA see the brilliant portrait drawn by Frank Thomas, *What is the Matter with Kansas?* (New York, Macmillan, 2004).

parties? – but that their preferred audience is still the independent middle class.[38]

The hypothesis is confirmed by the successes enjoyed by the 'Tea Party movement' in America.[39] Everywhere polemical antipolitics stands out, but it is above all the middle classes which are anxious. In America, as in Europe, segments of middle-class minorities are willing to mobilise and there is no lack of political entrepreneurs ready to exploit their anxiety. The protest uses the repertoires that the local political market offers them. Immigration and the anti-tax protest have both proved rather successful on both sides of the Atlantic.

In the 1920s the European middle classes were convinced that the enemy was the working class. Today the enemies are others. In the postwar period not only the working class, but also the middle classes were consolidated sociologically and reassured politically, thanks to policies of full employment, work opportunities and welfare protection. It was an extraordinary operation of social and political engineering, as well as, despite the radical change of direction, the welfare reforms promoted by neo-liberal politics, that generated insecurity and instability. These sentiments have since been mobilised in the name of the people. Too bad if the people, as that of so-called populists, are this time *ethnos* and not *demos*![40] Intolerance against islamists, gypsies and immigrants is an excellent surrogate for antisemitism.

We can naturally object that the new extreme right respects the electoral verdict and the rules of democracy. But perhaps they have simply learnt to use these rules, and even to reinterpret them. In opposition to constitutional democracy, i.e. the rule of law, the separation of powers, the limitations to the majority principle, the new extreme right proposes a model of plebiscitary democracy that rejects all these things and gives primacy to the declarations of the sovereign people and the leadership invested by it. Indeed, a very singular democratic fundamentalism has made its appearance. Democratic rules and principles have been emptied of their meaning, indicating a disturbing impatience with democracy understood as a confrontation and conciliation among different ideas, interests and parties. Shrewdly used, today the democratic rules allow citizens to put away the black and brown shirts, and the truncheons, and nevertheless, betray democratic principles.

If this is really how things stand, then the use of the populism as a concept is not only inappropriate, but even treacherous. It is inappropriate to classify an infantile syndrome of democracy such as South-American populism – approxi-

---

38 Of course, there are also those who argue that things go rather differently. See Pascal Perrineau (ed.), *L'engagement politique. Déclin ou mutation* (Paris, Presses de la Fondation nationale des Sciences politiques, 1994). For a more recent contribution see Daniel Oesch, 'Explaining Workers' Support for Right-Wing Populist Parties in Western Europe: Evidence from Austria, Belgium, France, Norway and Switzerland, *International Political Science Review* 29(3), 2008, 349–373.

39 Theda Skocpol, Vanessa Williamson, *The Tea Party and the Remaking of Republican Conservatism* (New York, Oxford University Press, 2012).

40 Pier Paolo Portinaro, *Breviario di politica* (Brescia, Morcelliana, 2009, pp. 55–63).

mate in procedure, but roughly democratic in substance – and a senile pathology, witnessed by parties that are rather different. At the same time, when recycling the term populism, the risk is that of euphemism.

The first to use the term was Pierre-André Taguieff, an authoritative French scholar of antisemitism, who in the 1980s registered, with some concern, the reappearance of old ghosts and their electoral growth, and tried to give this a label, and to highlight its particular traits.[41] The *Front National* rejected violence explicitly, it respected the rules of the game, and above all it was French. Was Taguieff's choice by any chance shaped by the old claim made by France's political and intellectual *milieux* of their country's allergy to fascism?[42] In recompense, there is reason to believe that the bearers of the label, that had immediate success in the media, received it with pleasure and have worn it with enthusiasm, consequently refining their discourse. They have been called populists, rather than with much less honourable appellatives: why not profit from it?

The risk of misunderstanding is exacerbated by the fact that the term populism is also frequently applied to whoever shows some interest in the problems of the popular classes and proposes redistributive policies in their favour.[43] If populism consists of vibrant critical stances toward politicians, what prevents whoever wants from accusing all those who openly place the issue of the morality of politics at the centre of their discourse of populism? The term populism risks lumping too many things together and underestimating the racism, intolerance and aggressive nationalism preached by the new extreme right. At the same time, is it not politically rather risky to claim that the so-called populists have a privileged representation of the working class?[44]

We may feel reassured thinking that the noisy and rough tones adopted by the new extreme right are the effect of the constraints placed on it by mediatised politics. As outsiders, they adapt zealously to the media's predilection for the exasperated conflict. And this adjustment is very fruitful. The so-called populists like to display a great mobilising capacity, but even if they mobilise limited minorities, the media coverage amplifies them well beyond their actual weight.[45] The

---

41 Paul-André Taguieff uses the formula of 'national-populism'. See *L'illusion populiste. De l'archaïque au médiatique* (Paris, Berg International, 2002).

42 Michel Dobry (ed.), *Le mythe de l'allergie française au fascisme* (Paris, Albin Michel, 2003).

43 In France an article in *Le Nouvel Observateur* (3 July 2008) entitled 'Un Le Pen à l'envers' carried an interview with an eminent political scientist, Pascal Perrineau, that compared Le Pen and Olivier Besancenot, leader of the *Ligue communiste révolutionnaire.*

44 Does calling them populist also bear witness to how much the working classes have become unpopular with those who professionally coin labels and those who were once its spokespersons? The question is raised by Philippe Riutort in 'Importer Berlusconi. Le déchiffrement de l'expérience politique de Bernard Tapie à la lumière du "populisme" italien' *Politix*, 77 2007, 153–171.

45 On the role of Fox News and the business world, close to the Republican Party, in the success enjoyed by the 'tea parties', see Skocpol, Williamson, *The Tea Party.*

problem is that words are never spoken in vain, especially in front of television cameras, and someone, somewhere, will assimilate them. Finally, we cannot also rule out that similar words indicate deeper extremist impulses, which may have been brought to the surface by the failure of the condemnation of antidemocratic discourse, that has become less rigorous than in the past.

To confuse observers even more the new extreme right has even learnt to use the language of rights. One can hear discourses that demand the protection of the cultural and material heritage of the people, its values, history, religion, landscape, security (against imported criminality) and wealth as rights. But is evoking rights and repudiating physical violence – albeit not without some breaches – and substituting it with verbal aggression, enough to become democratically credible?

Nevertheless, we need to observe the fruitful, and not always implicit, partnership which exists between the pseudo-populists and the parties of the conventional right, and which also has some precedents. Not infrequently one has the impression that the pseudo-populists say what is unpronounceable for others. Given the weakness of contrasting action, this has the effect of making banal some democratically unpalatable words. Parties of the conventional right have also reviewed their own political offer importing issues and tone from the new extreme right as was the case of Sarkozy's presidential campaigns.[46] In Denmark and Italy pseudo-populists have even joined government coalitions with them. And what about when some rather severe proposal for dealing with immigration and criminality find an audience in other parts of the political spectrum?

Civil society

Regarding outsiders and antipolitics from above, civil society also merits some attention. It may seem bizarre to classify civil society in this way, were it not for its political ambitions, that have rapidly transformed it. What was only a concept and rhetoric half a century ago has now become an alternative political space and actor. It has subsequently been promoted to a protagonist of political life and government action – then denominated 'governance' – which actively participates in one and the other, although in an original form and pretending not to have ambitions of power.

The political vocation of civil society, the idea of a space for spontaneous politicisation outside the state, has roots that go back a long way. Its antecedents include the first glimmers of associative behaviour discovered by Tocqueville in America, the nineteenth-century opposition of the *pays réel* to the *pays legal*

---

46 For the French case see the special issue *Mouvements* 4(52), 2007, dedicated to *La new droite. Une révolution conservatrice à la française?*, with articles by Claire Artufel, Joseph Confavreux, Bruno Cousin, Renaud Epstein, Michel Kokoreff, Jade Lindgaard, Christian Mouhanna, Anne-Sophie Petitfils, Marc Saint-Upéry, Pierre Tevanian and Tommaso Vitale.

in France and Italy, and above all the public sphere of which Jürgen Habermas painted a fascinating and problematic picture.[47] There was a time when even parties were a part of civil society, or, at least, this was Gramsci's idea. Later on, from around the 1960s onwards, once public opinion appeared to have been infiltrated by the media, whose critical capacity was conditioned by clear interdependencies with politics and economics, the term civil society has proved effective to indicate those forms of political action that overflow beyond the borders of conventional politics, like social movements.[48]

The theoretical roots of the concept are ancient and noble. Ferguson, Locke, Hegel, Tocqueville and Gramsci are its illustrious envoys.[49] But it was only from the 1970s that civil society has been re-proposed in the political lexicon, as a constellation of associative forms, legitimated by their voluntary, spontaneous and informal nature. As the object of growing theoretical interest, that has thoroughly updated the concept,[50] and by the scoop-hungry media, the decisive recognition of civil society, despite its inspiration that was critical towards official politics, has come from politics itself.

Once the initial bewilderment has been overcome, politicians too have hosted the arguments of civil society in public debate, have legitimated its forms of self-organisation, and have even renewed their own ranks by co-opting leading militants when it suits them. If civil society was initially perceived as being in competition with parties, later on the competition continued, but politicians tried to establish a profitable division of labour with it: they started to consider civil society as a space where all forms of extrapolitical action and antipolitical criticism, including social movements, can be enclosed, in order to officiate, regulate and integrate them. Since the 1970s, according to Bruno Jobert, politics, with the assistance of the theory, has even legitimised civil society, drawing up at least three different models.[51]

In the early 1980s the neo-conservative model imagined civil society as a sphere where individuals, to order to be freed from the destructive dependence on welfare, convened to restore traditional family and religious ties. Contrasted with the

---

47 Jürgen Habermas, *The Structural Transformation of the Public Sphere: An Inquiry into a Category of Bourgeois Society* (Cambridge MA, MIT Press, 1991).

48 For an original historical review for France see Hélène Hatzfeld, *Faire de la politique autrement. Les expériences inachevées des années 1970* (Rennes, Presses universitaires de Rennes, 2005).

49 Norberto Bobbio, 'La società civile', in *Stato, governo, società. Per una teoria generale della politica* (Turin, Einaudi, 1985).

50 For a general overview, see Michael Edwards (ed.), *The Oxford Handbook of Civil Society* (Oxford, Oxford University Press, 2009).

51 Bruno Jobert, 'Contending Civil Society Frameworks: Beyond the Tutelary Model', in Bruno Jobert, Beate Kohler-Koch (eds.), *Changing Images of Civil Society: From Protest to Governance* (London, Routledge, 2008). In the same volume see Hélène Michel, 'Incantations and Uses of Civil Society by the European Commission'.

state and with the big interest organisations, civil society had the task of supervising the transparency and morality of public action and the quality of public services from below, encouraging users to behave as responsible and aware consumers.

According to a second perspective, in the 1990s, persuaded that the free market exercised a corrosive effect on social life, the theorists of the 'third way' and social capital, perceived civil society as the world of voluntary associations, the no-profit sector and NGOs. Civil society became the virtuous *locus* of trust, solidarity and community ties. On the one hand, it is through these ties that civil society puts pressure on the state and public powers. On the other hand, civil society has been requested also to produce welfare services to replace those provided by the state in a way which is considered bureaucratic, inefficient, invasive and costly. The return to the state and its bureaucratic procedures was ruled out. But the state was invited to encourage civil society, to offer organisational and financial support, and to maintain its structure discretely. This second model thus represents civil society as an essential instrument of empowerment and of responsible citizenship.

A third and more recent 'integrative' model promotes civil society as a protagonist of new forms of social dialogue. It is the social space where new arenas of debate are established. It is also where not only the reserves of competence and available civicism are mobilised, but where the weaker interests are aggregated in order to involve them in the definition of public interest and in drafting collective choices. It is again the job of the public authority to create the right conditions for civil society to accomplish this task, by encouraging participation, and by adopting educative and informative policies dedicated to the more disadvantaged categories.

It is under such changeable forms that civil society has been received with all the honours in the *Who's Who* of politically relevant actors. After having recognised it, politicians celebrate it, consult it, negotiate with it and delegate key competences to it. For its part, civil society confirms its otherness, encouraging and conveying antipolitical resentment and critical entreaties, but also shows that it is ready to cooperate. Beyond being a low-cost appendage of the welfare state, useful to supply public services especially locally, and even asked to supply alternative, and low-cost, employment opportunities, civil society is thus another form of 'politics by other means'.

By adopting a perspective similar to that of post-materialist theorists, and taking the idea of democracy enshrined in constitutional documents as obsolete, Pierre Rosanvallon, whilst not ignoring the limits, has recognised in civil society and in the apparently chronic discontent with politics, the elements of a combative 'counter-democracy' and a system of indirect power. This tends to function 'against' rather than 'for', but civil society may prove extremely useful in overseeing and monitoring elected leadership.[52] Nevertheless how much does civil society

---

52 Pierre Rosanvallon, *Counter-Democracy: Politics in an Age of Distrust* (Cambridge, Cambridge University Press, 2008).

match its own rhetoric? Although it may be good for the health of democratic regimes, is it the appropriate antidote to the difficulties experienced by them? Can civil society really reanimate relations between citizens and politics?[53] And if so, can this instrument be exported for the benefit of new, or not yet consolidated, democracies?

There is good reason to believe that civil society is also a homeopathic remedy for forms of more unpleasant conflict. Its declared extraneousness to politics and the displacement that it imprints on the axis of conflict helps conceal earlier hostility between the well-off social strata and the working classes.[54] The reputation of autonomy and spontaneity of civil society, also raises many doubts. It certainly attracts disinterested militants, helps the weakest, assists the terminally ill, combats the racket and mafias, protects small savers and consumers and promotes innovative forms of consumption. Within civil society there are those who march for peace, who defend the environment and cultural patrimony against big infrastructural projects and urban speculation, or who help the most unfortunate populations of the planet. But, first of all, nothing is too spontaneous. Supporting civic activism is a highly professionalised activism. The more successful episodes of civil society mobilisation use refined organisational and communicative competences, often coming from the political market or from big organisations such as churches or trade unions, that invest in the cause of the day. To no lesser degree, civil society depends on the media and the media's predilection for spectacular claims inevitably orients it: minority rights or Nimby movements attract more audience than the wage demands of industrial workers.[55]

There is also reason to doubt the contrast between the disinterest of civil society and the particularism of parties and organised interests. We should ask whether the Hegelian representation of civil society, as a sphere of the particular, and of the private 'systems of needs', is not more reliable. Civil society remains a heterogeneous agglomeration insensitive to unitary objectives and shared actions and its structure runs the risk of generating segmentation, to the detriment of broader and more durable forms of solidarity and involvement. Moreover, according to the theory of social capital, there are two types of it: 'bridging' and 'bonding'. The first unites, the second excludes.[56] The distinction also fits civil society. Despite the excessive homage paid to its noble qualities, we must not underestimate the risk

---

53 The question is raised for instance by Iris M. Young, *Inclusion and Democracy* (Oxford, Oxford University Press, 2000, pp. 154–187).

54 Jean-Pierre Gaudin, *Pourquoi la gouvernance?* (Paris, Presses di SciencesPo, 2007). On the non-Western experience see Kanishka Jayasuriya, Kevin Hewison, 'The Antipolitics of Good Governance', *Critical Asian Studies* 36(4), 2004, 571–590.

55 Erik Neveu, *Sociologie des mouvements sociaux* (Paris, La Découverte, 2005, pp. 102–106).

56 Robert D. Putnam, *Bowling Alone. The Collapse and Survival of American Community* (New York, Simon & Schuster, 2000, p. 23).

that civil society could also turn out to be uncivil, privatistic and tribal.[57]

Civil society does not deserve to be assimilated with the pseudo-populist right merely because it often engages in discourses critical of politics. Its tones are at times exasperated, the language may be provocative, and the protest noisy, but civil society normally registers demands for 'another politics' which should be inclusive and not exclusive, solidaristic, participatory and more genuinely democratic. Yet, this does not solve the problem of how to classify some forms of fundamentalist-type religious associationism, or local committees which have recently emerged to defend urban communities against immigrants.[58] Once the rhetoric of civil society has persuaded citizens of the incapacity of official politics to deal with problems and has authorised them to 'do-it-yourself', who guarantees that this rhetoric will not, in the end, marry issues of the pseudo-populist right? We have already observed some disturbing examples of intolerance in which the local committees have been involved. The risk that an 'uncivil society' consolidates is not at all remote.

---

57 Ota De Leonardis reports this risk in *In un diverso welfare* (Milan, Feltrinelli, 1998).

58 Donatella Della Porta, 'Immigration and Protest: New Challenges for Italian Democracy', *South European Society and Politics* 5(3), 2000, 108–132.

chapter nine | a political class

A recycled concept

The divide between governors and the governed that democracy had promised to bridge, or at least reduce, seems to be opening up once again. Whether it has really expanded, or whether this is simply what is being reported, that sanctions the expansion in public debate and theory, is the impressive revival on a universal scale of the rather old concept of 'political class'. The term was coined by the antiparliamentary polemic that flourished between the nineteenth and twentieth century, and its use was virtually limited to the experience of the representative regime in Italy.

It was Gaetano Mosca who fathered the concept and for whom '*classe politica*' was the 'organised minority' that opposes and rules the 'disorganised majority' in all societies. Mosca's ambition was to formulate a general theory of society as an alternative to that of Marx. This is the reason why Mosca, adopted the term 'class'. His theory was in any case, based on a radical antidemocratic prejudice, that is, if it is always a minority that governs in democracy, then democracy is a sham. At the same time, the parliamentary regime has some inherent and unavoidable weaknesses.

Dwelling on these flaws, Gaetano Mosca turned out to be an obstinately conservative intellectual. In his opinion the electoral principle upset society's natural hierarchies. Moreover, the recruitment of the governors through an electoral competition generated incentives for the competitors to listen to the claims of particular interests and even induced them to solicit particular interests themselves. Mosca held that the electoral principle rewarded those politicians most able to manipulate public opinion and, in the case of parties, to manipulate the less-educated classes. In the specific Italian context at the close of the nineteenth century this was the reason why, according to him, the style and interests of politicians converged to the point where they constituted a class of their own, distinct from the rest of society.[1]

The background of Mosca's theory were the difficulties of Italian parliamentarism. Nevertheless, between the nineteenth and twentieth century, similar criti-

---

1   Gaetano Mosca carried out a careful analysis in *Sulla teorica dei governi e sul governo parlamentare* (Palermo, Loescher, 1884). See also Mosca's classic work, *The Ruling Class* (New York, McGraw-Hill, [1896] 1939). See Alfio Mastropaolo, 'La double théorie de la classe politique de Gaetano Mosca', *Revue de politique comparée* 11(4), 2004, 611–630.

cisms were also frequent outside Italy. Denigration of the parliamentary regime and its protagonists was very lively in France during the Third Republic, where it alternated between the moderate and the ironic, but always conservative, tones of Robert de Jouvenel's *La République des camarades,* the technocratic leanings of André Tardieu's *La profession parlementaire* and the monarchic and authoritarian antiparliamentarism of Charles Maurras.[2]

The German situation was not very different. An energetic antiparliamentary feeling had also caught on in Germany, where it would flourish under the Weimar republic. At that moment an effective competitive regime was established and critics were directed against mass parties. Some solid arguments against parties had already been polemically expressed by Robert Michels. In his research on political parties first published in 1910, Michels formulated his 'iron law of oligarchy',[3] claiming a tight link with the thought of Mosca in order to ennoble it. But it will be Carl Schmitt who will combine antiparliamentarism with the anti-party polemic. The charge made by Schmitt against parties, not without citing Michels, was that they abrogated the valued deliberative customs of liberal parliamentarism.[4]

In the totally different context of America in the early 1940s, Joseph A. Schumpeter also severely criticised electoral democracy, even if he avoided authoritarian temptations. Raising the question of the shared interests of political professionals and condemning their opportunistic behaviour in the hope of election or re-election, he put forward proposals which dealt exclusively with balancing the electoral principle.

Once democracy had been restored the theme of politicians' common interests reappeared, focusing the polemic again on parties. In Italy during the 1950s it was a respected jurist and newspaper columnist, Giuseppe Maranini, who revived the theme of political class, coining the neologism of 'partitocracy',[5] syntonising with the French public debate during the transition from the Fourth to the Fifth Republic.[6]

---

2   Robert de Jouvenel, *La république des camarades* (Paris, Grasset, 1914); André Tardieu, *La profession parlementaire* (Paris, Flammarion, 1937).

3   Robert Michels, *Political Parties: A Sociological Study of the Oligarchical Tendencies of Modern Democracy* (New York, Free Press, [1911] 1962).

4   The crossed citations of Michels and Schmitt are interesting. Schmitt cites Michels in *The Crisis of Parliamentary Democracy* (Cambridge MA, MIT Press, [1923] 1985, 89). Michels pays him homage in the foreword to the second German edition of his book *Zur Soziologie des Parteiwesens in der modernen Demokratie* (Stuttgart, Alfred Kröner Verlag, 1925). Schmitt also cited Mosca, whose work and political positions he knew well. On antiparliamentarism in Germany see Sandrine Baume, 'Le Parlement face à ses adversaires. La réplique allemande au désenchantement démocratique dans l'entre-deux-guerres', *Revue française de science politique* 56(6), 2006, 985–998.

5   Giuseppe Maranini, *Miti e realtà della democrazia* (Turin, Comunità, 1958).

6   We have already recalled Michel Debré, *grand commis*, gaullist and enduring protagonist of the political life of the Fifth Republic, *Ces princes qui nous gouvernent* (Paris, Plon, 1957). In France

Not long after the anti-party polemic reappeared in the German Federal Republic.[7]

A quarter of a century later, an incisive development in the dispute over parties and party personnel was marked by the very influential perspective of rational choice theory. In addition to indicting state intervention, this accused electoral personnel of serious intrinsic vices: an inability to withstand the claims of interest-holders, and being subject to the invincible attraction of 'pork barrel politics' and 'log-rolling'. That is, the exchange of favours with the high risk of corruption that it entails. The point of contact between this analysis and the older antiparliamentarian controversy is that both consider similar defects to be ineradicable, but in the wake of Schumpeter the treatment prescribed by rational choice is simply a strict containment of electoral politics.[8]

In conclusion, the representation of politics as a sphere dominated by the interests of its professional operators is not confined to Italy. Nevertheless, for a long while the concept of 'political class' has remained an exclusive of Mosca and, more specifically, of Mosca in Italian. Even the translations in a foreign language avoid being literal. The English translation used the expression 'ruling class',[9] without damaging the hearing enjoyed by the theory or preventing it from feeding a strong elitist current present in the political science.[10] Yet, even without citing Gaetano Mosca, the term 'class' had already been used by James Bryce in *The American Commonwealth*, where he proposed a detailed account of the creation of a political personnel professionally dedicated to politics in the United States, and that he referred to as the 'governing class', and incidentally also 'political class'.[11] But the example had no follow-up. The more generic expressions 'ruling class' and 'elite'[12] had more success. The latter was in circulation in the social sciences thanks

---

during this period antiparliamentarism/antipartyism had even become a party in the shape of Poujadism: see Stanley Hoffmann, *Le Mouvement Poujade* (Colin, Paris, 1956).

7   On the German polemic, considering innovation and differences with respect to the prewar anti-party polemic, see Susan E. Scarrow, 'Politicians Against Parties: Anti-party Arguments as Weapons for Change in Germany', *European Journal of Political Research* 29(3), 1996, 291–311.

8   James M. Buchanan, Gordon H. Tullock, *The Calculus of Consent: Logical Foundations of Constitutional Democracy* (Ann Arbor, University of Michigan Press, 1962).

9   See also one of the first American readers of Gaetano Mosca: James Burnham, *The Machiavellians. Defenders of freedom* (Putnam & Co, London, 1943). The German translation is similar: *Die herrschende Klasse, Grundlagen der politischen Wissenschaft* (Bern, Verlag A. Francke AG / Munich, Leo Lehnen, 1950).

10 On the interesting courses of thought of Mosca and Pareto in the USA, that intersect with the pluralist tradition, see Mario Grynszpan, 'La théorie des élites aux Etats-Unis: conditions sociales de réception et d'appropriation', *Genèses* 37, 1999, 27–43.

11 Lord James Bryce, *The American Commonwealth* (New York, Cosimo, [1888] 2007, vol. 2, pp. 53–68).

12 For a reflection on the concept of an elite and its success, as well as related concepts and the problems of similar research, see William Genieys, 'Nouveaux regards sur les élites du politique',

to an author of greater international renown than Mosca, Vilfredo Pareto,[13] who distinguished between different types of elite and especially between a governing and a non-governing elite, even if not a political one. Some decades later, Charles W. Mills talks of 'power elites' when describing and denouncing the military-industrial complex that upheld so-called democratic regimes overseas,[14] and even the formula 'political elite' has had some success.[15] The only one to stick to a literal translation of Mosca's expression was Raymond Aron.[16] In general, beyond the term 'elite', terms such as 'leadership' or 'ruling class', seemed more appropriate.

We can suppose that the social sciences preferred not to distinguish too precisely those who play political roles with respect to the rest of the 'ruling class', either because democracy expects similar roles to be held temporarily, or because in democratic regimes political leadership normally has a pluralistic and socially heterogeneous configuration, even with significant restrictions.[17] Therefore, how can we not consider the significance of the recognition of the concept of political class from the early 1990s, with its translation into other languages? The current conditions of democratic regimes are nothing like what Mosca describes. Yet, scholars, journalists and all sorts of political actors talk of 'politische klasse', 'classe politique', 'clase politica', and 'political class'.[18] Is there by any chance an

---

Revue française de science politique 56(1), 2006, 121–147.

13 Vilfredo Pareto, *The Mind and Society: A Treatise on General Sociology* (New York, Dover Publications, [1916] 1963, vol. 3, pp. 1422–1424).

14 Charles W. Mills, *The Power Elite* (Oxford, Oxford University Press, 1956). In this tradition see George W. Domhoff, *The Power Elite and the State: How Policy is Made in America* (New York, Aldine de Gruyter, 1990). The concept 'power elite' is also used by Thomas Bottomore in *Elites and Society* (London, Watts, 1964).

15 Geraint Parry, *Political Elites* (London, Allen & Unwin, 1969).

16 For a critical reflection on the concept of class, social and political, see Raymond Aron, 'Classe sociale, classe politique, classe dirigeante', *Archives Européennes de Sociologie* 1(2), 1960, 260–281.

17 There is no entry on 'political class' in the *International Encyclopaedia of Social Sciences* (New York, Macmillan & Free Press, 1968), or the *Dizionario di politica* (Norberto Bobbio, Nicola Matteucci, Gianfranco Pasquino, Turin, UTET, 2004). The concept has finally been accepted in the *International Encyclopedia of Political Science*, see Maurizio Cotta, 'Political Class' in Bertrand Badie, Dirk Berg-Schlosser and Leonardo Morlino (eds.), vol. 6, (London, Sage, 2011, pp. 1950–1960. At the Fourth World Congress of Sociology held in Stresa in 1959, when a group of scholars who were well-known or becoming well-known, including Norberto Bobbio, George E. Catlin, Joseph LaPalombara, Georges Lavau, James H. Meisel and Alain Touraine, held a workshop on political elites, the concept of political class was immediately discarded, and the discussion focussed on the concept of elite. The idea that a democratic and pluralist society could recognise the presence of a social group in some way coherent, that could monopolise political power, met with greater diffidence. See various authors, *Le élites politiche* (Bari, Laterza, 1961).

18 Among the publications of an essayist-journalistic nature, see Pierre Pellissier, *Tous nuls: portrait*

unconscious desire to revive the negative bias of Mosca's formula?

It is obvious to ask whether by any chance the antipolitical atmosphere that we currently breathe has favoured the reawakening of the never-resolved controversy over representative democratic regimes. But we should ask whether this has also generated a new and self-seeking misunderstanding, aimed at inciting the discontent of the governed against politicians. Nevertheless, we cannot either rule out the hypothesis that the behaviour and conduct of politicians has changed, justifying their representation *qua* social group, morally mediocre, beneficiaries of unjust privileges and united among themselves at the expense of the citizens.

An unfulfilled promise

In principle, in democracy all citizens are equally entitled to govern. All rigid and pre-established inequalities are ruled out and governors and governed are theoretically interchangeable. This is the best guarantee that the actions of governors will meet the expectations and needs of the governed and that political posts do not become positions of long-term privilege. In reality we know that it is the nature of the people, its numbers, heterogeneity and incompetence, that make this promise unrealisable. Political representation is one of the basic tools used to deal with this problem, but it always had a very difficult task. Representation is required to represent and not represent at the same time.[19] But how can a body of representatives where each pretends to really represent electors, or the interests that sustain them, reconcile their responsibility to govern and the infinite and contradictory claims of the represented?[20]

---

craché de la classe politique (Paris, Denoël, 1990); François Bazin, Joseph Macé-Scaron, Les politocrates: vie, moeurs et coutumes de la classe politique (Paris, Seuil, 1993); Hans H. von Arnim, Fetter Bauch regiert nicht gern. Die politische Klasse – selbstbezogen und abgehoben (Munich, Kindler, 1997); Eric O'Keefe, Who Rules America: the People vs. the Political Class (Spring Green, Citizen Government Foundation, 1999); Peter Oborne, The Triumph of the Political Class (London, Simon & Schuster, 2007). For more strictly academic works see Klaus von Beyme, Die politische Klasse im Parteienstaat (Frankfurt a.M., Suhrkamp, 1993); Hilke Rebenstorf, Die politische Klasse: zur Entwicklung und Reproduktion einer Funktionselite (Frankfurt, Campus, 1995); Hans-Dieter Klingemann, Richard Stöss, Bernhard Wessels (eds.), Politische Klasse und politische Institutionen: Probleme und Perspektiven der Elitenforschung: Dietrich Herzog zum 60. Geburtstag (Opladen, Westdeutscher Verlag, 1991); Jens Borchert, Jürgen Zeiss (eds.), The Political Class in Advanced Democracies: A Comparative Handbook (Oxford, Oxford University Press, 2003); and Lutz Golsch, Die Politische Klasse im Parlament: Politische Professionalisierung Von Hinterbanklern Im Deutschen Bundestag (Baden-Baden, Nomos, 1998).

19 Edmund S. Morgan illustrates this dilemma brilliantly in, 'Government by Fiction: The Idea of Representation', *Yale Review* 72, 1983, 321–339.

20 On the dual task of representation, see Giovanni Sartori, 'Representational Systems', in

If the theory is very sensitive to this need, it is much more difficult to satisfy it and to announce this to electors. What candidate for an elected post could ever prevail over his competitors without generating any expectations, without taking on any commitments, and without openly refusing any commission when offered? Burke explained the reasons to the electors of Bristol, but when he tried to contradict them he was not re-elected. One of the problems is the fact that it is inevitable among the ranks of politics – but also among the ranks of the media, of civil society, of organised interests, or somewhere else – that some actor or competitor will appear who demands a more authentic form of representation. Can a government that legitimates itself as a government of the people ever legitimately prohibit the people, empirically understood, from expressing its will? The cyclical accusation of not representing enough, or of representing excessively, is therefore the unavoidable destiny of representation and of democratic politics.

European classic theory, notwithstanding its articulations, tried to solve the problem defining political representation as a form of radical abstraction. The representatives should represent the people as a whole. It is clearly an unrealistic pledge. The American doctrine of representation, inspired by Madison, is more realistic. It openly recognises that the represented have pre-political will and ends", and admits that local constituencies influence representatives, but just invites the latter not to satisfy particular interests excessively. To obtain this Madison pledged the constitution of a republic of broad dimensions, where factions would inevitably multiply, but also balance reciprocally, to be finally decanted in the representative assemblies.[21] It is nevertheless difficult to establish a balance. When Europeans were thundering against the clientelistic distortions of representative government, in America declarations were being made against machine politics, bossism and patronage, later followed by a bitter polemic against lobbies and against the advantages enjoyed by big interest groups.[22] For one reason or another, the destiny of representation is infelicitous everywhere.

What seems to be the most effective remedy against the pluralistic pressures of the governed and the intrinsic contradictions of representative theory is thus the practice of politics itself. It is not a question of a conscious remedy, but of a relatively well-known social mechanism. As a body of activity, politics and political struggle require *ad hoc* skills: speaking in public, drafting laws, advocating causes, negotiating compromises among opposing interests, and above all battling for electoral consensus. Not only do all these skills need protracted training and ex-

---

International Enciclopaedia of Social Sciences (New York, Macmillan & Free Press, 1968, vol. 13, pp. 465–474).

21 James Madison, 'Federalist 10', in Alexander Hamilton, James Madison, John Jay, *The Federalist* edited by Lawrence Goldman (Oxford, Oxford University Press, [1788] 2008).

22 Martin Shefter, *Political Parties and the State. The American Historical Experience* (Princeton NJ, Princeton University Press, 1994). But see also Elmer E. Schattschneider, *The Semi-sovereign People: A Realist's View of Democracy in America* (Chicago, Holt, Rinehart & Winston, 1960).

perience, but politics consequently becomes a full-time commitment, confirming Schumpeter's observation. 'If we wish to face facts squarely – he wrote – we must recognize that in modern democracies …politics will unavoidably be a career'.[23]

Professional commitment gradually established therefore a new route of access to the state and also to the upper levels of society, differentiated from previous access: via nobility, landowning rights, property, industrial or financial activity, through the civil service, the religious sphere or via knowledge and expertise. At the same time, the shared experience in terms of expertise, cultural and relational capital, even between opposing political forces, brings politicians closer together. This does not necessarily unite them, but it sets them apart from their world of origin and gives them a common horizon.[24] In other words, politics circumscribes a 'field' of its own, to use Bourdieu's terminology, not very different from what occurs in other spheres of collective life: religious, artistic, juridical, academic or entrepreneurial.[25]

Political life limits a separate social space also through the interdependencies that it generates among its operators. Interacting among themselves, they influence and shape each other reciprocally.[26] The political field dictates rules of

23 Joseph A. Schumpeter, *Capitalism, Socialism and Democracy* (New York/London, Harper & Brothers, 1942, p. 285

24 On professional politics and politicians see Max Weber's classic essay 'The Profession and Vocation of Politics' in Peter Lassman, Ronald Speirs (eds.), *Max Weber: Political Writings* (Cambridge, Cambridge University Press, [1918] 1994). Weber knew the work of Bryce and also that of Moises Ostrogorski on American parties: see Ostrogorski's *Democracy and the Organization of Political Parties* (Garden City NY, Doubleday, [1902] 1964). See also Daniel Gaxie, *Les professionnels de la politique* (Paris, Seuil, 1973); Alfio Mastropaolo, *Saggio sul professionismo politico* (Milan, Angeli, 1984); Michel Offerlé (ed.), *La profession politique. XIXe–XXe siècles* (Paris, Belin, 1999); Jens Borchert, *Die Professionalisierung der Politik. Zur Notwendigkeiteines Ärgernisses* (Frankfurt, Campus, 2003); Anthony King, 'The Rise of the Career Politician in Britain—And its Consequences', *British Journal of Political Science* 11(3), 1981, 249–285; and Jens Borchert, 'Political Professionalism and Representative Democracy: Common History, Irresolvable Linkage and Inherent Tensions', in Kari Palonen, Tuija Pulkkinen, José Maria Rosales (eds.), *The Ashgate Research Companion to the Politics of Democratization in Europe* (Aldershot, Ashgate, 2008).

25 On the theory of 'political field', see Pierre Bourdieu, 'Political Representation. Elements of a Theory of the Political Field', in Bourdieu, *Language and Symbolic Power* (Cambridge MA, Harvard University Press, 1991), and *Propos sur le champ politique* (Lyon, Presses universitaires de Lyon, 2000).

26 To the constitution of the 'political field', through the interdependencies that are created among the elected, but also among those who collaborate in various ways in their election, can be applied the considerations of Norbert Elias on the birth and development of court life during the reign of Louis XIV. See *The Court Society* (Dublin, University of Dublin Press, [1969] 2006). Referring to Elias' work, see Éric Phélippeau's, 'Sociogenèse de la profession politique', in Alain Garrigou, Bernard Lacroix (eds), *Norbert Elias, la politique et l'histoire* (Paris, La Découverte, 1997).

behaviour and generates languages, habits, interests, as well as conflicts, hierarchies and solidarities, which are extraneous and often incomprehensible for an external observer. Here too, politicians share their specific way of representing themselves and their activity. Finally, the stakes disputed by politicians – power, visibility, prestige, position – are unifying factors as well as the antagonisms that divide them.[27]

Quoting Schumpeter once again, this is the reason why 'politicians so often fail to serve the interest of their class or the groups with which they are personally connected'.[28] Therefore, he explained, there is no political or administrative move and no policy measure that is not conditioned by calculations of the convenience of whoever carries out the one or adopts the other. In other words, their professional reproduction, together with the maximisation of electoral consensus and public posts, and the benefits that these generate, are pre-eminent interests for politicians.[29]

As happens for any profession, nothing allows us to underestimate the moral remuneration that politicians may also expect for their job.[30] Quoting Weber, politics can be a profession, without ceasing to be a 'vocation'. And it is also part of the politician's job to represent the good of the social body as their major concern: they have after all a professional 'interest in disinterestedness.'[31] The difficulty lies in the fact that this does not prevent whoever it suits the opportunity to stigmatise politicians and their separation from the political field. Are they compatible with something like democracy, whose very name evokes precisely the lack of any difference between rulers and ruled?

To solve the problem, politicians work very hard themselves to legitimate and consolidate their diversity using the instruments in their possession. These include specific symbols and rites such as the halls of power, official ceremonies, and the positions and qualities attributed to them. But politicians also use electoral rules and institutional design. The most recent innovation is the reinterpretation of majoritarian democracy and adversary politics, which transfers – unofficially, but it is becoming increasingly official —the destination of the representative mandate.

---

27 'There is less difference between two deputies where one is revolutionary and the other is not, than between two revolutionaries, where one is a deputy and the other is not', wrote de Jouvenel in *La République des Camarades*, p. 17.

28 Schumpeter, *Capitalism, Socialism and Democracy*, p. 273.

29 Phélippeau, 'Sociogenèse de la profession politique'.

30 On the motivations for a political career, see Daniel Gaxie, 'Rétributions du militantisme et paradoxes de l'action collective', *Swiss Political Science Review* 11(1), 2005, 157–188 and Patrick Lehingue, 'Vocation, art, métier ou profession? Codification et étiquetage des activités politiques', in Offerlé (ed.), *La profession politique*.

31 On political relevance that has the expectation of morality and of disinterest for the political world, see Pierre Bourdieu, in *Pascalian Meditations* (Stanford, Stanford University Press, 2000, pp. 124–126).

The receiver of the mandate is not primarily the parliament and parties, but the executive, or rather, the head of the executive. In this way, the change of agent radically modifies even the physiognomy of the principal, i.e. the voters. The aim is to simplify work: no longer a plurality of representatives, or parties, representing a plurality of separate social bodies, that compete and negotiate. In its place there is a unified collectivity of electors-consumers asked to choose between two fully exchangeable representatives.[32]

Unfortunately for politicians, the real world remains still much more complex. First of all society remains plural. Secondly, the kind of issues they are requested to deal with, but also the need for the media to attract audience and for politicians to raise the media's attention, have polarised political competition in an unexpected way and provoked sharper divisions within public opinion.[33] In third place, the latest redesign of democratic institutions is intended to free politicians more from conditioning by interest, but the result has been selective. If on the one hand, it has reduced the influence of those interests that manifest themselves, thanks to the big numbers, it has however, on the other hand, made politicians more sensitive to the requests of other interests, those who are able to exert their influence out of electoral support. This too is a drawback, even if there are good reasons to suspect that this last was not only an unexpected consequence, but an outcome that somebody wanted.

The so widely disapproved resistance of the 'established' politicians to the entry of 'outsiders' is an other obvious consequence of their professional condition. But this does not mean that their resistance always works. The political field is rich in attractions and there is no lack of outsiders, sometimes with vast resources accumulated elsewhere, who want to invest in it and to enter the political field. It may then happen that, pulled along by antipolitical rhetoric, politicians defend themselves by conducting, and advertising, recruitment campaigns for new political personnel, coming for instance from civil society. In fact, the opening up of the political field has become a very fashionable cause. Therefore politicians themselves cyclically promise an opening up, and cautiously work towards this, so as to better protect its closure or, at least, its internal hierarchies.

This is in any case one of the reasons why, in addition to being contested, the differentiation of the political field is in continual flux. In the same way the stratifications, equilibria and divisions that take shape in the sub-fields of the political field are changeable. There are marked differences between one situation and another. They depend on varying political techniques, representations of politics, or historical context in which political competition occurs, and by its characteristics

---

32 This is after all the so-called presidentialisation of parliamentary regimes. See Thomas Poguntke, Paul Webb (eds.), *The Presidentialisation of Parliamentary Regimes. A Comparative Study of Modern Democracies* (Oxford, Oxford University Press, 2005).

33 Amy Gutmann, Dennis Thompson, *The Spirit of Compromise. Why Governing Demands it and Campaigning Undermines it* (Princeton NJ, Princeton University Press, 2012).

and the relations, conflictual and otherwise, that the political field has with other spheres. Sometimes politics is a more inclusive space, and at other times it is more exclusive.

The capacity of the political field to reproduce itself is in any case very high. Sometimes it manages to do this even in spite of dramatic and protracted discontinuity. Italian fascism lasted twenty years, but a rather consistent number of the pre-fascist political personnel, reappeared on the scene. The return of old leaders, ousted by fascism, was predictable. What was less predictable was the reappearance of intermediate levels and local notables. When old actors happened to be dead, sons, younger brothers and relations often took their place, testifying to the high propensity of personal political capital to be transmitted via familial ties. It would be interesting to see whether similar strands of continuity are recognisable in other cases.

However, if the self-maintaining capacity of the political field is confirmed in this way, not even this extensive continuity validates the representation of politicians as a separate social class. Despite its separateness and the privileges secured by its officials and office-holders, the political world has always been, and remains, sufficiently heterogeneous and conflictual to make the use of the concept of class in the political sphere rather unconvincing. It was already a polemical simplification in the days of Gaetano Mosca, when the degree of heterogeneity of politicians was much less than it is now. Its rediscovery is primarily another sign of the period of discontent, real or presumed, of democratic regimes.

Between trust and corruption

The autonomy of the political field is at the same time a sociological effect, a constraint and a resource for politicians. More than any limitation of the theory, or any institutional mechanism, it is a practical adjustment which guarantees a degree of autonomy, albeit problematic and contested, to the governors from the governed, and which allows the former to do their job. This generates unavoidable tension with the democratic principle, but politicians are not in the least unprepared for this. The politicians' trade is also to give substance to a trait of the representative mandate that is essential for theory. That is, the trust of the represented in their representatives, or that the latter stir up in the former.[34]

In both the real world and in theory, representation implies an element of trust, even if in the real world it is the representative who constitutes the represented. Trust must be cultivated and continuously confirmed, also because it is the best antidote to the criticism raised by the autonomy of the political field.[35] The latter

---

34 Hanna F. Pitkin, *The Concept of Representation* (Berkeley, University of California Press, 1967, p. 138).

35 For an in-depth analysis see Daniel Gaxie, *La démocratie représentative* (Paris, Montchretien,

is more tolerable the more the governed recognise themselves in politicians and trust their actions. In other words, the autonomy of politicians also depends on a pledge of trust that the latter offer to the former. Electors are not all equally aware, but there is a sufficiently large number of them to make it wiser for politicians to establish a relation of trust with them, even in a form that has evolved much over time.

In regimes with restricted suffrage fresh with memories of the *ancien régime*, the identification between politicians, who were notables, and their electors was based on the personal capital of social authority and prestige of the former, and the expectations of protection and generosity of the latter. This was not just a banal exchange of votes for services, but the elector had to be persuaded that the notable would invest his influence, relational networks and even his own private patrimony to the advantage of his electors.[36]

Historically speaking, this mix of paternalism, protection and personal friendship that goes by the name of clientelism, and that varies according to circumstances, has been challenged by the processes of centralisation typical of the modern state. Evoking principles such as public interest and the equality of citizens before the law, personal local relations have been disqualified as immoral and anachronistic by the centralising elites and by mass parties which counter them with the impersonal services of the state and its Weberian bureaucracies. In reality, not only is it a utilitarian prejudice that reduces personal relationships to an exchange of favours and a distorted form of distribution of resources, but the morally dubious nature of clientelism is not self-evident. Not only did the notable remain a notable even without an electoral mandate, and still disposed his protective activity, but relations between notables and clients were, as a rule, legitimate for both.

It was parties that arranged an alternative formula to trust in the notables, replacing their paternalism by a fraternal image, not entirely without some element of paternalism. Elected and electors, leadership and militants, felt they belonged to the same political and associative circle. Sharing the same cause and fighting for it side by side – in socialist parties the expression 'comrade' indicated this condition – representatives and represented, but also party leadership and membership, tried to establish an egalitarian relationship that was symbolically and empirically confirmed through so-called 'descriptive representation',[37] where the party was careful to recruit at least part of its leadership, cadres and representatives, from the social groups that it intended to represent.

The descriptive representation gradually lessened the nearer we come to the top party executive, even though the executive will was still careful to emphasise it. By the early 1900s, Robert Michels reported how elected and party executives

---

2004).

36 For a valuable research on the mechanisms of representation by notables see Éric Phélippeau, *L'Invention de l'homme politique moderne. Mackau, l'Orne et la République* (Paris, Belin, 2002).

37 The definition is Pitkin's in *The Concept of Representation*, p. 60.

of working-class origin tended to become more bourgeois as their political career sociologically distanced them from their original social background, in terms of lifestyle and representation of interests. For Michels it was also politically intolerable that the political field conditioned who became part of it, but his disappointment as a socialist militant, prevented him from fully understanding the effects of the phenomenon. Even if this did not correspond to all democratic expectations, the access of new social strata to the political hierarchy was, in any case, a sign of change. The development of democratic regimes shows how the renewal of political hierarchies has also pulled policy renewal in its wake. Because the popular parties wanted to maintain the favour of their electors, they had to satisfy their expectations. It is certain that the parties themselves stirred up these expectations, but after all they had to start detecting real needs.

In order to avoid criticisms like those of Michels, descriptive representation was a symbolic pledge of their intentions. Obviously, descriptive representation turned out to be insufficient and had to be supplemented. A popular party could not recruit its representatives solely from the working classes, where it was harder to find the necessary competences to fit an electoral mandate. Nonetheless, when these competences were found elsewhere – for example, among the intellectual categories – the party would assert the criterion of political trustworthiness, commitment to values and the party programme, and would at the same time, concern itself that its cadres and leaders shared the experiences, needs, lifestyles of their electors. It is difficult to say how much this sharing was real and how much was apparent. But the image that leaders and cadres gave was carefully monitored in order to preserve the party's reputation as a circle of mutually recognised equals.

The notables' model of trust and the party model were not reciprocally exclusive. Mass parties officially rejected the notables' practices, redefining the meaning of the vote, and making it the free expression of the will of the elector. Yet, when it suited them, parties for a long time tolerated and instrumentalised clientelistic forms of trust.[38] One of the crucial features of the latest transformation of political parties has however been the rejection of their associative habits. This has complicated the mechanisms which create the bonds of trust between politicians and citizens a great deal, even calling into question whether it is still feasible to institute them.

The narrative of democratic malaise confirms this difficulty met by politicians, which, albeit in different ways, still solicits the trust of the governed, starting with the renewal of descriptive representation. In the political field one of the main causes for concern is the absence of women, and measures are introduced to fa-

---

38 Jean-Louis Briquet, Frédéric Sawicki (eds.), *Le clientélisme politique dans les sociétés contemporaines* (Paris, Puf, 1998), and Simona Piattoni (ed.), *Clientelism, Interests and Democratic Representation. The European Experience in Historical and Comparative Perspective* (Cambridge, Cambridge University Press, 2001). See also Marc Abélès, *Anthropologie de l'État* (Paris, Payot, 2005, pp. 128–135).

vour them, and the theory complies with this objective.[39] In some countries the issue of representation for linguistic or ethnic minorities has been raised. On the other hand, if parties pay great attention to renewing their ranks, what is neglected is the form of descriptive representation which benefited the working class.[40] In popular and socialist parties, the party machine was the basic channel of recruitment and vertical mobility. Once the party machine is deactivated, the representation of the working class is considerably reduced.

It is probable that party leaderships have persuaded themselves that the reasons why they once enlarged their pool of recruitment are nowadays outdated. Once social conflict had declined, why elect figures from the working classes to parliament?[41] It is more profitable to promote other qualities and to assert 'substantive representation'.[42] This favours the representation of interests and promotes representatives and governors able to deal with the problems in line with their own competences and professional curricula. Currently, entrepreneurs enjoy much success, and have the advantage of autonomous financial resources with which to deal with political competition.

Without solid and ramified organisational structures, contemporary parties reserve their collective political capital for party leaders and executives, while ordinary candidates are normally allowed the use of the party brand-name, and are invited to manage with the resources of social visibility and their own private financial means, or perhaps with the support of some associative network or lobby, favouring as a result, the individualisation – and de-institutionalisation – of political careers.

The course of the political career has been profoundly redefined by the latest transformation of parties. Once parties insisted on a lengthy and tiring apprenticeship to develop and train party cadres, to test their competence, and above all, to ensure their reliability and loyalty. The *cursus honorum* standard provided for promotion from the periphery towards the centre and from lower positions to higher ones. Now the number of lateral entries directly from the professions to

---

39 For a review of female representation see Joni Lovenduski, *Feminizing Politics* (Cambridge, Polity Press, 2005, pp. 12–44).

40 On the problems that raised the emargination from representation of weak social groups see Anne Phillips, *The Politics of Presence* (New York, Clarendon, 1995).

41 Daniel Gaxie, Laurent Godmer, 'Cultural Capital and Political Selection: Educational Backgrounds of Parliamentarians', in Heinrich Best, Maurizio Cotta (eds.), *Parliamentary Representatives in Europe 1848–2000* (Oxford, Oxford University Press, 2007, vol. 2, pp. 106–135). See also Heinrich Best, Maurizio Cotta (eds.), *Parliamentary Representatives in Europe, 1848–2000* (Oxford, Oxford University Press, 2000). Between the 1940s and late 1990s in the French parliament deputies of working-class origin fell from 10 per cent to 2 per cent, in Germany from 8 per cent to 2 per cent and in Britain from 25 per cent to 5 per cent. One can object that the working classes have shrunk everywhere, but this shrinking of their representation is not proportional.

42 Pitkin, *The Concept of Representation,* p. 209.

politics, has multiplied,[43] and once their first election is won, politicians base their ambitions on the increase of their own personal political capital, thanks also to the position held.[44]

Another form of representation now cultivated by politics is 'symbolic representation',[45] based on the virtue of civil society, mediatic notoriety, social visibility, professional success and the economic status of candidates. The display of social success through the media is a much valued instrument for generating identification and trust with electors and therefore an investment in a politician's career.

In short, contemporary parties make the prospect of establishing relations of equal trust, based on a shared cause, more remote. This does not necessarily occur because politicians disparage causes. Few politicians are willing to admit that they only engage in politics for their own benefit. But it is clear that something significant occurred in the transition from parties that valued and organised party membership to parties that discourage it.

Under the new conditions, entrusting politics to professionals is thus more vulnerable and suspect than ever. Initially the reputation of professional politicians was poor,[46] but this had improved markedly with mass parties, at least for their public. Currently it is again on the decline. It is one thing to accept that a militant was chosen according to the criteria of descriptive representation or for a full-time commitment in a representative institution or party machine. It is quite another thing to consider politics as a professional activity, and thus a private interest like any other activity, rewarded by taxpayers thanks to public funding.

The fact that politicians are increasingly concerned to accredit themselves – it remains to be seen with what success – as temporarily 'on loan' to politics is by no means accidental. What is strange is that politicians do not give as much attention to dispelling the democratically inconvenient image of the too close relations between the political field and the economic spheres. Not only do the prospects of access to the political field of the better-off social strata seem likely to increase, but the vicinity of political leadership and the economic-financial *milieux* has been banalised. With the assimilation of lifestyles and standards of living among the upper classes, politicians openly flaunt their familiarity with the world of business, despite the fact that a fierce and complicated power struggle is taking place with the latter.

Everything leads us to think that the increased interest of business *milieux* for elective posts corresponds to an intent to capitalise on the benefits reaped by post-Fordism, by the financialisation of the economy and by globalisation. In this sense the economic needs of mediatised politics are of great help. The work of the

---

43   King, 'The Rise of the Career Politician in Britain', pp. 249–285.

44   On more recent developments see Borchert, *Die Professionalisierung der Politik.*

45   Pitkin, *The Concept of Representation,* p. 92.

46   Dominique Damamme, 'Professionnel de la politique, un métier peu avouable', in Offerlé, *La profession polititique.*

media and opinion polls requires substantial investment, thus making the political field more vulnerable to being conditioned by whoever possesses the necessary financial resources. Yet, democratically speaking, the mingling of business and politics still causes perplexity, political and otherwise.

After all, one of the traits of modernity is that political authority is free from patrimonialism: it is not a private good, but a public good. This means that positions of power in the public and private spheres must be kept separate. A distinguished American liberal like Michael Walzer declared that, as a normative principle, in a democratic regime positions and resources of power must be neither cumulative nor convertible.[47] In the light of the rules of the game this perspective is debatable and there are even those who claim in favour of the private financing of electoral campaigns. The ability to collect private funds legally would confirm a candidate's reliability, anticipating electoral competition, seeing that the decisive stake is no longer the vote of citizens, but the financial resources necessary to stand as a candidate.[48] Despite this, a basic mission of democratic regimes, on which they base their legitimation, is to demonstrate the fluidity of social hierarchies, or to show that power is not all concentrated in the hands of the most qualified in terms of income, education or prestige. Democratic regimes must show that power really can be attributed according to other criteria, and that democracy works to facilitate access to all sorts of power. Given this, how can the general public be enamoured of politicians? There are too many reasons to suspect them of transforming politics into private interests and forming rigid hierarchies, while the public opinion seems quite aware of the *rapprochement* taking place between the hierarchies of politics and those of economic interests.

More enlightened democratic regimes have introduced norms to protect against possible conflicts of interest, even with the help of theory, to codify a deontology of politics, albeit with rather modest results. Philosophers, political scientists, economists have made substantial professional gains, thanks to this issue, and even thriving national and international institutions have been set up to measure order and cultivate public morality.[49] But we should ask whether this submission of politics to ethics is not just an instrument to better mask the greater submission of politics to economics, and perhaps another way to standardise institutions and political practices on a global scale.[50]

---

47 Michael Walzer, *Spheres of Justice. A Defense of Pluralism and Equality* (New York, Basic Books, 1983, pp. 129–164).

48 Philip Bobbitt, *The Shield of Achilles. War, Peace and the Course of History* (New York, Knopf, 2002, pp. 238–240).

49 Transparency International is exemplary, with its severe style ranking of different countries on the basis, albeit rather debatable, of the perception of morality of some categories, e.g. entrepreneurs. On such, the 'policy of morality', see Alessandro Pizzorno, *Il velo della diversità. Studi su razionalita e riconoscimento* (Milan, Feltrinelli, 2009, pp. 336–338).

50 Béatrice Hibou, *Anatomie politique de la domination* (Paris, La Découverte, 2011, pp. 49–55).

The paradox is that among those who more tenaciously raise the issues of politicians and their morality and corruption, and who have recently made it an omnipresent issue in public discourse and political competition, are those who benefit most from the current condition of politicians' weakness: the media and the economic powers. The decisional leeway of politicians has been reduced to the benefit of the entrepreneurial *milieux*. Not satisfied with this reduction, the latter, in an attempt to make their responsibilities less visible and to create problems for politics, tend to make a big show of the argument, whereas in reality if politicians are normally on the side of the corrupt, then entrepreneurs are normally on the side of the corruptor.

In reality, morality and corruption are other well-known examples of contested borders. There have been substantial attempts to fix these boundaries and to distinguish what is lawful from what is not, and to standardise the typologies of crime and repressive practices, but agreement is never universal. What is now illicit, was licit in the past. What is illicit in one place, is not illicit in another, and what is illicit for some, is not illicit for all. Not everything that is legally sanctioned is sanctioned by general public opinion and even those who apply the law, such as the courts, have different opinions on what to sanction and how to do it. Not only is it hard to interpret and apply any rule, but corruption is also invisible and the actors often possess vast reserves of complicity which protect them. There are also situations where corruption is an explicitly political theme and others where it is simply treated as a legal or police issue. There is an important difference between the two situations, also on the level of electoral outcomes.

The difficulties of defining corruption obviously suits both the corruptor and corrupted. But it also suits those making the accusations in the light of political criteria – politicians, business and the media. All compete to formulate complex strategies of ranking, trivialisation, diversion, and to re-script norms and procedures. Above all one of the many paradoxes of democratic politics is on the one hand the centrality of corruption in public discourse and, on the other, its limited impact on voters.

Surveys and qualitative investigations testify to a widespread expectation of morality, a deep-rooted diffidence towards the behaviour of politicians, a fairly good capacity to judge single political figures, as well as a general tendency to represent politicians as a social group that share a serious moral defect. In spite of this, electoral choice seems rather indifferent to similar verdicts. Except for exceptional situations, when voters are specifically interrogated on the point, the intensity of the criticism of the practices, defined as corrupt, varies noticeably. Some practices are considered unacceptable, whilst others are considered debatable, but pardonable. There are forms of illicit conduct that voters justify evoking the state of necessity, such as the need to speed-up a procedure, and others made tolerable by political struggle. Like every other opinion of politics, expectations of public morality are conditioned by political preferences, the competence of electors, the idea they have of the political situation – if they consider it more or less dramatic – and the type of relations they have with the political field. In the last instance, we should not be surprised if voters are not particularly reactive even to certified episodes of corruption and sensational scandals. If anything, electors declare that they vote on the basis of the available political supply: the words that politicians utter and the interests that they protect. After all, is their argument, they have to vote for someone![51]

From representation to accountability

Claiming that trust in politicians is on the decline is not so different from reporting the growth of the electorate's dissatisfaction with them. The first affirmation is no less uncertain than the second. Instead, it is more likely that generating trust has simply become a more laborious task for politicians than in the past. Not that it was always easy, but current techniques have become more complicated. There is no prevailing technique and today's politicians search for trust, from time to time, in different ways and with a great deal of effort: they can mobilise shared values and interests, use media appeal, evoke technical competence or the support of civil society, confirm clientelistic protections and raise antipolitical accusations. What makes the condition of politicians particularly difficult is also the widespread habit among the media to broadcast their supposed approval by the public, measured by opinion polls in real time.

It is certainly true that even if we take the malaise revealed by opinion polls seriously, this does not imply the active rejection of authority. Discontent may feed street protest, but must be kept distinct from rebellion. Despite this, in the democratic rhetoric the reputation of mistrust that surrounds them is, to say the least, uncomfortable for politicians and anyone can instrumentalise it. We already raised the question several times: given the ease with which it can be exploited, who can resist the temptation to do so?

In this way the narrative of malaise and mistrust has become a weapon not only of the day-to-day political struggle, but also a means to achieve other ends.

---

51 Pierre Lascoumes makes valuable remarks on the issue, beginning with the problem of defining corruption, but also its relevance in the public debate and its instrumental use by politics. See *Corruptions* (Paris, Presses de SciencesPo, 2004). For a detailed review of citizens' reactions and their apparent insensibility, see Philippe Bézes, Pierre Lascoumes, 'Enjeux et usages des enquêtes sur les représentations des atteintes à la probité publique', *Revue française de science politique* 55(5/6), 2005, 757–786. By the same authors, see the intriguing qualitative research in 'Les formes de jugement du politique. Principes moraux, principes d'action et régistre légal', *L'Année sociologique* 54(1), 2009, 109–147. See also Pierre Lascoumes, *Favoritisme et corruption à la française* (Paris, Presses de SciencesPo, 2010). It's worth reminding that in the elections following the Watergate scandal only 5.5 per cent of Republican electors switched to the Democrats, against 3.4 per cent of Democrats who voted Republican: see Donald Green, Bradley Palmquist, Eric Schickler, *Partisan Hearts and Minds: Political Parties and the Social Identity of Voters* (New Haven CT, Yale University Press, p. 40, pp.133 – 136).

Among other things, it is used to introduce institutional adjustments, inspired by the post-democratic paradigm, like the spread and reinterpretation of majoritarian democracy we just mentioned. Above all, in addition to reducing the governed to clients – consumers and tax-payers – the paradigm wanted to re-script the role of politicians. In the season of party membership and the circles of equal recognition politicians had a dual mission: to change the state of the world, promoting the collective interest of their principal, and to supply public services according to the needs of the broader collectivity. Today's politicians are primarily requested to adopt a managerial style in government, to balance the budget and to supply services functional to the state of the economy.[52]

In line with these developments – and perhaps in order to neutralise the embarrassing critical implications of the concept of political class and other similar representations – theory has again stepped in, scientifically embellishing the more recent displays of the autonomy of the political field, and its institutional adjustments. Once declared obsolete, these tasks include introducing the concept of 'accountability'.[53]

Accountability is not exactly a theoretical new entry, but for a long time the term was only used occasionally to indicate the duty of the elected to justify their actions to electors. Previously, the fact that such a justification corresponded to the logic of representation and the representative mandate was so taken for granted, the concept was not much used. A re-reading of Hanna F. Pitkin's book shows that the lexicon of representation was already expansive.[54] What is the point of complicating it? The theory already prescribed taking the needs of the electorate into account. That is, it stressed responsiveness,[55] reconciling this with the responsibility of government, and also implied that governors had to be answerable for their actions.[56] Even if the mandate is a fiction, it is obvious that the agent should offer at least some report to his principal.

For a long time the audit was done by the parties, which managed to carry out the tasks of both controller and controlled. Parties constituted, arranged and organised expectations and demands of large segments of the electorate, which they transmitted to governors. The latter came from their ranks, but this did not prevent the parties from exercising an *ex post* control, also in order to regulate the reactions of the governed. The replacement of the party model that allowed this with a model where the mediatic dimension is predominant, revolutionised the dialectic between elected and electors and favoured the discovery of 'accountability'.

The term governance comes from the language of the business sector, where

---

52 See the arguments concerning what he calls the 'market-state' raised by Bobbitt, *The Shield of Achilles*, pp. 213–242.

53 See the debate in Adam Przeworski, Susan C. Stokes, Bernard Marin (eds.), *Democracy, Accountability and Representation* (Cambridge, Cambridge University Press, 1999).

54 This included accountability: see Pitkin, *The Concept of Representation*, pp. 55–59.

55 Pitkin, *The Concept of Representation*, p. 113.

56 Sartori, 'Representational Systems'.

it was used to stipulate the limits of the mandate conferred on management by shareholders. As well as governance, accountability too is a term imported from the language of business. In this language, accountability was used to stipulate the limits of the mandate conferred on management by shareholders. Thanks to New Public Management, it was later applied to public administration, before becoming the acknowledged parameter to measure the legitimacy and trustworthiness of democratic governors.[57]

With full respect for the post-democratic paradigm, and for the narrative of the vote as judgement, accountability officially establishes a link between the performance of governors and the expectations placed on them for the future by the governed.[58] Within post-Fordist firms, the mandate that a manager receives from shareholders has nothing to do with either productive techniques or the organisation of work. It is simply to make a profit. In much the same way, with the last metamorphosis of representation, once an abstract mandate to govern has been conferred, accountability promises a verdict on how it has been exercised, indicating electoral outcomes as an instrument of measurement, insofar as it reveals customer satisfaction.

It is certainly plausible that more than one reason has made the previous forms of representation obsolete and encouraged a renewal. Beyond the transformation of parties and the action of the media, there is the social dispersion of the big collectivities and reference identities (class, religion, etc.), together with increasing pluralism, especially cultural pluralism, the de-territorialisation of political authority and the pre-eminence of supranational and democratically heterodox institutions, such as those of the European Union.[59] We need to prove, however, that this is sufficient reason to abandon the idea of representation as a bottom-up process, replacing it with the image of a top-down process, and to replace input-oriented legitimation with output-oriented legitimation.[60]

The redefinition of the concept of representation intends to help representatives withstand the demands of electors and of their competitors in the business world and the media. We should not forget that the pressure of the latter has become particularly acute since the pressure of the big numbers, channelled by parties, no longer intervenes to balance them. Officially defining the work of politicians as a reply not to the requests of the represented, but to an abstract demand of

---

57 Philippe C. Schmitter, 'The Quality of Democracy: The Ambiguous Virtues of Accountability', *Journal of Democracy* 15(4), 2004, 48–60.

58 John Dunn, 'Situating Democratic Political Accountability', in Przeworski, Stokes, Manin (eds.), *Democracy, Accountability and Representation*

59 Rudy B. Andeweg, 'Beyond Representativeness? Trends in Political Representation', *European Review* 11 (2), 2003, 147–161.

60 The trade-off between the two forms of legitimation implies another one: that between the government 'by' the people and the government 'for' the people. See Fritz Scharpf, *Governing in Europe: Effective and Democratic?* (Oxford, Oxford University Press, 1999).

good government, is a symbolic move to reduce the costs of representation: either as an offer of services to the represented, or as an act to constitute and maintain the represented. Promising to be accountable, and asking to be judged on their achievements, should allow politicians to be less complacent with electors and perhaps more selective in relations with organised interests. But is this exchange as virtuous as promised?

In fact, when theory comes to the aid of politics coining the concept of accountability, its aim is not just to present a conceptual expedient, but to demonstrate a certain rigour in its precepts. To talk of accountability means meeting severe conditions. Theory prescribes, before award or punishment, information and motivation of the choices of politicians.[61] Citizens must be adequately informed about policies adopted by decision-makers and their reasons, on which to pass a conscious verdict. Politicians must also be fully responsible for their actions, identifiable as agents by those to whom they are responsible, and must be effectively sanctionable for their actions, and expect to be sanctioned. Yet, what guarantees are there that democratic regimes will be able to meet such conditions?

Supporters of accountability will observe that incumbents can lose the elections and this is proof that electors punish them. But how many cases are there where electoral defeat sanctions governors who have failed? In the real world incumbents enjoy a broad advantage and an electoral defeat, no less than the turnover of power, depends on plenty of variables. Losing the elections is not always a sanction. On average, ordinary citizens are not particularly interested in politics or sufficiently competent; they vote inertially and do not really express any verdict. By contrast, incumbents have powerful instruments to adulterate the information supplied to the public, in the same way that they can manipulate the image of their performance with the help of the media and opinion polls. Symmetrical adulterations and manipulations can be made by their opponents. And what about the enormous financial investments made during electoral campaigns to condition the opinions of the electors?

The repertoires of arguments which policy-makers in office can use to accredit policies and condition successive judgements is very rich. Taking the cuts of public expenditure as an example, this can be presented as inevitable, with no alternative and imposed by external actors. Policy-makers can argue that the sacrifices demanded are temporary, or they can be disguised in a mix of more acceptable provisions. The responsibility can still be placed on the bad government of previous incumbents, or on the scarce collaboration of the opposition or local governments and so on.

Finally, public policies are not just more or less appropriate responses to objectively identified issues. Raising an issue, no less than finding a solution, is the stake of a political struggle. It is in itself a complex and disputed political issue.

---

61 Andreas Schedler, 'Conceptualizing Accountability' in Andreas Schedler, Larry Diamond, Marc F. Plattner (eds.), *The Self-Restraining State: Power and Accountability in New Democracies* (Boulder/London, Lynne Rienner, 1999).

Plenty of issues could not be raised or others could be raised instead – involving politicians, experts, civil servants, organised interests, etc.[62] On what grounds should policies be evaluated? All this explains why accountability has accumulated such an incisive critical literature in such a short time.[63]

There are plenty of excellent reasons to object that requirements of accountability are inapplicable, and to consider accountability a fiction no more credible than representation. Yet, this does not discourage the theory a great deal. Taking note of the slim chances of a reliable retrospective judgement on the part of electors – so-called 'vertical accountability' – theory has a ready remedy: 'horizontal accountability'.[64] This is not very different from what was once defined as checks-and-balances, but with some promising additions.

Horizontal accountability is also entrusted to public opinion and the media that animate it, together with civil society, judicial power and the many non-partisan and non-elected institutions which inundate today's democratic regimes. Policy analysts are now recruited to evaluate policies and their implementation 'scientifically'. Recently there has been an explosion in the number of democratic audit agencies. These certify the democratic reliability of elements of government, relieving citizens of this onerous and impracticable responsibility.[65] Political scientists are finally at work to define democratic 'quality' and to test universal indicators.[66] When they reach their goal, electoral procedures will be maintained – how can at least a part of the governors be selected otherwise? – but their task could be democratically minimised. It might be not too far away from the moment when some agency specialised in democratic rating will be operational.

After all, financial ratings agencies are already scrutinising and passing judgement on the action of elected authorities. Paradoxically the latter seem willing to accept their verdicts and their tightening of the electoral principle.[67] Recent events

---

62 Hal K. Colebatch, *Policy* (Philadelphia, Open University Press, 2002).

63 Very convincing critical arguments are raised by José M. Maravall, 'Accountability and Manipulations', in Przeworski, Stokes, Marin (eds.), *Democracy, Accountability and Representation.*

64 Guillermo A. O'Donnell, 'Horizontal Accountability in New Democracies', *Journal of Democracy* 9(3), 1998, 112–126.

65 This is still not the 'triple A' of rating agencies. A promising example is World Audit, a non-profit agency that receives information from agencies such as Freedom House, Transparency International, Amnesty International, Human Rights Watch and The International Commission of Jurists (www.worldaudit.org).

66 Larry Diamond, Leonardo Morlino (eds.), *Assessing the Quality of Democracy. Theory and Empirical Analysis* (Baltimore MD, Johns Hopkins University Press, 2005).

67 Introducing a balanced budget amendment into their constitutional texts, i.e. treating it as a basic democratic requisite, many European democracies are willing to satisfy the demands both of the EU authorities and also of financial audit agencies. After all, in doing so they recognise the authority of the latter to rate them also politically.

in Europe show how, even without any grand theoretical architecture, elective authority has not only failed in its ambition to gain real autonomy with respect to electoral conditioning, but may also be subject to much more stringent dictates of non-elected authorities, Greece being a case in point. Although we can ennoble these dictates classifying them as horizontal accountability, it is unlikely that democratic regimes derive any advantage.

In addition to being a useful tool to control pluralism, on the factual level the basic merit of political representation has always been its capacity to promote mutual listening between governors and governed. Elections have been considered important opportunities both for the electors to listen to the candidates, and for the candidates to listen to electors. This may not be enough, and indeed the circuit of official elective representation has always been flanked by forms of spontaneous and non-elected representation. Yet, the insufficiency of official elected representation is not a good reason to declare its task redundant and to hope for the advent of new forms of official representation, not supported by elections.[68] No doubt politicians have other opportunities besides elections to listen to claims and interests, in the same way that social, cultural and political pluralism and individuals manage to be heard in other ways. But these are symbolically less effective and, above all, elective representation provides other award-winning services which it is perhaps, better not to relinquish light-heartedly.

Another crucial service made by electoral liturgies was to represent the democratic collectivity to itself, accrediting it with a common constituted will, starting from a condition of pluralism and contrasting opinions and interests. This too is a way in which the representative – understood this time as the entire body of the elected – constitutes the represented, understood as the people as a whole. Not less relevant is the opportunity to count itself given to the people. The opinion of the majority is an expedient and is not worth more than the opinion of the minorities. But if the support of numbers does not make a political choice appropriate, it is still a symbolic confirmation of the equality among citizens as holders of equal power, which also confirms the horizontal bond that unites them. Numbers do not exist alone, and, although reducing electors to a numerical series is a politically and democratically debatable simplification, not without its drawbacks, in recompense it confirms the image of a collective body where individuals are part of that body.

On the other hand, once electoral procedures have been downgraded in favour of forms of non-elected representation, and once electoral representation is presented as a mere retrospective judgement, or as accountability, new problems arise. Not only is there a dissolution of the image of a common will, but there is

---

68 On non-electoral representation, see Dario Castiglione, Mark Warren, *Rethinking Democratic Representation: Eight Theoretical Issues* (Centre for the Study of Democratic Institutions, University of British Columbia, 2006), and Michael Saward, *The Representative Claim* (Oxford, Oxford University Press, 2010).

also the failure of the principle, no less unrealistic, but symbolically valuable, according to which democratic governors rule exclusively on the basis of their mandate and in the interests of the governed.[69]

To date, elections, political representation and democracy have legitimated and supported each other reciprocally. The struggle for representation has always been fierce and many have claimed to be spokesperson for the people, or for a part of the people. Without basing itself on electoral procedures, representation would retrogress to its medieval past, when it represented autonomous estates. As we have seen, this does not prevent anyone who might be interested from claiming to represent somebody or something else. Nevertheless, the more electoral representation is devalued, the more democracy becomes an interaction between the representatives of different interests, legitimating the fact that the resources available to them condition their capacity to negotiate.

It is a question of preferences, which are all legitimate in democracy, but it is without doubt that it is the weakest social strata which run the greatest risk of being marginalised from a politics entrusted prominently to similar mechanisms, and to non-elected representatives, or to authorities whose elected origin has been sterilised. In conclusion, accountability might then be among the announcements of a renewed form of democracy that tacitly revokes the minimum rules dictated by Bobbio. Once the symbolic link between the actions of governors and official displays of the popular will has been cut, what is left of its rules? And what will this democracy be like, we should ask? Indeed, can we still call it democracy at all?

---

69 This is what reminds us Paul Veyne, 'Did the Greeks Know Democracy?', *Economy and Society* 34(2), 2005, 334.

chapter ten | correctives

Democracy is also an armistice

After the second world war, European societies were, or were about to become, industrial societies, and were politically represented as class societies. Theory and politics characterised the relations between classes in two different ways: willing to collaborate or against. It may have been the memory of the great social and political battles of the 1920s, of the Depression, of the war itself, together with the competition of communist regimes, and the shift of equilibria among the forces in the field. It may have been that the structure of political opportunities did not back the renewal of violent conflict. The fact is that in the second postwar period what had previously proved impossible, actually succeeded.[1]

The physiognomy of actors in social conflict had changed, as had their cultural and symbolic resources, their way of representing themselves and the situation in which they acted, the weapons considered legitimate for use, beginning with collective action. In this way class conflict was brought under control. The postwar consensus allowed protagonists of collective life such as classes, trade unions and the business sector, to realise an 'armistice', where no one could take the upper hand.[2] An armistice, however, is not peace and had the circumstances changed, someone would certainly have profited.

To recap, the postwar consensus had two basic and interdependent clauses, consecrated by the postwar constitutional charters, recomposing the heterogeneous values and interests of different actors. According to the first clause, pluralistic democracy became a political horizon shared by all actors, who were authorised to compete in asserting their own vision of the world, on the condition that they renounced violence. Among other things, the armistice meant recognising the legitimacy of collective action organised by parties (and trade unions). The second clause of the armistice accepted the market economy, but with the proviso that the state would compensate the inequalities that this might generate. A future, with the triumph of socialism, was not ruled out, but political actors in favour of this were committed not to pursue it using violent means.

---

1   On the concept of structure of political opportunities, see Sidney Tarrow, *Power in Movement: Social Movements, Collective Action and Politics* (Cambridge, Cambridge University Press, 1994).

2   Mario Dogliani, 'Costituzione (dottrine generali)', *Diritto. Enciclopedia giuridica del Sole 24 Ore* (Milan, edizioni Il Sole 24 Ore, 2007).

The unexpected economic growth of the postwar period produced a great many resources, redistributed from the wealthier to the less wealthy classes, and reinforced the armistice. In the mid-1950s, Ralf Dahrendorf defined class antagonism a thing of the past and represented social conflict as an institutionalised power conflict.[3]

The upper classes had not abdicated either power or wealth, but had merely agreed to share some part of it. This meant limits to property rights, higher taxation and a more limited market autonomy. The state intervened to compensate. In addition to mediating work conflicts, it supported growth and carried out a valuable anti-cyclical action to help the private sector. The lower and middle classes were guaranteed opportunities for employment, income, consumption and welfare services, while democracy facilitated access to the political and administrative elites.

The armistice did not exclude critical representations of society, or intense social conflict, especially labour conflicts, yet it functioned for a quarter of a century, until the end of the 1970s when the upper classes, business and their political representatives were persuaded that the risk of social conflict was not so high or so damaging and that there was no longer a need to treat their opponents with such consideration. Growth was blocked, or this was the prevailing opinion, and the idea that defeating the crisis would mean revising the rules of democratic regimes and capitalist economies was highly successful.

What weakened the former protagonists of collective action and modified political equilibria were the effects of dispersion stimulated first by material well-being, and then by post-Fordism and globalisation, primarily through the labour market. Representing society as a body of individuals and not as a class society was another successful move. In all probability, the way in which actors, politicians, businessmen, the media and intellectuals dealt with the conflict was very influential. They contested its utility, appropriateness and legitimacy and denied that it was still a politically exploitable weapon, even in its more disciplined forms.

In the 1970s several episodes of violent conflict flared up in several countries and brought the concept of terrorism to the fore. This sort of violence involved the world of work only marginally, but it was nevertheless an occasion to question, not only the forms of protest and struggle, redefining the concept of violence, and, beginning with the right to strike, but the conflict itself.[4]

---

3   Ralph Dahrendorf, *Class and Class Conflict in Industrial Society* (Stanford, Stanford University Press, 1959).

4   The concepts of protest and violence are politically and juridically contingent. In the 1980s nearly all democratic regimes introduced norms which limited the right to strike, particularly in the public services. The British miners' strike set a precedent when the union and its leadership were criminalised, in a context where the government intentionally and publicly raised the issue of the violent degeneration of industrial conflict: see Phil Scraton, 'If You Want a Riot, Change the Law: The Implications of the 1985 White Paper on Public Order', *Journal of Law and Society* 12(3), 1985, 385–393. For an important contribution on the neutralisation of conflict and on the drawbacks of this neutralisation for democracy, see Chantal Mouffe, *On the Political* (London,

The political actors more in favour of the armistice that was stipulated in the mid-century, that is, the working-class parties and trade unions, had taken on responsibility of government, and were convinced to adopt an unbiased, non-conflictual, but systemic perspective. In view of the conditions of Western economies and the new policy direction, working-class parties may have thought this only meant cutting back the excesses and privileges which were no longer affordable, and that it was time to reinstate the authority of governors and to restore dynamism to the private sector, in order to relaunch growth and development. The postwar armistice would have lasted, however, especially if development had regained energy.

There is also reason to think that the working-class parties remained prisoners of the internal dynamics of the political field, with its propensity to sustain itself, and to reproduce itself electorally. This was, together with the opportunity that access to government offered, to discourage potential competitors capable of siphoning off their electoral clientele. Did they simply miscalculate, or was this the only possible calculation considering both their political responsibilities and their political culture? The fact is that, in accepting the restitution of total autonomy to the private sector from state regulation, in discarding the language of conflict, and in relinquishing their most powerful weapon, collective action, not only were they weakened, but the entire political field was weakened.

This marked the start of a new cycle, characterised by different social and political equilibria and by a new armistice, even if this was not stipulated as solemnly as the first. On the one hand, the protagonists confirmed the democratic rules. But these, reinterpreted in the light of the post-democratic paradigm, function in a completely different way. On the other hand, a rethinking of the role of the state and of welfare policies became legitimate.

In spite of this, conflict continued. It was parcelled out and concealed, but not cancelled. Protests continued and calls for strikes followed. The difference being that their character was now defensive, because the direction of the conflict had changed. The vertical conflict between the upper class and working class was no longer bottom-up, but top-down. It was less noisy and less visible, but it was also a fierce redistributive conflict in reverse. The private sector, firms, private managers, but also the public ones, the free professions – the list is not exhaustive – have benefited from an impressive redistribution of wealth and power.[5]

At the same time new and rather underhand forms of horizontal conflict were taking place in the rest of society. The geography of these conflicts is extremely complicated: autonomous workers *vs.* dependent workers, employees in technologically advanced sectors *vs.* those in sectors in decline, fully guaranteed

---

Routledge, 2005).

5   In a provocative pamphlet, François Ruffin cites Warren Buffett, supposed to be the richest man on the planet: 'The war between classes is a fact, but it is my class, that of the rich, that leads it and is winning'. See *La guerre des classes* (Paris, Fayard, 2008).

employees *vs.* the precariously employed and the unemployed, private-sector workers *vs.* public-sector workers, the young *vs.* the old, the most disadvantaged social categories in need of welfare services *vs.* those convinced of being able to manage without, rich regions *vs.* poor regions, and native citizens *vs.* immigrants. All of them are insidious and exhausting conflicts that set those who believe that they hold certain privileges against those who have none, and those who are in bad shape against those who are even worse off.

Similar divisions are also weapons for the upper classes, who already have arms galore with which to affirm themselves, but who still encourage them. During the first postwar cycle, the world of work was considered too politically strong and the risk of collision was avoided, whereas in the second postwar cycle the same amount of energy was put into keeping the labour force and the trade unions in a condition of dispersion and weakness. This is why, once the earlier forms of conflict had been discouraged, new forms developed. Theory and politics continually evoke the parlous state of social cohesion and promote it as an electoral issue. But they often forget that deviance is also a form of social conflict.[5] At the times of Fordism, marches and strikes rarely flared up, but when they did their tones could be bitter, and violence could not be fully ruled out, but they were quite different from much of today's displays of social unrest – from burnt out cars in French *banlieues* in Autumn 2004 to English riots in August 2011 – which is the result of social and cultural marginalisation, the decline of key agencies of primary and secondary socialisation, such as the family and public education, and the lack of forms of collective action capable of channelling dissent.

It is not just a question of social unrest and the defiance that follows. Among the governed, democracy seems to have induced an awareness, albeit rather approximate, of their right to be taken into consideration by those who govern. There are continual displays of defiance produced not only by the vast and chaotic constellation of movements, committees and associations, but also by ordinary citizens. Their defiance is selective and temporary and often falls back on territorial affiliations, such as neighbourhood, municipality or valley: the Nimby mobilisations are an excellent example. But, even if the conflicts this provokes can be classified under the reassuring label of civil society, they remain conflicts and an uncomfortable challenge for the rulers.

Those in government set up complex modes of adaptation to this state of affairs. Protest may become a normal component of public life and even be incorporated into a coalition of interests for or against a specific political measure, sometimes right from the start.[7] Governance is, after all, a technique used by public powers to manage these new social conflicts, even if it does not necessarily resolve them and the rigid resistance of scattered, but not irrelevant, segments of society remains a cause of tension and has its delegitimising impact on who governs.

---

6   Stéphane Beaud, Michel Pialoux, *Violences urbaines, violences sociales* (Paris, Fayard, 2003).

7   Claire Dupuy, Charlotte Halpern, 'Les politiques publiques face à leurs protestataires', *Revue française de science politique* 54(4), 2009, 701–722.

At first sight governors show detachment and self-assurance. When protest starts they are not slow to use the force of the state. What however remains is their problematic reputation for the malaise of the governed. Post-modern politics credits itself with being managerial and problem-solving, but this reputation is not particularly easy-to-wear. Consequently the restyling which democratic regimes underwent in the closing decades of the twentieth century demands further adjustments.

Similar adjustments are not necessarily opportunistic. If some are, and distractions are adopted to deflect attention, others are supported by compelling theoretical reflections on democracy's shortcomings. Sometimes the remedies arrive from below, or outside, official politics. Theory often plays a functional role for politics, but it is not entirely at its service. There are a great many theorists who remain independent and maintain their critical spirit. However, these proposals of adjustment merit attention and the following sections deal with those traceable to two main rhetorics: the 'transcendency of the social body', and the 'protagonism of active citizenship'. The first insists on the symbolic dimension, the second also consists of institutional mechanisms that serve to make it operative and credible.

The transcendency of the social body

Age-old tools which had fallen into disuse have been retrieved from the lumber-rooms of politics and put back into use. Thus, in America and then in Europe religious faith and traditional morality have first of all been rediscovered to help cement collective life. On the one hand religion has been brought back in fashion as a reserve of shared values and as a valued guarantee of morality. On the other hand politicians exploit the integrative capacity of religious institutions.

We have already noted the antipolitical use of religion made by Jimmy Carter and it is again in America that we find a solid link between religious fundamentalism and the Republican Party.[8] But in Europe too, albeit less manifestly, religion has re-entered the lists. Margaret Thatcher, *avant garde* as ever, was the first sign of this. Her conservative revolution parted company from the postwar consensus in preaching individual values, but also by reinstating conventional authority, such as the family and religion.[9] From then on the fashion slowly took root.

Encouraged by a shrewd use of the media, in many places religious institutions and beliefs are enjoying an unexpected revival. This does not occur everywhere or even to the same degree. Northern Europe seems less receptive than Southern

---

8   Emilio Gentile, *God's Democracy. American Religion after September 11* (Westport, Prager, 2008). For a colourful account of the success of the fundamentalist Republican right, see Thomas Frank, *What is the Matter with Kansas? How Conservatives Won the Heart of America* (New York, Macmillan, 2004).

9   Graeme Smith, 'Margaret Thatchers's Christian Faith: A Case Study in Political Theology', *Journal of Religious Ethics* 35(2), 2007, 233–257.

Europe. But there are situations where traditional and new religious beliefs and institutions compete with political ones with considerable success, using their own powerful organisational instruments. Is this a reawakening of spirituality, or simply the use of a receptive and integrative capacity, discarded by politics?

It is probable that the tension between modernity and religion, articulated by theories of secularisation was not as powerful as imagined.[10] But we still need to understand what the renewed audience of religion means: is it due to the moral disorientation of contemporary society,[11] or to the failure of the great secular narratives, or in response to a need for reassurance and protection by those social groups most afflicted by 'existential insecurity'?[12] What is certain is that politicians increasingly appeal to religion for help and that the latter reacts willingly. The religious authorities may even theorise that the rules and principles of democracy are inherently fragile and in need of external support.[13]

Italian affairs, complicated by the presence of the Vatican, cannot be taken as an example, but there are plenty of other episodes that merit mention. While in office Tony Blair made continual reference to religion,[14] and European Union institutions make a quite intense use of religion to balance out their over-utilitarian and colourless image.[15] Then it is worth quoting Sarkozy's attempt to import the conservative revolution to France and calling into question nothing less than the time-honoured and respected principle of republican secularism.[16]

Whether or not providing a service for politics, not necessarily free of charge, is compatible with the values professed by religious institutions is a question for these institutions to answer. It is their problem whether they offer genuinely new

---

10 For example José Casanova, *Public Religions in the Modern World* (Chicago IL, University of Chicago Press, 1994).

11 Tzvetan Todorov, *The Conquest of America: the Question of the Other* (New York, Harper & Row, 1984, p. 251).

12 Ronald Inglehart, Pippa Norris, *Sacred and Secular: Religion and Politics Worldwide* (Cambridge, Cambridge University Press, 2004, p. 275). Inglehart and Norris also apply this explanation to the USA, given the situation of welfare.

13 This is the case of Pope Benedict XVI, who has referred to the theory of Ernst-Wolfgang Böckenförde several times. See 'Die Entstehung des Staates als Vorgang der Säkularisation', in Böckenförde, *Recht, Staat, Freiheit* (Frankfurt a.M., Suhrkamp, [1967] 1991, p. 112). The debate continued: see Jürgen Habermas and Joseph Ratzinger, *The Dialectics of Secularization: On Reason and Religion* (San Francisco, Ignatius Press, 2005).

14 Peter M. Scott, Chris R. Baker, Elaine L. Graham (eds.), *Remoralizing Britain? Political, Ethical and Theological Perspectives on New Labour* (London, Continuum, 2009).

15 Bérengère Massignon, 'The European Compromise: Between Immanence and Transcendence', *Social Compass* 54(4), 2007, 573–582.

16 Recognising a principle of social cohesion in religion, Sarkozy even wrote a book, before becoming president: *La République, les religions, l'espérance* (Paris, Le Cerf, 2004). On 20 December 2007 he delivered an exacting discourse in the Basilica of St. John Lateran in Rome in the presence of Benedict XVI.

moral standards, or are simply being used as a bonding agent for identity or as an associative opportunity. For democracy, however, the use of religion poses more serious problems. If the legitimacy of the intervention of religion in the public debate is not debatable, what is problematic for democracy is the unmitigated reflection that the religious discourse sometimes assumes. Religious fundamentalism has recently been attributed to Islam,[17] but is actually characteristic also of some Christian sects and, at times, of Catholicism itself. In what way is this reconciled to safeguarding democratic principles such as mutual respect and the recognition of pluralism?

This attempt to rediscover a transcendent collective dimension can also be ascribed to the domineering reappearance in public discourse of the nation and its supporting liturgy. It first reappeared in the West in response to migratory pressure, secessionist ambitions, serious international tensions or the so-called terrorist threat. Postwar cosmopolitanism, the establishment of the UN, the process of European integration, the international vocation of large parties, together with an awareness of disasters caused by nationalism, had blurred the concept. But for at least a quarter of a century the nation has once again been an argument used by politicians to relegitimate themselves in the eyes of their citizens.

For some parties, such as the pseudo-populists, the term 'nation' has replaced 'race' and authorises the aggressive use of the rhetoric of identity,[18] frequently dressed up as the claim to a collective right to protect. Immigration certainly constitutes a serious and two-sided challenge. On the one hand, it is inevitable that the new ethnic, cultural and religious minorities will demand to be recognised. On the other hand, especially in the absence of appropriate material and symbolic policies of integration, which are difficult and costly to apply, it is clear that this recognition will meet with resistance. There is concern, however, when the political establishment renews its offer of services to the governed, rediscovering the nationalistic rhetoric, with the organicistic bias that may accompany it, eventually combining it with the rhetoric of the enemy – and the rhetoric of risk or emergency – and making a short-circuit between migratory processes, unemployment, security and even the terrorist threat.

---

17 One of the great *trompe-l'oeil* of our times is the incompatibility of Islam and democracy, and Islam and pluralism. The debate is fierce and liable to be biased. We are indebted to Edward W. Said, Palestinian and Christian (by birth), for a fascinating attempt to immunise us against the anti-Islamic bias in *Reflections on Exile and other Essays* (Cambridge MA, Harvard University Press, 2000). For an empirical analysis that stresses the inadequacy and instrumentality of some opinions on Islam, see Jean-François Bayart, *L'islam républicain. Ankara, Téhéran, Dakar* (Paris, Albin Michel, 2010).

18 On the identity and excessive and debatable use of this concept see the criticisms of Jean-François Bayart, *L'illusion identitaire* (Paris, Fayard, 1996). Samuel P. Huntington gives a good example of a risky use of the concept in his last book, *Who Are We? The Challenges to America's National Identity* (New York, Simon & Schuster, 2004) where he invites the USA to build up a strong religious, cultural and moral identity.

Instead of being a remedy, the rhetoric of culture in danger is a form of political marketing for more severe police measures, which are damaging to individual freedom,[19] and encourages the radicalisation of a part of the electorate on the right. What is particularly striking is how the 'war against terrorism', instead of being a chance to reflect on the causes of terrorism and how to prevent it, has simply replaced the old dualism between the free world and communist regimes, with a new dualism between the West and the Islamic world.

Another problem is the redundant and indiscriminate use of the language of rights. This is a spin-off from the success of 'constitutional' democracy and its aim is to set more severe limits to power in order to protect individual rights. In fact, the priority asserted by the language of rights has its own drawbacks. The first is that the redundant cataloguing of rights may set them against each other. When the rights of man and citizen are fragmented in women's rights, linguistic or racial minority rights, homosexuals' rights, and perhaps the rights of embryos, non-smokers and so forth, the attention that some obtain from public powers may reduce the attention given to others, facilitating operations of distraction by the public powers. How should we respond, in other words, when in public discourse the totally legitimate rights of homosexuals are used to overshadow the restrictions on public expenditure or the scarce attention of governments to working conditions or pensioners or women? The second risk is that individuals protected by rights, tend to perceive themselves not as parts of a collective body that shares, albeit contractually, interests and values, but as isolated individuals, who as rightholders, give up collective political action and turn to courts. Perhaps this too is a way for neo-liberal individualism to model and condition its potential opponents?[20]

Using its own means, theory has also contributed to the reconstruction of horizontal ties within the collective body, or at least the symbolic ones. Clearly, theory is never politically neutral. It is not neutral when it decides to reconstruct horizontal bonds either inclusively or exclusively. The latter is the case of a rather fashionable theory, rich in spin-offs in public discourse, such as 'communitarianism'. This originally developed to protect minorities. Its aim was to react to liberal individualism: both to its materialist version based on the market, and to its neo-contractualist version championed by John Rawls. Communitarianism emphasises the importance of identity, memory and tradition, together with the embeddedness of the individual in a community firmly unified by common, historically established values and by a shared moral idea of good, as well as by institutions such as the family and religion.[21] Although burdened by an undesirable organicis-

---

19 Didier Bigo, Laurent Bonelli, Thomas Deltombe (eds.), *Au nom du 11 septembre* (Paris, La Découverte, 2008).

20 Alain Brossat, *La démocratie immunitaire* (Paris, La Dispute, 2003) and Antoine Garapon, *La raison du moindre État. Le néolibéralisme et la justice* (Paris, Jacob, 2010).

21 For a presentation of communitarianism, see Amitai Etzioni (ed.), *The Essential Communitarian Reader* (Lanham NJ, Rowman and Littlefield Publishers, 1998).

tic and anti-universal claim, communitarianism, of which there are also moderate versions, has not been short of an audience. First and foremost, it was part of the nationalistic revival, but it also pressed for policies to reconstruct communitarian ties. That is, ties to benefit families and to encourage work, which in turn inspired welfare reforms in the United States and Britain.

The problem with communitarianism is its mistrust of pluralism and its tendency to exclude whoever is not part of what is defined as the community. It is precisely this sort of problem that has been opposed by other theories that preach solidarity and reciprocity obligations among citizens but in a rather different way. This is the case of 'republicanism', whose several versions are all aimed at reconstructing social ties by exalting civic virtue and positive freedom. In other words, republicanism recognises active involvement in public life as a new principle of cohesion, while proposing a new and more exacting definition of freedom as the 'absence of domination'.[22]

In the environs of republicanism we can often find thinkers who want to purify and refine the concept of patriotism, and who rediscover the link between this concept and universal values, solemnly assembled in constitutional texts in the mid-twentieth century in the form of 'patriotism of the constitution'.[23] Encouraging people to develop civic commitment and mutual respect, and to participate, is laudable, as is tracing the collective memory of shared values and narratives, but these precepts have the defect of rejecting any reflection on factors that corrode collective life and exacerbate its inequalities. To stitch up the split between governors and governed is it really just a question of some uplifting civic or patriotic call, or it would be a case of balancing the inequalities produced by the market?

The question also applies to contributions to sociology and political science, which are often inspired by communitarianism and republicanism, and makes large use of concepts such as 'network' or 'social capital', sharing the formula of active citizenship, reciprocal trust, common values and trying to apply this in terms of social engineering and public policies. Once they have archived the model of society structured by classes and widespread interests, or thanks to economic development and democratic institutions, the social sciences empirically reveal the decline of collective ties. Consequently they invite the public powers to cultivate ties of reciprocity, relations of trust, willingness to cooperate among citizens, as well as the adoption of useful policy measures where these do not exist, or the removal of obstacles that limit their functioning, thus replacing the costly paternalism of the welfare state.[24] As already noted, the formula appears so convincing

---

22 Among many, see Philipp Pettit, *Republicanism. A Theory of Freedom and Government* (Oxford, Clarendon Press, 1997).

23 The concept has been re-examined and reformulated several times by Jürgen Habermas in *The Post-National Constellation* (Cambridge, Polity Press, 2001).

24 Critically, see Mark Bevir, 'Institutionalism and the Third Way' in Adcock, Bevir, Stimson (eds.), *Modern Political Science: Anglo-American Exchanges since 1880* (Princeton NJ, Princeton

that developed democracies not only apply it to themselves, but even export it. But are associations and local networks – a question which we have already asked – sufficient to cope with the social damages typical of late modernity, together with the many grounds for tension that afflict democratic regimes?

The protagonism of active citizenship

The republican exhortation to civic-mindedness and the theory of social capital are entitled to be considered as the connecting link with another great rhetoric currently in circulation: that of active citizenship through associationism. The two are connected by the sacred icon of Alexis de Tocqueville. This is a paradoxical destiny for a conservative who was rather pessimistic about the future of democracy in general, and of American democracy in particular, even though he valued its inventions. Nevertheless, Tocqueville still seems to inspire a civic rhetoric, articulated in different ways, supported by a rich theoretical formulation, and by practical experiments of incontestable interests. In this way what we could define as the 'neo-democratic' paradigm has taken shape, providing for substantive revisions primarily on the side of procedures. That is, associations, together with local self-government, governance, civil society and deliberative practices are promoted to basic democratic mechanisms to balance the elitist verticality of the post-democratic paradigm and its applications.

The theoretical contributions traceable to the neo-democratic paradigm are many and heterogeneous. The distinctive trait of this paradigm, with respect to the empirical investigations of political science on which the post-democratic paradigm rested, is the rediscovery of 'practical reason' – or of normative political philosophy – which aims to revitalise democracy through an ethical theory anchored in non-traditional, but shared values. This does not mean that the scientific study of politics is put aside. The neo-democratic paradigm has stimulated a striking mass of valuable empirical research, around the fertile themes of social capital, governance and deliberative democracy. In spite of this, the theoretical starting points of greater importance for this paradigm may very well be the normative ones offered by John Rawls and Jürgen Habermas.

In the case of Rawls,[25] the vital element of his thought, at least in its early version, is the exhumation of the social contract. Hans Kelsen considered compromise as a principle of caution that preserved the diversity of the parts and started from the relations of force among them. In contrast, what Rawls has in mind is an ethically-based social contract. In line with his politico-cultural extraction, consti-

---

University Press, 2007). With reference also to international civil society, see Jean-François Bayart in *Le gouvernement du monde. Une critique politique de la globalisation* (Paris, Fayard, 2004, pp. 96–109).

25 John Rawls, *A Theory of Justice* (Cambridge, Harvard University Press, 1972).

tuted by the experience of the New Deal, in the early version of Rawls' thought there are two principles on which both a just society and the social contract should be based: the principle of equality, that provides the maximum freedom of each, compatible with the equal freedom of all; and the principle of difference, where the only legitimate inequalities are those which benefit the most disadvantaged.

Rawls' proposal has been subject to endless criticism, starting with its lack of attention for the plurality and heterogeneity of contending concepts of 'good', and has been, not incorrectly, accused of abstractness. How many human beings are realistically willing to share the viewpoint of a sophisticated American intellectual academic? In spite of this, in the difficult juncture of the 1970s, it was precisely the attempt to stabilise ethically the gains made by the welfare state – sheltering it from politico-electoral competition – made by a scholar distant from the political world, but of firm democratic convictions, that stood out as an interesting alternative to neo-liberalism and the post-democratic paradigm.

In the long run, the Rawls who exerted more practical influence nevertheless is the Rawls who focuses later on the concept of 'overlapping consensus' in the pages of *Political Liberalism*.[26] Putting his own theory on the same level as other comprehensive doctrines – or conceptions of the good – that lacerate pluralistic society, what Rawls demands of each doctrine is that it reconciles rationality and reasonableness, tolerance and mutual respect, so as to establish an equitable, stable and peaceful cohabitation, that keeps the motives for division in the private sphere. Everyone has their own principles of justice and it will be difficult to unify them in a shared conception of the good. Therefore the problem of pluralistic cohabitation can be resolved not by censuring pluralism, but by convincing the parts to apply the dictates of public reason reciprocally. When it comes to political issues, the parts should divest themselves of their particular viewpoint and adopt an impartial perspective that recognises and safeguards basic rights and freedoms. The problem is that as a similar proposal, which is not lacking in ambition, it is no less abstract than that of a social contract. Rawls himself shows how ambitious and unrealistic it is when he reserves its application to the choices of the Supreme Court.

The second great icon of neo-democratic paradigm is Jürgen Habermas.[27] Twenty-five years after Rawls, Habermas proposed exploiting the potential of linguistic communication as a constitutive element of the interdependency among human beings and hence oriented towards agreement. He believes the exchange of rational arguments, in the pursuit of 'consensus' through reciprocal understanding and persuasion among free and equal citizens, to be the means to remove the grounds for moral and political conflict, and to restore meaning to celebrated concepts in the democratic tradition such as citizenship, popular sovereignty and solidarity.

---

26 Rawls, *Political Liberalism* (New York, Columbia University Press, 1993).

27 Jürgen Habermas, *Between Facts and Norms. Contributions to a Discourse Theory of Law and Democracy* (Cambridge MA, MIT Press, 1996).

Habermas does not resign himself to the idea that society be given over exclusively to the systemic capacity of integration of the capitalist economy and bureaucratic organisation. At the same time, he recognises the coincidence between the authors and addressees of norms – such as the subjects of liberal democracy – as the sole form of rational legitimation of the modern right. In exercising popular sovereignty, the rights of man and those of the citizen are no longer an external bond for making political decisions, according to the individualist perspective, but the status that participants in public discourse must mutually recognise, so that this discourse can fully unfold and produce legitimate effects. While compromise is the fruit of bargaining among the parts that act strategically and accept it for different reasons, consensus is rationally motivated and based on reasons that convince the parts in the same way. For Habermas consensus must be pursued in the public sphere, where opinion is shaped, while the majority principle can be applied in places where the 'will' takes shape, i.e. political decisions.

There are good reasons to consider this as an excessively trusting and strained theory of the opportunities offered by communication, and a overestimation of the opportunity to resolve the tension between basic rights and popular sovereignty. This has not stopped Habermas' theory from offering, together with that of Rawls, a great many pointers towards more recent reflections on democracy and its symbolic reopening to the governed, after the post-democratic paradigm – and related institutional reforms – had worked to radically diminish their role.

In fact, governance can already be understood as an innovation which moves in such a direction, insofar as it is a procedure based on dialogue and consensus, that encourages citizens to participate, especially through associations. The value of associations has also been increased by the successful theory of social capital, and they have even been placed at the centre of a specific theory of 'associative democracy'.[28] Once the inadequacy of regulatory principles which previously held up advanced democracies has been ascertained, associative democracy suggests a reassessment of spontaneous associative ties and linkages. Where these are lacking, it is desirable to promote them and to allot them the task of providing some services currently monopolised by welfare. Paul Hirst, who has done more than anyone else to formulate this theory, argues that once the concepts of 'public' and state have been decoupled, why non confer a public status on citizens who organise themselves independently and on the ties that consequently structure society?

---

28 Erik O. Wright (ed.), *Associations and Democracy* (London, Verso, 1992) and Paul Q. Hirst, *Associative Democracy* (Cambridge, Polity Press, 1993) and *From Statism to Pluralism* (Oxford, Polity Press, 1997).

Yet, also associative democracy comes in for criticism.[29] In much the same way as governance, it not only views associations as strategic actors rather than as interdependent entities, but also the democratic character of associations is doubtful: there are as many non-democratic associations as democratic ones. Moreover, it is hard to imagine how to coordinate them once they have multiplied, without supposing a state-type authority. Finally, as in other cases, there are problems for the less educated, less well-off and politically less competent social strata. These may not be insuperable —after all any experience can be a good occasion to learn – but nor are they easy to overcome.

Another essential rediscovery of democratic correctives by theory and hence by politics is what is indicated on the whole with the formula 'participatory democracy',[30] to distinguish it from 'direct democracy', which partially reappears thanks to the referendum. Roughly speaking, the roots of participatory democracy go back to the 1970s, when the appearance of civil society was followed by the first attempts to raise its value, not only as actors, but also as a *locus* of political participation. At the time, one of the ideas of participation was to erode the spaces of official politics and to constitute an alternative. It was the progeny of a period of intense collective mobilisation and presented critical rather than managerial motions in an attempt to guide democracy.[31] The attempt failed, but the new forms of participation remained on the political agenda, and theory went on to address it until new experiments were made, stimulated above all by the theories of social capital and the 'third way'.

Not necessarily laying claim to similar ancestors, theory and politics began to design institutional mechanisms, which, more than substituting the traditional procedures of representation and government, attempt to correct and integrate them, actively involving citizens in policy-making. Of all the possible mechanisms the most ambitious, and theoretically most elaborate, are the procedures of deliberative democracy.

---

29 For a critical perspective on associative democracy, and on the limits of associationism, see Mark E. Warren, *Association and Democracy* (Princeton NJ, Princeton University Press, 2001). Warren does not deny the democratic potential but stresses the risk that democratic associations generate, even with the best intentions, non-democratic effects. See also Theda Skocpol in *Diminished Democracies. From Membership to Management in American Civil Life* (Norman, University of Oklahoma Press, 2003), and Matthew A. Crenson, Benjamin Ginsberg, *Downsizing Democracy. How America Sidelined its Citizens and Privatized its Public* (Baltimore MD, Johns Hopkins University Press, 2002), on the dispersive effects of short range, local or specialised associationism.

30 For a synthetic, stimulating and persuasive analysis see Jean-Pierre Gaudin, *La démocratie partecipative* (Paris, Colin, 2008).

31 For an original and historical review of France see Hélène Hatzfeld, *Faire de la politique autrement. Les expériences inachevées des années 1970* (Rennes, Presses universitaires de Rennes, 2005).

According to its theorists, the basic assumption of deliberation is the inverse of that of rational choice. Actor preferences are not only exogenous and predefined, but socially positioned and not in the least rigid.[32] Deliberation consists of setting up what are normally assembly-like situations, which are supposed to have a potential to modify the participants' preferences and to make them converge. Deliberative theory agrees with the Rawlsian notion of breaking with any higher religious, political, intellectual or moral authority, and any interpretation of reality that allows a safe ranking of preferences, interests and values. It agrees also with Habermas' appraisal of public discussion. Consequently, deliberative theorists suggest a laborious and compelling decisional technique, above all in terms of time. This invites citizens to publicly compare and sharpen their own preferences, so as to mature a rational consensus around collective decisions. The public debate is expected to oblige participants to censure any egoistic or discreditable motivation and to only manifest those grounds which are publicly acceptable, thus facilitating the re-composition of differences.[33]

Moreover, deliberation is also a technique of collective learning, which helps mitigate the informative asymmetries between discussants, increases awareness of the issues being discussed, the available solutions and their consequences. Deliberation reduces media interference and is particularly suitable in situations where experts' opinions conflict or are unable to produce a solution. Deliberation also encourages actors to come up with solutions not previously contemplated, or to re-evaluate other previously discarded solutions. Above all, it is an opportunity to debate different points of view rationally, and hence to stimulate a considered examination of opposed arguments. It also allows interlocutors to get to know each other, and to establish relations of mutual respect and trust, which help to cool dissent and reinforce the legitimacy of decisions. Although bearers of values and different interests, perhaps in conflict, participants in a deliberative process should be induced to recognise the existence of differing opinions and accept their legitimacy.[34] It is difficult to say what the public echo is of this recognition. At the same time, whoever is involved has the opportunity to compare *alla pari*, to learn from interlocutors, to formulate choices more widely shared than those adopted using the majority principle.

---

32 Jon Elster, 'The Market and the Forum: Three Varieties of Political Theory', in Jon Elster, Aanund Hylland (eds.), *Foundations of Social Choice Theory* (Cambridge, Cambridge University Press, 1986) and Claus Offe, 'Micro-aspects of Democratic Theory: What Makes for the Deliberative Competence of Citizens', in Axel Hadenius (ed.), *Democracy. Victory and Crisis* (Cambridge, Cambridge University Press, 1997).

33 See Jon Elster (ed.), *Deliberative Democracy* (Cambridge, Cambridge University Press, 1998).

34 For a catalogue of the virtues of deliberation see Jon Elster, 'Introduction', in *Deliberative Democracy*, 1998*b* and Loïc Blondiaux, *Le nouvel ésprit de la démocratie* (Paris, Seuil, 2008, 32–34).

The first attempts to marry deliberation and participation took place spontaneously at Porto Alegre in Brazil. In 1988 the local administration, led by a coalition
headed by the *Partido dos Trabalhadores* and prompted by the world of associations, set in motion an experiment in participatory budgeting. This involved
even the poorest citizens through assemblies and debates where they set municipal
policy lines on the issues of taxation, investment and public services. From then
on the technique has spread around the planet.[35] Since then deliberative theory
generated an impressive fall-out of initiatives. Juries, conferences, forums, town
meetings, neighbourhood assemblies, deliberative polls,[36] public debates and on-
line consultations have sounded out citizens on all sorts of policies: from public
budgeting to infrastructure, and from welfare and environmental policy, to the
Nimby syndrome.

Yet, even these procedures come in for criticism. Leaving aside the most
obvious, i.e. that they are also instruments of government, of conflict discipline
and control, a specific weakness of deliberative motions is that they only allow
monothematic decisions. A single question is addressed, but once deliberated, the
assembly dissolves. But there are also many practical hitches, starting with conditions of access. With deliberation anyone who is interested in the issue being
discussed can participate. But who decides who is interested? Second, the impulse
to set deliberative procedures in motion normally depends on the political authorities. The protagonists are private actors, but we should not underestimate the
probability of instrumentalisation and manipulation, from both above and below.
Surely there is also the risk of elected authorities and political actors advocating
a deliberative consultation just in order to selectively mobilise a limited public of
citizens and to discourage other forms of political action, and even to divert the
potential of participation and protest to their own advantage.

And how will the decisions taken by a deliberative motion be received and applied? If elected authorities maintain the monopoly of the final decision, how can
we prevent deliberation from becoming a formal exhibition with limited practical
results? If this were not enough, we should not forget that all public policies are
part of a context in which other policies are adopted. Consequently, there are also
problems of compatibility with other decisions, which only the public authorities
can resolve, and the inevitable fear that deliberation will be reduced to a rite which
simply legitimates or contains dissent.

We should not omit the role of professionals: the experts who assist with the
deliberative procedure in merit of the arguments, and the facilitators who help in

---

35 On Porto Alegre, see Marion Gret, Yves Sintomer, *Porto Alegre. L'espoir d'une autre démocratie*
    (Paris, La Découverte, 2002). Among the many publications, see Yves Sintomer, Carsten Herzberg,
    Anja Röcke, *Les budgets participatifs en Europe: Des services publics au service du public* (Paris,
    La Découverte, 2008), and Jules Talpin, *Schools of Democracy* (Colchester, ECPR Press, 2011).

36 On deliberative polls see James Fiskin, *Democracy and Deliberation: New Directions in
    Democratic Reform* (New Haven CT, Yale University Press, 1991).

questions of procedure. The former can obviously condition choices and select information. But the latter can also do so, considering they are requested to animate the deliberation, to set the agenda, to collect documents and to organise expert hearings, to give the word to different parts and to verbalise debates. All these are operations that participants in deliberation are not able either to conduct alone, or to control. Even if the role of facilitator is as professional and neutral, how much could it still disturb the authenticity of deliberation? Surely the increasing professionalisation of such an activity raises doubts about the procedure.[37]

Yet, other criticisms can be made. Who guarantees that conflicts will become more reconcilable? Rational discourse, where each sets out their own reasons and where there is a perspective of reciprocal persuasion, can help civilise conflict management, but direct confrontation may also make it irreconcilable. Furthermore, where in the real world of heterogeneous and diverging interests are the confines between deliberation and negotiation, and between compromise and consensus? Supposing that actors orient themselves sincerely towards understanding and reciprocity, are citizens really capable of what they are being called for? The procedure works to reduce the inequalities of competence and information, or to bring socially heterogeneous *milieux* nearer to one another, but the undertaking is still challenging. Deliberation, especially if repeated, can reduce the asymmetries of information and knowledge, but that does not mean that it does. It is, after all, a procedure made to measure for the educated middle classes. It calls for the ability to discuss and convince, often in public. Not everyone has these qualities, and they cannot always be acquired in a citizens' jury or a neighbourhood assembly. On the contrary, there is a high risk of a hierarchisation of the public, and that those who are most politically skilled, and who have most experience in debate and argumentation, will condition those who are less skilled and less experienced.[38]

It is no coincidence that some deliberative theorists also suggest measures to promote the ability of the most disadvantaged to take part on a par in deliberation. Re-proposing welfare as a constituent element of democracy means adopting measures to remove inequalities of class, race, gender and culture that limit the freedom of individuals and their expressive capacity. Deliberative theory thus turns to the public powers, which are openly requested to promote the realisation of ideal deliberative conditions, where those willing to take part in the deliberation are placed on an equal footing.[39]

---

37 Luigi Bobbio emphasises how the results differ depending on the situation where deliberation takes place, the interests involved, and the characteristics of the actors: 'Types of Deliberation', *Journal of Public Deliberation* 6(2), 2010: http://services.bepress.com/jpd/vol6/iss2/art1

38 Among the many critiques of the impact of inequalities of deliberation, see Lynn M. Sanders, 'Against Deliberation', *Political Theory* 25(3), 1997, 347–376.

39 James Bohman, *Public Deliberation. Pluralism, Complexity, and Democracy* (Cambridge MA, MIT Press, 1996, pp. 132–142).

It goes without saying that satisfying similar claims is more difficult than con-voking a deliberative meeting. Despite this, deliberative procedures always have some point in their favour and a greater use of them may be desirable. It is unlikely that deliberation has an epistemic value and allows actors to reach better or wiser decisions. But every time policy-makers agree to use its techniques, they are, if nothing else, recognising the problematic nature of their relations with citizens. In particular, they are admitting the importance of listening to their needs, and of including them less superficially in public and collective life.

Furthermore, re-proposing the principle of 'government through discussion'[40] which is the basis of modern parliamentarism, deliberative procedures officially re-discover a principle recently undervalued by the post-democratic paradigm and by the new practice it inspired of majoritarian democracy, but historically rich in mer-its. This is compromise in dealing with conflicts.[41] At the same time, deliberative democracy pays public homage to other, often disregarded, principles such as mu-tual respect and tolerance, and to the idea that citizens constitute a collective body, divided on the level of values and interests, but nonetheless willing to live together.

In deliberation we see the reappearance of the idea of a common good at least as a normative ideal, and of democracy as a principle of pluralistic cohabitation. Unfortunately, intolerance is once again a part of our political landscape. Even lib-eral-democratic values are susceptible to being interpreted from a fundamentalist perspective. But if, on the one hand, we run similar risks, on the other, it is encour-aging that someone somewhere is working to oppose them. Of course, on condition that the corrective is not reduced to a mere distraction which ends up avoiding any sort of partisan dialectic and any form of social conflict or large-scale mobilisation.

In the 1970s the participatory motions were overpoliticised, and today's ex-amples want them underpoliticised. Even deliberative procedures can constitute an instrument to neutralise and delegitimate official politics. Whoever participates is prescribed, if divested of any sense of belonging or political affiliation. Is it by chance that democratic regimes, once they reach the peak of elitist evolution, dress up to make some participatory show, but nothing else?

It is too early to make definitive judgements. Deliberation is based on an idyl-lic representation of actors' motivations and is easily instrumentalised. Yet, it has some worthwhile objectives and can be a valuable instrument of information and conciliation. Policy-makers consider it with a great deal of interest and appropriate it, and we can suspect they do so because they have to. The governed are increas-ingly less remissive. They do not rebel, but they often find a noisy way to make

---

40 For a definition, see Ernest Barker in *Principles of Social and Political Theory* (Oxford, Oxford University Press, 1963). See also Bernard Manin, *Principles of Representative Government* (Cambridge, Cambridge University Press, 1995).

41 Amy Gutmann, Dennis Thompson, *The Spirit of Compromise. Why Governing Demands it and Campaigning Undermines it* (Princeton, Princeton University Press, 2012).

their ideas heard. Governors may as well let them deliberate.[42] But things will not necessarily remain like this.

We should never forget that the model where policies begin by singling out a problem and perseveres in looking for a solution, and concludes with its implementation, is extremely unlikely. The same model is even more unlikely if applied to extremely complex policies such as those dealing with democratic procedures. In other words, not only is it uncertain that participatory innovations achieve the publicly declared objectives of their promoters, but it is no less uncertain that they attain the unconfessed objective of making the impact of greater participation innocuous. As always, a complex power struggle emerges around these innovations among a crowd of competing actors with diverging ambitions, whose outcomes are extremely uncertain. Nothing prevents these innovations from being the preliminary moves, beyond rule renewal, towards an enhanced way of understanding democracy. Who knows if the rediscovery of discarded principles, such as public debate and reciprocal persuasion at the low levels of the democratic regime,[43] will even exceed the expectations of its promoters, and disappoint whoever wants to instrumentalise it? Could deliberation favour the emergence of a wave of public feeling and a new reform of democratic institutions, that might undermine the now widespread managerial idea of government action?[44]

Meanwhile, in democratic regimes between the low levels and high levels, the renewal of procedures has promoted above all a new hybridisation between democracy and non-democracy. At the low levels we have governance, civil society and instruments of participatory democracy that promise to offer citizens a voice and a new and effective opportunity to be heard. Pluralism is even encouraged, provided that its multiple parts must remain separate and do not coalesce. This is the reason why governors try to select the voices of the governed that they do not consider too awkward, to the detriment of others, who they prefer to remain silent. The problem is that this claim is not always fulfilled and that sometimes the actors demonstrate an unexpected capacity for resistance and protest.

Instead, at the high levels, democratic regimes pretend to reduce the representation of pluralism simplifying political competition around two main all-inclusive, generic and interchangeable political alignments. Yet, this does not mean at all that such an attempt to depoliticise electoral democracy – or to politicise it in a different way – are succeeding, or that it is enough to reduce competition for

---

42 For an interesting perspective see Thomas Fromentin and Stéphanie Wojcik (eds.), *Le profane en politique. Compétences et engagements du citoyen* (Paris, L'Harmattan, 2008).

43 This can also occur at the high levels, because at times there is an attempt to deal with questions that are crucial in our era using similar procedures, concealing another form of non-elected representation: see Michel Callon, Pierre Lascoumes, Yannick Barthe, *Agir dans un monde incertain. Essai sur la démocratie technique* (Paris, Seuil, 2001).

44 See, a little over-optimistically, Loïc Blondiaux, *Le nouvel ésprit de la démocratie* (Paris, Seuil, 2008).

power at the high levels. Parliament, local government and organised interests are still the *loci* where power is disputed and they are certainly not silent spectators. Neither is the constellation of public authorities and regulatory agencies. Some authorities are old, such as the judiciary, and others, such as the public, private, national and supranational unelected authorities, are new, and each moves according to its own logic.

In other words, the new arrangement of the high levels is anything but peaceful and orderly. A deaf and bitter conflictuality opposes the electorally invested authorities and the unelected institutions. The task of the latter is to limit the range of action of the former, to verify their performance, to assure their morality, meanwhile asserting that their superior technical competence is the best protection of citizens' interests.

What is certain is that the higher levels of democratic regime try to distance themselves from lower levels, despite paying them every sort of homage. Yet, the lower levels, albeit in a discontinuous and contradictory way, lay siege to the higher ones. According to Rosanvallon, this is 'counter-democracy',[45] while John Keane, summing up the contrasting pressures in the higher and lower levels, defines it as a 'monitory democracy'.[46] But how effective are these forms of balancing that interweave at all levels of democratic regimes?

Taken together, what is currently taking place is a striking transformation of democratic regimes whose outcomes are difficult to predict, but whose scope is arguably comparable to the transformation imposed on representative regimes by universal suffrage. The only difference being that, at first sight, the transformation appears to have gone in the opposite direction. Despite the rethoric of active citizenship, are we by any chance observing a revenge against universal suffrage, without even bothering to revoke it?

---

45 Pierre Rosanvallon, *Counter-Democracy: Politics in an Age of Distrust* (Cambridge, Cambridge University Press, 2008).

46 John Keane, *The Life and Death of Democracy* (London, Simon & Schuster, 2009).

| epilogue

> '... we must be careful here. The ministers of knowledge have always as-
> sumed that the whole universe was threatened by the very changes that
> affected their ideologies and their positions. They transmute the misfortune
> of their theories into theories of misfortune. When they transform their
> bewilderment into "catastrophes", when they seek to enclose the people
> in the "panic" of their discourses, are they once more necessarily right?'

Michel de Certeau, *The Practice of Everyday Life*, 1980

The more the diagnosis is uncertain, debatable and aware of its shortcomings, the more difficult it is to reach a conclusion. Nothing would, therefore, allow us to imagine a therapeutic proposal, with respect to a state of democracy that seems acceptable according to its current definition, even if unsatisfactory for the greater part of its alleged beneficiaries. It is not even a foregone conclusion that one of the tasks of the social sciences is to make forecasts and dictate therapies, although they do it continuously. This is why this volume is without a conclusion.

Through a peculiar mixture of institutions – elections, basic freedoms, parlia-ments – modern representative regimes, and then democratic regimes, meant to associate the governed with government. This invention now carries the name of democracy. Yet, even if we limit the boundaries of the people, this task of as-sociation was not too easy to realise. Therefore democracies accommodated with a purely symbolic and indirect association of the governed. The running of the state and the responsibilities of government were removed from the hands of the sovereign by the grace of God and became the stake of a legitimate contest. In designating governors through competitive elections, the governed at least had a way to express their preferences.

Experience shows that not even this was very easy, or without drawbacks for the governors. This is the reason why the contest not only admitted only those com-petitors who supplied adequate guarantees of reliability, but also invented plenty of ways to keep the governed at a safe distance, rendering their voice more remote and less troublesome. It was to be expected. Democracy is a technology of power. It can certainly promise to cancel power or to limit it, but power is still power.

Yet, nothing is ever promised in vain. The attempts to keep down the costs of association of the governed encountered *ab initio* a basic obstacle. After all, the association of the governed suits governors as regards obtaining legitimacy, but also information, collaboration and the reduction of the grounds for conflict or for improving conflict management. But once the governed were entitled to govern, albeit indirectly, they felt authorised to be more demanding and raised the cost of their collaboration: if the people are sovereign, why should they not have expectations as regards the action of the governors?

Where the governed did not think this, there were those who would think this in their place. The competition for power – and consensus – that representative and democratic regimes instituted has always meant that the governed found, in the circle of governors, or among those aspiring to become governors, advocates ready to represent them – i.e. recognise and defend their causes – obviously in order to gain some advantage in terms of consensus and power. Even had the governed not been so demanding, someone would have induced them to be.

Yet, what occurred to the governors of late modernity is that a complicated mass of reasons, or a singular array of disparate events, put new instruments at their disposal to reduce the costs of association with the governed and primarily to subdue the advocates of potentially troublesome causes, particularly those of the lower and weaker strata. Recently, these strata have found few advocates willing to defend them.

The long ascent of the professional hierarchies of politics no longer depends on the ability to mobilise the big numbers. At the same time, a new conviction about the state of the world, and how best to deal with its problems, has largely prevailed. The more troublesome and heterodox interests – those demanding that democracy guarantee more equality and justice by redistributing power and wealth – have been disqualified, and even the more well-intentioned advocates no longer consider them sufficiently remunerative to take on. At the same time, there is now a very widespread opinion that it is not the task of politics to make the world different from what it actually is. Once the great ideological inebriation wears off, there will be those who sustain that pragmatism has finally replaced ideology. Yet, there is reason to believe that politics has only stopped making promises, since there are sufficient less costly and less demanding ways to keep the governed at bay. What we should not forget is that in reality politics acts, and contributes to change, also when it claims to not to. For instance, letting the market act in its place.

Apparently this does not authorise us to speak of 'betrayed democracy', at least in the meaning generally attributed to the term. There are many ways of making democracy, especially if one believes that it consists of some minimum rules. What was in force in the past was termed democracy, as is what is in force today. In spite of this, once the rules of the game have been readjusted without too much noise, and once society has changed, democracy may look in good shape *per se*, but probably the same cannot be said for its outcomes, at least from the point of view of the large majority of the governed.

Even democracy and its rules constitute a policy. Establishing democracy, maintaining it and revising it is an exacting policy, even a very exacting one. Thus, like all policies, democracy is primarily the fruit of the power struggle, and the expedience of politicians and other political and social actors. In the postwar period a particular variant of democracy prevailed. In the course of a quarter of a century or little more, this was substituted with a different variant. Among the many reasons for change there is the democratic regime itself, together with postwar economic growth and the welfare state. It was the success of postwar democracy that contributed to reshape the profile of *homo democraticus*. It is at this point that the range of solidarity that the adaptive and conflictual reactions generated by industrial society started to be undermined.

This reshaping has been confirmed and reinforced by the individualistic and utilitarian culture of neo-liberalism. This culture has been ennobled by rights, or tempered by civil society and communitarianism. But people's behaviour is not indifferent to social norms. The *homo democraticus* shaped by solidaristic-type political cultures – socialist or not – and by the classist representation of society, that contrasted the inequalities and pluralism generated by modernity and industrialisation, has been archived. Once disqualified from full employment and social justice, today's *homo democraticus* is identified with the client-customer of what remains of welfare, with the taxpayer and, clearly, with the holder of legally defendable rights within constitutional democracy. The individuals are not too malleable, but neither are they are they too rigid.

We should ask whether the tenacity with which the use of the term democracy is defended is willing to emphasise continuity rather than concealing a rupture. Today the substance of what is willing to be exclusively formal democracy has become the privilege of the few, and this is confirmed by all the indicators of social inequality. The conditioning of particularistic interests has been defined as unacceptable, not so much in the name of the general interest, but in the name of the efficiency of government action. Thus, democratic procedures have been renewed. Only that, while the interests of the business *milieux* have benefited, the interests of the many have been damaged. A terrible collateral damage is that, once the interests of a large part of the governed have been neutralised, often someone tries to stimulate their worst instincts. For years now, governors have not taken decisive steps to tackle unemployment and the decay of employment, which is euphemistically called flexibility. On the contrary, the request of law-and-order policies are often considered as electorally profitable, even if the risk to stimulate intolerance towards immigrants is very high. Was this outcome inevitable?

Democracy was invented as a mechanism to help govern complex societies, that ill tolerate the rigidity of autocracy. But its modest, and rather variable, redistribution of power between governors and governed is by no means a gift. It is a laborious, fragile and certainly not definitive balance, that must be confirmed day by day. This even applies, let us remember, for today's rather anorexic variant of democracy. We should ask ourselves whether, when society was more prosperous in what Hobsbawn, in an excess of nostalgia, referred to as 'the golden age',[1] the advocates who represented a not indifferent part of the governed proved unable to play ahead.

It is perfectly conceivable that the unique constellation of events, and the extraordinary availability of resources that favoured that particular season of democracy, and the balance of power on which it was based in the mid-twentieth century, would sooner or later disappear. Nevertheless, while there were those who exploited the opportunities offered by social and cultural change to disperse the

---

1   Eric J. Hobsbawn, *The Age of Extremes: The Short Twentieth Century, 1914–1991* (London, Michael Joseph, London, 1994).

big numbers, the advocates who based their own professional success on the vote of the popular classes paid scant attention to what was happening. Perhaps they were convinced that the benefits, won at a high price, were by then irreversible. Or, very probably, they were persuaded that their electors had no alternative but to vote for them.

There is nothing to indicate with any certainty that it would have been possible to safeguard the precedent democratic armistice and its inspiring principles. Perhaps there should have been a more timely formulation of a new scale of values and a new culture, less concerned with private consumption and the protection of welfare, and more concerned with persisting inequalities. Welfare was also born from a need for social justice, or has at least been legitimated in these terms. In any case, with time, the advocates of social justice not only took welfare for granted, but did not realise that the same rhetoric of autonomy, difference, authenticity and rights could actually corrode it. These last values should perhaps have been declined in such a way as to make them more resistant to a utilitarian interpretation of individualism.

To remedy the overload of expectations, the redesigning of the techniques of government of democratic societies did not stop at the transfer of broad functions of government from the state to the market or civil society. Democratic regimes were redesigned so as to reduce the political demands and offers of representation, promising to make the action of government institutions more efficient. Taking a look around, today the results are not dazzling. Perhaps it was a serious error to recognise democratic maturity in a trade-off between an exasperated pluralism beyond the borders of political institutions and in a rationed pluralism within those borders.

Once good democratic manners had been interiorised, social peace seemed to have descended on democratic societies, or almost.[2] Why then maintain a powerful apparatus to mobilise consensus as political parties, that was perceived as a cost? Reinforcing the division of work between representatives and represented, between professionals of politics and ordinary citizens, appeared to be more expedient: for politicians, the monopoly of politics and of the political competition; for citizens, their armour of rights, their affairs and private pleasures and, possibly, the fragrant virtues of civil society. Considering that the cultural level of the population had grown, in the same way as the material conditions of life, it might have been possible to render citizens more responsible. Hiding the difficulties would be stupid. Professional politics – sometimes masked by non-politics and antipolitics – has however played the old game of consolidating its primacy and tightening the circle of political actors who count with success.

Among other things: if the deontology of politicians allows them to cultivate their own career ambitions, and their own private advantage undisturbed, it is clear that even the governed will adjust to this. When the basic principle that holds

---

2   I fully share the reserves expressed by Chantal Mouffe in *On the Political* (New York/London, Routledge, 2005).

collective life is the utility of each, and the first to adopt this principle are those who govern, it is legitimate that the governed also think of their own private advantage. The problem of political morality has always existed. It is nevertheless very risky when the mask of hypocrisy falls away and politics is revealed as nothing other than a utilitarian and uninhibited competition for particularistic gains. If democracy is already mediocre on account of its personnel, it necessarily becomes mediocre, and uncivil, for whoever observes it and draws dire examples from it.

Under these conditions, if the author of this volume – who with his own values and interpretative instruments also takes his modest part in the complicated democratic game – is allowed to present a forecast on the future state of the world, it would be best to venture just one. Contrary to those who hold that democracy currently enjoys more than acceptable health, democracy is indeed a noble cause, but at the moment it is also a 'lost cause'.[3] This is a very drastic verdict and we must be cautious in formulating it. In reality, given that the term democracy is polysemic, it is more reasonable to hold that what is lost is not democracy *per se*, but only a certain of way of understanding it.

If democracy is the government of the people, then the people has never been so badly treated or counted so little as today. Never, as now, have democratic leaderships conceded so little to a large majority of their fellow citizens. It is some time since the hierarchies of politics have been so submissive to those of business and finance, when they are not actually identified with them. With rare exceptions, in more developed democratic regimes, today's economic crisis is exacerbating, often dramatically, the already existing difficulties suffered by broad segments of the population.

Greece is always cited as the happy cradle of democracy, but now it risks becoming, if not its tomb, at least the herald of its disappearance. Athenian democracy was indeed something completely different, but there is a tragic irony in what today's Greeks are experiencing, perhaps as the guinea pig for tomorrow's democracy. It has been reported that the disregard of the will of the Greek people, and the generalised impoverishment to which they have been condemned, are exclusively for their own good. Nevertheless, seeing what has happened in Greece, and how, can we really hold that the government of the people is a cause that can be won?

No lost cause, however, is lost forever while there is even a single individual who withstands resignation.[4] Although their application has proved imperfect, the inspiring principles of democracy – freedom, equality and mutual respect – and the desire to make conflicts among human beings peacefully negotiable, to contain and civilise power by placing it at the service of the collective body, are of inesti-

---

3   It is worth reading the reflections of someone who knew a lot about it, having had the opportunity to meditate on it throughout his life. See Edward W. Said, 'On Lost Causes', in *Reflections on Exile and Other Essays* (Cambridge MA, Harvard University Press, 2000). I am indebted to it for many of the following arguments.

4   Said quotes Theodor W. Adorno: see 'On Lost Causes'.

mable value and still deserve to be cultivated, in the hope that politics can do so. Yet, we need to be realistic. At the moment, the signs are not promising. There is very good reason to believe that the standard of living in more advanced societies is likely to decline further. The success of the 'golden age' also depended on some extraordinary advantages enjoyed by these societies in the past. These included an extremely favourable international environment from the economic and political perspective. Today the terms of trade are no longer unconditionally auspicious for Western countries and the international environment has become more complicated. The decline of earlier international hegemonies could be a great opportunity to establish a new negotiated and fair equilibrium, but it may also imply further risks.

The average standard of life of non-Western populations does not seem to have improved much after the removal of old and unjust protective barriers. In some places things have improved, but inequalities between states are increasing, and in many places conditions are worsening. Globalisation foresees exchanges, reciprocal influence and convergences that may also be fertile, but at the same time stir up imperial ambitions, dramatic hostilities and new forms of exploitation. The prevailing idea is that states, regions and cities are competing. Nowadays this raises the more successful among them, or those considered more successful, to the level of a standard. But competition offers advantages to winners and disasters to losers. It means adopting the technologies, lifestyles and forms of government, of whoever is considered more advanced, whilst relinquishing our own specificity. There are exceptions, but the standard being imposed is a powerful, even if not too visible, mechanism of dominion.

As regards developed countries, globalisation clearly makes it difficult for them to compete with emerging countries over labour costs. But apart from placing some modest hope in more technologically advanced production, where emerging countries are rapidly catching up, no developed country seems inclined to take into consideration another possible withdrawal strategy with respect to the present one, which foresees the impoverishment of the many, in exchange for the disproportionate enrichment of the few. On the contrary, can we imagine an ordered withdrawal, whose costs are equally divided? For example why not cutting defense spending or increasing fiscal pressure on the wealthy strata, on rents and luxury goods, so as to substantially reduce the burden on the lower and middle strata, starting with safeguarding public services, essential to guarantee a decent quality of life? If austerity is a necessary ill, why not distribute it in a way which is less socially unbalanced?

Continuing on the road taken for over a quarter of a century, we should also ask ourselves whether democracy – also in its current soft version – will manage to resist the evident widening of, not only material, but also cultural and political, inequalities and the growth of disorder. It is a difficult question, because the worsening of living conditions is a complex phenomena. Not everyone is worse off, not everyone is worse off in all aspects of their existence, and not everyone is aware of being worse off. The labour market now functions in low-gear and dependent workers are evidently weakened, but if consumption drops for some, it remains relatively high for others. There are segments of society that benefit, regions become more prosperous and pieces of individual existence that are promoted. We should not forget that the condition of women has improved, civil rights are widespread and no-one regrets the disciplinary institutions of Fordist society. Furthermore, there has been no lack of mechanisms to embellish or disguise the more dramatic suffering, pushing it to the margins of collective life, or reducing it to statistics, perhaps together with some proof of compassionate solidarity. The media have even transformed the display of the luxury of the rich into a form of popular consolation.

The sufferings of the world, near or far, are filtered, and frequently leave the observer undisturbed, or are allowed to impact individually and silently. This is another sign of the times. The spectacular fund-raising for one or other unfortunate category, victims of a catastrophe, or war, or cancer, or hunger, are very successful and are generally seen as an uplifting proof of solidarity. Thus we are ready to applaud all the good causes sponsored by the media. In recompense, the images of inequality, that have become habitual in our daily life, have until now only occasionally stirred generalised motions of indignation.

We should note that a large part of the citizenry does not even have a memory of the preceding democratic age. For others, well-being was so belated, modest and short-lived that it stopped them from appreciating the improvement when it arrived, and understanding when it began to decline. Too many citizens were resigned before, and have remained resigned. Yet, another part, that could appreciate well-being, perhaps after having fought so hard to obtain it, and has seen it vanish, bear its loss because the decline has been slow until now, or because it is shared.

For those who feel defeated there is also a powerful mechanism that explains how resignation is the conviction that defeat is not individual, but societal. Losing alone rankles. You must examine yourself, even if it is only to be absolved and to ascribe the fault to others. Whereas a collective defeat is easier to bear, involves fate and can even be liberating: 'things have gone badly, but from now on I'll cope on my own'.

The inability to formulate a convincing diagnosis of the state of the world is also part of the defeat. Or rather, there is no lack of diagnoses, but it is difficult to recognise them and to suggest them, instead of the prevailing diagnosis. We need advocates able to negate the fatality of what occurs. Instead the old advocates are content to live off their earnings and thus the issue of equality, although not cancelled, has been put aside. If anything, the number of scapegoats has multiplied – politics itself, immigrants, some professional categories, like teachers or civil servants – pointed to by advocates who plead other, less noble and even patently ignoble, causes. Words that the memory of fascist dictatorships had made unutterable until yesterday, are now repeated with impunity in the public arena, while the signs of indifference to democratic values and principles abound, and are no less risky than aversion. Is there a link between the scant generosity of democratic regimes towards citizens and the meagre sensibility that many citizens show in practice? To what else can we to attribute the awakening of the old ghosts of intolerance and racism?

Yet, although the democratic cause has been left to decline, this does not mean that the situation must necessarily turn out badly. The prospect of a new, less dismal, season is not ruled out. The great collective energies that once managed to mobilise seem to have vanished, but even in their gaseous state something survives and could re-condense. The submission of the governed is more obvious than rebellion. When it works, power does not need to use force. Its most effective arms are persuasion, manipulation, seduction and corruption. Yet, this does not rule out forms of unwillingness or resistance and protest which, even if sporadic or short-lived, always cause embarrassment.

Democracy rarely punishes incapable or dishonest governors. The incumbent always has enough cards in the hand to remain. This does not mean that citizens do not complain against an order of things deemed incompatible with what they have learnt to consider their due from democracy.[5] Thus, democratic regimes have been forced to accept that citizens, at least, discuss, and even set up proper spaces for them. But this is certainly not enough to contain discontent. Until now discussion, protest, resistance and particle by particle defiance, have only involved minorities and the effect has been contained. But the movements of protest around the planet should not be underestimated.

Unfortunately there are also events that stir up very little indignation. People protest in the street or on the web against the impoverishment caused by financial speculation, unemployment or the drop in salaries, but are not equally ready to denounce the fate of immigrants, and the terrible television spectacle of overloaded boats full of wretched people who land on the southern shores of the Mediterranean, or are brutally returned to Africa. Neither is there equal protest against the slaughter carried out in some not too distant corner of the planet. But even closer to home, in the most wretched part of Naples, overrun by uncollected rubbish, local residents called for the eviction of the Roma and applauded those who set fire to their makeshift homes.

Nonetheless, mass education and the new forms of information and communication still have great potential. Collective life continues not only to spread new forms of political action, albeit rather haphazardly, but also it generates solidaristic feelings of great value. Despite the lack of a shared diagnosis on the state of the world, critical reflection is dynamic and is also a political actor not to be underestimated. Fortunately, the age in which democracy was interpreted extensively has not been an isolated episode. However ambiguous and trivialised, the culture of rights remains a resource. The same can be said of the growing, albeit wavering, awareness of environmental damage despite its current prevailing individualistic interpretation. And even if brutal repression is frequent, it is difficult to remove protest permanently with non-democratic techniques.

Power has never been unidirectional or unequivocal. Governors depend on the governed no less than the other way around. There is never a definitive equilibri-

---

5   It is what we could define as 'a moral economy of democracy' borrowing the language of Edward P. Thompson. See 'The Moral Economy of the English Crowd in the 18th Century', *Past & Present* 50(1), 1971, 76–136.

um. It takes only a very small shock to change it. A minority governing a majority always has a tough job. It is only the rhetoric of power that hides the fact. Thus, irrespective of attempts to facilitate the task, the job of governing is always demanding. The beauty of human things is that no power struggle is ever definitively lost and that the most desperate lost causes sometimes turn out winners.

The end-of-decade financial crisis had been predicted, but few imagined precisely when it would happen, or that it would be so devastating and that the damage would spread so far. To date, it does not seem to have dented the trust that a large part of the political, business and intellectual establishment places in the mix between a little democracy and a lot of market. States intervened massively, but still the most frequently heard formula is that the problem is not the market, but the need for a stricter respect for its rules – stabilise the market and the economy will prosper as before.

Neo-liberal policies did apparently save developed economies in the crisis of the 1970s, and put large parts of the planet on the road to development. But in the last thirty years, there has not been a single moment that can be defined as glorious, and the final balance of the social, environmental, and even moral cost of the pretended relaunching of the market economy, is not in the least, flattering. Thus the present circumstances may very well be what will make previous certainties crack, where critical thought starts to bite again, when new horizons of possibility open up for these reactions – of power – that every power necessarily inspires. Political ideas now abandoned on the margins of political life – e.g. equality, social justice, general interest, shared destinies and social risks, etc. – could return to the fore and point the use of democratic rules in a new direction. Obviously such circumstances also offer opportunities for the enemies of democracy, but this does not mean that they will have the upper hand. Even if the limitations of democracy prohibit it as being conceited, this is why the game of democracy remains open and deserves to be played.

As democracy is an imperfect human invention, its present state is not surprising. What is surprising, however, is the scant awareness of the extraordinary nature of such a modest, imperfect and highly changeable invention. Democracy, and its principles, have old enemies that have gained new energy from its current difficulties, also because the present seems to have absorbed the future. Today, in the political sphere, there are few who cultivate the myth of mutual aid or the common good, which was a myth, or a normative ideal, but that for all, especially governors, constituted an invitation to avoid the uninhibited pursuit of one's own particularism.

Yet, as we said at the beginning, although inauspicious presentiments prevail, they are not the only ones and nothing is pre-determined. The worst could happen, or not. Who knows? No-one had foreseen the present situation, if not in a casual and fragmented way. Even if in our narratives the present appears as the legitimate progeny of the past, nobody had really planned it. The same applies to the future. Indeed, an order of things, less conditioned by privilege is no longer either unreasonable or more improbable than what we have to live with nowadays. In the history of modernity the negation of interlinking social interdependencies that shape human beings is cyclical. It is therefore unlikely that the current condition, where negation prevails, will last *ad infinitum*. We can virtually rule out the abolition of privilege, but perhaps it can be weakened. It happened in a not too distant past and it can happen again.

There are many signs indicating a change of season. This does not necessarily mean a return to the earlier season of welfare state. Society, to use Polanyi's terminology, is quite capable of finding other mechanisms than the state to defend itself. For those who observe them, these signs, so peremptorily contrasted not only by the beneficiaries of the new equilibria, but also by powerful limitations, give good reasons to be discouraged. But this may be a defect of short sightedness. Therefore, the account presented here is really without a conclusion, and if anything, ends with the invitation to resist resignation. The lost cause of democracy – its egalitarian variant, but not only – could still rally. There are signs of change that we can see and there are most probably many others we cannot see, simply because our lenses do not focus well. The current condition of democratic society, and of the world around it, is as always, unstable. Yet, as always, there is no shortage of men and women who not only reason and debate, but who are also willing to be captivated by democracy. If optimism is often foolish, pessimism is more often obtuse.

index